THE ROOTS
OF AMERICAN ORDER

THE ROOTS
OF AMERICAN
ORDER

RUSSELL KIRK

Epilogue by Frank Shakespeare

THIRD EDITION

REGNERY GATEWAY
Washington, DC

Library of Congress Cataloging-in-Publication Data

Kirk, Russell.
The roots of American order / Russell Kirk.—3rd ed.
p.   cm.
Includes bibliographical references and index.
ISBN 0-89526-755-1
1. Political science—History.   2. Law—History and criticism.
I. Title.
JA81.K55   1990
320′.09—dc20   90-43184
                                                                    CIP

Published in the United States by
Regnery Gateway
1130 17th Street, NW
Washington, DC 20036

Distributed to the trade by
National Book Network
4720-A Boston Way
Lanham, MD 20706

1992 printing
Printed on acid free paper
Manufactured in the United States of America

10 9 8 7 6 5 4

*The third edition of this book is dedicated
in memory of Marjorie Rachel Kirk,
my mother*

CONTENTS

VII

Covenant of private conscience and insight. The second Isaiah foretells that Israel shall be as a light to the nations. Summary of the prophets' labors. The enduring truth of the Law and the Prophets.

Under God in Time and History, 38

Sacred history and secular history. Understanding the Old Testament. The Hebrews become aware of eternity. Hellenic "linear" time and Hebraic "psychic" time. God's intervention in time. The Hebrew concept of order. Disorder as the rejection of divine wisdom. Universal recognition of certain natural laws. Revelation as the foundation of order: illustration from the Danakil people.

The Old Testament and the New America, 45

The Puritans' parallels with the Hebrews. Calvinism, in various forms, shaped American character. The Old Testament and American social realism. American democracy and the transplanted legacy of Israel.

Chapter III: Glory and Ruin: the Greek World, 51

The One Betraying Flaw of the Hellenes, 51

Ancient Greece no happy model for American politics. Greek *hubris*, arrogance. The Greek genius. Causes of Greek political failure. Inadequacy of the Greek religion; its darker side. Akragas and the chthonian deities. Turbulence of Greek society.

Solon and the Athenian Polity, 60

Solon as an exemplar for Americans. Solon's enduring achievement. His background and character. Athens' decline late in the seventh century B.C. The Laws of Draco. Social ills of Athens. Solon and righteous order, *eunomia*. Solon reforms the constitution of Athens: economic and political renewal. Solon resigns power. Solon's ethical basis for order: the spiritual statesman. The tyranny of Peisistratus in Athens. Solon happy in the hour of his death.

And That House Fell, 67

Greek tyrannies of the late sixth century B.C.; growth of democracies. New Athenian constitution of Cleisthenes. The Greeks hard pressed from east and west; Greek victories over enemies; beginning of Greece's Great Age. Ascendancy of Pericles in Athens; Athenian civilization. Injustice of Athens as a cause of the Peloponnesian War. Athens falls before Spartan power, after failure of the Syracusan expedition. Carthage destroys Akragas. The Greek order of the *polis* begins to dissolve.

The Cave and the Dust-Storm, 73

Limited direct influence of Plato and Aristotle upon early Americans. Ideas of those philosophers permeated western civilization nevertheless. Socrates' life and death. Plato and his Academy; his endeavor. Plato no Utopian. Plato's vain attempts at Syracuse. His ambition to restore order in the soul and order in the republic. Meanings of "philodoxer" and "philosopher". The Greek sophists. The meaning of the word "soul". Homer's concepts of the soul and of order. Hesiod on these subjects. The search for righteousness through tragedy. Protagoras and "man as the measure of all things." The reply of Socrates and Plato to the sophists: God as the measure of all things. Plato speaks in symbol and parable.

Chapter IV: Virtue and Power: the Roman Tension, 97

CONTENTS

aristocracy of New England, founded on commerce, shipping, and learning. Example of the Winthrop family. English culture and manners set the tone for America. Persistence of American idea of the gentleman into democratic times.

Representative Assemblies and Local Autonomy, 323

Lack of system in Britain's colonial administration. Taxes levied by colonial assemblies. Those assemblies sprang up naturally, and were recognized by the Crown. Function of colonial governors; their limited powers. The assemblies not radical; dominated by landed proprietors usually. Local government in Virginia: the counties; great power of justices of the peace through the county courts. New England's town meetings: the township system. Enlargement of participation in town meetings. Autonomy of English colonies contrasted with Spanish practice. The seeds of democracy in colonial government. American freedom and order grew organically.

The New World's Christianity, 332

Tocqueville on religion in America. Moralistic routine before 1734. Description of the Quakers in Pennsylvania. Political collapse of the Holy Experiment after 1756. John Wesley in America. "Enthusiasm" in the eighteenth century. The rise of Deism: Wesley's struggle against it. Whitefield's preaching in America. Character of Jonathan Edwards; difficulties in Northampton. Edwards turns back the clock. Originality of his thought: praise by Mackintosh. Sin a negative. Swift spread of Edwards' influence. America would have been ungovernable without Christian belief.

Chapter X: Eighteenth-Century Intellects, 347

Constitutional Order: Montesquieu, 347

Public men are influenced strongly by books published during their own formative years. The French Enlightenment: its mentality scarcely penetrated to America. Montesquieu frequently quoted at Constitutional Convention. Montesquieu's urbane talents. His influence conservative in England and America, though not in France. Laws are relationships. Montesquieu a relativist in law, but not an opponent of natural-law teaching, in its Ciceronian sense. Law is not despotic: Montesquieu's reply to Hobbes. Laws grow out of social experience. Ordered freedom maintained by separation of powers and by checks and balances. Need for a "depository of laws". Americans sympathetic to Montesquieu's ideas.

Skeptical Realism: Hume, 358

Hume admired by Hamilton and Franklin, detested by Adams and Jefferson. Hume's amiability. A Tory by accident? Hume's puncturing of the balloon of Pure Reason. Analysis of his *Human Understanding*. Morality, says Hume, is obedience to rules of approbation and disapprobation. Hume's formidable assault on the "social compact". Human association results neither from compact nor from force. Hume's dislike of fanatics, religious and philosophical. He would not have been pleased by some of his eminent disciples. His influence upon James Madison. Reasons for his American popularity.

The Laws of England: Blackstone, 368

Sir William Blackstone the chief source of legal knowledge in America during Revolutionary and Constitutional era. Mingled character of Blackstone on natural law. A champion of

FOREWORD

This book, the first edition of which was published in 1974, is an endeavor to help in the restoring of historical consciousness among Americans.

"Happy are the people whose annals are tiresome," Montesquieu wrote. He meant that such a folk must have enjoyed peace for a great while: the Swiss since the era of the French Revolution are our best example of a people so blessed.

But the annals of the United States, and of the civilization in which America participates, are far from tiresome—even though they may be taught tiresomely. Lacking a knowledge of how we arrived where we stand today, lacking that deeper love of country which is nurtured by a knowledge of the past, lacking the apprehension that we all take part in a great historical continuity—why, a people so deprived will not dare much, sacrifice much, or take long views. With them, creature comforts will be everything; yet, historical consciousness wanting, in the long run they must lose their creature comforts too.

At every level of instruction, from kindergarten through graduate school, the serious study of history has been declining for half a century and more. From time to time, foundations and learned societies, and newspapers and magazines, growing alarmed at the drift toward ignorance of anything not featured on television, publish surveys of the extent to which the rising generation has sunk into a Sargasso Sea of ignorance of the past.

In 1975, some months after the first edition of *The Roots of American Order* appeared, Dr. Richard S. Kirkendall, executive secretary of the Organization of American Historians, presented an interesting report on the decay of historical studies. Since then, various other such analyses have been published; all have been disheartening.

Professor Kirkendall's report, "The Status of History in the Public Schools", proved "if proof is necessary, that history is in crisis and that history's crisis is not merely a part of the large difficulties of academic life at the present time." One of the chief causes of the decline of interest in history, Dr. Kirkendall and his colleagues found, was the notion that history "is not a practical subject." Here one thinks of Albert Jay Nock's essay "The Value of Useless Knowledge", in which he argues that although historical knowledge has no immediately utilitarian application, nevertheless it is the most *valuable* of all intellectual disciplines.

"Signs of improvement are scarce," Dr. Kirkendall reported in 1975. And since then, although the Organization of American Historians and other associations occasionally have dredged up a few cheering crumbs of historical revival, in general we are no better off in this discipline than we were before we commenced celebrating the Bicentenary of the United States.

One of the livelier historical writers of our time, Dr. John Lukacs, has argued that we are entering upon an era when historical literature will supplant the novel and other forms of humane letters. Let us devoutly hope so.

We learn from history that we learn nothing from history, Hegel wrote. Perhaps that hard truth may revive our historical consciousness, after experience of adversity. When the gods of the copybook headings with fire and slaughter return, sometimes chastened men and women perceive afresh that they should have heeded the records of human endeavor and misadventure—which we call history.

T. S. Eliot remarked once that we have been condemning the rising generation to a new form of provincialism: to the provinciality of time, which imprisons men and women in their own little present moment. Eliot perceived that most of what we know is learnt through history—public or personal history. For only the past is knowable—civilization's past and our family's past. Upon the rippling surface of the deep well of the past lies an evanescent film that we call the present, dissolving and sinking even as one reads these phrases; while the future, diverting although it may be as subject for speculation, remains quite unknowable. If ignorant of the past, we drift bewildered on the well's surface, momentarily; and then sink to oblivion.

As a widespread social phenomenon, the unhistorical or antihistorical attitude is peculiar to our era. It parallels the widespread seeming indifference to the reality of the soul and the prospect of the life everlasting. Quite conceivably men and women uninterested in the soul may forfeit their own souls, and a people uninterested in their history may cease to have a history, or to remain a people.

In the hope of opening eyes to the perceptions that historical knowledge may convey, and of waking minds to the energy and color of the historical imagination, this third, and perhaps final, edition of *The Roots of American Order* is published. This book is no exercise in antiquarianism; not the sort of history that might have been written by Walter Scott's Dr. Dryasdust. Rather, this book enlarges upon Santayana's admonition that those who ignore the past are condemned to repeat it. It may be added that those who understand the past can prepare prudently for a tolerable future.

Will the moral and social order that Americans have known for two centuries and more endure throughout the twenty-first century? That may depend upon whether enough men and women in these United States, informed by study of the institutions and convictions that have been developed over three thousand years, make up their minds to stand by the Permanent Things.

—Russell Kirk
Piety Hill
Mecosta, Michigan

THE ROOTS
OF AMERICAN ORDER

CHAPTER I
ORDER,
THE FIRST NEED OF ALL

T wo centuries after the founding of the new nation called the United States of America, we need to renew our understanding of the beliefs and the laws which give form to American society. Our own society, like that of any other people, is held together by what is called an "order". The character of that order is the subject of this book. What is "order"?

Imagine a man travelling through the night, without a guide, thinking continually of the direction he wishes to follow. That is the image of a human being in search of order, says Simone Weil, a woman who suffered much: "Such a traveller's way is lit by a great hope." Order is the path we follow, or the pattern by which we live with purpose and meaning. Above even food and shelter, she continues, we must have order. The human condition is insufferable unless we perceive a harmony, an order, in existence. "Order is the first need of all."[1]

Before a person can live tolerably with himself or with others, he must know order. If we lack order in the soul and order in society, we dwell "in a land of darkness, as darkness itself," the Book of Job puts it; "and of the shadow of death, without any order, and where light is as darkness."

When she wrote figuratively of a man travelling alone through the night, Simone Weil was thinking of herself. All through her brief life of thirty-three years, she sought to order her soul. She was French, Jewish, and Christian. In search of spiritual order, she studied Greek and Indian philosophy, Sanskrit, the Christian mystics, quantum theory. She worked in fields and factories so that she might come to understand and to share the life of hard toil.

And at the same time, Simone Weil was thinking of social order in the modern world. Her slim book *The Need for Roots* has the subtitle "Prelude to a Declaration of Duties toward Mankind." She wrote it while exiled from France, then occupied by German troops; she wrote it at the request of the French provisional government in exile, as a study of how the French, should they be liberated from the Nazi domination, might find anew the roots of their order and so live together in peace and justice.

Spiritual doubt and social disorder Simone Weil knew all too well. To understand the Spanish civil war, in 1936 she spent several weeks with the Republican army on the Catalonian front, a searing experience that haunted her to her death. To share the sufferings of her compatriots in occupied France, she determined in 1943 to eat not more daily than the subjugated French were allowed; she was then in an English sanitorium, in wretched health—and, in effect, she starved herself to death. Her several books were published after her death.

Our twentieth century, Simone Weil wrote, is a time of disorder very like the disorder of Greece in the fifth century before Christ. In her words, "It is as though we had returned to the age of Protagoras and the Sophists, the age when the art of persuasion—whose modern equivalent is advertising slogans, publicity, propaganda meetings, the press, the cinema, and radio—took the place of thought and controlled the fate of cities and accomplished coups d'état. So the ninth book of Plato's *Republic* reads like a description of contemporary events."

This analogy of fifth-century Greece with our age is too true. One may add that our time of troubles also is like the disorder of the Roman republic in the first century before Christ, and like the catastrophic collapse of Roman civilization in the fifth century after Christ. As individuals and as a civilization—like that man without a guide in the darkness, like Simone Weil, like societies that are dust now—we people in the closing decades of the twentieth century grope for order.

Like many other concepts, perhaps the word "order" is best apprehended by looking at its opposite, "disorder." A disordered existence is a confused and miserable existence. If a society falls into general disorder, many of its members will cease to exist at all. And if the members of a society are disordered in spirit, the outward order of the commonwealth cannot endure.

We couple the words "law and order"; and indeed they are related, yet they are not identical. Laws arise out of a social order; they are the general rules which make possible the tolerable functioning of an order. Nevertheless an order is bigger than its laws, and many aspects of any social order are determined by beliefs and customs, rather than being governed by positive laws.

This word "order" means a systematic and harmonious arrangement—whether in one's own character or in the commonwealth. Also "order" signifies the performance of certain duties and the enjoyment of certain rights in a community: thus we use the phrase "the civil social order."

In this book, we examine the roots of order in the United States of America. Old and intricate, these roots give life to us all. We can distinguish two sorts of roots, intertwined: the roots of the moral order, of order in the soul; and the roots of the civil social order, of order in the republic.

Although to some extent we trace the history of civilization when we describe the origins of our order, this book is not a comprehensive survey of culture—that work having been done by others. Rather, this book emphasizes certain institutions and customs, and certain ideas and beliefs, which continue to nurture order in the person and order in the republic, down to our time. No study could be more relevant to our present discontents.

We examine, successively, the legacy of order received from the Hebrews; from the classical culture of the Greeks and the Romans; from the medieval world and the age of the Reformation, particularly in Britain; from the turbulent civilization of the seventeenth century; from the elegant civilization of the eighteenth century; and from America's colonial experience. We discuss both the beliefs and the institutions out of which American order has grown.

Seeking for the roots of order, we are led to four cities: Jerusalem, Athens, Rome, and London. In Washington or New York or Chicago or Los Angeles today, the order which Americans experience is derived from the experience of those four old cities. If our souls are disordered, we fall into abnormality, unable to control our impulses. If our commonwealth is disordered, we fall into anarchy, every man's hand against every other man's. For, as Richard Hooker wrote in the sixteenth century, "Without order, there is no living in public society, because the want thereof is the mother of confusion." This saving order is the product of more than three thousand years of human striving.

The "inner order" of the soul and the "outer order" of society being intimately linked, we discuss in this book both aspects of order. Without a high degree of private moral order among the American people, the reign of law could not have prevailed in this country. Without an orderly pattern of politics, American private character would have sunk into a ruinous egoism.

Order is the first need of the soul. It is not possible to love what one ought to love, unless we recognize some principles of order by which to govern ourselves.

Order is the first need of the commonwealth. It is not possible for us to live in peace with one another, unless we recognize some principle of order by which to do justice.

The good society is marked by a high degree of order, justice, and freedom. Among these, order has primacy: for justice cannot be enforced until a tolerable civil social order is attained, nor can freedom be anything better than violence until order gives us laws.

Once I was told by a scholar born in Russia of how he had come to understand through terrible events that order necessarily precedes justice and freedom. He had been a

Menshevik, or moderate Socialist, at the time of the Russian Revolution. When the Bolsheviks seized power in St. Petersburg, he fled to Odessa, on the Black Sea, where he found a great city in anarchy. Bands of young men commandeered street-cars and clattered wildly through the heart of Odessa, firing with rifles at any pedestrian, as though they were hunting pigeons. At any moment, one's apartment might be invaded by a casual criminal or fanatic, murdering for the sake of a loaf of bread. In this anarchy, justice and freedom were only words. "Then I learned that before we can know justice and freedom, we must have order," my friend said. "Much though I hated the Communists, I saw then that even the grim order of Communism is better than no order at all. Many might survive under Communism; no one could survive in general disorder."

In America, order and justice and freedom have developed together; but they can decay in parallel fashion. In every generation, some human beings bitterly defy the moral order and the social order. Although the hatred of order is suicidal, it must be reckoned with: ignore a fact, and that fact will be your master. Half a century ago, perceiving a widespread disintegration of private and public order, William Butler Yeats wrote of what had become the torment of much of the modern world:

> Things fall apart; the centre cannot hold;
> Mere anarchy is loosed upon the world,
> The blood-dimmed tide is loosed, and everywhere
> The ceremony of innocence is drowned;
> The best lack all conviction, while the worst
> Are full of passionate intensity.

During the past half-century, the center has failed to hold in many nations. Yet once revolution or war has demolished an established order, a people find it imperative to search for principles of order afresh, that they may survive. Once they have undone an old order, revolutionaries proceed to decree a new order—often an order harsher than the order which they had overthrown. Mankind cannot be governed long by sheer force.

No order ever has been perfect, and it is tempting to fancy

that we could create a new order nearer to our hearts' desire. A freshman once informed me that we have no need nowadays for the beliefs and institutions of yesteryear: he himself, he said, could outline a better moral system and a better political pattern than those we have inherited. I asked him if he could build a gasoline engine, say, without reference to anything mechanical now existing. He replied that he could not. I observed that moral and social concerns really are more delicate and complex than a mere mechanical contrivance—and that even should his novel order be superior, apparently, to the old order, still no one would accept it but himself and a few followers. For people take the proofs of mankind's experience as evidence of some soundness, and they tend to resist any new creation of some living person not conspicuously a better authority than themselves.

That undergraduate was not singular in his repudiation of the experience of a civilization. Our times resemble those of the concluding years of the Roman Republic, the age of Marcus Tullius Cicero. As disorder washed about him, Cicero examined the causes of private and public confusion. "Long before our time," he wrote in his treatise *The Republic*, "the customs of our ancestors molded admirable men, and in turn those eminent men upheld the ways and institutions of their forebears. Our age, however, inherited the Republic as if it were some beautiful painting of bygone ages, its colors already fading through great antiquity; and not only has our time neglected to freshen the colors of the picture, but we have failed to preserve its form and outlines."

Like Plato before him, Cicero understood that the problem of order is simultaneously personal and social: Roman men and Roman justice had declined together. It is so still. That is one reason why Plato and Cicero remain relevant to our present condition.

"To freshen the colors of the picture" is the purpose of this book. We are concerned here with the social experiences and the ideas that blended in America to form a pattern of inner and outer order, still enduring. The popular demand for "relevance" in college and university, nowadays, has some justification; and this book is meant to be relevant to the disputes of our present hour. Those who ignore history, says George Santayana, are condemned to repeat it. Those who neglect the roots of order, one may add, are compelled to water those roots desperately—after wandering in the parched wasteland of disorder.

Upon our knowledge of those roots may depend what sort of order America and the world will have by the end of this century. It may be the order of Aldous Huxley's *Brave New World*, rich and dehumanized; it may be the garrison-state controlled by ferocious ideology, as in George Orwell's *Nineteen-Eighty-Four*; or it may be an order renewed and improved, yet recognizably linked with the order that arose in Jerusalem, Athens, Rome, and London.

The higher kind of order, sheltering freedom and justice, declares the dignity of man. It affirms what G. K. Chesterton called "the democracy of the dead"—that is, it recognizes the judgments of men and women who have preceded us in time, as well as the opinions of people living at this moment. This higher kind of order is founded upon the practical experience of human beings over many centuries, and upon the judgments of men of vision and intellect who have preceded us in time.

Against this higher kind of order, there contend in our age various ideologies—fanatic political creeds, often advanced by violence. By definition, "ideology" means servitude to political dogmas, abstract ideas not founded upon historical experience. Ideology is inverted religion, and the ideologue is the sort of person whom the historian Jacob Burckhardt called the "terrible simplifier." Communism, fascism, and anarchism have been the most powerful of these ideologies. The simplistic appeal of ideological slogans continues to menace the more humane social orders of our time.

The American order of our day was not founded upon ideology. It was not manufactured: rather, it *grew*. This American order is not immutable, for it will change in one respect or another as the circumstances of social existence alter. American laws are not like the laws which Lycurgus gave to the Spartans, never to be altered at all. Nor do we Americans emulate another people of old Greece, the

Locrians—whose magistrates put a rope around the neck of any citizen who proposed a change in the laws. (If the reformer convinced the people of his wisdom, honors were heaped upon him; but if he did not persuade them that his proposals were desirable, he was hanged by the neck until dead.) As Edmund Burke said, change is the means of our preservation.

But also we must have permanence in some things, if change is to be improvement. Americans generally retain a respect for their old moral habits and their old political forms, because those habits and forms express their understanding of order. This attachment to certain enduring principles of order has done much to preserve America from the confused and violent change that plagues most modern nations.

No order is perfect: man himself being imperfect, presumably we never will make our way to Utopia. (If ever we arrived at Utopia, indeed, we might be infinitely bored with the place.) But if the roots of an order are healthy, that order may be reinvigorated and improved. If its roots are withered, "the dead tree gives no shelter." Permanence and progression are not enemies, for there can be no improvement except upon a sound foundation, and that foundation cannot endure unless it is progressively renewed. The traveller in the wasteland seeks the shelter of living order.[2] This book is meant to water roots, for the renewing of order and the betterment of justice and freedom. What Patrick Henry, in 1775, called "the lamp of experience" is our hope of order refreshed.

Notes

[1] Simone Weil, *The Need for Roots: Prelude to a Declaration of Duties toward Mankind* (translated by Arthur Wills, with a preface by T. S. Eliot; Boston: Beacon Press, 1952), p. 11. Also Simone Weil, *On Science, Necessity, and the Love of God*: (New York: Oxford University Press, 1968), pp. 63-64.

[2] For recent concepts of "order" discussed only briefly in this introductory chapter, see particularly Hans Barth, *The Idea of Order: Contributions to a Philosophy of Politics* (translated by Ernest W. Hankamer and William M. Newell; D. Reidel: Dordrecht, 1960); and Eric Voegelin, *The New Science of Politics* (Chicago: University of Chicago Press, 1952).

CHAPTER II
THE LAW
AND THE PROPHETS

From Mount Sinai to Massachusetts Bay

T he tap-root of American order runs deep into a Levantine desert; it began to grow some thirteen centuries before the birth of Jesus of Nazareth. Through Moses, prophet and law-giver, the moral principles that move the civilization of Europe and America and much more of the world first obtained clear expression.

To a wandering people of obscure origin, the Hebrews, or Children of Israel, occurred then a tremendous "leap in being": that is, by an extraordinary perception, the Israelites came to understand the human condition as it had not been understood before. Even earlier than the time of Moses, the Israelites had experienced the moral workings of an unseen power, which had spoken to the consciousness of Noah and of Abraham. But through Moses, the Hebrews learned more distinctly that there watched over them an all-powerful intelligence or spirit which gave them their moral nature. In their sacred book called Exodus, later, the Jews who were the Israelites' descendants would set down the revelation which Moses received from Yahweh, or Jehovah, the unseen Lord of all.

"Revelation" means the unveiling of truths that men could not have obtained from simple experience in this world.

It is a communication of knowledge from some source that transcends ordinary human perception. To the Israelites, Moses made known that there exists but one God, Jehovah; that God had made a covenant or compact with His people; that He had decreed laws by which they should live. From that revelation have grown modern ethics and modern social institutions and much besides.

"Exodus" means departure: the Israelites were departing from Egypt into Palestine. Also they were departing from the old moral order of the cosmological empires—from that old order's capricious deities and arbitrary priest-kings—into a new moral order which would be called, later, the faith of Judaism. Later still, this moral order revealed at Sinai would become the foundation of the moral order called Christianity.

Some twenty-nine centuries after Moses heard the voice from the burning bush, a smaller band of wanderers would embark upon another exodus, farther in distance but swifter in time than the exodus of the Israelites. The people of this later exodus were the Puritans, sailing for the New World, and their ablest leader was John Winthrop. On the deck of the ship *Arbella*, halfway between England and Cape Cod, in the year 1630, Winthrop preached a lay sermon, to remind his fellow-voyagers how they had made a covenant with the God of Israel.

"We must delight in each other, make others' conditions our own, rejoice together, mourn together, labor and suffer together," Winthrop said: "always having before our eyes our commission and community in the work, our community as members of the same body. So shall we keep the unity of the spirit in the bond of peace, the Lord will be our God and delight to dwell among us, as His own people, and will command a blessing upon us in all our ways, so that we shall see much more of His wisdom, power, goodness, and truth than formerly we have been acquainted with.

"We shall find that the God of Israel is among us, when ten of us shall be able to resist a thousand of our enemies, when He shall make us a praise and glory, that men shall say of succeeding plantation, 'The Lord make it like that of New England.' For we must consider that we shall be as a city upon a hill, the eyes of all people are upon us. So that if we

shall deal falsely with our God in this work we have undertaken, and so cause Him to withdraw His present help from
us, we shall be made a story and a by-word throughout the
world; we shall open the mouths of enemies to speak evil of
the ways of God and all professors for God's sake; we shall
shame the faces of many of God's worthy servants, and cause
their prayers to be turned into curses upon us, till we be consumed out of the good land whither we are going."[1]

These words of Winthrop are in the spirit of what the Jews
called the Torah, the Law. The moral commandments revealed to Moses upon Mount Sinai were broken by the Israelites
almost as soon as they were made known; the principles of
order reaffirmed by Winthrop were violated by the settlers in
New England not long after the landing in Massachusetts.
Yet without knowledge of that moral order, the men of ancient Israel and Judah could not have lived in community.
And so it is with the people of modern America, and of lands
which inherit the moral understanding of Judaism or of
Christianity.

Even the simplest human communities cannot endure
without some form of laws, consciously held and enforced.
Ants and bees may coöperate by instinct; men must have
revelation and reason. What we call "biblical law" was not
the first code of justice. Long before Moses and his brother
Aaron led the Hebrew people out of Egypt, codes of law had
been promulgated among the Babylonians, the Sumerians,
the Akkadians, the Assyrians, and the Hittites. Yet it is the
Law made known through Moses that has survived, and
which still works upon the society in which we live.

The Israelites of the Exodus were a people without
writing, nomads who left no archeological evidence behind
them; they were far less civilized than certain other peoples of
that age; indeed, having had no cities, they cannot properly
be called civilized at all. We can know Moses and the people
whom he led only through the Pentateuch, the first five books
of what Christians call the Old Testament. The Moses of that
sacred history was a "charismatic leader," a man of especial
spiritual gifts, who perceived and expressed truths which until
then had been glimpsed only dimly, if at all.

In the dawn of every religion, some such figure as Moses

may be discerned: the "seer" who sees what others cannot see. The seer communicates such truth to his followers, teaching them how to order their lives and to live together in community. The other creeds of the ancient world are dust and ashes now, but the Decalogue of Moses and the understanding of man's existence under God which Moses communicated to the people remain a living power, the source of order.

All the aspects of any civilization arise out of a people's religion: its politics, its economics, its arts, its sciences, even its simple crafts are the by-products of religious insights and a religious cult. For until human beings are tied together by some common faith, and share certain moral principles, they prey upon one another. In the common worship of the cult, a community forms. At the heart of every culture is a body of ethics, of distinctions between good and evil; and in the beginning, at least, those distinctions are founded upon the authority of revealed religion. Not until a people have come to share religious belief are they able to work together satisfactorily, or even to make sense of the world in which they find themselves. Thus all order—even the ideological order of modern totalist states, professing atheism—could not have come into existence, had it not grown out of general belief in truths that are perceived by the moral imagination.

This religious origin of private and public order has been described afresh in the twentieth century by such historians as Christopher Dawson, Eric Voegelin, and Arnold Toynbee. The first social organization, beyond mere family groups, is the cult that seeks to communicate with supernatural powers.

Animals survive by instinct; true human beings cannot. Possessing reason, even primitive men ask questions. They find themselves, as did the Israelites in the desert of Sinai, in a condition of danger, suffering, and ignorance. Led perhaps by some man of marvelous insights, they join together in seeking answers to their questions. So the cult, the religious association, comes into existence. Men try, through the cult, to acquire protection and knowledge from a power that is more than human. Without such communication, they cannot survive on the human level—and perhaps not even on the animal level.

This truth may be more readily understood in the troubled twentieth century that it was in the nineteenth. Under tribulation, men come to realize that they are feeble and imperfect, if they try to stand by themselves. They recognize their failings—what the Hebrews called their sinfulness.

"The nineteenth-century myth of inevitable and perpetual progress **has** been exploded by the impact of world wars, with their demonstration that autonomous man cannot solve the vast problems of racial and cultural conflict, economic welfare and political order," R. B. Y. Scott writes. "He is overwhelmed by his own machinery, and by social torrents set loose through his unwillingness to affirm his solidarity with his fellow men. The judgments of God are manifest in the world of today. The time has come to bring home to men that these are right judgments on human sin; that men bear these consequences inevitably, because they are morally responsible beings who have denied their own nature in denying their responsibility to their neighbors."[2]

It was so with the Israelites of the Exodus. Their problems of personal and social order, at bottom, were similar to the problems of order we confront today. How may human beings live with their own weaknesses and ruinous impulses? Can they turn to a source of goodness and wisdom that surpasses mere human talents? The revelation which came to Moses was in answer to perennial human longings. What is man doing in this hard world—man, with his vague aspirations and his power of reflection? How may a community live together in order and peace? Through Moses there came a response to these implicit questions, and that response endures in the twentieth century after Christ.

The Moses of the Pentateuch was a man acquainted with the civilization of Egypt at its higher levels, and so better prepared than the nomads whom he led in confronting these perplexities of private and public order. Yet the vision of order which he describes was more than the order which then existed in Egypt. That is why it has endured to our time.

When the fugitive Israelites struggled to survive in the ghastly desert of Sinai, between Egypt and Palestine, Moses ascended Mount Sinai—as desolate today as it was then, except that an ancient Christian monastery stands there now.

Almost nowhere does physical nature seem more hostile to mankind than in Sinai, though the armies of Israel and Egypt have fought for that waste in recent years. Yet upon the Mount, a bush or tree burst into flame, and a voice said to Moses' consciousness, "I am that am." To Moses, a mortal human being, a timeless Power spoke. The Creator made Himself known to His creatures, telling them of His intention for them.

What Moses experienced and expressed was something more than what we call "intuition" and something more than even what we call "vision." Moses' perception was transcendent—that is, Moses perceived the nature of being through some means beyond the limits of human rationality and private experience. Moses was enabled to express truths about the human condition which could not have come out of his environment or even from the collective experience of the Israelites. This transcending of the five human senses and of memory, this communion with a source of wisdom more than human, is what we mean by the word "revelation".

So far as words could express his overwhelming experience of transcendence, Moses made known to the Israelites the existence of the Other, the divine Presence, the supreme being who had revealed Himself upon Mount Sinai: the existence of One whom they came to call Yahweh (incorrectly translated as "Jehovah" in English). Yahweh, Moses told the people, is the Lord of all creation; He is God, and no other gods exist. (Three centuries before the birth of Christ, the Jews would cease even to utter the word "Yahweh", lest they seem blasphemous, and would substitute other titles for the Lord.) Coming down from his solitary communion upon Mount Sinai with the eternal One, Moses gave Yahweh's commandments to the Children of Israel. He told them how to order their lives, and how to dwell together in community: that is, Moses communicated the principles of personal and social order. From outside human experience, the Spirit had spoken.

We cannot well understand order and disorder in America today, or elsewhere in the world, unless we know something of the beliefs and the experiences of the Hebrew people in a remote land and a remote time. In the lines of T. S. Eliot, "The communication of the dead is tongued with fire beyond the language of the living." Through Moses, long dead, meaning came into human existence. Our modern moral order, at least in what is called the West, runs back to the burning bush on Sinai.

American *political* institutions owe little, directly, to the example and the experience of the Israelites or the Jews. True, the Puritans of Massachusetts Bay endeavored to establish a "Bible state"; but in its extreme form that experiment endured only three years; even in its modified aspect it lasted merely for two generations. Nevertheless, the American *moral* order could not have come into existence at all, had it not been for the legacy left by Israel.

In the whole of John Adams' political writings, which draw heavily upon Greek and Roman political experience, there is no account of the states of Israel and Judah. It was not that Adams, a descendant of the Puritans, ignored the patrimony of the Hebrews: rather, he understood that the *political* experience of Israel and Judah was irrelevant to American circumstances. "I will insist that the Hebrews have done more to civilize men than any other nation," Adams wrote in 1809. "If I were an atheist, and believed in blind eternal fate, I should still believe that fate had ordained the Jews to be the most essential instrument for civilizing the nations. If I were an atheist of the other sect, who believe or pretend to believe that all is ordered by chance, I should believe that chance had ordered the Jews to preserve and propagate to all mankind the doctrine of a supreme, intelligent, wise, almighty sovereign of the universe, which I believe to be the great essential principle of all morality, and consequently of all civilization."[3]

As Adams understood, it is the prophets of Israel and Judah, not the kings, who teach us the meaning of order. Israel and Judah were petty states not very different in political structure from some other petty states of the ancient Levant; as states, they perished under the might of the vast empires that had menaced them from their beginnings. It is not Jerusalem the political capital that signifies much; it is

Jerusalem—repeatedly ruined and depopulated, but always rising from the ashes—as Zion, the home of the name of God, that looms immense. To look at the spiritual experience of the Hebrews and the Jews in adequate perspective, however, it is well first to review briefly the political history of the kingdom that had Jerusalem for its capital.

Jerusalem: Disaster and Triumph

For nearly two centuries after Moses had led the Israelites to the threshold of the promised land of Canaan, the Hebrew tribes were engaged in occupying Palestine—sometimes by peaceful penetration, sometimes by conquest. At the height of their territorial power, Israel and Judah combined would occupy an area little bigger than modern Belgium. Joined in a loose confederation, the tribes were led by judges, or charismatic chieftains, whose duty it was to restore righteousness; these judges inherited the office of Moses.

About the year 1030 B.C., the Israelites chose a king, that they might withstand better the military power of their enemies. The kings of Israel and Judah would not claim to be divine, unlike the rulers of the Oriental empires in that age: at most, they declared that the Lord approved of them. Saul, the first king, fell to his ruin before his young rival David. Leading a band of mercenaries, David took the old Jebusite city of Jerusalem, and founded there both the religious sanctuary of the Israelites and their political capital. ("Zion" originally meant the hill on which David established Yahweh's shrine and built a palace.) The kingdom of a united Israel lasted only through the reigns of David and his son Solomon; after the year 926, this realm was split into a northern kingdom and a southern—into Israel (or Samaria) and Judah.

The kingdom of Israel, with its capital at Samaria, was five times the size of its southern rival, and included ten of the twelve Hebrew tribes. But after two centuries, it was crushed by the Assyrians, and the enslaved "Lost Ten Tribes" vanished forever into the heart of the Assyrian empire. Little Judah, nevertheless, survived until the year 587 (or, in a broken condition, a trifle longer), going down at last before the might of the Chaldeans of Babylon; the people of Judah, too, or most of them, were carried away into bondage.

In the year 538 B.C., a remnant of the Jews (as the descendants of the Israelites are called after their Babylonian captivity) were permitted to return to Jerusalem, where they rebuilt their Temple, or sanctuary of Jehovah, about 520. A people militarily weak and often impoverished, governed for centuries by high priests and later by kings or princes half Greek in their culture, the Jews of the Return were dominated successively by the Persians, the Greeks, the Hellenistic empires of Syria and Egypt, and the Romans. Under these foreign masters, some degree of autonomy was possessed by the Jews until the Romans crushed the revolt of the Jewish Zealots in the year 70 A.D. Then again the Jews were expelled from their sacred city and dispersed throughout the civilized world. Not until almost the middle of the twentieth century would there arise again in Palestine a state governed by people of Jewish stock.

This is a long grim history of civil war, foreign oppression, fire and slaughter. If the subjects of the monarchies of Israel and Judah, and of the later Jewish states, knew something more of freedom and justice than did the people of neighboring states, that was in part because their kings were too feeble, and too much harassed by enemies on their frontiers, to rule with absolute authority.

What chiefly distinguished the Israelites and their successors the Jews from the political order of the despotisms by which they were surrounded, however, was the existence of a partial check upon the civil authority. For before the Babylonian Captivity, the great prophets restrained the kings' ambitions, and during the Hellenistic and Roman overlordships the people were protected by the Sanhedrin, or court of religious elders. Yet no one writes of the "political genius of the Jews" after the fashion in which historians praise the Greek and Roman contributions to worldly order.

The Israelites almost might be called a non-political people: they developed no political theories of a secular sort, and no enduring practical political institutions on a national scale—though their local communities, clan and town, outlasted their monarchy and (until the Diaspora, or uprooting of the Jews) outlasted alien dominations. Their one clear political principle was a religious doctrine. Jehovah is King, they declared, and true laws are Jehovah's laws. Judges, kings, and high priests, the powers of this earth, are but surrogates of Jehovah at best, indulged by Him or sometimes made instruments of His wrath. "The human rulers of this people are chosen, accepted, or tolerated by God," as Roland de Vaux puts it, "but they remain subordinate to him and they are judged by the degree of their fidelity to the indissoluble covenant between Yahweh and his people. In their view of things the State, which in practice means the monarchy, is merely an accessory element; in actual fact Israel lived without it for the greater part of its history."[4]

This, then, is the high contribution of Israel to modern social order: the understanding that all true law comes from God, and that God is the source of order and justice. But of practical political establishments in Israel or Judah or the later Jewish principalities, nothing remains.

It is no wonder that the New England Puritans failed to establish a latter-day Bible state, on an Old Testament pattern, for that ideal state of justice and charity never really had existed in Israel and Judah; and the Jewish "theocracy" after the Babylonian exile could not be imitated successfully in seventeenth-century America, a land and an age profoundly different. The twentieth-century democracy of Israel, with its secular parties and western parliamentary structure, bears no resemblance to the Kingdom or to post-exile theocracy. Even had Israel and Judah not been overwhelmed by Nineveh and Babylon, the temporal order of those little kingdoms did not possess strength sufficient to endure long without thoroughgoing alteration.

Yet though scattered and persecuted, the Jewish people survived. When all the other civilizations and creeds of the ancient world have disappeared, Jewish faith and Jewish culture have persisted to our time, permeating the societies of many lands and reasserting their vigor. Similarly, the holy city of

Jerusalem did not die, though Nineveh and Babylon and Memphis and Susa and Antioch, and other mighty imperial capitals of the ancient world, were destroyed utterly. The buildings of Jerusalem might be razed, the city's walls thrown down, its population put to the sword; still, under Byzantine and Arab and Crusader and Turk, the Jew would find his way back to the sanctuary of Zion, lamenting beside the Wailing Wall that was said to be a fragment of the ancient Temple, renewing community on those blood-soaked sacred hills.

From its foundation, the hill-town of Jerusalem was a fortress. Almost impossible to storm except from the north, and repeatedly strengthened by military works, this city would sustain sieges century after century—falling after desperate resistance against overwhelming odds, yet always restored after some interval. Only as a fortress did the place enjoy natural advantage: it did not lie upon the principal ancient trade routes, there was little water, the country round about was infertile; the city had no industry, and its commerce was such as a place of pilgrimage and minor political capital could attract.

For all that, this unlikely spot became the most holy ground for three great religions, so that the city on its plateau, nearly surrounded by deserts, magnetically drew back inhabitants after destruction, though mighty Babylon lay covered by the sands and the old capitals of Egypt gave way to Greek Alexandria. Jerusalem was denounced by the prophets for wickedness and hardness of heart, but the city was condemned so fiercely only because it was loved so passionately.

Where the Temple built by Solomon stood once, there rises today the Dome of the Rock, the Mosque of Omar, erected by the Moslems in 688 A.D. The Temple, with its most sacred chamber the Holy of Holies, was the reason for Jerusalem's symbolic power over all Jews; the palaces of King David and his successors were as nothing by the side of the Temple. Jerusalem, said the prophets and the priests, was the throne and dwelling of Jehovah: all the nations of the earth would come there to worship the one true God. And so it came to pass.

Out of Jerusalem, said the prophets, flows the river of life.

This is the eternal city: salvation radiates from Jerusalem, for here God meets with man. Beyond the confines of time, Jerusalem will be the city of moral perfection and of joy. The material Jerusalem, down through the centuries, was squalid enough in one age or another. Yet the Jerusalem of prophecy—the symbolic Jerusalem, holy Zion—is the city of divine wisdom in which man is freed from sin.

So it was with the political order of the Israelites and the ancient Jews—imperfect at its best, weighed in the balance and found wanting. But the moral order of Israel, the sanctuary of the soul, has transcended time and circumstances. It lives in the modern world. The Bible is the record of the growth of that moral order.* Although America is no Bible state, without some knowledge of the Bible the fabric of American order cannot be understood tolerably well. Therefore the meaning of the Old Testament—which to many people in the twentieth century must seem a confused and confusing account of remote times and forgotten wars—is the subject of the next portion of this chapter.

The God of Justice

There is but one God; and He is just. That is the essence of the legacy of Israel. It may be platitudinous to say this, but the important thing about platitudes is that they are true—which is why they have become platitudes.

Through Moses, this fundamental understanding of the just God was given clear expression. But it was known before

---

* By definition, the Old Testament is a collection of sacred writings in Hebrew, declared by the Jewish Scribes to have been composed under divine inspiration. "Testament" means "covenant" or "contract" under God. Probably the division and arrangement of the Bible with which most people are familiar was the labor of Stephen Langton, at the University of Paris, about the year 1228 A.D. Attempts to make the Bible more easily readable by large deletions and rearrangements often have reflected the editors' preferences and prejudices. Thomas Jefferson made such an attempt at sorting out the sayings of Jesus from the Gospels; but the result was chiefly a calculated reinforcement of Jefferson's own Deism.

the voice spoke upon Sinai. In its most dramatic form, that truth is examined in the Book of Job.

As we know it in the Old Testament, the story of Job appears to have been set down during the Babylonian captivity of the Jews, about the time of Isaiah II. Yet its origin is immensely older—running back to an age more than two thousand years before the birth of Jesus. In the Book of Job one finds no mention of the Israelites. What are we to make of God's ways toward man? That question was asked many centuries before the Israelites came out of Egypt, and a voice from the whirlwind answered it.

God permits Satan to try the faith of a good man, Job, a kind of desert sheik. Deprived by Satan, the Evil One, of his children and his goods, Job sits like a leper upon a dunghill, afflicted by a loathsome disease. He is made what the Arabs call *sidi bu zibbula*—old father of the dunghill, outcast and despised. His wife tells him to curse God and die. Indeed he longs for death, but he will not renounce the Lord.

Job has been a just man: he has not lusted after virgins, acquired wealth wrongly, committed adultery, mistreated his slaves, refused charity to the poor, widowed, and orphaned, worshipped strange gods, rejoiced at enemies' misfortunes, thrust strangers into the street, or abused his land and his tenants. Yet God has decreed, or permitted, that Job should suffer beyond endurance. Why?

To Job amongst the ashes come his "comforters", friends who know only the letter of the law, with their smug and narrow interpretations of the ways of God. Job has offended against God, or else does not submit himself meekly to God's justice, they tell the sufferer. It is as if Job were upon trial. Can he not find a mediator with God, or even summon God to witness?

Then, to the confounding of the comforters, God does speak from a whirl of dust. Job has been more right than his comforters, God reveals; yet Job too has been wrong. The Lord of creation reminds Job that His ways are beyond human comprehension: Job has fallen into presumption by attempting to understand the will of God. To this revelation the tormented Job submits himself meekly. It is not for man to

adjudge God, as if God and man were litigants. With this submission, Job's faith is made perfect. And in the end, there is
restored to Job twice what he had before his loss.

Such faith in God's ultimate justice, a true perception
coming down to the Children of Israel from the dawn of conscience, distinguished the Hebrews from the other peoples of
the ancient world. The gods of Israel's neighbors were many,
and they had little to do with justice. The "Baals" of Syria
and Mesopotamia were local deities, propitiated sometimes
by human sacrifice; they were arbitrary gods, in no kinship
with human beings; no universal sovereignty was claimed for
them. The gods of Assyria and Phoenicia and other nations
were voracious and dreadful. The gods of Egypt were strange
to the point of lunacy. The gods of the Greeks were mere per-
sonified forces of nature, whose passions and caprices no man
would think of emulating. Greece excepted, those other
nations called their rulers divine beings. But for Israel, the
king was Jehovah's steward at most: the Israelites had their
priests and their kings, but not priest-kings.

With their loathsome rites, their temple prostitutes, their
indifference to justice, these alien religions were abhorrent to
the Children of Israel. Unlike these false gods, Jehovah was
not a mere force of nature, or the patron of a clan. His relation
to Israel was *ethical*, from the time He spoke from the burning
bush. He was the God of the Covenant: of an eternal pact
between Him and His chosen people, a compact renewed by
every worshipper at every formal sacrifice to Jehovah.
Although man was made in God's image, man was forbidden
to create any molten image of Jehovah, lest Israel come to
worship idols rather than the reality of God. When, at the
final ruin of the Jewish state, Roman soldiers burst into the
Temple and tore away the veil of the innermost sanctuary,
they were astonished to find no image there. Israel alone knew
that no man might look upon the face of the Creator.

From the eighteenth century onward, humanitarian
writers have protested that Yahweh, God of Israel, was merciless. But to so argue is to ignore the strange gods of those
centuries. To those who lived by His laws, Jehovah was infinitely kind; in time, Israel learned through the prophets that

24

God was not the lord of justice only, but also a deity loving His people and to be loved by them. Nothing of that sort could be said of the pagan gods: no worshipper of Astarte or Moloch or Ashur or even Zeus thought of his deity as the author of law for man, or fancied that a terrible and unpredictable divine force could be loved. Those ages considered, Jehovah was gentle, by the side of the false gods.

Only Jehovah had made with man a covenant—a solemn bond between greater and lesser, revealed to men chosen by the Lord. To Noah, some knowledge of this Covenant was communicated; to Abraham, a further understanding; to Moses, a large revelation. The God who decreed the Covenant was a God who had made known the ways of justice among men. Potentially at least, the world that God had created was a world of order. That order had been broken by man's willful sinfulness, beginning with the disobedience of Adam and Eve in the Garden. "For the imagination of man's heart is evil from his youth," the Lord declares in the book of Genesis.*

"In Adam's fall we sinned all": that is the first line of the Puritans' *New England Primer*, the first book printed in North America. That doctrine was part of New England's legacy from Israel. What is called the "doctrine of original sin" passed from Judaism into Christianity, and became in time a fundamental principle with the Christian settlers in early America.

Man had fallen, the Israelites believed: that is, man had fallen away from what God intended man to be. The story of the Garden of Eden was a representation of that Fall. Although some understanding that man had sinned and fallen away from his better nature may be traced dimly in other religions of the ancient Near East, only in the faith of

---

* Here, as usually in these chapters, the English translation is from the "King James" Bible, the oldest one still in common use. The recent Jerusalem Bible expresses Genesis 8:21 thus: "Never again will I curse the earth because of man, because his heart contrives evil from his infancy." On translations of the Scriptures, see Ward Allen (ed.), *Translating for King James* (Nashville: Vanderbilt University Press, 1969); and Dewey M. Beegle, *God's Word into English* (New York: Harper, 1960).

Israel had, that conviction a dominating place. To Israel, "sin," in essence, was rebellion—insurrection against God by breaking the Covenant, or rebellion against moral and social order by failure to fulfill one's obligations. The people of Israel learned that violence and fraud are embedded in fallen human nature, and may be restrained only by obedience to divine authority. Their own fierce history confirmed this: the story of man's fall into sin was repeated in every generation. It was sin that set the men of Israel and Judah at one another's throats even in their hours of desperate common peril. Just after the Babylonians carried off the inhabitants of Jerusalem to captivity, the remnant of the people left in Judea fell to ruinous civil strife—one proof among many of the depravity afflicting even God's chosen people.

Yet in His mercy, Jehovah had given His people an opportunity to redeem themselves. If they would abide by the Covenant He had communicated to Moses, they might be saved from the destroying clutch of sin. The Law was not a punishment or an oppressive burden imposed upon the people: on the contrary, it was the precious gift of Jehovah, by which Israel might exist in justice. The Law of Jehovah was the means for living with one's self and living with one's neighbors; it was the means for regaining order in the soul and in the community.

Modern people, relatively secure, generally take it for granted that some sort of order is at work in the world. They assume, however vaguely, that certain principles of justice exist, and that life has purpose of some sort. But before the people of Israel experienced their "leap in being," by which they learned of the just God and His laws, no confidence prevailed anywhere that an abiding order governed the universe. Everything that happened might be chance, accident; the gods were ferocious or whimsical; those gods laid down no clear principles for the conduct of human life. At best, the pagan gods did as they pleased with human beings, regardless of justice. As Hesiod wrote of the chief of the Greek gods,

> Zeus rules the world, and with resistless sway
> Takes back tomorrow what he grants today.

True, the ancient civilizations desperately desired some principles of private and public order. One can make out an attempt to reach such principles in certain Greek myths; and the Egyptians, or some of them, endeavored to find ethical authority that would make life worth living. In the Egyptian "Coffin Text" entitled "Dispute over Suicide," written about the year 2,000 B.C., we find an awareness by the nameless author that all men are guilty of the disorder that afflicts society, and that only by participating in the divine essence of existence can a person—who is both man and soul—work to redeem the people from their degradation.[5] The quest for enduring order is a natural and necessary search among any people. But the first real success in that quest was achieved by Israel, and that surprising triumph has not been forgotten by mankind.

To the Israelites, the One God revealed himself: that is, divine wisdom and power were made known to Israel by a deliberate act of God. Divine authority informed a people how they should live. The terror of existence without object or rule was dissipated by the revelation that man is not alone in the universe; that an Other exists; and that Other is the One God, who makes it possible for human beings to be something better than the beasts that perish. Through the revelation of order in the universe, men and women are given the possibility of becoming fully human—of finding pattern and purpose in existence, unlike dogs that live from day to day only.

So the Ten Commandments, the Decalogue, are not a set of harsh prohibitions imposed by an arbitrary tribal deity. Instead, they are liberating rules that enable a people to diminish the tyranny of sin; that teach a people how to live with one another and in relation with God, how to restrain violence and fraud, how to know justice and to raise themselves above the level of predatory animals.

Those Commandments are simple enough. They declare that there exists a Supreme Being; that all other "gods" are false; that material images delude; that God's name must not be used for evil purposes; that one day of the week should be devoted to contemplation of the divine; that parents must be honored; that murder and adultery and theft are evil; that in a process at law, one must not lie; that the inner desire for another's possessions is sinful. These principles are not the whole of morality, of course; but they are essential to morality. And they are as true for a complex modern civilization as they were for desert wanderers.

Through Moses, the Israelites received a body of lesser laws, still observed in large part by Orthodox Jews. Long later, after the remnant of the people of Judah had returned from their Babylonian exile, these rules and the revelations of the Hebrew prophets were written down in the Torah, the code of divine law, so that the Jews might govern their whole daily existence by religious principles. The Torah, and the rabbis who expounded it, would hold the Judaic faith and observance together while all the other creeds and religious communities of the ancient world dissolved. So it is that the Jews are known as the people of the Law; they possessed the Law before they possessed the Book, or the Bible.

The Law is not merely the decree of a monarch who may pretend to divine powers—that the Israelites learned. The Law is not merely a body of convenient customs and usages that men have developed for themselves. The Law is not the instrument of oppression by a class or a hierarchy. For the true Law is derived from the Covenant that God has made and reaffirmed with his people. The Law is revealed to save man from self-destruction; to redeem man from sin and its consequences; to keep man from becoming a Cain, his hand against every man's; to enable man to resemble the God in whose image he was created.

Throughout western civilization, and indeed in some degree through the later world, the Hebraic understanding of Covenant and Law would spread, in forms both religious and secular. The idea of an enduring Covenant, or compact, whether between God and people or merely between man and man, took various styles in various lands and ages; it passed into medieval society through Christian teaching, and became essential to the social order of Britain, from which society most settlers in North America came. This concept and reality of Covenant was not confined to those American colonies—notably the New England settlements and Pennsylvania—which were fundamentally religious in their motive. Like the people of Israel and Judah, the Americans broke solemn covenants repeatedly; but like Israel, America nevertheless knew that without a covenant, the people would be lost.

And from Israel, even more than from the Roman juris-consults, America inherited an understanding of the sanctity of law. Certain root principles of justice exist, arising from the nature which God has conferred upon man; law is a means for realizing those principles, so far as we can. That assumption was in the minds of the men who wrote the Declaration of Independence and the Constitution of the United States. A conviction of man's sinfulness, and of the need for laws to restrain every man's will and appetite, influenced the legislators of the colonies and of the Republic. Thomas Jefferson, rationalist though he was, declared that in matters of political power, one must not trust in the alleged goodness of man, but "bind him down with the chains of the Constitution."

A principal difference between the American Revolution and the French Revolution was this: the American revolutionaries in general held a biblical view of man and his bent toward sin, while the French revolutionaries in general attempted to substitute for the biblical understanding an optimistic doctrine of human goodness advanced by the philosophes of the rationalistic Enlightenment. The American view led to the Constitution of 1787; the French view, to the Terror and to a new autocracy. The American Constitution is a practical secular covenant, drawn up by men who (with few exceptions) believed in a sacred Covenant, designed to restrain the human tendencies toward violence and fraud; the American Constitution is a fundamental law deliberately meant to place checks upon will and appetite. The French innovators would endure no such checks upon popular impulses; they ended under a far more arbitrary domination.

Israel's knowledge of the Law merely commenced with the experience under God imaginatively described in the books of Genesis and Exodus. This knowledge was broadened and deepened by a succession of prophets. The power of the prophets diminished with the fall of Jerusalem to the armies of Babylon, and ended in the first century of the Christian era. Without venturing rashly here into the labyrinths of biblical scholarship, it is possible to describe the prophets' enduring significance for modern men, and to suggest how deeply interwoven with the fabric of American order this prophetic teaching remains.

Righteousness and Wrath

The word "prophet" means a speaker—one who is called by God to speak to the people and to those in the seats of the mighty. Through the grace and favor of God, a prophet foretold the purpose of God; but he was not a magician, a soothsayer, or a man who predicted in detail the course of events. To put it another way, the Hebrew prophets were men endowed with moral imagination, convinced that Jehovah had commanded them to speak in His name, to tell the people of divine wrath and divine mercy.

"The Hebrew prophets kept the personality of God—kept it triumphantly, and abolished all other claimants to Godhead," T. R. Glover says. "God is personal, and God is one; God is righteous, and God is king—they are four great tenets on which to base any religion, and they were not lightly won. They were the outcome of experience, hard, bitter, and disillusioning—a gain acquired by the loss of all kinds of hopes and beliefs, national and personal, tested in every way that man or devil can invent for the testing of belief. . . . They made righteousness a thing no more of ritual and taboo but of attitude and conduct and spirit. They set religion free from ancient follies and reviving horrors."[6]

Moses was a prophet, and so was Samuel, the last of the judges of Israel. Here, however, we are concerned chiefly with the prophets of the eighth and seventh centuries before Christ, to whom was given courage to rebuke kings and to threaten a whole people with the anger of God. These were the solitary figures later recognized as true prophets, to whom Jehovah had revealed His will—though often they were without public honor in their own time. Amos, Hosea, the first Isaiah, Micah, Jeremiah, Habakkuk, and the second Isaiah have no counterparts in other religions. They were deeply involved in the wars and the domestic discontents of their age, but their message has transcended the events that compelled them to speak.

Israelites and Jews knew that many false prophets had gone forth into the land: court prophets attached to a royal household (though some of these might be true prophets, nevertheless); "sons of prophets," or wandering bands of enthusiasts; prophets who mistook their mere dreams for divine revelation; charlatans and demagogues who pretended to have gained the prophetic afflatus—that is, to have obtained supernatural communication of knowledge. But the false prophets were forgotten, and the true prophets endured.

Although the mouthpiece of God, each of the great prophets spoke in his own style. By their passion, their eloquence, their fearlessness, and their vindication through events, later generations weighed these prophets and found them truly the servants of Jehovah. In the earlier years of Israel, they were called seers—men who perceived what ordinary vision could not apprehend.

Out of their knowledge of the history and traditions and literature of Israel, these men spoke to their generation, reminding Israel of the Covenant and of Jehovah's wrath and purpose. But they spoke from something more than knowledge of the past. They had been inspired by God (often to their own alarm and astonishment) to announce His judgments. They transcended sensory perception and the realm of matter. They were media or conductors, so to speak, for the voice of the Other.

Their insights—or, rather, their communications from a power more than human—were not gained in dreams: God had addressed their minds directly. When they foretold tribulations, because of disobedience to Jehovah, those tribulations soon occurred. When they described the mercy of God, and the relations in which man should stand to his Creator, the resounding persuasiveness of their voices moved the minds and hearts of posterity, if not of those who met the prophets face to face.

The first prophet to set down in writing his revealed hard truths was Amos, who left his herds and his sycamore trees near the town of Tekoa at the command of Jehovah. Making his way to the high sanctuary of Bethel, in Samaria, about 765 B.C., this countryman—no more, apparently, than a shepherd or peasant—denounced king and people for having fallen away from the Covenant. To the high priest, Amos denied that he was a prophet—meaning that he was no professional foreteller of events, but instead a man overwhelmed by God. The luxury, the corruption, the injustice, the smugness of Israel he assailed, telling his hearers that the king would be put to the sword and the people carried into slavery; that the high priest of Bethel would die in exile, his children slain, and his wife made a harlot. What wonder that priests and people drove him out of Bethel? Yet those judgments came to pass.

What signifies most in Amos is his declaration that Jehovah is the God of all peoples, not of Israel only. The Covenant itself is the expression of a justice in the universe that existed long before Moses ascended Mount Sinai; the Israelites, true, are Jehovah's chosen people, in that God has chosen to instruct them directly, and not others; but for that very reason, God demands of Israel a righteousness greater than that of other nations. Amos tells of the anger of God with Tyre, Edom, Syria, Philistia, Amon, and Moab, states faithless and pitiless; but God's wrath with Israel is not less, for Israel has broken the Law. Ignoring the commandments of the Lord, Israel had trusted in sacrifices and rituals to appease Jehovah; so the Lord must chastise His people for sin and folly. There is but one God; and He is Lord of all nations, sparing none, forgetting none.

Like the earlier prophets, Amos delivers a commination for the abuse of power by kings. This conflict runs through the whole history of Israel and Judah. Occasionally a king would seek the counsel of a prophet and ask his blessing—ask, perhaps, for his intercession with the Lord; but commonly the prophets stood in unyielding opposition to royal policies. At the heart of this encounter, often, was this dilemma: the kings of Israel and Judah found it prudent to treat with the monarchs of neighboring states, to take other kings' daughters in marriage, to tolerate the cults of those alien nations within Israel, to form and break alliances with powers that knew not the Law. How might the little kingdoms of Israel and Judah survive without such unhallowed dealings? Trust in the Lord God, replied the prophets. But the kings knew the edge of Assyrian or Babylonian or Egyptian swords and spears. Down to the fall of Jerusalem, this struggle between king and prophet was not resolved.

"The ways of the Lord are right, and the just shall walk in them," the prophet Hosea, another countryman, declared to Samaria, in the late decades of the eighth century, "but the transgressors shall fall therein." Like Amos, but more than Amos, Hosea told of what must be, if Israel should continue to disobey the Law; and yet Hosea implied that this punishment might be revoked by God, should Israel return to obedience. (What the prophets "foretold," ordinarily, were probabilities, not immutable destinies.) For the Lord is compassionate: as a loving and dutiful husband forgives and redeems a licentious wife, so Jehovah seeks to save his people from the fruits of sin. Let the kingdom of Israel cease from harlotry; let Israel abjure alliances with Assyria or Egypt; and then the Lord will forgive and save.

As Samaria sank toward oblivion, in Judah there spoke Isaiah ben Amos, as high in station as Amos and Hosea had been lowly. The first prophet Isaiah told King Ahaz, in the name of the Lord, not to court the terrible Assyrians. Egypt and Assyria, the mortar and pestle of war, might devastate Judah, but a remnant of the chosen people would endure and return. And at the end of time, the world will be transformed; justice will triumph; Zion will be perfected; the people who have kept faith with Jehovah will be rewarded. Put no trust in worldly powers; let Judah stand still while imperial hosts are arming. Near the end of the eighth century, Isaiah described the divine order in history. By the mercy of the Lord, Judah should be saved from Sennacherib's sword, but the cunning and worldly-wise should be confounded: "Woe unto them that seek deep to hide their counsel from the Lord, and their words are in the dark, and they say, Who seeth us? and who knoweth us?.... For the terrible one is brought to nought, and the scorner is consumed, and all that watch for iniquity are cut off."

In that same age, the prophet Micah exhorted the sinner to accept God's anger: the Lord, infinitely compassionate, will raise up those who have been chastened. Jerusalem will fall, but not forever. That catastrophe was not far distant. The prophet Habakkuk, called during the reign of King Jehoiakim, at the end of the seventh century and the beginning of the sixth, inquired why God had permitted the Chaldeans of Babylon to harass Judah and other nations so frightfully. And he found his answer: the Chaldeans had enforced the judgment of Jehovah upon the nations; the sinful were punished through the agency of the sinful. "The righteous shall live by his faith," the Lord told His prophet: wait on the Lord, rejoicing in Him. In the end, the righteous shall be redeemed.

Jeremiah, most tormented of the prophets, lived through the reigns of several kings, and he survived the devastation of Jerusalem that he had foretold. Standing in the court of the Temple, terrified at his dread call from God but fearless before the people, Jeremiah declared to the princes and the multitude that the Temple should be destroyed and the city lie desolate, unless Judah should repent and amend its ways. "This man is worthy to die, for he hath prophesied against this city, as ye have heard with your ears," the priests and the court prophets cried. But the princes saved Jeremiah, and his message was sent to King Jehoiakim—who burnt it.

Jeremiah declared that Judah must submit to Babylon, as a punishment decreed for sins; he would not pray for Jerusalem in her last extremity, for his master was not the king, but God. When the Babylonians took the city in the year 587, after a siege of more than a year and a half, they released the prophet from the dungeon into which King Zedekiah had thrust him. And then Nebuchadnezzar's soldiery sacked fallen Jerusalem; they burnt the Temple and the royal palace, threw down the city's walls, and carried off the people into bondage.

And yet Israel was not destroyed, Jeremiah prophesied; for Jehovah had made a new Covenant with his people. "After these days, saith Jehovah, I will put my law in their inward parts, and in their heart will I write it; and I will be their God, and they shall be my people. And they shall teach no more every man his neighbor, and every man his brother, saying, Know Jehovah: for they all shall know me, from the least of them unto the greatest of them, saith Jehovah: for I will forgive their iniquity, and their sin I will remember no more."

The old Covenant, that is, had worked upon the nation; the new Covenant would work upon the individual person, through conscience and private insight. Jehovah did not need His house upon Zion, nor did He need the kingdom of Judah, as He had not needed Samaria. He was the Lord of Hosts, and through the hearts and minds of those faithful to Him would He bring Israel to redemption; captives though they were, His people would spread the truth of Jehovah throughout the world. The Supreme Person would accomplish His will through a multitude of persons, not through a political state.

The last of the major prophets was the second Isaiah, living long after the first Isaiah (though his writings are Chapters 40 to 66 of the Book of Isaiah). He prophesied during the Babylonian Captivity, saying that mighty Babylon would fall before the power of Persia, and that the chosen people would be liberated by the conquering Cyrus. Upon the palace wall of Belshazzar, regent of Babylon, appeared the puzzling words *mene, mene, tekel, upharsin**; Babylon did fall in a single night; and the second Isaiah (or the nameless prophet so designated) had foretold, the remnant of Judah returned to Jerusalem.

This was a healing prophecy. It is possible to know God, if one does not aspire to understand him utterly: "For my thoughts are not your thoughts, neither are your ways my

---

* "And this is the writing that was written, MENE, MENE, TEKEL, UPHARSIN. This is the interpretation of the thing: MENE; God hath numbered thy kingdom, and finished it. TEKEL; Thou art weighed in the balances, and art found wanting. PERES; Thy kingdom is divided, and given to the Medes and Persians."

—Daniel 5:25-28

ways, saith the Lord. For as the heavens are higher than the earth, so are my ways higher than your ways, and my thoughts than your thoughts." Israel had been the Lord's suffering servant, the representative of mankind; for the sins of all mankind had Israel been chastised. Now the remnant of Israel should be raised up, and the truth of the Lord should go forth to the Gentiles, Israel serving as a light to the nations. At the sins and the tribulations of Israel, the Lord had suffered like a woman in childbirth. Now He will comfort His people, for He loves them.

From first to last, the prophets often were detested by the kings, hated and menaced by the people; like Israel, they were suffering servants. They pointed the way to the salvation of man; man rejected them. Now God himself would intervene more directly in the world, the second Isaiah promised: God would send a new servant, with the divine spirit upon him, to establish justice in the earth.

What are we to make of these prophets, from Amos to the second Isaiah? If they were speaking only to the kings and the people of two petty Levantine states that fell to bits, the prophets would matter little enough in the history of mankind. If that were all, then the prophets failed, for even the restored Jerusalem of the Return went down to dust and ashes later. But in truth, the prophets were speaking to all men, in all times.

"The prophet was an individual who said No to his society, condemning its habits and assumptions, its complacency, waywardness, and syncretism," Abraham Heschel observes. "He was often compelled to proclaim the very opposite of what his heart expected. His fundamental objective was to reconcile man and God. Why do the two need reconciliation?" Why, because of man's overweening pride, man's resentment at God's intervention in history, man's abuse of freedom. Though Jews and Christians declare that no true prophets have been called for the past nineteen centuries, the old prophets endure.* "It is for us to decide whether freedom

---

* Moslems proclaim Mohammed as the greatest of the prophets, of course; and the Mormons believe Joseph Smith to have been a latter-day prophet.

is self-assertion or response to a demand; whether the ultimate situation is conflict or concern."[7]

Through interpretation of Jehovah's ways with Israel, through their search for meaning in Israel's historical experience under God, the prophets descried order in the world. Early they perceived that man is made in the image of a Person who is invisible: the Lord of Creation, transcending matter and time. Out of His love, that Lord has prescribed ethical principles by which God's people may live in community, so that they will not be as the beasts that perish. The Children of Israel first knew God as the Lord of Israel; presently they came to know Him as the Lord of all nations; late, they knew Him for the Lord who works upon every human heart. He is the Lord of Justice, and the Lord of Mercy. Those who obey Him will be saved, redeemed from sin, suffer though they may in their time; at the end of days, theirs shall be the victory. The man who loves the Lord will obtain order in his soul, and the nation that is meek before the Lord will obtain order in the commonwealth. Without knowledge of the Lord, there can be only the outer darkness, where there is wailing and gnashing of teeth.

The Law and the Prophets gave clear ethical meaning to human existence; that is why the order of modern society is founded upon them. All the sins of man that Amos denounced are with mankind still: ghastly violence, corruption of justice, oppression of the weak, selfish indulgence, hypocrisy, ruinous complacency. Although thirty-three centuries have passed since Moses heard the voice of Jehovah, mankind in general has not succeeded satisfactorily in ordering either soul or commonwealth. Yet without the principles of order made known by the Law and the Prophets, modern man could not recognize standards for the person and the republic.

The common people of Israel understood only imperfectly the Law and the Prophets; the average man of the twentieth century understands them no better. Were it not for the legacy of Israel, nevertheless, the human condition would be unendurable for many. Like the ancient Egyptian of the "Dispute over Suicide," men would ask themselves whether it is not better to die by one's own hand than to live amidst corruption. Without the Law and the Prophets, order in existence could not endure.

Under God in Time and History

In the preceding account of Israel and of the sources of Jewish and Christian belief, the character of the Law and the teachings of the prophets have been set down as they were understood by nearly all the early settlers in America, and by the vast majority of Americans at the time of the framing of the Constitution of the United States. Historically speaking, such are the Hebraic roots of American order, whether or not the reader of this book wholly accepts the Law and the Prophets. To undertake Jewish or Christian apologetics— that is, to undertake a theological defense of these beliefs on the basis of reason—is beyond our present purpose and beyond the limitations of space.

To many Americans in the twentieth century, the Old Testament may seem a puzzling and confused narration, in part incredible, in part irrelevant to the condition of modern man. No whale could have swallowed Jonah, any high-school student may object. The "historical Moses" may have been rather different from the Moses of Exodus, modern scholarship may suggest. During the past century, the decline of popular knowledge of the Bible, particularly of the Old Testament, has made it more difficult to relate the Hebraic experience to modern questions of order. For that matter, the Bible never was easy to understand.*

---

* Sir Arthur Quiller-Couch ingeniously compared the books of the Bible with works of English literature, suggesting that with the best of intentions, strong impediments have been placed between the common reader and the understanding of sacred literature.

Let us imagine—as Quiller-Couch suggested in 1920—"a volume including the great books of our literature all bound together in some such order as this: *Paradise Lost,* Darwin's *Descent of Man, The Anglo-Saxon Chronicle*, Walter Map, Mill *On Liberty*, Hooker's *Ecclesiastical Polity, The Annual Register*, Froissart, Adam Smith's *Wealth of Nations, Domesday Book,*

But what we need to bear in mind, if we wish to grasp the connection between the experience of order in biblical times and the experience of order in our own age, is that there exist two distinct forms of history: sacred history, and secular history. Sacred history consists of an account of mankind's experience with God; secular history consists of an account of mankind's experience in mundane affairs. The first form of history often can be expressed only through imagery—through parables, allegories, and the "high dream" of poetry. The second form of history, dealing with worldly events, tries to confine itself to such verifiable records and narrations as are available. Historians in either form must possess imagination, if their products are to have enduring significance.

Necessarily, sacred history describes through images, "as in a glass, darkly." For man's experiences of transcendence—man's sudden rare perceptions of a reality that cannot be measured accurately by his limited five senses—are unlike man's experiences of battles, diplomatic conferences, or elections. The poet sometimes obtains a glimpse of truth, which he then endeavors to test as best he can by his rational faculties: so it is with the scientist, too. And so it was with the

---

Le Morte d'Arthur, Campbell's *Lives of the Lord Chancellors*, Boswell's Johnson, Barbour's *The Bruce*, Hakluyt's *Voyages*, Clarendon, Macaulay, the plays of Shakespeare, Shelley's *Prometheus Unbound*, *The Faerie Queen*, Palgrave's *Golden Treasury*, Bacon's *Essays*, Swinburne's *Poems and Ballads*, FitzGerald's *Omar Khayyam*, Wordsworth, Browning, *Sartor Resartus*, Burton's *Anatomy of Melancholy*, Burke's *Letters on a Regicide Peace*, *Ossian*, *Piers Plowman*, Burke's *Thoughts on the Present Discontents*, Quarles, Newman's *Apologia*, Donne's *Sermons*, Ruskin, Blake, *The Deserted Village*, *Manfred*, Blair's *Grave*, *The Complaint of Deor*, Bailey's *Festus*, Thompson's *Hound of Heaven*.

"Will you next imagine that in this volume most of the authors' names are lost; that, of the few that survive, a number have found their way into the wrong places; that Ruskin for example is credited with *Sartor Resartus*; that *Laus Veneris* and *Dolores* are ascribed to Queen Elizabeth, *The Anatomy of Melancholy* to Charles II; and that, as for the titles, these were never invented by the authors, but by a Committee?

"Will you still go on to imagine that all the poetry is printed as prose; while all the long paragraphs of prose are broken up into short verses, so that they resemble the little passages set out for parsing or analysis in an examination paper?" (See Sir Arthur Quiller-Couch, *On the Art of Reading*, Cambridge University Press, 1920, pp. 154-55.)

prophets. In the seventeenth century, the great mathematician and philosopher Pascal had one intense experience of religious transcendence. What he had experienced in the depths of the soul, below the limits of ordinary consciousness, he could not put into words, though he was a master of prose. All he could say was "Fire, fire, fire!"

Therefore the Old Testament, a sacred history, ought not to be read as if it were simply an account of everyday events. Often it is symbolic and poetical, for many truths are most accurately expressed in symbol. The story of Jonah, for instance, really is a kind of parable: it teaches how a people, through their religious faith, may preserve their identity even though conquered and enslaved by some immense power—as if a man were to be swallowed by a sea monster. Just so the Jews, through faith in Jehovah, survived their Babylonian Captivity.

Similarly, it is not a conceivable "historical Moses" —unknown to us, because no documents or even artifacts or bones survive from that remote time and that obscure people—who really matters. The important Moses is the figure portrayed by the scribes—the man who experienced a "leap in being," who was granted moments of transcendence perhaps comparable to Pascal's, who through that experience was enabled to describe the Law for the Hebrews. One might as well search for "the historical Don Quixote de la Mancha." Even if somehow it could be shown that Cervantes had in mind a particular Spaniard of his acquaintance whom he used as model for his immortal character, it would not be the "historical" Quixote who would matter to the twentieth century: the significant Quixote is the Knight of the Sorrowful Countenance of Cervantes' novel. As Mark Twain said of Homer, the *Iliad* was written either by Homer or by another man with the same name. So it is with Moses and the Law.

Although a good deal of secular history is intermingled with the sacred history of the Bible, the Old Testament's purpose is not to present a chronicle of political and military events, but rather to describe in a variety of ways, and by various hands, how the Hebrews were made aware of the existence of Jehovah, and of Jehovah's laws, and of the Covenant that joins God and man. To criticize the Old Testament as if it were an attempt at chronological recording in the modern sense is to mistake its whole character.

By the truths about the human condition that were revealed from the lips of Moses and of the prophets, the Hebrews became aware of eternity. This is not easy for us to understand. For modern men generally think of what we call "time" much as the Greeks thought of time: that is, time seems "linear," extending in a kind of line from some point in remote antiquity to the present. But the Hebrews thought of time as "psychic"—that is, related to the soul, to spiritual experience. For God, all things are eternally present: God is not bound by human conventions of "time." What occurred to Moses and the prophets was a breakthrough in time, so to speak: for certain moments, or rather in certain abrupt experiences, time and the timeless coincided, and the Hebrews were given a glimpse of God's eternity. This is expressed by Thorleif Boman:

"For us space is like a great container that stores, arranges, and holds everything together; space is also the place where we live, breathe, and can expand freely. Time played a similar role for the Hebrews. Their consciousness is like a container in which their whole life from childhood on and the realities which they experienced or of which they had heard are stored. Because every person is and remains identical with himself, a consolidating unity adheres to each person's psychical content which could be expressed thus: all this is my world, my existence. A man who lives from the psychical impressions that the external world makes upon him has a world in his consciousness; he lives in time, but even while he actually lives in time, moments and intervals of time play a very subordinate role. It is the same I that once played as a child, went to school as a youth, and entered competitive life; body and appearance have changed, life's experiences have come, but the man himself, i.e. his consciousness, has remained the same self. Seen from the inside his personal experiences form a unity, a world; in that world he moves freely and with ease. Thus even while the Hebrew lives in time, time-distinctions play a very trifling role for him. Even in the divine consciousness all time-measurement disappears, because Yahweh remains identical with himself."[8]

For the Hebrew, then, in essence time is not simply a progression of events, marked by deaths and births. The true significance of time is its psychic relationship with eternity. One may say that what matters about time is the intensity of psychic consciousness in certain moments, not mere duration. For the Hebrew prophet, and for the Hebrew and the Jew who understood the prophet, then, to survive physically as an individual is not the aim of existence. The Hebrew's "time" is not merely the days and nights of individual life, but rather the existence of a people under God. God is outside of "time," even though time is His creation: for God, all events in the history of a people are simultaneously present. God is not bound by "past" or "future" or "present."

That being so, Hebrew thinkers are not much concerned with the question of personal immortality. The survival of the Hebrew *people*, chosen by God, is the burning concern of the prophets. The individual living in this moment is one of those people: he shares in the past of the people, and shares in their future. The order of the people, under the Covenant with God, transcends the momentary desires of any individual. If men are to be saved, they will be saved as persons among the people of God, not as isolated individuals.

With the revelation to Moses, made fuller by the prophets, God had broken into time. Thereafter the Hebrews, or those among them who understood the Law and the Prophets, held a view of history and the human condition very different from that of other peoples. "The God who became manifest through the Exodus deliverance obviously was not subject to any time but was rather a sovereign lord of time, or, to put it differently, a God transcending time," Gerhart Niemeyer writes. ". . . Furthermore, an eternal God manifested by a pinpointed intervention in time must be a God of purpose, will, and intelligence, rather than merely a god of cosmic potency. As manifested by His action in the past, He must be a God of judgment and redemption. . . . So now time became, in a way, an ocean inhibited by men, interrupted by the single island that was thrown up through God's past intervention." And God might intervene again.[9]

This brief disgression about the Hebrew concept of time is closely related to the concept of order—and, through Jewish and Christian teaching, to the idea of order which still underlies America's personal and social order. If God is purposeful, consciously willing, intelligent, just, and redeeming—why, then man is foolish if he does not seek to know this Being: to understand the human condition, one tries to know God. If such is God's nature, then the "time" which matters is the time in which men commune with God and fulfill His purposes. Through God, man enters into eternity, redeemed from sin. If this is true, surely history takes on a new meaning: history becomes the life of a people in their search for God, or their flight from God. And accounts of the doings of captains and kings are important only so far as those events relate to God's purposes with mankind.

If one accepts the reality of a just and loving God, whose eternity is the escape from the shackles of time and the sufferings of this world, it must follow that a people should enter into the order which God has designed for them. If God has ordained an order for the soul or the person, and an order for the community, to flout that order is a destructive act of disobedience, by which a man would make himself a prisoner of time. It was this conviction which steeled the Hebrews and the Jews to live by the Law, despite all sufferings and all temptations.

Under fierce trials, often the Jews of the Diaspora must have asked themselves this question: what evidence exists that Moses and the prophets perceived clearly and spoke truly? They found pragmatic evidence, the evidence of the experience of their people: the fact that they had survived as a people, when other peoples had perished. In the passage of the centuries, they saw not only Jews, but Christians and Moslems, still living by the essence of Hebraic revelation; they saw even new secular philosophies and ideologies permeated by the Law, though the philosophers and ideologues might try to deny it. This might not be perfect evidence of the truth, but all evidence for things beyond the five senses is imperfect: survival and continuing relevance to the human condition are the best practical tests to determine whether a body of belief is right or wrong.

And, as Jeremiah had prophesied, Jehovah had put His law in their inward parts, and written it upon their hearts. In exile, their national community broken, they perceived the reality of God inwardly, through their worship. Personal knowledge of God's existence and justice and love, of God's eternity, entered into their lives—if as in a glass, darkly. But for that knowledge and that confidence, they would have perished altogether.

From the experience of the Jews in history, within the confines of time, it is possible to learn why men submit themselves to a personal order and a social order. To go to the heart of the matter, why do human beings conform to a prescribed personal order, when often their immediate pleasure and advantage would be served by disregarding that personal order? Why do they conform to a prescribed social order, when often they seem to have much to gain by breaking the laws?

The fundamental reason for such obedience is this: God has willed such an order, and that order is for man's great benefit. If a man defies that order, he becomes something less than human: he separates himself from the God who brought him into existence, and who offers him eternity. Disorder is rejection of divine wisdom and justice and love. So for the sake of sustaining that order, and of playing his part in it, a man who believes in the Law and the Prophets will sacrifice everything worldly. It is better that a man should die in time than that a people should perish for eternity.

It is the Hebraic order which has come down through the centuries to the American Republic—if altered by intervening circumstances and beliefs. God, the Lord of history, the timeless One, became known at Mount Sinai. His Law still is the source of order, even when the forms of that law have been secularized.

Other peoples have inherited other moral orders: such an order, for instance, as Gautama, the Buddha, communicated to India. Yet the rudiments of order seem everywhere similar. C. S. Lewis, in *The Abolition of Man*, collects parallel passages from a variety of religions and philosophies that illustrate the existence of a Natural Law universally recognized. He finds common acceptance, though variously expressed, of a law of general beneficence; a law of special beneficence; duties to parents, elders, ancestors; a law of justice; a law of magnanimity. Revelation in the Old Testament perhaps is not the only form that revelation has taken; but it is the form of revealed truth upon which American order depends.[10]

Revelation, in one form or another, everywhere has been the foundation of private and public order. It is not altogether surprising that the primitive Children of Israel, in an Arabian desert, should have experienced profound moral revelations; for such insights are not unknown among the moral leaders of peoples who remain primitive to the present day. In 1928, a small party led by a British explorer, L. M. Nesbitt, was trapped by a band of fierce Danakils in the Danakil Depression of Africa. They were saved from massacre by a kind of Danakil prophet, a very ancient man named Suni Maa, who lived by a moral order that the young men of his clan could not apprehend. Nesbitt asked this "living skeleton" if the lives of the explorers were in danger.

"In great danger indeed," replied Suni Maa, "especially with the younger men who are avaricious, and whose short life has not yet raised them above the soil to which they cling. They do not know that there are things, not of this world, but mysterious and superior, and worthy of being sought to the exclusion of everything else."[11]

Such perception of a truth beyond the senses, expressed in this century by a Danakil seer, was the revelation that Moses delivered to the Children of Israel. As the Hebrews learned, there exists a moral order which transcends time. In both its Christian and its Jewish forms, the order of Sinai still gives vitality to America.

The Old Testament and the New America

In colonial America, everyone with the rudiments of schooling knew one book thoroughly: the Bible. And the Old Testament mattered as much as the New, for the American colonies were founded in a time of renewed Hebrew scholarship, and the Calvinistic character of Christian faith in early America emphasized the legacy of Israel.

Marcionism—the heresy that Christians ought to cast aside Jewish doctrines—had no adherents in early America.* Only a handful of Jews settled in the colonies before the Revolution, and not a great many until the later decades of the nineteenth century; yet the patrimony of Israel was more powerful in America than in Europe.

The New England Puritans not only ordered their commonwealth by the Ten Commandments and the books of Leviticus and Deuteronomy, but constantly drew parallels between themselves and the people of Israel and Judah. The Puritans thought of themselves as experiencing afresh, under God, the tribulations and the successes of the Hebrew people. "For answers to their problems," says Daniel Boorstin, "they drew as readily on Exodus, Kings, or Romans, as on the less narrative portions of the Bible. Their peculiar circumstances and their flair for the dramatic led them to see special significance in these narrative passages. The basic reality in their life was the analogy with the Children of Israel. They conceived that by going out into the Wilderness, they were reliving the story of Exodus and not merely obeying an explicit command to go into the wilderness. For them the Bible was less a body of legislation than a set of binding precedents."[12]

New England's intellectual leadership, which would give that region an influence over the United States disproportionate to New England's population, transmitted this understanding of the Hebrew patrimony far beyond the New England colonies. But also the teachings of John Calvin of Geneva, so strongly imprinted upon the Congregational churches of New England, worked as well (if less intensely) upon the other American colonies. The Presbyterians—Scottish, Scotch-Irish, and English—who came to the middle and

---

* Marcion, about the middle of the second century of the Christian era, taught that Christians ought to subscribe only to the "pure gospel" of Saint Paul, and that the Yahweh of the Jews really was not God, but the Demiurge, under whom mankind suffered until the coming of Christ.

southern colonies also were disciples of Calvin; even the Anglican settlers, until the middle of the seventeenth century, often emphasized the Calvinistic element in the doctrines of the Church of England.[13] The Baptists, too, were moved by Calvin.

John Calvin's Hebrew scholarship, and his expounding of the doctrine of sin and human depravity, impressed the Old Testament aspect of Christianity more strongly upon America than upon European states or other lands where Christians were in the majority. And of course the Lutherans, the Methodists, the Quakers, and other Christian bodies in the American colonies did not neglect the Old Testament, though they might tend to give it less weight than did the Calvinists.

"Because freedom from slavery and oppression were dominant themes in the Old Testament," Neal Riemer writes, the legacy of Israel and Judah nourished American liberty. "It warned—as in the story of the Tower of Babel—against Man's attempt to be God. It forced Man—as in the story of Adam and Eve—to recognize his mortality and fallibility and to appreciate that there can be no Utopia on earth. Again and again, it inveighed against the belief that Utopia can be captured and made concrete in idolatry. On the other hand, however, it left ample room for effort to make life better. This is the central meaning, as I read it, of God's Covenant with Noah and its reaffirmation with Abraham, with Moses, and with the later prophets."[14]

So the Old Testament helped to make social realists of the early Americans. As Edmund Burke would declare at the end of the colonial period, the religion of most of the Americans was "the dissidence of dissent, and the Protestantism of the Protestant religion"—suffused with the spirit of liberty. But it was not from the Law and the Prophets that the Americans dissented; the Calvinists' quarrel was not with the Children of Israel, but with the prerogatives of the Church of England. Generally the Calvinists believed more fervently in the authority of the Old Testament than Martin Luther had; the idea of the Covenant colored all their political convictions.

Clinton Rossiter expresses succinctly the cardinal point

that American democratic society rests upon Puritan and other Calvinistic beliefs—and through those, in no small part upon the experience of Israel under God. "For all its faults and falterings, for all the distance it has yet to travel," Rossiter states, "American democracy has been and remains a highly *moral* adventure. Whatever doubts may exist about the sources of this democracy, there can be none about the chief source of the morality that gives it life and substance. . . . " From this Puritan inheritance, this transplanted Hebrew tradition, there come "the contract and all its corollaries; the higher law as something more than a 'brooding omnipresence in the sky'; the concept of the competent and responsible individual; certain key ingredients of economic individualism; the insistence on a citizenry educated to understand its rights and duties; and the middle-class virtues, that high plateau of moral stability on which, so Americans believe, successful democracy must always build."[15]

Of course Puritanism, and the other forms of Calvinism in America, were Christian in essence, not renewed Judaism merely. And the stern Calvinism of the early colonial years would be modified, presently, by the growth of a less Calvinistic Anglicanism, by the influence of Lutheranism, by the coming of millions of Catholic immigrants in the nineteenth century, and by the arrival of masses of immigrants of other confessions or persuasions. As generation succeeded generation, moreover, the New Englanders themselves would relax the strictness of the founders of Massachusetts Bay Colony.

That said, nevertheless American political theory and institutions, and the American moral order, cannot be well understood, or maintained, or renewed, without repairing to the Law and the Prophets. "In God we trust," the motto of the United States, is a reaffirmation of the Covenants made with Noah and Abraham and Moses and the Children of Israel, down to the last days of prophecy. The earthly Jerusalem never was an immense city: far more Jews live in New York City today than there were inhabitants of all Palestine at the height of Solomon's glory. But the eternal Jerusalem, the city of spirit, still has more to do with American order than has

48

even Boston which the Puritans founded, or New York which the Dutch founded, or Washington which arose out of a political compromise between Jeffersonians and Hamiltonians. Faith and hope may endure when earthly cities are reduced to rubble: that, indeed, is a principal lesson from the experience of Israel under God.

Notes

[1] John Winthrop, "A Model of Christian Charity", in Perry Miller (ed.), *The American Puritans: their Prose and Poetry* (New York: ·Doubleday, 1956), pp. 78-83. See also *Winthrop's Journal "History of New England"*, edited by James Kendall Hosmer (New York: Barnes and Noble, 1908 and 1966), Vol. I, pp. 24-50.

[2] R. B. Y. Scott, *The Relevance of the Prophets* (New York: Macmillan, 1968), p. 225.

[3] John Adams to F. A. Vanderkemp, February 16, 1809, in C. F. Adams (ed.), *The Works of John Adams* (Boston: Little, Brown, 1854), Vol. IX, pp. 609-10.

[4] Roland de Vaux, *Ancient Israel* (New York: McGraw-Hill, 1961), Vol. I, p. 99.

[5] See James B. Pritchard (ed.), *Ancient Near Eastern Texts relating to the Old Testament* (second edition, Princeton: Princeton University Press, 1955), pp. 405-07; also Eric Voegelin. *Israel and Revelation* (Baton Rouge: Louisiana State University Press, 1956), pp. 98-101.

[6] T. R. Glover, *Progress in Religion* (London: Student Christian Movement, 1922), pp. 143-4.

[7] Abraham J. Heschel, *The Prophets* (New York: Harper Torchbooks, 1971), Vol. II, p. xvii.

[8] Thorleif Boman, *Hebrew Thought compared with Greek* (translated by Jules L. Moreau; New York: W. W. Norton, 1960), pp. 137-38.

[9] Gerhart Niemeyer, *Between Nothingness and Paradise* (Baton Rouge: Louisiana State University Press, 1971), pp. 166-67.

[10] C. S. Lewis, *The Abolition of Man* (New York: Macmillan, 1947), pp. 51-61.

[11] L. M. Nesbitt, *Desert and Forest: the Exploration of Abyssinian Danakil* (London: Penguin Books, 1955), p. 269.

[12] Daniel Boorstin, *The Americans: the Colonial Experience* (New York: Random House, 1958), p. 19.

[13] On the power of Calvinism in early America, see C. Gregg Singer, *A Theological Interpretation of American History* (Nutley, N. J.: Craig Press, 1964), particularly the Introduction.

[14] Neal Riemer, *The Democratic Experiment: American Political Theory* (Princeton: D. Van Nostrand, 1967), p. 35.

[15] Clinton Rossiter, *Seedtime of the Republic: the Origin of the American Tradition of Political Liberty* (New York: Harcourt, Brace, 1953), p. 55.

CHAPTER III
GLORY AND RUIN:
THE GREEK WORLD

The One Betraying Flaw of the Hellenes

In philosophy, in warfare, in the early sciences, in poetry, in grace of manners, in rhetoric, in high cunning, the people who called themselves the Hellenes excelled all civilized folk who had preceded them in time; in certain things, they have not been equalled in achievement, all these centuries since the Greek *polis*, the city-state, lost its freedom. Yet the ancient Greeks failed in this: they never learned how to live together in peace and justice.

To most of the men who drew up the American Constitution, the ancient Greek commonwealths offered few precedents worth following—except in the sense that the blunders of Greek political experience provided some salutary negative lessons. For philosophy and the arts, we turn to the glory that was Greece, as for religion and ethics we turn to Israel; but for a pattern of politics we emulate neither.

It was clear to the men who founded the American Republic that they had inherited and developed a social order better than Athens or Syracuse or Sparta or Corinth had ever known. What they found valuable in the Greek experience or order was a cautionary tale of class conflict, disunity, internecine violence, private and public arrogance and selfishness, imperial vainglory, and civic collapse: what to shun.

Speculative in all things, the ancient Greeks debated and wrote endlessly about political constitutions; yet no Greek commonwealth ever succeeded in establishing a good constitution that would endure long—except perhaps for Sparta, a garrison state. The history of Athens, the city where the tragedies of Aeschylus and Sophocles and Euripides were written and first performed, was itself tragic, so that the best which may be said of Athens' political order is that many other Greek commonwealths suffered still worse ills. Nevertheless, what the Hellenes accomplished despite their political confusion remains astonishing.

"To one small people, covering in its original seat no more than a hand's-breadth of territory, it was given to create the principle of Progress, of movement onwards and not backwards or downwards, of destruction tending to construction," Sir Henry Maine wrote in 1876. "That people was the Greek. Except the blind forces of Nature, nothing moves in this world which is not Greek in its origin. A ferment spreading from that source has vitalized all the great progressive races of mankind, penetrating from one to another, and producing results according with its hidden and latent genius, and results of course often greater than any exhibited in Greece itself."[1]

If this praise seems a trifle exaggerated, still it is true that what we call "modern civilization" could not have come into existence without the Greek gifts. (It should be added that the Greeks themselves recognized no "principle of Progress," even if in fact they did bring about human progress: the Greek philosophers and poets and historians generally believed that there was nothing new under the sun—that human history would repeat over and over again, under new aspects and names, what humanity had suffered or achieved in earlier ages.) The Greeks had come near to conquering the known world; had they been able to develop any tolerable system of harmony and amity within their culture, they might have succeeded altogether. No other race has produced, within a brief period, so many brilliant individuals as did the Greek people at the height of their glory.

The Greeks had a word for everything, we say. One of

their most important words was *hubris*—meaning man's overweening arrogance, at which the gods grow wrathful. And no wonder; for fierce local pride, a ruthless lust for power, and arrogant individuality run catastrophically through Greek history. Their religion could not restrain them. That is why, despite all their endowments, at last the Greeks succumbed to less volatile peoples.

Notorious in the ancient world for their craftiness, often the Greeks overreached themselves, as individuals and as communities. "Never trust a Greek," Euripides wrote about 410 B.C. "Beware of Greeks bearing gifts," the Romans would say. The Hellenes were the cleverest people of antiquity, and the best soldiers; yet they spent their energies in destroying one another. It was impossible to unite the Greek city-states for any purpose, except in extreme emergency—if then. Leagues or confederacies of some of those states would be formed, from time to time—and would dissolve abruptly, out of the presumed immediate advantage of one or another of the partners. "Greeks tell the truth," a Russian proverb runs, "but only once a year."

During the period in which the Israelites invaded Palestine, the waves of people called the Hellenes were conquering the Greek mainland and the islands, submerging remnants of an earlier civilization in those lands. When the Israelites were struggling against the power of the Philistines, the Greeks were sacking Troy, in Asia Minor. About the time when the Assyrians destroyed the northern kingdom of Israel, the Greeks were founding colonies throughout the Mediterranean, eventually all the way from Spain to Egypt, or from the Black Sea to Libya. The great age of Greece, the age of the culture of Athens, began not long after the independence of the Children of Israel had ended.

Liberal historians and literary men of the eighteenth and nineteenth centuries idealized the Greek civilization that they knew through its literary remains and the broken fragments of its architecture and sculpture. Greece in general, and Athens in particular, those writers praised somewhat extravagantly as the birthplace of freedom, the sanctuary of the good and the beautiful, the source of rationality, the home of sweetness and light. This enthusiasm was neither wholly unjustified nor altogether sound. Most leaders of the French Revolution indulged an indiscriminate admiration for classical Greece and Rome. But the leaders of the American Revolution, and of the early years of the American Republic, seasoned their classical tastes with several grains of salt.

So far as they turned to classical examples for political justification or guidance, Americans paid more attention to the Roman Republic than they did to the Greek cities; and upon them, the direct influence of the Greek historian Polybius—writing about the Roman constitution—probably was greater than the combined influence of Plato's and Aristotle's political theories. The founders of the United States, many of them lawyers and nearly all of them men with considerable practical experience of public life in colonial and Revolutionary America, perceived that the institutions of a Greek *polis*, compact in territory and small in population, could not be imitated successfully in the sprawling expanse of the American Republic; but the Roman Senate might be another matter. Some of the American leaders, from colonial times up to the Civil War, had read the Greek and Roman historians in the classical languages; many more had read those works in translation, or at least in abridgements. Most of them were well aware that whatever the accomplishments of the Greeks in the realm of the mind, strong and equitable political order had not been a Greek accomplishment.

Even today, looking up to the Acropolis of Athens, one sympathizes with the adulation of Greek civilization that prevailed among educated people through the eighteenth and nineteenth centuries. If a civilization is to be judged by its beauty, the Greeks never have been excelled. The wrecked temple called the Parthenon remains glorious, though a stone skeleton; the carved maidens of the Erechtheum have a tranquillity that the living Athenians never knew; the whole splendid complex that Pericles created whispers in ghostly fashion of noble aspirations and perfected taste—though the Crusaders made a castle of these monuments, and the Turks later converted the sanctuary of Athena into a patchwork fortress. Down the centuries, the Acropolis was plundered by its conquerors: the very frieze of the Parthenon was stripped off at the end of the eighteenth century, to repose in the British Museum. Although now only the shadow of a shade, the Acropolis' loveliness lingers as evidence of Greek imagination. Almost at the beginning of things, the Greeks knew everything. But how did they come to know it?

No one has answered that question satisfactorily. We do know the causes of the Greeks' political failure. This Periclean architectural splendor was erected with funds filched from allies of Athens; in one aspect, it was the manifestation of a rapacious imperialism that led to the massacre of other Greeks luckless enough to have trusted to Athenian honor. The fiscal extravagance of building those temples upon the Acropolis was a principal cause of the Peloponnesian War, and the work was completed only two years before Athens surrendered to Sparta. Americans who had read Thucydides' history, perhaps in Thomas Hobbes' translation, knew that this beauty had been bought with the price of blood. Pericles' democratic imperialism had been succeeded by demagoguery, by oligarchy, and by defeat at the hands of old enemies. What is called by historians the "Great Age" of Athens lasted less than fifty years; American statists looked for greater permanence.

After all, the Parthenon was not built by a spirit of sweetness and light only, but also by a civic ambition that knew few scruples. And the gods worshipped upon the Acropolis—even wise Athena herself—were feeble models for a good social order. Alfred Zimmern, one of the more influential writers on Greek political institutions, remarks that the work of the Greek political thinkers "was vitiated by their failure to realize the extent and urgency of the claims of the individual soul. Men must be spiritually free before they can co-operate politically on the highest terms. In the last analysis the weakness of Greek political speculation can be traced back to the weakness of Greek religion."[2]

How far, indeed, did the Olympian or "Homeric" deities of the Acropolis—those gods to whom magnificent temples were dedicated in every Greek city—offer true freedom of spirit to the Greek citizen? Those temples, and the gods' images that stood within, were symbols of civic pride, and often of civic arrogance; these were "official" gods, but they did not speak to private conscience, or nourish the human longing for immortality, or clearly declare a norm for what men and women ought to be.* At Athens, one sees the broken monuments of the Olympian deities; and formerly, at least, many writers mistook the stone aloofness and tranquillity of the Olympian gods for the spirit of the old Greeks themselves. But the power of the Olympian mythology diminished rapidly in the "Great Age" of Greece—though some of its insights passed into the religious philosophy of Plato.

There was more to Greek religious yearning than the state cult of the Olympians. Greek spiritual impulse had a side at once darker, more pathetic, and more satisfying to certain emotions than ever the idealized images of Zeus and Athena and Poseidon and Apollo could be. For a time, the Homeric religion, the Olympian mythology infused with spirit, partially obscured this earlier and more mystical religion; but after the "Great Age," the old yearning would manifest itself again, and the Olympian civic cults would diminish in vitality.

One still glimpses something of this other faith at Delphi—or better still, in a way, at one of the grand Greek cities of Sicily, ancient Akragas. And what one glimpses is not the rationalism, the sweetness and light, which yesteryear's admirers of Hellenic culture mistook for the whole of the Greek religious consciousness.

---

* There is marvelous insight in the *Iliad* and the *Odyssey*. But unlike the Hebrew religion, which grew and unfolded over many centuries, the Greek religion did not develop beyond an early high promise—or rather, when Greek popular faith began to seem inadequate, it was supplanted by philosophy. Greek religion itself never rose higher than Homer. "The first great manifestation of spirit is the Homeric religion, which is simultaneously the first great manifestation of nature," Walter F. Otto writes. "In later Greece the spirit continued to emerge in manifold aspects, but never in so original a form as in this religion of the living spirit. With it Hellenism uttered its eternal word concerning the world." (Walter F. Otto, *The Homeric Gods: the Spiritual Significance of Greek Religion*, translated by Moses Hadas; New York: Pantheon, 1954, p. 159.)

Early in the fifth century before Christ, the poet Pindar called Akragas the most beautiful of mortal cities. Nowadays the town is called Agrigento; and though decayed, with no suggestion of Greek genius in its modern population, the place has beauty still. From the cathedral, which stands on what once was the acropolis, or citadel, of Akragas, one looks across a valley full of ruins and almond trees, toward an opposite ridge that still is surmounted by classical temples of the sixth and fifth centuries before Christ.

Here, with a splendid prospect of the sea, are the shrines of the civic deities, protectors of the *polis* of Akragas: temples dedicated to Zeus, to Hera, to Heracles, to other Olympians. That of Zeus, overthrown by an earthquake during classical times, was one of the three biggest temples in all the Greek world—so vast in design that the people of Akragas, nearly ruined by its cost, never succeeded in roofing most of it before it fell. The city's southern wall runs close by these tall columns; it seems as if the Akragantines had set the temples of their gods upon this height to impress upon approaching enemies some sense of the mightiness of the gods who watched over fair Akragas. But these Olympians failed their city, for Carthage lay directly across the sea; and in time the Carthaginians would storm Akragas and set fire to these temples of golden stone.

How far the folk of Akragas put their trust in the gods of Olympus is uncertain. For underneath that city lies a monstrous labyrinth of watercourses and strange passages, all the work of man: cold air from those subterranean regions rises from an aperture in the Piazza del Purgatorio, turning to vapor in the Sicilian sun. Out of worship of something, that labyrinth was created—but not out of devotion to the Olympians. Under the brow of a hill, distant from the civic temples of the city's southern ridge, one still can enter the cavern-fane of Demeter and Kore, older than the Greek city itself— dedicated to chthonian deities, dark gods of earth and underground waters, of death and rebirth and fertility. Was not the faith of the common man of Hellenic times, even during the Great Age perhaps, an appeal to these shadowy powers, more than to the beautiful carven or cast abstractions set high upon the hill?*

From first to last, many among the Greeks prayed to the chthonian deities under the earth, or turned to the mystery-cults of Orpheus or of Dionysius, rejecting the rational, substantial world. Some, among these the traveller Pausanias in the second century before Christ, found courage enough to crawl down into the cave of Trophonios, the earth god—there to learn the future. (A considerable time after emerging from those dark terrors of the temple-cave of Trophonios, Pausanias found that he was able to laugh again.)

The Greek god of law and order was Apollo, the spirit of sunlit reason. But against the ordered world of Apollo there contended powerfully the Greek god Dionysius, the spirit of passion, unrest, release. In the most famous of Greek shrines, at Delphi, the temples of those two great gods stood side by side. Might the presence of the god of order restrain the magic of the god of excess?

If the Greek religion was not so gentle and sunlit as nineteenth-century writers often fancied it to have been, neither was the Greek civil social order tranquil: Apollo struggled with Dionysius. At Akragas, the city's first hideous tyrant, Phalaris, is said to have roasted his enemies in a fur-

---

* Unless one understands something of the Greek religion, one is liable to misinterpret Greek tragedy, always religious in character. Thus some modern critics and dramatists often represent Sophocles' *Antigone* as a kind of "civil rights" tract, with the ruler Creon as the embodiment of oppressive government and the girl Antigone as the symbol of personal liberty. One may find, as did Aristotle, a groping toward "natural law" in *Antigone*. Yet the tragedy is no political polemic. For the Greeks never conceived of liberty *outside* the *polis*, the state, or even in opposition to the state: Socrates would not assert legal rights against the Athenian democracy. Sophocles' Creon is not a tyrant, but only a leader of the *polis* in danger of becoming a tyrant; Antigone is not enunciating some new theory of law in opposition to the state and to the *nomos*, or tradition of law. Actually, Antigone speaks for the claim of the chthonian deities, whose cult demands that her brother's body must be ceremonially buried; Creon represents the civic cult of the Olympian deities, with its demand for obedience to public order. Sophocles did not look upon either claim as wrong or unjust, in itself; rather, his tragedy describes the conflict of loyalties and duties, the clash of religious impulses that cannot be reconciled easily.

nace of brass shaped like a bull. Throughout its independence, Akragas alternated between despotism and anarchy —and so it was with most other Greek cities. Out of Akragas' population of more than two hundred thousand people, at the height of this *polis*, the large majority were slaves, many from Africa. (Among Greek political thinkers, only Plato was able to hint at a commonwealth not supported by slavery—and then only in the dream-realm of his early *Republic*.) In most cities, the common expectation of the ablebodied average citizen (despite the Greeks being a remarkably healthy race) was that he might die by violence while still fairly young. Even in luxurious Akragas, these Greek lovers of beauty were hardy men, accustomed to spear and sword; doubtless they would have been astonished at the idyllic description of their existence which secure scholars would sketch centuries later.*

Neither those wonderful representations of the Olympians in human form, in every city's civic temples, nor the cults of darkness, mystery, and domestic hopes, closer to many Greeks hearts, could give to the Greeks such a principle of personal and public order as Jehovah had given to Israel. The Olympian and the chthonian deities came to blows repeatedly, quite as every Greek *polis* stood ready for war against barbarians and against other Greek cities of similar origins and institutions, should advantage seem to lie in aggression. Within every city, class hostilities, political feuds, and private ambitions rent the fabric of civil social order every few years. The democracies were no less violent than were the tyrannies and the oligarchies. To the Greeks, "freedom" meant primarily the independence of their own city-state, not personal liberty in any high degree. Their passionate attachment to the immediate place of their birth was at once their strength and their undoing; while the picturesqueness of their religion did not provide them with a coherent moral order.

---

* In general, nevertheless, the Greeks abhorred torture, and they would not permit it to be represented in the theater. They were capable of putting to the sword the whole male population of military age in captured cities, but they stopped short of inflicting deliberate physical cruelties in cold blood.

Solon and the Athenian Polity

And yet these Greeks of ancient times contributed more to the American understanding of order than at first meets the mind's eye. Although the Greeks never achieved enduring justice for themselves, that was not for want of trying. Some of them, statesmen and philosophers, indirectly shaped American institutions. The Greek architect of order most impressive to Americans of their country's formative years was Solon.

About the time when Jeremiah was prophesying the destruction of Jerusalem by Nebuchadnezzar, there rose to authority in Athens the poet Solon, whom later Greeks would revere as one of the Seven Sages. Two centuries afterward, Plato would write that had Solon persisted in his elegiacs and iambics, he might have equalled or excelled Homer or Hesiod as a religious poet. But Solon turned to statecraft; he became the towering lawgiver of Athens. The Constitution of the United States, adopted nearly twenty-four centuries after Solon gave a new constitution to Athens, has in it some tincture of Solon's prudence.

Americans of the eighteenth century knew Solon through the pages of the Greek biographer and moralist Plutarch (A.D. 46-120), whom a few of them had read in the Greek, but whom many encountered in the stirring translations of North or of Dryden. Through his *Lives of the Noble Grecians and Romans*, Plutarch came to influence Americans' thought more (with the possible exception of Cicero) than did any other classical writer. Of all Plutarch's parallel lives, none seemed more relevant to the necessities of the infant American republic than did his life of Solon.

Dr. Benjamin Rush, Philadelphia physician, scholar, and signer of the Declaration of Independence, was no hearty admirer of the curriculum of classical studies generally. Yet Rush dreamed a dream in which three lawgivers came to him, and the first said, "I am Solon."* Rush thought it would be

---

* The other two lawgivers of Rush's dream were William Penn and Numa Pompilius, the Roman counterpart of Solon.

better to teach American boys the Bible and Judaic studies, intensively, than to expend time upon Greek and Roman mythology; but he knew Solon's worth. And the innovating radical Tom Paine, who usually seemed more critical of classical learning than was Rush, admiringly paraphrased Solon's principle that popular government was at its best when "the least injury done to the meanest individual was considered an insult to the whole Constitution."[3]

The Americans of Rush's and Paine's time perceived that Plato and Aristotle, those grand names, had written as men denied power, when the Greek *polis* already was decadent. But Solon had been such a one as the American leaders themselves, called to high authority, endeavoring in the dawn of what would become a mighty state to forge a permanent framework of just institutions.

Poet, philosopher, religious teacher, patriot, hero, and practical leader of men, Solon possessed the intellect and the character for which the founders of the United States sought in their own generation. It is not surprising that in the jargon of American daily journalism, "solon" has become a cant term for "legislator." Had Solon never lived, perhaps the American Constitution would have come into existence nevertheless; but that document might have been less strongly marked by the concepts of "checks and balances," of compromise among interests and classes, and of "mixed government," that Solon expressed and in considerable degree established in rising Athens. Long after Solon, these principles would be re-expressed by Plato, Aristotle, Polybius, Cicero, and other classical writers on politics; they would enter into the theory and the fabric of constitutional government throughout western Europe and (in a diversity of forms) throughout the New World.

Solon, the son of a spendthrift father of good family, was born perhaps fifty years before the Babylonians took Jerusalem, and he lived for three decades after that destruction—which event presumably did not loom large for him. He was a man of vision, a seer: he implied that truths were imparted to him from a source beyond his private rationality, and in that he was like a prophet. His practical accomplishment, though large, did not matter so much as the high example of probity that he set, and the moral imagination which he introduced into the political order.

In the later years of the seventh century before Christ, Athens had lost a part of that dominant strength on the mainland of Greece which she had possessed as early as the tenth century. Corinth, Sparta, and her immediate neighbor Megara threatened to eclipse her; although the population of Attica (the territory immediately controlled by Athens) was large, Athens' political organization was relatively feeble. No longer ruled by kings, Athens was tormented by civil feuds. The harsh laws enacted by Draco, beginning in the year 621, had restored order for some years, but had widened the perilous breach between social classes. Athens during Solon's youth was an aristocratic state, with both the virtues and the vices of that condition of society. It had become true of Athenians that the love of money was the root of all evil.

The wealthy landowners desired still greater possessions; the poorer classes, envious, desired what they had not the ability to employ intelligently. More immediately, the laws of Draco, though protecting property, had pushed the poor to the wall. Of the free citizens of Athens, many had fallen hopelessly into debt and were compelled to pay to their creditors one-sixth of the income from their property—the margin between a competence and grinding penury. The lot of the numerous artisans or craftsmen in Attica—nearly all of whom, being descended from aliens, did not enjoy full citizenship—was worse still, for they and their wives and children could be sold into slavery if they did not meet obligations to their creditors; thousands, indeed, had been so sold abroad. In such conditions, rebellion might be expected. Whether the rebels should win or lose, the *polis* of Athens would be torn apart, and left defenseless before external enemies. Despite wealth, population, and culture, Athens still was governed by a constitution that had developed in a simpler tribal society. Might a man of genius be found who could restore true community to the Athenians?

Such a one was the ethical poet Solon. This man proclaimed that only through righteous order, *eunomia*, may the commonwealth endure. The leaders of the people have been corrupt and unrighteous, Solon wrote in one of his elegies. They have affronted *Dike*, or Justice, and Justice will take vengeance unless the commonwealth mends its ways.* Before affairs came to crisis in Athens, Solon had made his mark as patriot and diplomat, regaining the island of Salamis for Athens, and standing above political faction. A merchant, he had travelled much. His being an inspired poet counted for more with the ancient Greeks than it would with modern American voters.

In the year 594, Solon was elected "eponymous archon," or chief civil magistrate of Athens. The condition of the commonwealth being desperate by this time, everyone—the middle classes, the rich, the poor—agreed to confer upon Solon the authority of "arbiter" or "reformer of the constitution," with power to do whatever he might find necessary in political and economic concerns. Entrusted with such authority, nearly any other Greek would have made himself tyrant. Yet Solon, rejecting opportunity to seize absolute rule and vast wealth, healed Athenian society.

His practical reforms may be touched upon here. In economic policy, Solon abolished the old law that had permitted a person to mortgage his own body; he liberated all people who had been sold into slavery for debt, ransoming and bringing back from abroad those who had been shipped into other countries. He rejected the demand of the radicals that all lands be divided equally among Athenians, but he reduced debts and took measures to diminish the concentration of land-holding. He revised and revalued the coinage, and reduced the rate of interest. Without seizing the property

---

* The Greek word *dike* (pronounced dī-kē) signifies justice, compensation for evils or damage suffered, and legal proceedings. The Greek word for law is *nomos*, meaning custom, convention, constitutional law, or positive law. For good definitions of such terms, see F. E. Peters, *Greek Philosophical Terms: a Historical Lexicon* (New York University Press, 1967).

For a perceptive and succinct description of the Greek understanding of justice and law, see Huntington Cairns, *Law and Its Premises*, the twentieth Benjamin N. Cardozo Lecture (New York: Association of the Bar of the City of New York, 1962). "Since law has its source in the world as a system of order," Dr. Cairns writes, "that system necessarily sets limits to what is sound and correct in the legal realm."

of the wealthy, he succeeded in improving the condition of the poor and in restoring a tolerable economic balance in the commonwealth.

As for the political constitution, Solon affirmed the reality of a "polity"—that is, of a system of government which respects the interests and the rights of all classes and elements in a commonwealth. The reformed order which he brought about was neither an aristocracy nor a democracy, but a "mixed" government. He abolished the requirement of good birth for holding office, instead establishing qualifications and duties on the basis of wealth, as determined by annual income. Four classes of citizens were recognized, the wealthier being permitted to hold higher offices, the poorer to take lesser posts. These classes were related to military service, and thereafter the military strength of Athens depended principally upon the men of the middle classes, who could pay for the armor and weapons necessary for their service as heavy-armed infantrymen.

Solon increased the powers of the Assembly, or popular congregation of all free citizens. Executive authority, however, he left in the hands of the old Council of the Areopagus, a kind of senate recruited from former religious, military, and civil magistrates. To make the Assembly more effective, Solon created a new Council of Four Hundred, to prepare and guide the Assembly's business. These old and new councils, Solon wrote, would save the Assembly from rashness: "The ship of state, riding upon two anchors, will pitch less in the surf and make the people less turbulent."

He admitted to Athenian citizenship foreigners who would rear their sons to follow a trade or a craft in Attica, or who had been exiled permanently from their native cities; he encouraged Athenians to enter crafts and commerce. Before long, the effect of these measures was to make Athens the leading Greek state in manufacturing and commerce.

To the Athenians, Solon had given a measure of democracy, but in the process had made himself unpopular with many—including some whom he had benefited greatly. There were those who heaped contempt upon him because he had not made himself absolute master of the city nor enriched himself at public expense. To them he replied in a sardonic poem:

> Solon surely was a dreamer, and a man of simple mind;
> When the gods would give him fortune, he of his own will declined;
> When the net was full of fishes, over-heavy thinking it,
> He declined to haul it up, through want of heart and want of wit.
> Had I but that chance of riches and of kingship, for one day,
> I would give my skin for flaying, and my house to die away.

Solon had not sought power; he resigned power readily.

Having promulgated his code, Solon (who declared that his laws would bind the *polis* for a hundred years) left the city for a decade, probably both to see whether the people would abide by the new constitution in his absence, and to avoid the complaints and the mockery of those who found fault with his creation. By this time he was about fifty-two years old. He would return to Athens; but just now it is well to look at the ethical basis for order which Solon had described in his poems and exemplified in his life.

Zeus, the supreme god, is just, said Solon; it is men who bring disasters upon themselves. Zeus watches, and his justice works retribution upon the evildoer; aye, and not upon the evildoer only, but upon his children and his neighbors, for divine wrath afflicts a whole state.

Men labor under private illusions; they hope for what is most unlikely, and demand what should be left to Fate. The frantic pursuit of wealth commonly leads to follies and crimes:

> Wealth would I have, but wealth by wrong procure
> I would not; justice, e'en if slow, is sure.

Honor, not possessions, should be sought by the virtuous man—that honor which comes from excellence. Renounce illusion, pursue justice, and seek to obey the gods, to whom we owe the wonder of life.

As a man must order his private life, abandoning illusion, so the commonwealth must seek a harmonious existence: justice consists in the harmonious arrangement of social duties and right. The righteous man maintains his desires and his responsibilities in balance, and so it is with the state. Classes and factions must restrain themselves, if the *polis* is to endure; righteous laws reconcile the claims of different social groups, and that was what Solon had accomplished through his constitutional reforms:

> Such power I gave the people as might do,
> Abridged not what they had, nor lavished new;
> Those that were great in wealth and high in place
> My counsel likewise kept from all disgrace.
> Before them both I kept my shield of might,
> And let not either touch the other's right.

A man may teach as much by what he is as by what he says; and so it was with Solon. When he left Athens for ten years of wandering, he declared that he would be judged by Time, not by the men of his own hour. By Time has he been judged and found noble and righteous. "He created the type of the lawgiver, the *nomothetes*, in the classical sense, not for Hellas only, but as a model for mankind," Eric Voegelin writes of Solon. "He was a statesman, not above the parties, but between them; he shared the passions *of* the people and thus could make himself accepted as one of them in politics; and he could act with authority as the statesman *for* the people, because in his soul those passions had submitted to universal order. The Eunomia he created in the polis was the Eunomia of his soul. In his person came to life the protoype of the spiritual statesman."[4]

Most men have a rough way with principles of righteousness. No sooner had Solon gone abroad than self-seekers endeavored to break in upon his reformed constitution. By the year 561, an early friend of Solon's, Peisistratus, succeeded by cunning in making himself tyrant of Athens.*

---

* In one of the most wily of Greek ruses, Peisistratus dressed a beautiful young woman, extraordinarily tall, in armor like that of the goddess Athena; she rode to the Acropolis in a chariot, with Peisistratus reverently following, and was admitted to the fortress as a divine being. Once got inside as devotees of the presumed goddess, Peisistratus and his accomplices could not be ejected by the magistrates. The Athenians may have been the least superstitious of the Greeks, but their rationality was not always proof against impostors.

He was dislodged, but would return to power. Solon had returned to his native city in the midst of these new troubles. He opposed Peisistratus with his accustomed intrepidity; when all other adversaries of the usurper fled, old Solon went into the marketplace and exhorted the citizens to overthrow the tyrant. No one stood by him, so Solon returned to his house, laid his weapons in the porch, and declared that he had done with public affairs; he would not flee. It was the folly of the citizens, he told his countrymen, that had surrendered the Acropolis a second time to Peisistratus; men's vices, not the gods' malice, undo righteousness:

> If now you suffer, do not blame the Powers,
> For they are good, and all the fault was ours;
> All the strongholds you put into his hands,
> And now his slaves must do what he commands.

Aside from his usurping of authority, the clever Peisistratus turned out to be a friend to the constitution that Solon had instituted; in some respects he even strengthened its generous provisions, and persuaded Solon to give him advice. At the end of his life, Solon began to write a long poem about the fabled island of Atlantis; but he was nearly eighty years old, the age to which he had desired to survive, and the task was too arduous for him. Herodotus would write that Solon, in his travels, had told King Croesus of Lydia that no man should call himself happy until the hour of his death: "In every matter it behoves us to mark well the end: for oftentimes God gives men a gleam of happiness, and then plunges them into ruin." But Solon himself had ordered his soul and his acts consonant with the order of the universe. Dying full of years and honors, and leaving a model of righteousness to mankind, Solon was happy in the hour of his death, if ever man was.

And That House Fell

That righteousness which Solon had labored to quicken in public concerns as in private, and that Athenian constitutional balance which might have been an example to all Greek commonwealths, were not destined to endure. For a time, true, it seemed as if rectitude and the mixed polity might prevail. The half-century that followed the death of Solon was a time of tyrants, for the most part, but often enlightened and prudent tyrants.* Athens and many of the Greek cities grew in prosperity, strength, and beauty.

Toward the end of the sixth century—at least in mainland Greece—the tyrants began to slip from power, and relatively democratic constitutions were proclaimed; in Athens, the sons of Peisistratus were overthrown in the year 510, chiefly through the might of Sparta, an old-fangled commonwealth that opposed both tyranny and democracy. When the Spartan garrison had been forced to withdraw from Athens, the nobleman Cleisthenes drew up a revised Athenian constitution more democratic than that of Solon, but influenced strongly by Solon's general principles, distributing powers carefully and, in Plutarch's words, "admirably adapted to promote unanimity and preserve the state." The tendency of the age was in the direction of greater civic liberty, of federations to resist barbarian enemies, and of a growing moral consciousness.

But the Greek states increasingly were menaced from east and from west. The Ionian Greeks of Asia Minor's coasts were subjugated first by the Lydians, then by the Persians; in Sicily, the terrible Carthaginians made headway against the Greek colonies, and the infant power of Rome began to press against the Greek cities of the Italian boot. By the year 490 B.C., the gigantic Persian empire commenced an invasion of Europe, and not long later the African commercial state of Carthage, with a large fleet and many mercenary troops, moved against the Greeks of the west.

Despite odds, the Greeks triumphed in east and in west. Miltiades and Themistocles of Athens crushed the Persian

---

* Although most Greeks professed to detest tyranny, many desired to become tyrants themselves. "Tyranny," in its Hellenic sense, means illegal assumption of power; a tyrant was not necessarily cruel, and few Greek despots were stupid. In their early stages, at least, new tyrannies commonly were popular with the poorer classes. Aristotle describes tyranny as a degenerate form of kingship.

hosts at Marathon and Salamis. Theron, tyrant of Akragas, aided by Gelon, tyrant of Syracuse, overwhelmed the Carthaginian army at Himera, saving Sicily, it is said, on the very day when the Athenian naval victory off Salamis ended the Persian invasion of mainland Greece. So commenced Greece's "Great Age"—generally reckoned as enduring only three-quarters of a century, if so long.

It would be an age of brilliant culture—and of military atrocities. The political and intellectual leaders of the young United States, long later, would profit by this tragic experience of the Greeks of the fifth century; for then most educated Americans read Plutarch attentively, and some read the overwhelming history of Thucydides, the Athenian general who beheld the end of the Great Age and understood the reasons for Greek failure. The Great Age of Greece was a democratic period, in Athens and many other states: that was one reason why few American politicians, until the time of Andrew Jackson, chose to proclaim themselves democrats.

For Athens, the most brilliant and most democratic of Greek states, bears the heaviest responsibility for that suicidal conflict called the Peloponnesian War. It was the folly and injustice of Athens, in considerable part—Athens' failure to achieve righteous order in the democratic commonwealth—that left Greece, by the end of the fifth century, impoverished and feeble before barbarian adversaries.*

About the year 461, the democratic leader in Athens, Ephialtes, broke the power of the Council of the Areopagus and in general abolished the checks upon popular sovereignty that had been part of Solon's "mixed government," retained substantially by Cleisthenes. In law, political power thus passed to the commercial and industrial population, and to Athens' numerous seafaring citizens, who had increased under the policies of the naval commander Themistocles; the more aristocratic or the middle-class Athenians called these "the sailor rabble." A politician of remarkable talents,

---

* To the Greeks, a barbarian was anyone who did not speak Greek and share Greek culture—indeed, almost any people who did not participate in the Olympic games might be regarded as barbarous.

Pericles, completed Ephialtes' work and made the mass of Athenians effective masters of public policy. From 443 to 429, Pericles led the Athenian democracy—at first with astonishing gains for the Athenian state.

Defeating her rivals at sea and on land, Athens built an empire and grew rich. Himself a man of intellectual power and taste, Pericles encouraged at Athens the philosophers, the architects, the artists of the Great Age. The Acropolis, devastated during the Persian war, was rebuilt in that magnificence still visible today, heedless of cost. Between the defeat of the Persians at Salamis and the end of the Peloponnesian War, Athens could boast of nurturing or attracting more men of original intellectual or artistic gifts than ever before had been gathered in one country; perhaps, indeed, no such congregation of talents has occurred anywhere since then. The dramatists Aeschylus, Sophocles, Euripides, and Aristophanes were eminent citizens of the Athenian *polis* during the Great Age. This was the time, too, of the historians Herodotus and Thucydides and Xenophon; of Phidias and Ictinus and others in the arts; of the beginning of Athens' schools of philosphy (Pericles inviting to his city such famous sophists as Protagoras and Hippias), with Socrates as the fearless teacher and martyr of the Great Age.

Yet all this splendor of culture soon was overwhelmed by political and military disaster. Puffed up by pride and greed, afflicted by that arrogance which the Greeks called *hubris*, the Athenian democracy abandoned Solon's righteousness for the prizes of empire. The smaller states which had been Athens' allies were reduced to servitude, and these victims called Athens "the tyrant city"—meaning that, however democratic at home, Athens abroad became the devourer of other cities' freedom. For survival, many of the Greek cities combined against Athens. When her opponents were joined by the military power of Sparta, Athens fell desperately into the long struggle for supremacy of the Peloponnesian War, from the year 431 to 404.

That war ended when, after a ghastly siege, a Spartan garrison occupied the Acropolis of Athens. Thucydides wrote that the city of Athens, like some tragic hero, fell from inner flaws. The Athenian democracy had been rash, selfish, and merciless, devastating even neutral states; Athens' immense resources had been squandered in extravagant undertakings, and the Athenian people had elevated to leadership demagogues and self-seeking adventurers, while exiling or rejecting or misemploying those men of integrity and ability who might have saved the *polis*. Lacking unity of purpose, self-control, and prudence, the Athenians had flung away everything they had gained since Solon had restored justice in the commonwealth.*

The war had been decided not in Attica or the Peloponnesus, but in distant Sicily. There Syracuse, the strongest and most populous Greek city of the west, had been chosen as the victim of Athenian ambition. The Athenian Assembly had voted enthusiastically to dispatch its navy and a large proportion of its troops on what was little better than a piratical raid, with enormous Syracusan loot in prospect. But the Syracusans had been reinforced by a Spartan fleet and a Spartan army. After months of fighting, what remained of the Athenian force in Sicily had surrendered to the Syracusans and Spartans in September, 413. The captured Athenians were flung into the stone-quarries outside Syracuse, and of all the men who had gone out from Attica, next to none ever returned. After that debacle, the surrender of Athens had been merely a matter of waning energies and hopes.

Popular government had been discredited in Athens by the folly of this Syracusan expedition, and the civil war had weakened all Greek city-states, even those that had remained neutral in the struggle. On the fringes of the Greek world, the barbarian powers exulted in the Greeks' disunity. The Carthaginians determined to conquer the whole of Greek Sicily; having captured Selinus and Himera, they laid siege to

---

* The failings of Athenian democracy were remarked by several leading Americans of the Revolutionary and Constitutional period. Benjamin Rush, for instance, wrote that Sparta, with its "compound legislature," enjoyed five hundred years of freedom, by contrast with the instability and domestic violence of pure democracy in Athens. (Spartan liberty meant freedom for the Spartans, of course—not for the subject peoples of Lacedaemonia, or for the serfs called helots.)

Akragas, the second strongest city of Sicily (after Syracuse), and the first in splendor and beauty.

Akragas fell to Carthage little more than a year before Athens surrendered to Sparta, and the ruin of that "most lovely of mortal cities" suggests how failure to find enduring principles of order undid the Greeks everywhere. The philosopher Empedocles had said that his fellow-citizens of Akragas built as if they thought themselves immortal, but lived as luxuriously as if they expected to die on the morrow. Even as the Carthaginians made ready their troops and ships for the invasion of southern Sicily, one private citizen of Akragas, named Gellius, was so rich that he splendidly entertained every visitor to the city; once he gave impromptu hospitality to five hundred cavalrymen from Gela who had arrived rain-soaked, "and provided them all forthwith from his own stores with outer and inner garments." When the Carthaginians besieged Akragas, the city's senate decreed that citizen-soldiers on watch should not use more than two pillows and three blankets. One recalls the warning of Solon against the appetite for excessive wealth.

Akragas had gathered mercenaries and troops from other Greek cities of Sicily. But these failed them; the Akragantines believed that their allies and the Spartan commander of the mercenaries had been bribed by Carthage. Abandoned by their doubtful friends, the terrified people of Akragas fled out of their wonderful city one night in December, 406; entering the next day, the soldiery of Carthage slaughtered what free citizens had not escaped. The generous Gellius and his friends, preferring death to exile, took refuge in the temple of Athena; when all was lost, they set fire to the building and died there. After using Akragas as their winter headquarters, the Carthaginians burnt the place. The temple of Hera, still standing, bears on its columns the mark of that Punic fire. "And that house fell, and great was the fall of that house."

So it came to pass, in the eastern Mediterranean and the western, that the order of the Greek *polis* began to dissolve. Torn by factional disputes within every city, unable to unite effectively against barbarian adversaries, subject to the lust for power without responsibility, intent too often upon private gain at the expense of the common good, the Greeks could not maintain their freedom. The traditional morality was giving way before new notions and new circumstances; the old generation and the new were at loggerheads.

The decay of the righteous order which Solon had described in his poems had led to the fall of Athens and the fall of Akragas. By an effort of imagination and intellect, might righteousness be regained? That question became the obsession of Plato and of Aristotle.

The Cave and the Dust-Storm

Although Plato and Aristotle have exerted upon what we call "Western civilization" more influence than have any other philosophers, it would be mistaken to claim for them a powerful direct influence over the minds of the men who made the American Republic. Plato's Republic—his "best state" —never was of this world, nor could it have been. Indeed, Plato and Aristotle loom larger in the twentieth century than they did in the eighteenth, so far as Americans are concerned.

He had learned from Plato two things only, John Adams declared: that hiccoughs are a cure for sneezing, and that husbandmen and artisans should not be exempted from military service. To the men of the Revolutionary and Constitutional era in America, their own colonial experience—and their British inheritance of ordered liberty—meant more than could Plato's and Aristotle's meditations on the failure of the Greek city-state. The Americans were looking for practical models of sound government, applicable to American circumstances; those could not be found readily in the pages of Plato, nor was Aristotle's treatise on politics directly relevant to many of their problems.

As a more subtle influence, nevertheless, the thought of the founder of the Academy and the thought of the first systematic organizer of knowledge worked strongly upon the Americans. The ideas of Plato and Aristotle had permeated the European civilization from which the colonists had come. Those ideas had passed into the civilization of Rome, and then into medieval culture, and so into the mind of Europe and of America after Renaissance and Reformation—redoubled, in Plato's case, after the Renaissance.

More, Hellenic thought had been woven inextricably into the fabric of Christian teaching, so that it was next to impossible to distinguish Judaic threads from Greek: Saint Paul, and the Greek and Latin Fathers of the Church, had united the patrimony of Jerusalem and the patrimony of Athens. The New Testament, written in Greek, is full of Platonic insights; one cannot fully appreciate Saint Augustine's City of God without knowing Plato's Republic; and Aristotle's works dominated the learning of the medieval Church.

So it is not merely in occasional references to Plato's or Aristotle's classifications of forms of government that one detects the influence of those two philosophers upon the American mind. It is Plato's and Aristotle's analyses of the human condition, rather, and their theories of justice, that have been incorporated into American concepts of order. The general cast of mind of the leading men of America bore the stamp of Hellenic ethics and metaphysics; in the eighteenth century, and for much of the nineteenth, formal education in America was so attached to classical learning that nobody who had passed through grammar school could be thoroughly ignorant of the teachings of Plato and Aristotle, any more than he could have been innocent of knowledge of Moses or Isaiah.

The name of Socrates was as familiar to the men who signed the Declaration and the Constitution as was the name of King Alfred, say. Whether or not the Americans made much of Plato's mystical doctrines, the example of Socrates moved them: and they knew Socrates through Plato's dialogues.

Socrates had died for the truth, and for his century, and for the people who put him to death, and for the sake of enduring law. Athens' defeat in the Peloponnesian War had overthrown the democratic constitution temporarily. Then there had come to power, for a brief interval, the Athenian oligarchy called the "Thirty Tyrants"—among them several men who had been pupils of the teacher Socrates. When the democratic party in Athens put down the Thirty, the restored democracy was in a mood anything but temperate. All criticism of the democracy was forbidden; anyone who taught what seemed innovating did so at his peril. In the year 399, the philosopher Socrates was accused before the Athenian jury (drawn from the democratic Assembly) of "not worshiping the gods whom the city worships, introducing religious innovations, and corrupting the young men."

Socrates, who always had exhorted his pupils to obey the laws of Athens, and who had been a valiant citizen-soldier, was a man of virtue and wisdom. But the democracy of Athens did not understand his teachings, which were intended to renew private and public morality. By a narrow majority, he was found guilty. Although he could have chosen exile, if he had fled he would have been false to the truth, to his city, and to himself; so he chose to suffer death, drinking the poison cup of hemlock that was brought to him. By his end, Socrates became to the classical world nearly what Jesus of Nazareth, crucified, would become to the Christian world. Plato's dialogues *The Apology, Crito,* and *Phaedo,* describing Socrates' last days, were received almost as sacred books by the educated men of classical times.

After their master had taken poison, Plato and other followers of Socrates sought refuge abroad. Some years later, Plato returned to Athens, and there established in the grove of Academe what came to be known as the Academy—a school of higher studies, or rudimentary university. When advanced in years, Plato twice made voyages to Syracuse, hoping to transform society in that great city of the West, and so to save Greek civilization. When he died in Athens, more than eighty years old, Plato had failed to redeem his time. But as a man of intellect and imagination, he had accomplished a labor far more enduring than was that of the captains and the kings of the fourth century.

Like Socrates before him, Plato endeavored to renew the vitality of Greek society by deepening its religious understanding. In the depths of the soul, he sought for a truth beyond matter and time; in his intricate dialogues, he ex-

75

pressed poetically the truths he perceived. In one degree or another, the philosophers and many of the public men of Greece and Rome and the Hellenistic empires, for hundreds of years after Plato's death, accepted his communication of truths apprehended. But the mass of men understood him even less than the Athenian jury had understood Socrates, so that not until the popular triumph of Christianity did Plato's insights begin to move the world as he had hoped they might.

Though Plato was a man of vision, he was no impractical dreamer. Yet as Paul Elmer More remarks, the word "Platonism" has become almost synonymous, in many quarters, with the word "Utopianism". "It is a fact, sad and indisputable," says More, "that no one is more likely to call himself, or to be called by his admirers, a Platonist than the reformer with a futile scheme for the regeneration of the world, or the dreamer who has spurned the realities of human nature for some illusion of easy perfection, or the romantic visionary who has set the spontaneity of fancy above the rational imagination, or the 'fair soul' who has withdrawn from the conflict of life into the indulgence of a morbid introspection, or the votary of faith as a law abrogating the sterner law of works and retribution. Half the enthusiasts and inspired maniacs of society have shielded themselves under the aegis of the great Athenian."[5]

As More adds, Plato himself was not that sort of Platonist: Plato was no projector of fantastic schemes, but instead a man intent upon opening other men's eyes to the higher realities of human existence. Most men—so Plato suggests in his "myth of the cave"—do not perceive true reality. As if they were prisoners chained forever in a cavern, they see only shadows on a stony wall, and mistake those shadows for living objects of the actual world outside. Should one of their number escape, and then return with tidings of what he had found in daylight, they would think he lied and deserved to die.

The way of the man of vision and righteousness is not easy. In *The Republic*, Socrates speaks of such a man in a decadent and violent age: "He is like one who, in the storm of dust and sleet which the driving wind hurries along, retires under the shelter of a wall; and seeing the rest of mankind full of wickedness, he is content, if only he can live his own life and be pure from evil or unrighteousness, and depart in peace and good will, with bright hopes." Those hopes were for immortality of the soul.

But Plato did not sit always in the shelter of a wall. His voyages to Syracuse are only the more conspicuous examples of his endeavor to accomplish an immense reform—a reform in the soul and a reform in the republic. He sought much of his life for a philosopher-ruler, a second Solon, who might restore righteousness through wisdom and example. Had the cities of Hellas been able to unite under such a leader of heroic mold—under a leader of Syracuse, perhaps—they might have worked those moral and social reforms, and have prepared that common defense, which could have preserved Greek liberty and genius.

As the glory of Athens had gone down to agony in the quarries of Syracuse, Plato longed to raise up that glory again, even with Syracuse as its center. But the philosopher-king could not be found. Socrates had died for the sake of speaking the truth; in searching for the philosopher-king, Plato came near to a destruction like his master's. Young Dionysius II, king of Syracuse, was weak and vicious, baulking even at study of geometry under Plato. The high-minded Dion, Plato's Syracusan friend, overthrew the younger Dionysius; but Dion was imprudent and vacillating at the crisis of his fate, and so was murdered by another pupil of Plato. For want of a human instrument, the Syracusan hope of the Greek commonwealths was lost. The wisdom and virtue necessary for contending successfully against a sea of troubles rarely are found united in one man.

In his mundane effort, then, Plato failed. But in his intellectual effort—his erection of the symbols of reality, with God as the measure of all things—he triumphed after death. He could not cleanse his world, but it would have become a worse world more swiftly had not Plato taught those who would listen to him.

Plato's whole endeavor was the recovery of order: order in the soul, order in the *polis*. He knew that these two kinds of order are not identical, and yet cannot be separated altogether. The central truth in Plato's writings is his doctrine of the soul. To understand that doctrine, we must glance at the opposing opinions which Plato confronted.

The word "philosopher" means "lover of wisdom." Also there is a Greek word to describe the philosopher's opponent: that word is "philodoxer," meaning "lover of opinion"—that is, an opinionated man suffering from vain wishes, who passionately pursues illusion. Out of the *doxa,* the false opinion fanatically held, comes disorder in the soul and disorder in the body politic. How may this disorder be checked? By *eunomia,* Solon had said: that is, by righteous order, by disciplined harmony of a man's soul, which makes "all things proper and sensible in the affairs of men."

We are handicapped in such discussions by our imperfect terms, tools that snap in the hand. For nowadays, in our language, there is no English word to express adequately the concept of "philodoxer," the man whose desires override his righteousness. We do have the word "sophist," derived from the Greek, which expresses in part the concept of a preacher of the *doxa.* Plato struggled against the Sophists, professed teachers of wisdom who actually were teachers of the way to worldly success in Greece.

The typical Sophist of the fifth and fourth centuries before Christ did not take the health of the soul into his reckoning of success. But if man does not restore order in his soul, Plato reasoned, then order cannot be restored in the state. Opposing the Sophists, Plato offered the decadent Greek society—which had lost faith in its religion, its traditions, its old customs—a means for making possible once more the life of the soul and the life of the civilization of Hellas.

From the rise of civilization onward, there had been men—poets, prophets, philosophers—who had groped for knowledge of the soul. What is the soul? In the dictionary's definition, it is "a substantial entity believed to be that in each person which lives, feels, thinks, and wills." It is the essence of a human being—what moves his body and gives him his self-consciousness. Though bound up with the physical body, the soul is not identical with that body. The soul is "you" and "I". We are aware of a personal identity which is not simply a name or a collection of organic tissues. If we are moral beings, it is because we have souls: that is, a spirit within each of us, the soul, somehow permeates or directs mind and body. It is the soul which distinguishes human beings from inanimate objects, plants, and the lower animals.

So far as we know, speculation about the soul first arose in ancient Egypt; we already have mentioned an Egyptian dialogue of a man with his soul, concerning suicide. Plato probably was influenced by Egyptian concepts of the soul, and possibly by Hebrew ideas, though we cannot be sure of that.

Centuries before Plato, the early Greek poet-philosophers had tried to understand the soul—and the soul's relationship to order in private and public existence. Homer (who lived at the end of the tenth century or the beginning of the ninth century before Christ, probably) perceived the soul only dimly, at best. In *The Odyssey*, Homer portrays the soul of the dead chieftain Achilles, slain at Troy, in the underground realm of Hades. Achilles' soul, and the other souls of the dead there, are pale unhappy things; Achilles had rather be the meanest slave in Boetia than king among these shadows. The Greeks of Homer's time apprehended only the *psyche*, the life-force that departs with death, never to live after but in dreams. To Homer, a dead man was but a *soma*, a corpse.

And yet Homer, living in a confused and violent time when the civilization of Hellas was beginning to rise upon the ruins of the earlier Mycenean civilization, did perceive that his society was disordered because the souls of men were disordered. He recognized that man's soul is the center of his passions, but also the center of his ability to order and judge knowledge. He sought to bring the human soul into harmony with some divine order—with the intention of the Olympian gods for mankind. Though the soul, for Homer, virtually may perish when the body perishes, still it is the soul which impels a living man to do right or do wrong.

In the ninth century before Christ, probably, the poet Hesiod tried to describe the divine justice which orders the universe. By mighty struggles, he wrote, Zeus had brought out of Chaos a precarious order in the universe. Zeus had sent

Force and Power to restrain Prometheus from persuading men to act as if they were gods. Yet for Hesiod, as for Homer, the soul was "opaque," indistinct; he did not know how it might enter into communion with divine wisdom.

With the philosopher Heraclitus (about the beginning of the fifth century), the Greek understanding of the soul was enlarged. That understanding runs through the tragedies of Aeschylus and Sophocles, during Athens' Great Age. For those dramatists, tragedy, a religious drama, was a means for opening the soul to the conflicting demands of *Dike* (Justice). The tragic hero must search his soul, that he may know the way of righteousness and how he has fallen from that path.

At the moment when the tragic drama towered over Athens, nevertheless, the philodoxers or Sophists already were at their work. The greatest of these was Protagoras. "Man is the measure of all things," Protagoras taught. He was by no means wholly a philodoxer, for Protagoras declared that reverence and justice must live in the soul of every man, or else the commonwealth would perish; for Protagoras a man with a diseased soul brought disease to the *polis*, and ought to be put to death if, after five years of reformatory education, he should turn out incorrigible.

Yet the general ethical tendency of the Sophists is sufficiently suggested in our word "sophistry," meaning "clever but misleading reasoning." Amid the disorder of the fifth and fourth centuries in Hellas, there arose the figures of the philodoxers, the Sophists, "realistic," sardonic, driven by *pleonexia* (the lust for power), discarding *peitho* (righteous persuasion) in favor of trickery or intimidation; impelled by their passions and low interests, their illusions, even at the moment they claimed to speak as practical logicians and champions of common sense. For fees, the Sophists taught the young men of Athens and other Greek cities the way to material success, especially through public speaking before the assembly or in cases at law. The typical Sophist took Protagoras' phrase "man is the measure of all things" to mean that no individual man is responsible to any transcendent moral authority for his actions.

Against the disciples of Protagoras, Socrates and Plato affirmed that God is the measure of all things. Here was the supreme Greek "leap in being," comparable to that of the Hebrew prophets. Man must order his soul in conformity with divine laws, Plato said; only thus can order in society be obtained. Here Plato followed in the footsteps of Solon, who had said that the *doxa*, the passion of life, must be disciplined for the sake of order, *eunomia*.

Although a lucid writer, Plato is a most complex thinker, and has been more commented upon than any other philosopher in the history of ideas. Plato writes in symbols, for there is no other way in which transcendent knowledge can be expressed. At its highest level, the truth about man and his condition must be religious truth, and in some degree mystery. (As a twentieth-century writer, G. K. Chesterton, has put it, all life is an allegory, and can be understood only in parable.) Plato is seeking transcendent reality; his work is a leap in being, a glimpse of an eternal order, divinely ordained, which we must try to imitate in our souls and our social institutions. For this, like the Hebrew prophets and, later, Jesus of Nazareth, Plato found it necessary to speak in symbol and parable.

Still, one may suggest here, in bald prose, Plato's fundamental principles. First of all, Plato proclaims the immortality of the individual soul, temporarily confined and corrupted in this world. The cleansing liberation of that soul ought to be our chief object here on earth; we must free ourselves from false loves and degrading appetites, that we may conform to the *nomos*, the law, of a transcendent God. The soul, separable from the body, endures forever.

With burning conviction, Plato teaches that there exist divine moral laws, not easy to apprehend, but operating upon all mankind. He refutes the argument of some Sophists that there is no distinction between virtue and vice, and he affirms that God, not man, is the measure of all things.

He says that the true reality lies in Ideas, the realm of intellect and imagination, by which matter is moved. We humans are not mere creatures of physical nature, at the mercy of Fate and Fortune: by the exercise of reason, we may know something of the truth and follow that truth.

To make these principles more clear, it is well to examine briefly Plato's most controversial dialogue, *The Republic*. Plato's theories of justice and order have been variously criticized in different ages, the critics of any period tending to see in *The Republic, The Statesman,* and *The Laws* the reflection of opinions and events in their own time, and so to commend or denounce Plato as he seems to sympathize with, or to oppose, their own prejudices and interests. In the twentieth century, Plato has been denounced by some as a Communist; by others, as a Fascist. He was neither; he was not even an "idealist," as nineteenth-century critics took him to be.

For *The Republic* is misunderstood if it is approached as a treatise upon politics primarily. That discourse really offers a pattern for the soul's harmony. Plato believed that "society" is "man" written in larger letters. If we can conceive of a just society, perhaps we may discover something more important—the character of a just man. We can understand man's soul, Plato reasons, by comparing it with the harmony that ought to prevail in a good social commonwealth. Speaking through the mouth of Socrates, Plato says that the projected "best state" in *The Republic*, so far as it might be adapted at all to the existing world of the Greeks, must be modified to take on flesh. *The Republic* is an inquiry into the real nature of spiritual and social harmony. It is an analogy or allegory of personal order, not a model constitution—though it does suggest reforms in the state. Consider how a good *polis* would be ordered, Plato is saying; if we can imagine that, then perhaps we can imagine how a man should order his soul.

In the imaginary *polis* of *The Republic*, society is divided into three large classes. There are the philosopher-rulers, who enjoy no private property, and have even wives and children in common. (This provokes the accusation that Plato is a Communist.) These are the "Guardians," well educated, who guide the state.

Then comes the class of the fighting men, the defenders of the state; and the third class will be made up of the large majority of the people, the cultivators of the soil. Each class will have its own rewards: the guardians, contemplative leisure; the soldiers, military glory; the farmers, material gain. And each class shall confine itself to the performance of its peculiar duties. Every person will belong to the class, and do the sort of work, for which he is fitted by his nature.

Now this social scheme was irrelevant to American society in the eighteenth century; for that matter, it could not have been imposed upon any Greek city in the fourth century before Christ. But it ought not to be taken for a plan of prompt practical action.

What Plato really is discussing is not some fantastic political innovation, but Justice. The best possible society, Plato argues in effect, would be one in which every man should do the work for which he is best suited by his nature, and in which the more intelligent men would be guardians of the common good, under good laws. We strive for Justice, he reasons, not by following nature (*physis*), as some Sophists had declared; rather, Justice is to be approached by obeying the *nomos* (law or tradition).[6] What, in essence, is justice? Why, justice is "to each his own": that is, every person should perform the duties and receive the rewards that accord with his own nature. To put it another way, the just society is one in which every man goes about his own proper business, unselfishly, moved by a deep concern for the common good. If we form in our minds a concept of the just republic, perhaps we can begin to understand the character of the just man—and commence our social reform thus by reforming one individual, one's own soul.

Plato says that the human soul, like the commonwealth, has three parts. The commonwealth has its guardians, its soldiers, its farmers. The soul has its intellect, its will, its appetite. The intellect resembles the guardians; the will resembles the military; the appetite resembles the economic producers. Just as the guardians ought to lead the soldiers and the farmers, so the reason or intellect ought to control the will and the appetite in the soul. It is as if every man were driving a chariot: he has two horses, Will and Appetite, and they are directed by Reason.

So reform of the soul and reform of society must proceed in parallel fashion. But no reform at all can be possible if we fall prey to the vagrant impulses of will and appetite, or if we submit ourselves to the evil counsels of the typical Sophist. Only through reason can we order the soul and the commonwealth; and one of the tools of reason is the "myth" —that is, the fable or allegory or parable, the symbols of truth. In part at least, *The Republic* is such a myth or parable or analogy. To mistake that "best state" for a literal plan of prompt social reconstruction is to fall into the sort of intellectual confusion which Plato spent so much time exposing.

Had Plato outlined some scheme for social harmony more consonant with American circumstances, still it would have been too remote in time for application even fragmentarily in eighteenth- or nineteenth-century America. What men of genius give to later ages, however, is not social models to be slavishly imitated: what the great philosopher bequeaths is enduring insight, applicable to many circumstances. The Platonic doctrines which touch upon the permanent things are not outworn. The Platonic understanding of justice, for instance, was deeply implanted in the minds of the early American leaders—through its incorporation into Christian thought, through its embodiment in Roman jurisprudence, and through its expression in English law. For *The Republic*, and Plato's other "social" teachings, at heart are meant to teach men how to bring their souls into harmony with divine order. If human nature is a constant, such ideas are relevant to the human condition under a variety of social circumstances. Everything depends upon the state of the soul—which is meant for eternity.

These wonderful insights of Plato, absorbed into the core of classical and Christian culture, were passed down through many generations to modern times—to John Adams, for one, who actually learned more from Plato, through a kind of intellectual osmosis, than Adams recognized. How did Plato come to perceive these transcendent realities that he called Ideas? By profound meditation, for the most part: by entering into what, centuries later, would be called "the dark night of the soul," deeper than ordinary consciousness, until (in the words of a twentieth-century theologian, Rudolf Otto) the mystical thinker becomes "nothingness before an overpowering absolute might of some kind," aware of his dependence upon a Presence that cannot be described in words. It may be said that Plato experienced a kind of revelation, different in character from that of the Hebrew prophets, but as enduring: this is true especially of his perception of the human soul. Once expressed through Plato's reasoned discourses and his symbolic imagery, these insights became part of the general civilized consciousness.

Plato had been born in the year 427, four years after the Peloponnesian War began; he was twenty-eight when Socrates was put to death; at the age of sixty, he had endeavored to make a philosopher-king of the younger Dionysius; he died in 347, as King Philip of Macedon was about to march into Greece, ending the freedom of the Greek city-states. Plato had lived from the Great Age of Greece into Greek decadence. In his last dialogue, *The Laws*, he affirms, "It is God who is, for you and me, the measure of all things." God, it seemed, had weighed Hellas in His balance and had found it wanting.

Yet the example of Socrates, and the vision of Plato, endured so long as the classical world hung together at all—keeping alive some understanding of order and justice and freedom; reminding some men that there endures a realm of ideas more real than the realms of appetites; affirming that the unexamined life is not worth living; insisting that if men's souls are disordered, society becomes no better than a cave or a dust-storm. Blending with the revelation received by Israel and with the words that Jesus of Nazareth would utter nearly four centuries later, Platonic thought would begin to ferment, long after Plato's death, among peoples far beyond the confines of the Greek world.

Like Solon, Plato intended to write a long fable about legendary Atlantis; like Solon, he never did write it. Yet there existed beyond the Atlantic an unvisited land, after all, and it is more strange than any of Plato's myths that Plato's apprehension of order and justice should be a living influence among the people of that land, twenty-four centuries after the mystical philosopher's soul departed from Athens.

Aristotle and Political Forms

At the age of eighteen, Aristotle came to the Academy to study under Plato; those studies would continue for twenty years. The son of a physician to the king of Macedonia, Aristotle had been born at Stagira, a Greek city subject to the half-barbarous, half-hellenized Macedonian state. He wrote some treatises while still at the Academy. When Plato died, Aristotle began to wander about the Greek world, going first to Atarneus, in Asia Minor, where the tyrant Hermias (once a slave) became a friend, and later Aristotle married Hermias' sister. Hermias was an ally of King Philip of Macedon, then in the midst of his conquest of the Greek states; Artaxerxes Ochus, king of Persia, caught Hermias by treachery and crucified him.

This disaster sent Aristotle traveling again, about the Ionian Sea where Persia and Macedonia were jousting for supremacy. Because of his learning and his Macedonian connections, about the year 343 B.C. he was appointed by King Philip to be the tutor of Philip's son Alexander, then thirteen years old. For at least three years, the famous philosopher instructed in ethics and rhetoric the young man who was to conquer most of the known world. Alexander became regent in 340, while his father was away at his wars; Aristotle, living at his native city of Stagira—which Philip had sacked in 348, but restored at Aristotle's request—had leisure to meditate and write.

When Alexander became king of Macedonia, Aristotle, then fifty years old, returned to Athens and established a new school, the Lyceum, where he would teach and write until the death of Alexander, far away in Asia, in the year 323. Then the Athenian democracy, rising against Macedonian supremacy, accused Aristotle of impiety (really a trumped-up political charge), as their grandfathers had prosecuted Socrates. Not desiring to taste the cup of hemlock, Aristotle retreated to Euboea, where a few months later he died in exile, at the age of sixty-three.

Aristotle had seen the world turned upside down in his

own lifetime. He had been born in 384 B.C., when Sparta was the chief power of the Greek mainland, the tyrant Dionysius I was master of Sicily, and Macedonia still was a backward land, hard pressed by aggressive neighbors. He had gone to Athens in 362, at the time of the battle of Mantinea, where Spartans and Thebans slaughtered each other, opening the way for the future Macedonian conquest of Greece.

He had left the Academy in 347, the year when Philip intervened in the Sacred War in central Greece. He had become Alexander's tutor in 343, when Philip extended his power into Epirus. He had founded the Lyceum in Athens when Alexander took Thebes in a single night and destroyed that ancient city. He had written most of his scientific and ethical and political works while the invincible Alexander was conquering the Persian empire and carrying Greek culture all the way to the frontiers of India, and beyond. He died in the year when Athens surrendered to his friend Antipater, regent of Macedonia; when Demosthenes, the Athenian orator and patriot, was compelled to take poison; when Alexander's generals had commenced to carve up into Hellenistic empires the dead king's conquests. It had been a time of troubles and innovations on a colossal scale, Aristotle's age—comparable in more ways than one to the twentieth-century time of troubles that would commence about 1914 A.D.

Serious political thought frequently arises in such a time of troubles, when men of intellect find it necessary to examine the causes of general disorder and violence, and to propose remedies if they can. One enduring product of the triumph of Macedonia in Greece, Asia, and Egypt was Aristotle's *Politics*, which treatise he had begun to write about 357, but which still was unfinished when he died thirty-seven years later.

Poetic, ethical, and political truths endure longer than do scientific theories. In the ancient world and in medieval times, the systematic Aristotle was venerated, above all, as a "natural philosopher"—what we would call a physical scientist. And his scientific achievement was tremendous; but it has been supplanted by modern science, except in the sense that Aristotle's pioneering work in the scientific method, and some valuable suggestions and guesses of his, are stones in the foundation of twentieth-century science. Aristotle's scientific treatises, that is, remain chiefly of antiquarian interest today; but his *Poetics, Ethics, Politics,* and *Metaphysics* (or science of the divine) stand essential in the study of those several disciplines. On reading or re-reading those famous books—studied almost without interruption, in one part of the world or another, ever since they were published—one thinks of T. S. Eliot's apt defense of ancient writers. "Someone said," Eliot wrote in 1919, " 'The dead writers are remote from us because we *know* so much more than they did.' Precisely, and *they* are that which we know."[7]

In his ethical and political studies, Aristotle wrote as a man of the world, having traveled much and experienced much, and having been friend or adversary of many of the most powerful men of his time of troubles: calm though they may seem, the pages of the *Politics* and of the *Nicomachean Ethics* arose from the ruinous turbulence of the fourth century before Christ. Here we have space only to examine Aristotle's ethical and political teachings that affected the American order—which can be done coherently with relative ease, because for Aristotle, as for Plato, there existed no real dividing line between politics and ethics. We can do no more than mention here that Aristotle's metaphysics entered deeply, in medieval times, into the doctrines of the Christian Church—culminating in their incorporation into the *Summa Theologiae* of Saint Thomas Aquinas.

In the fields of ethics, politics, and metaphysics, considerable differences exist between the thought of Plato and the thought of Aristotle. Aristotle did not carry on Plato's lofty idea of the immortality of the soul, for instance; Aristotle treats the soul as if it were little more than a faculty or attribute of the body, like the "axness" of an axe. (Thomas Aquinas, following Aristotle and disagreeing with Plato, reasons that the soul cannot exist without the body—though in Heaven, the soul will enter into a "spiritual body.") Aristotle generally is regarded as the more "practical" of the two in ethical and political concerns; yet the roots of much that follows here in our analysis of Aristotle might be found in Plato's dialogues.

Man is gregarious, a social animal, says Aristotle. "A man

in solitude must be either a beast or a god." It is in community that human beings realize their aim in existence; they become fully human only by becoming civilized, and civilization means the life of the city. Man is made for action, and the highest form of action is thought. In the savage state, man thinks scarcely at all. Unless we are social beings, we are not fully human beings.

So it is that ethics and politics really form one study: they are two aspects of the science of the highest good for man. Ethics, Aristotle reasons, is that aspect of the study which emphasizes the individual's condition of mind, or his character; politics is that aspect which emphasizes the state as the means for attaining this highest human good.

Just when the sovereignty of the Greek *polis* was evaporating, Aristotle produced a closely-reasoned theory of order in the *polis*. For him, the Greek city-state was superior to any other form of social organization; yet that reality was expiring as he lectured. Even rudimentary morality must disintegrate, Aristotle believed, if the city-state should collapse—and in the classical world he was vindicated grimly by the event.

When the Greek states, submitting to Alexander, acknowledged Aristotle's conquering pupil as commander-in-chief of the Hellenic campaign against Persia, indeed they put an end to the old menace from the east. But also, in effect, they put an end to their autonomy, their creative power, and their very religious faith. Except for his hasty temper, Alexander was near to being the philosopher-king. Alexander declared that to Philip, his father, he owed life; to Aristotle, the good life. Yet it was this invincible disciple of Aristotle, through one of history's paradoxes, whose actions resulted in the ruin of the Hellenic ethics and the Hellenic politics that Aristotle praised and expounded.

"Nothing to excess": since Homeric times, that had been the cardinal principle in Greek morality. Applied to political forms by Aristotle (as, much earlier, by Solon) this belief is the chief contribution of Aristotle and his school to the understanding of order. It is expressed through Aristotle's doctrine of the mean, sometimes called the "Golden Mean."

This "mean" does not signify the average, the mediocre,

or that splitting of the difference which Aristotle called "the disputed middle." Nor does the "mean" always signify, necessarily, the best. Rather, the mean amounts to that harmony achieved by avoiding excesses and extremes; it is moderation, or balance, in private life and in public.

A truly happy life, Aristotle argues in his *Ethics*, is an existence of goodness, free from impediments—that is, reasonably secure from poverty, sickness, and restrictions. Such a life of moral excellence may be attained through observance of the mean. Be neither ascetic nor gluttonous: be temperate. Be neither cowardly nor rash: be prudently courageous. Be neither subservient nor arrogant: be self-respecting.

As it is with the individual, so is it with the state, in the practical science of politics. The majority of men (though not always the philosopher or the heroic leader) should find that the mean is the standard for their existence. And in politics, usually a state should settle for the mean of government. This political mean is not the best conceivable state, Aristotle makes clear; but though it is no perfect condition, still it is the most satisfactory condition of peace that a community is likely to realize.

To ascertain this political mean, one must understand what various forms of government are possible. So Aristotle examines many city-states of his own day or of earlier times. He distinguishes three forms of "right government" meant for the general welfare: monarchy, aristocracy, and the commonwealth. By monarchy, Aristotle signifies the leadership of one man of excellent virtue, under a body of laws which limit his power. By aristocracy, he signifies the predominance of a class of men of high birth, dutiful and filled with the spirit which later would be called *noblesse oblige*. By a commonwealth, he signifies the exercise of power by a majority—but a virtuous majority, respecting the lawful rights of all classes.

As for the deviations, democracy is rule by the crowd, for the benefit of the dominant majority; oligarchy is rule by a few for the good of that few; tyranny is unconstitutional assumption of power by one man for his own satisfaction. The defects of these degenerate forms of government are obvious enough. But also the "right governments" are difficult to maintain. What Aristotle advocates is a mixed government—the ingredients of the mixture varying with particular circumstances—to incorporate the virtues of the several forms.

In the *Ethics*, Aristotle calls this mixed government, this political mean, a timocracy—that is, government by responsible citizens who meet a property qualification for exercising the franchise. (Plato had extended this term "timocracy" to signify, also, a government by men of honor.) In the *Politics*, Aristotle uses the term "polity" rather than timocracy. This polity, ordinarily a mixture of aristocracy and commonwealth, or of oligarchy and democracy, is the mean because it tends to be dominated by the middle class. For his "middle class," Aristotle had in mind those citizens neither rich nor poor—not members of the grand aristocratic families, nor yet the *demos*, the mob of artisans and sailors without property. This middle class of Athens and of many other states supplied the heavy-armed infantry who bore the brunt of the city's campaigns on land; also this middle class was most productive economically, less rash than the other classes, and more stable in its family life. The middle classes had suffered most in the civil struggles of the Greeks; they would be the people most concerned to maintain a decent and enduring social order.

The term "polity" would join together various virtues of other forms of government. From oligarchy, the polity would adopt election of magistrates or public officials. (In the Greek democracies, officials ordinarily were chosen by sortition—that is, random selection in a lottery.) From democracy, the polity would take the sound principle that all free-born citizens should have some share in public decisions. Domination either by the selfish rich or the envious poor would be avoided; aristocratic violence and popular roguery would be restrained.

This polity is a community of friendship, founded upon common affections as well as upon common interests. In a state, men have everything to gain by peaceful coöperation, as if they were so many parts of a human body; yet through ignorance or appetite, they tend to ignore the mean and to rush to extremes that bring on destruction. Aristotle confesses that true polities rarely are encountered:

"In the first place, the middle class is in most states generally small; and the result is that as soon as one or other of the two main classes—the owners of property and the masses—gains the advantage, it oversteps the mean, and drawing the constitution in its own direction it institutes, as the case may be, either a democracy or an oligarchy.

"In the second place, factitious disputes and struggles readily arise between the masses and the rich; and no matter which side may win the day, it refuses to establish a constitution based on the common interest and the principle of equality, but, preferring to exact as the prize of victory a greater share of constitutional rights, it institutes, according to its principles, a democracy or an oligarchy.

"Thirdly, the policy of the two states which have held the ascendancy in Greece has been to blame. Each has paid an exclusive regard to its own type of constitution; the one has instituted democracies in the states under its control, and the other has set up oligarchies: each has looked to its own advantage, and neither to that of the states it controlled."[8]

This analysis was all too true, especially in its concluding strictures upon Athens and Sparta. But Aristotle's treatise did not bring about the growth of the polity. (Indeed, his *Politics* was not published until centuries after Aristotle's death, it appears—although earlier writings of his on politics, now lost, probably were widely read in his own time.) What followed upon the death of Alexander and the death of Aristotle was the death of the *polis*. Physically, some Greek cities endured a thousand years longer—but reduced to the condition of municipalities merely, no longer independent cities and virtually autonomous cultures. Macedonia and the Hellenistic empires of Asia dominated those cities at first; eventually all of them succumbed to Rome. Deprived of their freedom, they withered under the Roman peace. The spirit gradually went out of them; their creative powers trickled away; their prosperity shrank, and so did their population.[9]

In the Hellenistic world, everything depended upon central authority; in the earlier Hellenic world, everything had depended upon humane scale and local affections. Aristotle says that the maximum number of free citizens enjoying the franchise, for a true polity, was five thousand; Plato, influenced by the mathematical theories of Pythagoras, had put the number at five thousand and forty citizens.[10] Roam though they did, the Greeks never obtained what we call a "worldview." Their religion, their morality, their frames of government all were bound up with the compact little city, its dependent lands, and its protecting deities. Once forced into an alien imperial structure, they lost the vices of arrogance, but they acquired the vices of servility.

Dike, justice, became merely a question of the schools, to be debated idly at Athens. When Saint Paul preached in Roman times at that glorious city, he was received with civil sneers; men said to one another, "Who is this charlatan?" Gradually the Athenians lost the capacity for belief in anything, and only at Athens did Paul win no converts. It was the clever relativism of the Sophists, not the mystical insights of Plato or Aristotle's aspiration after the Supreme Good, which dominated the classical Greeks in their decadence. The schools of philosophy lingered on long, until in 529 A.D. the Emperor Justinian shut them; but they had ceased long before to say much that was relevant to enduring order.

Plato and Aristotle, nevertheless, would cross oceans in times to come. The leading men of America's formative years would find Aristotle's concept of the polity, in particular, still valuable to them. True, much of Aristotle's treatise was of historial interest chiefly. Far from being a land of city-states, the new United States had scarcely more than a half-dozen towns that could be called cities by anyone; neither the New England township nor the Virginian county government much resembled the *polis*. America had no aristocracy of birth, strictly speaking: not one English nobleman had settled permanently in the colonies, and no peerages had been bestowed upon colonials. Slavery—of a kind harsher than the Greek—America had, indeed; but in its early decades, America had no very large urban element like the rabble of the Greek cities or the Roman proletarians. The tendency of America was toward swift expansion and "a more perfect union," not toward the local devotion of the *polis*.

For all that, the community of friendship advocated by Aristotle became an American ideal; the reconciling of interests and classes was a conscious objective of theirs, too. And Aristotle's praise of the middle class was a kind of endorsement of American society, for from the beginning America was predominantly a middle-class society, in the sense that small independent farmers made up the bulk of the population in the New England and the Middle colonies. Even in the plantation South, the "yeoman farmer" held a majority of the franchises and was praised (by Virginians so different as Thomas Jefferson and John Randolph of Roanoke) as the chief support of a free society.[11] American towns, too, were dominated by small merchants and craftsmen; few Americans even thought of calling themselves either aristocrats or—until the 1820's—democrats. The middle was almost all-encompassing in America.

Thus the Greek idea of political and social balance, as the Americans found it expressed by Aristotle and Polybius and Plutarch, was incorporated directly into the American Constitution. But some other Greek beliefs found no favor in the new United States.

The Greeks' conviction that religion and culture must be bound up inseparably with the city-state went against the grain of American individualism. A pluralistic society even in its beginnings, America could agree on no national establishment of religion; the Greeks would have been astounded that such a nation-state, unconsecrated to the gods, could endure for a decade.

Yet in another sense, repeatedly pointed out by Alexis de Tocqueville, America was held together by a religious bond stronger than any the Greeks or the Romans had known: by a Christian faith that worked upon individual and family, rather than through a state cult. The failure of the Greeks to find an enduring popular religious sanction for the order of their civilization had been a main cause of the collapse of the world of the *polis*. The power of Christian teaching over private conscience made possible the American democratic society, vastly greater in extent and population than Old Greece. Hellenic thought, Platonic and Aristotelian, contributed to that American religious morality through the strong threads of Greek vision and reason which are woven into Christian doctrine.

Once political parties took form in the United States, both the disasters of Greek political experience and the achievements of Greek philosophy instructed the leaders of parties that their own new polity must be an enlarged form of Solon's "mixed government." Their own reading of Greek literature was reinforced by the classical examples contained in Montesquieu and other eighteenth-century writers. The American constitutions, indeed, would surpass Solon's in their elaborate checks and balances; they would establish for the nation and in the several states a system of representative government on the British pattern, rather than the "direct democracy" that had collapsed even in little Attica. And *nomos*, the inherited law, the instrument of justice, had few sophistical opponents in America.

The civilization that arose in Greece was not effaced altogether by its political catastrophe; Washington's classical architecture is some evidence of that. Still better evidence of the Greek genius is the incorporation of Greek philosophical and historical knowledge into American social institutions. Ideas are deathless, Plato had said often: material forms, which pass away and rise again in new aspects, are delusory. Surely the ideas of Hellas still breathe life into American order, though material Hellas has become remote and legendary for us as Atlantis seemed to Solon and to Plato.

Notes

¹ Sir Henry Maine, *Village Communities in the East and West* (third edition, London: John Murray, 1876), p. 238.

² Alfred E. Zimmern, "Political Thought", in R. W. Livingstone (ed.), *The Legacy of Greece* (Oxford: Clarendon Press,

1921), pp. 330-31; see also Zimmern, *The Greek Commonwealth: Politics and Economics in Fifth-Century Athens* (Oxford: Clarendon Press, 1911), particularly Chapter VIII.

[3] For Rush and Paine on classical authors, see Chapters VI and VII of Richard M. Gummere's *Seven Wise Men of Colonial America* (Cambridge, Mass.: Harvard University Press, 1967).

[4] Eric Voegelin, *The World of the Polis*, Volume II of *Order and History* (Baton Rouge: Louisiana State University Press, 1957), p. 199.

[5] Paul Elmer More, *Platonism* (third edition, Princeton: Princeton University Press, 1931), pp. 280-83.

[6] For a better understanding of the terms *physis* and *nomos*, see F. E. Peters, *Greek Philosophical Terms: a Historical Lexicon* (New York: New York University Press, 1967), pp. 131-2, 158-60.

[7] T. S. Eliot, "Tradition and the Individual Talent", in his *Selected Essays, 1917-1932* (New York: Harcourt, Brace, 1932), p. 6.

[8] Aristotle, *Politics*, Chapter XI, translation of Sir Ernest Barker (Oxford: Clarendon Press, 1948), p. 217.

[9] See George Findlay, *Greece under the Romans* (London: J.M. Dent, 1844), particularly Chapter I.

[10] Plato's calculation of the maximum number of citizens was influenced by his knowledge of the mathematical-mystical philosophy of Pythagoras. For Aristotle's deliberate rounding-off of the Platonic calculation, see Eric Voegelin, *Plato and Aristotle*, Vol. III of *Order and History* (Baton Rouge: Louisiana State University Press, 1957), pp. 293-4.

[11] On Virginian political institutions and controversies of the formative period of American history, see Charles Sydnor, *Gentlemen Freeholders: Political Practices in Washington's Virginia* (Chapel Hill: University of North Carolina Press, 1952); and Russell Kirk, *John Randolph of Roanoke: a Study in American Politics* (revised edition, Chicago: Regnery, 1964), particularly Chapter V.

CHAPTER IV
VIRTUE AND POWER:
THE ROMAN TENSION

The High Old Roman Virtue

In the year of the Declaration of Independence, Edward Gibbon published the first volume of his *Decline and Fall of the Roman Empire*. The grandeur that was Rome, suffusing Gibbon's chapters, worked strongly upon the imagination of the men who founded the United States. Between the Roman Republic and their own republican creation they perceived parallels, and other similarities would be discerned as America grew.

In 1764, Gibbon had conceived the idea of writing his great work, "as I sat musing amidst the ruins of the Capitol, while the bare-footed fryars were singing vespers in the Temple of Jupiter." One can rest today where Gibbon sat on the flight of marble steps leading to the ancient church of Santa Maria Aracoeli—the site of the Roman Temple of Jupiter—upon the Capitoline Hill. Upon this hill, Romulus established a village for fugitive slaves, about the middle of the eighth century before Christ, and here the founder of Rome built Jupiter's temple, now a Franciscan church. The descendants of Romulus' villagers would conquer the world—from Scotland to Mesopotamia, from Germany to Morocco—so that in three continents one still encounters the battered stone memorials of their Roman peace.

Yet it will not do to think of Roman civilization as a ruin only. All the way from the Roman Republic to the American Republic, a continuity runs. Go from the Capitol down into the heart of medieval Rome (once the Campus Martius of the Republic), round about the immense domed Pantheon that was built in the reign of Augustus, first of the Roman emperors: here civic life has persisted for more than two thousand years, even in the most frightful of times. Old Rome fell, but did not die. Rome of the consuls, of the emperors, and of the popes, the Eternal City, often devastated but never effaced, has given order to many nations.

Through its influence upon modern states—so John Henry Newman wrote—the Roman Empire lives today; and the Roman power is what Saint Paul described as "the power that withholds," the power that hinders the coming of total disorder, of the anarchy called in Christian teaching the reign of Antichrist. "We have actually before our eyes," Newman wrote in 1838, "as our fathers also in the generation before us, a fierce and lawless principle everywhere at work—a spirit of rebellion against God and man, which the powers of government in each country can barely keep under with their greatest efforts . . . at least we know from prophecy that the present framework of society and government, so far as it is the representative of Roman powers, is that which withholdeth, and Antichrist is that which will rise when this restraint fails."[1]

Certainly the Roman understanding of the rule of law still lives in the modern world, restraining destructive impulses. This Roman concept of law and obligation, as variously expressed by Polybius and Livy and Virgil and Cicero and the Stoics, passed into American political thought and jurisprudence, and is permanently embedded in the American Constitution.

The intricate structure of Roman law arose gradually from a little market-town on the Tiber, a settlement in its beginnings far more humble than Jerusalem or Athens. About the middle of the sixth century before Christ—about the time when old Solon returned to Athens, and when the Jews made their way back from Babylon to Jerusalem—the people of

Rome, then ruled by Etruscan kings, began to grow swiftly in culture and in power.

During the fourth century, Rome conquered the Latin cities that were her neighbors: from that struggle onward, Rome sent her legions abroad until, by the year 146 B.C., she had broken Carthage and had sown with salt the site of her African rival. To liberate the cities of Old Greece from Macedonia, the legions penetrated into eastern Europe; once established in Greece, which they occupied thoroughly, the Romans picked a quarrel with the Seleucid Empire and commenced their conquest of Asia. Later, led by Julius Caesar, the legions would conquer Gaul and land in Britain. By the late days of the Republic, the Roman commonwealth had no very powerful external enemies left to fight: almost in a fit of absence of mind, the Romans had become masters of all the Mediterranean lands and of vast territories to which the Mediterranean culture scarcely had penetrated before.

The secret of this universal triumph, said the admirers of the Romans, was the high old Roman virtue; and so said the Roman moralists themselves. "Virtue" means energetic manliness. The early Romans were a pious people, even though their religion itself was a simple faith, later to assimilate many elements from the Greek religion; they were earnest, tenacious, well-disciplined, frugal, often self-sacrificing when the state was in peril. A sense of duty and an attachment to honesty and honor worked upon their leading men. Those qualities would decay in later times, but even to the final ruin of the Roman system some men of the stern old Roman pattern might be found.

At the time when they defeated Carthage, the Romans were virtually incorruptible, the Greek statesman Polybius wrote: from their piety (which the skeptical Polybius attributed to their superstition) arose their integrity. "If, among the Greeks for example, a single talent only be entrusted to those who have the management of any of the public money; though they give ten written sureties, with as many seals, and twice as many witnesses, they are unable to discharge the trust reposed in them with integrity. But the Romans, on the other hand, who in the course of their magistracies, and in embassies, disburse the greatest sums, are prevailed on by the single obligation of an oath to perform their duty with inviolable honesty. And as, in other states, a man is rarely to be found whose hands are pure from public robbery; so, among the Romans, it is no less rare to discover one that is tainted with this crime."

For imagination and artistic genius, the Romans were inferior to the Greeks. But the Romans were a people of strong practical endowments, grand engineers, tireless political administrators, organizers of military success; most of all, they were men of law and strong social institutions, who gave to the world the *pax romana*, the Roman peace.

The best critic of the men who had conquered the world in little more than half a century was Polybius, a leading man of the Greek city of Megalopolis, who for years lived as a hostage of Rome, but who understood the Roman genius and became an influential counselor to the principal Romans. Polybius' historical analysis of Roman character and the Roman constitution, about the middle of the second century before Christ, was earnestly studied by the leaders of America's Constitutional Convention two thousand years later.*

Three chief elements composed the polity of the Roman Republic: the consular authority; the senate; and the *comitia*, or formal assemblies of the people. (To give the people a more immediate check upon the senate, popular tribunes were chosen, with power of veto upon senatorial actions.) The two consuls were the chief magistrates, with power almost absolute in time of war; the senate controlled the public purse and determined general policies in ordinary circumstances; the people, usually voting in "tribes," allotted rewards and punishments, elected magistrates, approved or rejected legislation, and determined peace or war, and alliances. (Such is Polybius' description of the Roman constitution during the Punic wars; the character of the *comitia* would begin to

---

* "Polybius was of special interest to the framers of the Constitution. They studied him intently as the leading authority on the Greek city-states. He is the ancient counterpart of historians like Spengler and Toynbee who analyze the cycles of progress and decay of nations." See Richard M. Gummere, *The American Colonial Mind and the Classical Tradition* (Cambridge, Massachusetts: Harvard University Press, 1963), pp.177-78.

decay not long after those wars, and the people would lose almost all their powers at the end of the Republic.)

This system incorporated both checks and balances upon political power, and provided for separation of political functions. The Roman constitution, said Polybius, was not formed upon abstractions, but developed out of the circumstances of the time of troubles in which the people of Rome found themselves. By the time of the second war with Carthage, that constitution stood at the height of its success. It was the "mixed government" praised by Aristotle, but which Aristotle had thought almost impossible to maintain on a grand scale.

The Roman constitution was not purely monarchical, or aristocratic, or democratic, though it contained features of all three patterns of government. At its height, this republican constitution had the high advantage of uniting all the citizens for strenuous public efforts. It was peculiarly suited for enabling men of strong practical talents to rise to authority. The Senate, whose domination increased in the later Republic, was made up of men—many from plebian families—who had risen through a regular series of civil and military offices, at the conclusion of which they were enrolled for life as senators.* The best of the senators were heroic; even the worst of them were able enough in more than one walk of life.

Two thousand years later, the reputation of the Roman constitution remained so high that the framers of the American constitution would emulate the Roman model as best they could. The Roman institutions of checks and balances in politics, and of separation of powers, would be imitated in the frame of government for the United States.

---

* The contest between "patricians" and "plebians" belongs to the early centuries of Roman history, not to the time of the Punic Wars or of the late Republic. The patricians were those Romans belonging to old families—descendants of the orginal settlers of Rome; many of the patricians were what we would call subsistence farmers. The plebians were descended from foreigners, conquered Latin peoples, and fugitives who settled in Rome. After all plebians were admitted to full Roman citizenship (about 286 B.C.), the distinction between those two orders retained little political significance. One may write, however, of the "senatorial class," founded more upon wealth and ability than upon ancestry—although in the later Republic and in the Empire, this senatorial class tended to perpetuate itself in power.

The American presidency would resemble somewhat the Roman consular *imperium*, and the senate of the United States was intended to function, in part, as had the senate of Rome. And yet that Roman constitution, which had given the Romans dominion over the civilized world, was beginning to decay even as Polybius wrote of it.

Polybius foresaw Rome's decadence. "All things are subject to decay and change," he wrote. "When a state, after having passed with safety through many and great dangers, arrives at the highest degree of power, and possesses an entire and undisputed sovereignty, it is manifest that the long continuance of prosperity must give birth to costly and luxurious manners, and that the minds of men will be heated with ambitious contests, and become too eager and aspiring in the pursuit of dignities. And as those evils are continually increased, the desire of power and rule, and the imagined ignominy of remaining in a subject state, will first begin to work the ruin of the republic; arrogance and luxury will afterwards advance it; and in the end the change will be completed by the people; when the avarice of some is found to injure and oppress them, and the ambition of others swells their vanity, and poisons them with flattering hopes. For then, being inflamed with rage, and following only the dictates of their passions, they no longer will submit to any control, or be contented with an equal share of the administration, in conjunction with their rules; but will draw to themselves the entire sovereignty and supreme direction of all affairs. When this is done, the government will assume indeed the fairest of all names, that of a free and popular state; but will in truth be the greatest of all evils, the government of the multitude."[2]

That process commenced after the Punic Wars, and resulted in devastating civil wars. Yet the typical Roman, disliking social and intellectual change, clung to what were called the *mores majorum*—the ancestral ways. There was much in the old Republic worth conserving. Under the *jus civile*, the civil law for Roman citizens, the Romans enjoyed immunities against arbitrary power, and protection of their property, that were rare in the ancient world: for all its severity, the Roman commonwealth knew ordered liberty.

It was a society held together, until late Republican years, by family ties stronger perhaps than any other Western society has known: the family was believed to be a spiritual continuity of the dead and the living and those yet unborn, united by blood. The authority of the *paterfamilias,* or head of the family (which ordinarily included many households), and of the family council, was tremendous; while the Roman matron, wife and mother, was held in a respect never accorded to women—with the exception, possibly, of Sparta—by any other society of ancient times.*

It was a society, until the Punic Wars, of small agricultural proprietors, industrious, god-fearing, patriotic, courageous. They were famous throughout the ancient world for their fortitude, their endurance under adversity. Aeneas, the legendary leader of the Latin peoples, was called always the "pious Aeneas," and the concept of piety lay at the heart of Roman culture.

In the twentieth century, this word "piety" generally implies strong religious observances; it meant that to the Romans, but also it meant more. A pious man, in the Roman understanding, was one who fulfilled his duties, religious and social—one who subordinated his own desires to the claims of others. "Piety is the foundation of all the other virtues," Cicero would write when the Republic was falling to its ruin.

A man was pious who gave the gods their due, through worship and sacrifice; who honored his father and his mother, and indeed all his ancestors; who stood by his friends; who was ready to die, if need be, for his country. A pious man, that is, submitted himself to things sacred, and believed unflinchingly that it was better to perish than to fail in his sacred duties. A society held together by such a cementing belief would offer strong resistance to forces of disintegration.

---

* At the very beginning of Rome, it is said, Romulus decreed strong protections for a wife. A husband could put aside his wife only for very grave cause, chiefly adultery; if he should expel her for lesser reason, the offending man was condemned to forfeit half his property to his abused wife and the other half to the goddess Ceres; should he sell his wife, the state would deliver him over to the infernal deities. Divorce was rare until the last century of the Republic, and in historical times (as distinguished from legends of ancient Rome) a man who turned away his wife even for serious cause might be punished by the censors—Roman magistrates who enforced public morality, in addition to taking the census of the tribes.

And yet the old Roman society had begun to break up even while Polybius praised it. The chief material cause of the Republic's decay appears to have been the military success of its armies and the expansion of Roman territories and power. The three Punic Wars ruined the majority of the Roman peasants, who died valiantly by hundreds of thousands; those who returned after years or decades of campaigning found themselves hopelessly in debt. With the conquest of Carthage and her dependencies, and later of Macedonia, Greece, Asia, Gaul, and other lands, innumerable slaves poured into Italy, further injuring the old economic pattern and forming an alien proletariat in the imperial city itself. From subjugated Greece, sophists and rhetoricians came to Rome; conservatives like the elder Cato detested them, for though they might elevate Roman culture, their philosophies undermined the old Roman *pietas*. Increasingly, the free Roman citizenry became little better than paupers, ready to follow some charismatic demagogue or ambitious military man; since the citizen-pauper had a vote, it became necessary increasingly to conciliate him by "bread and circuses"—public doles or subsidized food, gladiatorial shows and other public amusements, and public works and distributions that must be paid for by fresh conquests abroad.

Among any people, the moral order and the social order become so closely intertwined that it is most difficult to distinguish the causes of decadence. What had happened to the Republic? So Cicero inquired near the end of the old constitution. Was it that men were worse than formerly, or that bad laws had corrupted the commonwealth? Both baneful causes of decay could be traced, he argued: there cannot be a good commonwealth unless most citizens are virtuous, and the citizens find it difficult to hold by the old morality in a time of political disorder and corruption. There existed material reasons for the decline of the high old Roman virtue, but also that fall from virtue accelerated the political disintegration of the commonwealth.

So it came to pass that only thirteen years after the destruction of Carthage (146 B.C.), the Romans began to rend one another—class against class, allies against the claims of Rome, slaves against masters, provinces against Roman garrisons, general against general, Senate against People. Between the years 133 and 121, Tiberius and Caius Gracchus, as tribunes of the people, attempted fundamental reforms, setting aside the constitution; they were slain. This struggle divided the Romans into two ferocious parties—the Optimates, or "Best Men," and the Populares, or democratic partisans.

Against the centralizing power of Rome, the other Italian cities rebelled then, in the Social War of the years 90 to 88; the rebels were crushed at immense cost. Marius, a successful commander, took up the cause of the Populares, and was opposed in the field by Sulla, general of the Optimates; the Civil War which resulted dragged on hideously for seven years, and in the course of it immense tracts of farmland were confiscated or laid waste. Marius, backed by the first professional army that Rome had known, made himself master for a time; he fell from power, and when he regained the consulship at the end of his life, he took Rome and butchered his opponents. He was succeeded by the merciless dictator Sulla, champion of the Senate.

No sooner had Sulla restored a kind of order, than the Asiatic provinces were overrun by Mithridates, King of Pontus. Between the years 73 and 71, the slaves rose in arms, led by the gladiator Spartacus—the Servile War. Italy lay in misery.

Upon Sulla's death, the Senate regained some authority, but real power slipped into the hands of three men ill sorted—Pompey, who had reconquered Asia; Julius Caesar, a bankrupt young man of genius turned demagogue; rich Crassus, who had crushed the slaves' rising and had done well out of the civil struggles. This is the period of Roman history that was best known to Americans of the eighteenth century. It was the time of Marcus Tullius Cicero, philosopher and statesman, consul and rhetorician. Directly or indirectly, the mind and life of Cicero are bound up with the American understanding of order more than are the thought and action of any other man of classical times.

Cicero and the Law of Nature

Cicero was a man of brilliance who set his face against a military revolution, and lost, and paid with his life. It is only seemingly a paradox that the Americans of the Revolution and the new Constitution venerated this leader of resistance to violent change.

For Cicero was the spokesman of the idea of ordered liberty, for which the Americans were seeking. His writings were woven into the schooling Americans had received: the study of Cicero lay at the heart of the curriculum, both in Britain and in America, all during the seventeenth and eighteenth centuries. The rhetoric they had learned was Ciceronian, and the spaciousness of their own political oratory was modelled upon Cicero's. Besides, Cicero was the most famous lawyer of ancient times, and most American political leaders of the formative years had been introduced to the law, many being practicing lawyers. Finally, but most important, it was by Cicero that the doctrine of the law of nature had been expounded lucidly in the Roman age, and that juridical doctrine was essential to the founders of the American Republic.

Born into the order of *equites*, or knights (substantial middle-class citizens originally required to equip themselves as cavalrymen in the Roman forces), Cicero rose to the highest offices in the Roman Republic through his eloquence. He began his career by acting as advocate for men falsely accused by the followers of the dictator Sulla. In a corrupt time, Cicero was incorruptible; he had no equal as an orator; he mastered an immense body of knowledge. In 70 B.C., he prosecuted Verres, the Roman governor who had plundered Sicily; Verres fled abroad, and Cicero's reputation for probity and courage was established, together with his preeminence as a lawyer.

In the year 64, when he was consul, Cicero suppressed the plot of Catiline against the Republic, putting to death the chief conspirators. As a body, the Roman lawyers resisted the military men who aspired to dominate the Republic, and Cicero led that resistance. Julius Caesar courted Cicero's friendship, but the orator would not join him. For a year,

Cicero was the honest and able governor of the sprawling Asiatic province of Cilicia; upon his return to Rome, the collapse of the Republic was imminent.

In that crisis, Cicero sided with Pompey and the senators against Caesar; Pompey was defeated and killed. Refusing to assume command of the surviving senatorial forces, Cicero went back to Rome, where he was well received by the victorious dictator Caesar, and spent two years in political retirement, writing some of his best books. After Caesar was murdered, Cicero struggled to restore the constitution, denouncing Mark Antony in the Senate and trying to unite the provincial governors in resistance to the triumvirate that had succeeded Caesar. At last he was proscribed by Mark Antony and his colleagues, though Octavian (later Augustus) tried to remove Cicero's name from the list of the condemned.

Mark Antony's soldiers sought out Cicero at his seaside villa in December, 43, and ran him through. They carried his severed head and hands to the profligate adventurer Antony, whom they found at an election in the forum. Antony, in Plutarch's description, "commanded his head and hands to be fastened up over the rostra, where the orators spoke: a sight which the Roman people shuddered to behold, and they believed they saw there, not the face of Cicero, but the image of Antony's own soul."

With Cicero fell the Republic. Years later, Augustus, first of the emperors, found his little grandson reading one of Cicero's books, and said to him, "My child, this was a learned man, and a lover of his country."

As a model of republican virtue, Cicero meant much to the leaders of the infant American republic. And those leaders had read him closely—particularly his *Republic* (written between his return from exile in the year 57 and the outbreak of renewed civil war in 49 B.C.) and his *Duties* or *Offices* (composed during his enforced retirement under Caesar's dictatorship).* The better-schooled men among them knew

---

* Of *The Republic*, however, the Americans of Convention times knew only the portion called "The Dream of Scipio" and some fragments; for a fuller surviving manuscript of that book—much of which is missing even today—was not discovered until 1820, in the Vatican.

almost by heart Cicero's principal orations; and they were familiar, too, with his letters, which give an insight into Cicero the man more intimate than our knowledge of anyone else in ancient times. In Cicero's writings, they found powerfully expressed the idea of the law of nature, essential to an understanding of American social order; here they studied his book *The Laws.*

"True law is right reason in agreement with Nature," Cicero wrote in *The Republic;* "it is of universal application, unchanging and everlasting; it summons to duty by its commands, and averts from wrong-doing by its prohibitions. And it does not lay its commands or prohibitions upon good men in vain, although neither have any effect upon the wicked. It is a sin to try to alter this law, nor is it allowable to attempt to repeal a part of it, and it is impossible to abolish it entirely. We cannot be freed from its obligations by Senate or People, and we need not look outside ourselves for an expounder or interpreter of it. And there will not be different laws at Rome and at Athens, or different laws now and in the future, but one eternal and unchangeable law will be valid for all nations and for all times, and there will be one master and one rule, that is, God, over us all, for He is the author of this law, its promulgator, and its enforcing judge."[3]

Until Rome mastered the rest of Italy, the Roman people knew only the *jus civile,* the civil law for native-born Roman citizens. This was a complex body of customary laws, not ordinarily promulgated through formal enactment by Senate and People, but rather developing out of long usage among the Romans themselves—much as, many centuries later, the English common law would arise as a kind of organic growth, from the precedents set by decisions in particular cases at law. As this body of laws increased in complexity, it was regularized to some extent by the annual edicts of the praetors, or chief judicial officers of Rome—who almost might be called the Roman chief justices.

But once Rome extended her power over the whole of Italy, it became necessary to recognize—indeed, to create—a second body of laws, applicable to the multitudes of people who were not full Roman citizens, and therefore neither entitled to the privileges of Romans nor accustomed to the *jus civile*. This new body of laws came to be known as the *jus gentium*, the law of nations—meaning not international law, but instead a body of legal rules founded upon customs more or less common to non-Roman peoples. A second judicial officer, the *praetor peregrinus* (or judge for strangers), had jurisdiction over such cases.

Yet in many instances, it was found difficult to reconcile the differing forms of law prevailing among various "foreign" peoples, or to make those forms agree tolerably well with the Roman civil law. Therefore the praetors had to search for principles of justice that would apply reasonably to these cases of differing legal systems—principles founded upon ethical norms, the general opinion of mankind, and the nature of rational man; upon theories of universal justice. Thus there developed a third body of laws: the *jus naturale*, natural law, as distinguished both from customary law (whether the *jus civile* or the *jus gentium*) and from statutory law (or positive laws formally enacted by the People and confirmed by the Senate).

As a term of jurisprudence and politics, natural law may be defined as a loosely-knit body of rules of action prescribed by an authority superior to the political state. These rules are presumed to be derived from divine commandment, from the nature of man, or from the long experience of mankind in community.

On the one hand, natural law must be distinguished from positive or statutory law, decreed by the state; on the other hand, it must be distinguished from the "laws of nature" in the physical sciences—that is, from propositions expressing the regular order of certain natural phenomena, as in biology or physics. Also natural law sometimes is confused with assertions of "natural rights," which may or may not be founded upon Greek and Roman concepts of natural law.

Cicero's works, from his orations against Verres until the end, contain the most detailed of early discussions of natural law. The Ciceronian understanding of natural law, which still holds some power over men's minds, is this: human laws are only copies of eternal laws. Those eternal laws are peculiar to man, for only man, on earth, is a rational being. The test of validity for the state's laws is their conformity to reason.

To put this another way, natural law is the interpretation of customary or positive law in the light of general ethical principles. Natural law is not a written code, but rather a means for doing justice by referring to the general norms for mankind. In English law, this method is called "equity"; and, as Sir Henry Maine remarks, the English Chancery judges embedded in their lasting decisions whole texts from Roman writings on equity, though without publicly acknowledging their sources.

Recourse to the law of nature kept Roman law from becoming archaic as Roman society changed. "I know of no reason why the law of the Romans should be superior to the laws of the Hindoos," Maine writes, "unless the theory of Natural Law had given it a type of excellence different from the usual one. In this one exceptional instance, simplicity and symmetry were kept before the eyes of a society whose influence on mankind was destined to be prodigious from other causes, as the characteristics of an ideal and absolutely perfect law. It is impossible to overrate the importance to a nation or a profession of having a distinct object to aim at in the pursuit of improvement."[4] So, what with its harmonious character and facility for reasoned enlargement, the natural law of Rome came to outlast Rome's political structure.

As the praetors and jurisconsults (or authorities on law recognized by the Roman state) interpreted the *jus civile* and the *jus gentium* for generations and centuries after Cicero's death, the whole body of Roman law became imbued with the concept of a justice that is not man-decreed merely. In the early years of the Empire, the philosopher-statesman Seneca elaborated the idea of natural law that Cicero had introduced so eloquently. Even after Rome fell, natural-law principles would shape the systematic compilation of law published by the Emperor Justinian at Constantinople. Through the Church and the medieval Schoolmen, and especially through the work of the Bologna doctors of law and of Saint Thomas Aquinas, Ciceronian natural law dominated legal theory down to the seventeenth century. In southern Europe, these natural-law theories re-emerged after the "Dark Ages" of disorder; in the fullness of time, the natural-law element in Roman law would prevail in northern Europe and—through a subtle process of infiltration—would work even upon the independent common law of England, though English kings tried to keep out Roman theories.

The supreme law comes from God, Cicero wrote in his *Laws*. It originated before "any written law existed or any state had been established." The crowd defines law as written decrees, commanding or prohibiting; but the crowd errs. Learned men know that "Law is the highest reason, implanted in Nature, which commands what ought to be done and forbids the opposite. This reason, when firmly fixed and fully developed in the human mind, is Law. And so they believe that Law is intelligence, whose natural function it is to command right conduct and forbid wrongdoing. They think that this quality has derived its name in Greek from the idea of granting to every man his own, and in our language I believe it has been named from the idea of choosing.* For as they have attributed the idea of fairness to the word law, so we have given it that of selection, though both ideas properly belong to Law. Now if this is correct, as I think it to be in general, then the origin of Justice is to be found in Law; for Law is a natural force; it is the mind and reason of the intelligent man, the standard by which Justice and Injustice are measured."[5] Law, then, at base is a knowledge of the ethical norms for the human being.

If indeed true law is the right reason of the intelligent man, a divine gift, it must follow that the law of man's nature is superior to the *jus civile* or the *jus gentium*, superior to the praetor's edict, superior to the commands of Caesar or Antony. The law of the state ought to be consonant with the law of nature; one may appeal from the injustice of governors to the eternal law of ethical truth.

Now Marcus Tullius Cicero, so strongly attached to tradi-

---

* According to Cicero here, the Greek noun *nomos,* law, is derived from the Greek verb for "distribute"; and the Latin word for law, *lex,* comes from *lego,* meaning "to choose." Cicero therefore argues that a system of justice—that is, of choosing between justified and unjustified claims—grows out of human recognition of enduring natural laws.

tion and precedent, a man of constitutionality and order, was not arguing that we ought to challenge every customary or statutory law on the degree of its conformity to natural law. On the contrary, ordinary human laws are the means—however imperfect—by which we express our understanding of the enduring moral law. The natural law is not a fixed code in opposition to the law of the state: properly understood, the law of nature is the moral imagination, and that natural law enables us, through reason, to apply customary and statutory law humanely. The natural law, in Cicero's expression of it, is ethical principle interpreting the rules by which men live together in community.

Yet in times of sharp crisis, the true legality of governors may be tested by repairing to the law of nature. If a dictator, like Caesar—or a body of oligarchs, like the First and Second Triumvirates against which Cicero contended—has flouted or overthrown the constitution of a state, then their decrees do not have the moral force of true law. If the temporary masters of the state are unjust—that is, if they act contrary to the law of nature—men possessing right reason are under no moral obligation to obey them. "And indeed in civil strife," Cicero wrote in *The Republic*, "when virtue is of greater importance than numbers, I think the citizens ought to be weighed rather than counted."[6] The crowd, too, may act illegally and unjustly: one appeals from mob-law to that eternal law which is of divine inspiration. Between virtue and power, a tension exists always; and even should power be endorsed by a temporary majority, virtue ought not to yield.

Cicero was anything but a revolutionary. The doctrine of natural law, nevertheless, would be embraced in later centuries by men bent upon overthrowing an established political order; thus the signers of the American Declaration of Independence appealed to "Nature, and Nature's God." Ordinarily, magistrates employ concepts of the natural law to humanize, modernize, and harmonize an established body of customary law and positive legislation: the natural law is an instrument for progress, not a weapon of revolution.

When an entrenched order, for all that, has ceased to recognize in its positive laws the claims of a minority or even of a majority, then those in opposition will appeal to the moral law, the law of right reason, the law of man's nature, the source of justice. And with the natural law as their apology, the opposition may take up arms. Upon Ciceronian grounds, even in twentieth-century Germany—the country most strongly influenced by respect for positive law—the opponents of Hitler justified their resistance by invoking the constitution that Hitler had overthrown, and the laws of nature.[7] This conflict between the decrees of the total state and the moral law is even more intense in modern times than it was in the closing years of the Roman Republic.

"But for natural law," A.P. D'Entreves writes, "the petty laws of a small peasant community of peninsular Italy would never have become the universal law of an international civilization. But for natural law the great medieval synthesis of godly and worldly wisdom would not have been possible. But for natural law there would have been no American and no French revolution, nor would the great ideals of freedom and equality have found their way into the law-books after having found it into the hearts of men."[8]

With Cicero there perished the Roman Republic. To later times, however, Cicero passed on the heritage of the natural law, compounded of Greek theory and Roman practice. One heroic custom of the early Romans was to "devote" a man to the gods, that through his sacrifice the commonwealth might be forgiven for wrongdoing. To the *mores majorum*, and to the moral law, Cicero gave the last full measure of devotion. At times in his public life, Cicero had been timid or vacillating; yet at the end, the high old Roman virtue was his.

Imperial Splendor and Misery

Between the tawny river Tiber and the smart shopping streets of twentieth-century Rome lies the long-gutted hulk of the mausoleum of Gaius Julius Caesar Octavianus, upon whom the Senate conferred the title of Augustus—previously reserved for the gods. Octavian, or Augustus (for presently he assumed his title as his personal name) restored the Republic in name, and in fact became the first of the emperors.

To the exhausted Roman world, Octavian gave peace. He crushed Antony at the sea-battle of Actium, in the year 31 B.C.; four years later, the Senate declared him Princeps, or first citizen of the restored Republic. As imperator, or commander of the legions, he could have made himself absolute. But he preferred to furbish up republican forms, restoring the constitution after a fashion. He did protect the Senate, purging it of corruption; but with the *comitia*, or Assembly, the People, he found it necessary to abolish all but the name, taking tribunes' powers for his own office. For the Roman populace, the city mob that lived by bread and circuses, had become a proletariat. In the old Roman definition, a proletarian is a man who gives nothing to the state but his children. Rootless, impoverished, unemployed, fierce but cowardly, what had been the People had decayed into what was only a heavy burden upon the imperial city.

Had it not been for the dispassionate intelligence of Augustus, the Roman system might have collapsed altogether when the Republic fell. Resourceful as his uncle Julius Caesar had been, and wiser, Augustus effected a thoroughgoing reform of the Roman political structure, and did what he could to renew the moral vitality of all classes. In architecture and the arts, Augustan Rome rose to a splendor unknown in the West before; in prose, the age possessed a noble historian—Livy, who celebrated the Roman historical experience and awakened historical consciousness among the upper classes; in poetry, this was the time of Virgil and Horace, who eighteen centuries later would remain part of the heritage of all well-schooled Americans.

No body of political institutions endures forever, and it was Augustus' remarkable achievement that the structure he built did not tumble down until two centuries and a half had expired. If the Augustan system was no true republic, still it was in essence no despotism. Peace, prosperity, and a measure of freedom that system did maintain.

If an age is to be judged by the men of vision whom it nurtures, the "Golden Age" of Augustus is worthy of comparison with the Great Age of Greece. Among those men of genius, the name of Virgil stands first in the patrimony of our civilization.

Like Homer long before him and Dante long after, Publius Vergilius Maro was a religious poet, with a religious vision of what the world is meant to be. By evoking the legendary past of the Latin people, in the *Aeneid*, he aspired to consecrate anew the mission of Rome. He did not prevail altogether against the pride, the passion, and the concupiscence of his time; no poet can do that. Yet had there been no Virgil, rousing the consciences of some men of the Empire, the imperial system would have become far grosser and more ruthless than it was; and later ages would have understood less of human dignity.

Had it not been for Virgil, the society of the early Empire might have been consumed by its own materialism and egoism. Influenced probably by the mystical doctrines of the old Greek sage Pythagoras, Virgil perceived at work in Roman civilization a divine mission—a purpose for which the Christian word is "providential." Communicating that insight to the better minds of his age and of succeeding centuries, Virgil—though he was not born a Roman citizen —made of *Romanitas*, the Roman culture, an ideal that in part fulfilled his prophecy of Rome's mission.

T. S. Eliot, the foremost of twentieth-century poets, is the best interpreter of the foremost of Latin poets. There are to be found in Virgil's poetry, Eliot observes, three key words: *labor, pietas, fatum*. Whatever was good in imperial Rome lies in those words.

By *labor*, Virgil meant the dignity of labor—agricultural occupations in particular—for the person and the state. He set his face against what George Orwell calls the "strange, empty dream of idleness." He knew that we must find our happiness in work, or not at all. Here, says Eliot, Virgil expresses "something that we ought to find particularly intelligible just now, when urban agglomeration, the flight from the land, the pillage of the earth and the squandering of natural resources are beginning to attract attention." He passed on to Christianity, Eliot suggests, "the principle that action and contemplation, labor and prayer, are both essential to the life of the complete man."

By *pietas*, Virgil meant something larger than churchgoing or correctness toward one's parents. He meant a humility before the gods, a love of one's country, and a sense of duties that are not adequately expressed by any English word; and he gave this concept of *pietas* to an age groping for renewed purpose. As Eliot continues, "The Roman Empire which Virgil imagined and for which Aeneas worked out his destiny was not exactly the same as the Roman Empire of the legionaries, the pro-consuls and governors, the businessmen and speculators, the demagogues and generals. It was something greater, but something which exists because Virgil imagined it. It remains an ideal, but one which Virgil passed on to Christianity to develop and to cherish."

By *fatum*, Virgil meant the Roman imperial destiny —Rome's duty, imposed by unknowable powers, to bring peace to the world, to maintain the cause of order and justice and freedom, to withstand barbarism. "I think that he had few illusions and that he saw clearly both sides of every question—the case for the loser as well as the case for the winner. . . . " For Virgil, this mission was the real significance of Rome's history. "And do you really think that Virgil was mistaken?" Eliot inquires. "What Virgil proposed to his contemporaries was the highest ideal even for an unholy Roman Empire, for any merely temporal empire. We are all, so far as we inherit the civilization of Europe, still citizens of the Roman Empire. . . . "[9]

The Julian and Claudian emperors who succeeded Augustus were no disciples of Virgil. For some of the administrators and soldiers of imperial times, nevertheless, *labor* and *pietas* and *fatum* retained meaning. And upon the minds of Roman jurists and philosophers and men of letters, Virgil's ethical poetry was imprinted. No other name of the classical ages loomed so large as Virgil's in medieval times—though the vulgar mistook him for a magician. Indeed there is magic in Virgil's lines, but the magic that operates upon conscience rather than upon material objects. Recognizing Virgil as the purest soul of antiquity, thirteen centuries later Dante would choose that poet for his guide through the mysteries of Hell and Purgatory.

Virgil left his mark upon the Roman society. For the Rome of the depraved emperors, the slaughters in the Colosseum, the persecutions of the innocent, the ruinous wars in Asia, also was the Rome of the philosophers of fortitude. During the first century of the Christian era, the ideals of Virgil blended with the Stoic philosophy—imported from Greece, but transformed by the Romans into a belief more humane and strong—to make tolerable what otherwise would have been a social wasteland.

In a bloody age, Roman Stoicism held together the civil social order of imperial centralization, and taught a small circle of men the nature of true freedom. This religious philosophy attained in the first and second and third centuries after the birth of Christ a direct influence upon public policy. The subtle influence of that philosophy upon American civilization is not easily measured; but it endures, both in its own right and as "the porch to Christianity."

The Stoic philosophy was peculiarly congenial to the old Roman character, though it was unable to move deeply the mass of men in the Empire. Stoicism commences in a thoroughgoing materialism: this world we know is the only world, the Stoic declares, and everything in it, even the qualities called spiritual, has a material character. Yet this world is ruled by divine wisdom. God, the beneficent intelligence that directs all things, is everywhere present, and indeed is virtually identical with the universe. The duty of man is to ascertain the way of nature, the manner in which divine providence intends that man should live.

Conscience informs the wise man of what is good and what is evil. Most things, including fleshly enjoyments, are neither good nor evil, but simply indifferent. Conforming to rational nature, the Stoic looks upon all men, even the vicious and the imbecile, as his brothers, and he seeks their welfare. (Because all men are equal in God's sight, the Stoics reasoned, slavery is unjust.) We human beings are made for coöperation, like the hands, like the feet.

The philosopher lives upon a mountain, as it were

—superior to vanities, expecting little of his fellow-men, but sympathizing and helping. The Stoic does not complain at misfortune, for that would be to reproach God. He abjures ambition and performs his duties. And his aim is not happiness, but virtue.

Of these Stoics, Lucius Annaeus Seneca was the most eloquent. Statesman, moralist, and dramatist, he undertook the Stoic responsibility of serving the state. The most high-principled man of his time succeeded in rising to great office, paradoxically, under the most infamous of emperors, Nero. Whatever a man in office might do to uphold the ideas of *labor* and *pietas* and *fatum* under such an emperor, Seneca did. Yet in the end, Seneca came to agree with senatorial conspirators that for the sake of the commonwealth, Nero must die. Crushing that plot, Nero ordered his minister to commit suicide. Seneca and his wife died together; Nero did not long survive them.[10]

Seneca stood at the top of Roman society. The other principal philosopher at the time of the Julian and Claudian emperors was a crippled slave, Epictetus. He came of a humble family in the Hellenized town of Hierapolis, in Phrygia, and from his early years he was a slave to Epaphroditus, the freedman and favorite of Nero. Sickly from birth, Epictetus is said to have been tortured by his master, and to have learned from helpless suffering that happiness is the product of the will, not of external forces.

His dissolute master sent him to study under the philosopher Musonius Rufus—educated slaves being more valuable—and so the obscure Epictetus gained mastery over men's minds for centuries thereafter. Epaphroditus, who was secretary to Nero, was present at that emperor's sorry death, helping the fallen wretch to kill himself. This act of kindness, possibly the only one Epaphroditus ever performed, was his own undoing: for the ferocious Domitian, succeeding Nero in imperial authority, put the former favorite to death on account of it, declaring that no servant ought to presume to violate the divinity that hedges an emperor, even at the emperor's command. Epictetus seems to have been freed after his master's execution, but he was involved in the general expulsion of philosophers from Rome ordered by Domitian, and so took up residence in Epirus, where he held his school for many years, dying sometime during the reign of the magnificent Hadrian, whose friend he is believed to have been.

Freedom, Epictetus says, is to be found in obedience to the will of God, and in renouncing desire. Thus Epictetus, though in bondage much of his life, lived and died a man truly free; while Nero, his master's master, lived and died an abject slave to will and appetite, though to outward appearances the most fortunate man in the world. Disciplining his character, Epictetus rose to that immortal fame which, to the Stoics, was the only possible immortality.

The free mind of this slave-philosopher is reflected in his manly and pithy prose. His *Enchiridion,* or *Manual,* was compiled by the historian Arrian, a devoted pupil of that teacher, who set down the observations of his master. Intended to make available within a small compass the remarks of Epictetus most likely to form good character, the *Manual* duplicated, in part, the four books of Epictetus' *Discourses* that have come down to modern times.

"Two maxims we must ever bear in mind," Epictetus says: "that apart from the will there is nothing either good or bad, and that we must not try to anticipate or direct events, but merely accept them with intelligence." The guardian spirit within each of us, if we exert the will, may lead us to righteousness and free us from servitude to material objects and to men. The Emperor Domitian recognized in these Stoic principles an irreconcilable opposition to arbitrary power, and so expelled the philosophers from Rome.

Social regeneration does occur now and again in distressed societies, and the Virgilian and Stoic teachings had something to do with the coming of a better line of emperors, the Flavians; theirs was the Silver Age of Latin letters (69-96 A.D.)—the time of the stern historian Tacitus, who declared that the Romans in their expansion "create a wilderness, and call it peace." In their turn, the Flavians were followed by the "Five Good Emperors" (98-180 A.D.)—Nerva, Trajan, Hadrian, Antoninus Pius, and Marcus Aurelius. With the last, we turn to a philosopher-king.

Marcus Aurelius as Exemplar

Mankind always is looking for exemplars—that is, for models of character. Outside the pages of Plutarch, the classical exemplar who probably appealed most strongly to Americans of the eighteenth and nineteenth centuries was the Emperor Marcus Aurelius. From the first settlement of the English colonies, Marcus Aurelius had been read in America. Captain John Smith, commanding the train-bands of the first Virginians, cherished Marcus Aurelius above all other writers.

In modern Rome, the monumental constructions of the Antonine emperors still loom above the flood of motor-traffic. In the piazza before the Capitol stands the bronze effigy of Marcus Aurelius on horseback, the most nearly perfect equestrian statue of the ancient world surviving to our time. (It was spared from smelting for its metal in the Middle Ages because of a popular belief that it represented the Emperor Constantine, friend to Christians.) Eighteen centuries of Roman ferocity and rejoicing have passed in procession before this bronze rider.*

He was born Marcus Annius Verus, descended from two Roman families of distinction, in 121 A.D. The Emperor Hadrian, admiring the boy's generosity and piety, directed his heir-apparent, Antoninus Pius, to adopt the young man —together with Lucius Verus—and to train the two youths for mastery of the world. Epictetus' *Discourses* were put into the hands of the boy. This book incalculably affected the mind of the future emperor, making him into a thorough Stoic.

Hadrian's tomb, which in medieval times would become the Castle of Sant' Angelo, dominates the Tiber still;

---

* Nathaniel Hawthorne, in *The Marble Faun*, describes the statue: "It is the most majestic representation of the kingly character that ever the world has seen. A sight of the old heathen emperor is enough to create an evanescent sentiment of loyalty in a democratic bosom, so august does he look, so fit to rule, so worthy of man's profoundest homage and obedience, so inevitably attractive of his love."

Hadrian's humane policies would dominate the Empire for two more reigns after his death. Hadrian's will was done: Marcus Annius became Marcus Aurelius Antoninus, and was associated with his kindly foster-father in the government of the Empire, and knew at the age of seventeen that one day he must bear all the burdens of the world. "Power tends to corrupt," Lord Acton writes, "and absolute power corrupts absolutely." Yet it was not so with Marcus Aurelius, although Lucius Verus, for a time his colleague, succumbed to the temptations of the office.

Marcus Aurelius was invested with power as absolute, in effect, as any man ever had obtained outside the Asiatic despotisms. But he never ceased to restrain himself, and deferred in everything to the Senate, considering himself the servant of Senate and People. His imperial administration, lasting nineteen years, was marked by prudent and generous reforms at home, and by decisive victories on the Parthian and German frontiers. In all these, the Emperor himself was the commanding force.

"Every one of us wears mourning in his heart for Marcus Aurelius," says Ernest Renan, "as if he had died but yesterday. . . . Thanks to him, we can understand how those old Roman families, which had seen the reign of the bad emperors, still clung to their uprightness, their dignity, their sense of justice, their civic spirit, and, if I may say so, their republicanism. . . . The advent of the Antonines was simply the accession to power of the society whose righteous wrath has been transmitted to us by Tacitus, the society of good and wise men formed by the union of all those whom the despotism of the first Caesars had revolted."

Marcus Aurelius was a reforming conservative: "He invariably treated man as a moral being; he never affected, in the common fashion of would-be transcendental politicians, to take him for a machine or a means to an end. If unable to abrogate the atrocious penal code of his age, he softened its practice. . . . Seneca had said: 'All men, if you only go back to their beginnings, have the gods for their fathers.' On the morrow, Ulpian was to declare: 'By natural law all men are born free and equal . . .' "[11] In elevation of mind and qualities of military leadership, Marcus Aurelius was the "guardian" whom Plato had sought many generations earlier.

Marcus Aurelius' *Meditations,* one of the most intimate of all books (its real title being *Marcus Aurelius to Himself*), seems to many of its readers as if there were no gulf of time between the Emperor and us. Appreciation of Marcus Aurelius' reflections, however, is a modern thing, for his little book was not generally known until the sixteenth century. Ever since then, it has been read more than any other work of ancient philosophy, being relevant to the condition of men in every age who endure tribulation. Marcus Aurelius was less talented as a writer than was Seneca, but the personal character of his little book gives it a poignancy one encounters earlier in the letters of Cicero. Soldiers especially have encountered in Marcus Aurelius a conscience speaking to a conscience.

History leaves only one reproach upon this emperor's name, his persecution of the Christians. Yet this was undertaken out of honest motives, from a misunderstanding of Christian teaching and practice, caused by the excesses of fanatics on the fringe of the churches. It was not by intolerance that his policy was guided, but by a charity almost excessive.

"Pity is a vice," the first Stoic philosopher, Zeno, had said. But the Stoic Emperor, believing that wickedness was the consequence more of ignorance than of malevolence, was inclined to pardon the worst ingratitude. Out of pity, he tolerated the licentious Lucius Verus, and did not sufficiently restrain the brutality of his own son, Commodus. When Avidius Cassius, an able general, raised the standard of revolt in Asia, Marcus Aurelius offered to abdicate, for the sake of general peace. When Cassius' head was brought to him, he was grieved to have lost by assassination an opportunity to forgive the rebel; and rather than punish Cassius' supporters, he burnt all the rebel general's correspondence unread, as soon as it was delivered to him.

Everyone in America who read seriously, during the last quarter of the eighteenth century, knew the glowing description of the age of the Antonines with which Gibbon's *Decline and Fall of the Roman Empire* opens. It was a period of affluence, security, and splendor, during which the laws were enforced and many evils diminished. For all that, it was an age morally corrupt, the dying glow of a high culture, and the Emperor was saddened by the vices and follies of the millions of people entrusted to his charge. He surrounded himself with the most upright of the Romans, especially those families whose Stoicism, uniting with the high old Roman virtue, had been proof against the evil Caesars.

This high-principled domination would be dissolved only a few years after Marcus Aurelius, worn out at the age of fifty-nine, died in the midst of a campaign near Vienna, in the year 180. The moral degradation of the masses, the condition that led to the rule of the barracks-emperors, is glimpsed with a terrible clarity when one reads of Marcus Aurelius at the gladiatorial shows. Detesting those ghastly displays, still he was compelled by the force of depraved public opinion to be present and to receive the salutes of the doomed men below in the arena. Refusing to watch that slaughter, the Emperor read books, or gave audiences, during the shows. And the ninety thousand human brutes, the spectators packing the Colosseum, with the jackal-courage of anonymity, jeered him for his humanity.

He is thought to have written his *Meditations* during the last two years of the Marcomannic War, while he was engaged in fierce campaigns along the Danube—"the spider hunting the fly," in his own words. A successful commander, Marcus Aurelius flung back the Marcomanni and other German tribes, giving Rome and Italy two more centuries of survival, during which Christianity would rise to strength—so that the collapse of political order in the fifth century would not mean the destruction of the whole Roman heritage. Similarly, the Stoic philosophy of which Marcus Aurelius was a strong representative prepared the way for acceptance of Christian teaching in the dying Roman culture. And thus, as if he were the instrument of the Providence which he knew to govern this earth, the philosopher-king lived, unknowingly, for the sake of a religion that he persecuted.

God has designed a natural order for this world, Marcus Aurelius wrote. The duty of every man is to do his part in this order; to live willingly in community, helping others:

"If thou didst ever see a hand cut off, or a foot, or a head, lying anywhere apart from the rest of the body, such does a man make himself, as far as he can, who is not content with what happens, and separates himself from others, or does anything unsocial. Suppose that thou hast detached thyself from the natural unity—for thou wast made by nature a part, but now thou has cut thyself off—yet here there is this beautiful provision, that it is in thy power again to unite thyself. God has allowed this to no other part, after it has been separated and cut asunder, to come together again. But consider the kindness by which he has distinguished man, for he has put it in his power not to be separated at all from the universal; and when he has been separated, he has allowed him to return and to be united and to resume his place as a part."*

He lived not for himself, but to do his duty in public action. Despite the melancholy that runs through the *Meditations*, he performed his labor with a hopeful spirit. We see him struggling against the weakness of the flesh (he being then a sick man, desperately tired), as in his playful exhortations to himself to rise early in the morning, that he might do the work of a man. We see him preferring even the rough and dangerous life of the frontier camp to the sham and treachery of the imperial court. We hear him teaching himself to welcome the approach of death—because, in addition to other reasons, if a man were to live longer, he might become such a creature as the depraved men he encountered too often. The sense of the vanity of human wishes was with the Emperor always, but he bore it manfully:

"To go on being what you have been hitherto, to lead a life still so distracted and polluted, were stupidity and cowardice indeed, worthy of the mangled gladiators who, torn and disfigured, cry out to be remanded till the morrow, to be flung once more to the same fangs and claws. Enter your claim then to these few attributes (of good character). But if you find yourself falling away and beaten in the fight, be a man and get away to some quiet corner, where you can still hold on, or, in the last resort, take leave of life not angrily, but simply, freely,

---

* Quotations here from the *Meditations* are the translation of George Long (second edition, London, 1883)—an English classical scholar who greatly admired General Robert E. Lee.

modestly, achieving at least this much in life, brave leaving of it."

So Marcus Aurelius wrote while he broke the hordes of the Marcomanni and the Quadi beyond the Danube. His words would hearten many later men in their troubles.

Yet the Stoic philosophy, and the integrity of the Good Emperors, could not regenerate the Roman masses. Stoicism was a high and austere creed, too abstract and intellectual for popular acceptance. Even the imported Egyptian cult of Isis had more votaries, in those days, than did Stoicism. In the long run, the Christian faith which Saint Peter and Saint Paul had brought to Rome would renew the moral order, even though it could not save the state. But Christianity was a revealed religion, the worship of a crucified God, and it would touch the heart.

Marcus Aurelius' son and successor, the brawny Commodus, lived as if he were bent upon undoing his father's moral and political achievement. He proscribed distinguished Romans as Nero had done, fought with wild beasts and gladiators in the arena, and insisted that people worship him as the Roman Hercules. The imperial court dreaded its master. In the year 192, at the instigation of the Emperor's intimates, a wrestler strangled Commodus. For the following hundred years, the Empire would sink downward. The order of the soul being decayed, Rome could be governed only by force and a master.

These Ruins Are Inhabited

By the quays at the port of Split, in the country now called Yugoslavia, stands the gigantic Palace of Diocletian, half fortress, half villa; within its wall is a rabbit-warren of a medieval city. When the Avars and the Slavs overthrew the Roman power in Dalmatia, in the year 614 A.D., the citizens of the devastated city of Salona took refuge in the Palace, and a dense population has been living within those walls ever since.

This frowning palace was more than three centuries old

when the barbarian Avars and their subject peoples came over the mountains. It was built by the Emperor Diocletian, who had begun life as a rude peasant, the son of slaves, in the hills near Salona. After his abdication, Diocletian returned to this beautiful Adriatic shore to spend his declining years in a splendid retirement. Not the least of the strong Diocletian's achievements was that he could retire peacefully from the seat of the mighty: for most emperors of the third century had died by the sword, sometimes at the hands of their own troops. With Diocletian—acclaimed emperor by the Pannonian legions in the year 284—the structure that Augustus built came to its end. To save the state, Diocletian established a despotism, requiring all men to call him lord and to worship him as a god. The Senate was reduced to little better than a town-council, and Diocletian himself resided most of his reign at Nicomedia, in Asia Minor. Dividing the Empire into four immense regions, he appointed three colleagues to share power with him, so that the imperial authority might both defend the ravaged frontiers and carry on the interior administration of the Empire competently.

Under Diocletian, equality prevailed among the people of the Roman system—the equality of servitude, or of equal misery. Everyone was assigned heavy duties without corresponding rights. City magistrates were made personally responsible for the collection of taxes, and fixed inescapably in their posts; duties were passed on, compulsorily, from father to son. Peasants were reduced permanently to serfdom. Wages and prices were fixed, and everything was regulated by central authority—so far as that power could be enforced. Grinding taxation impoverished every class. For the concluding eight years of his reign, Diocletian relentlessly persecuted the Christians, they refusing to worship the divine emperor.

Yet Diocletian was not an evil emperor: on the contrary, he devoted himself to the defense of the Roman state, working himself to exhaustion. He was compelled to his harsh policies by harsher necessity. Only by doubling or tripling the size of the army, and by concentrating all power in the emperor and his colleagues, and by attempting to give that authority a divine sanction, could he hold back the barbarians on the frontiers and prevent for a time the internal disintegration of the Empire.

For Diocletian, wearing the diadem and dressed in gorgeous oriental robes, endeavored to shore up an empire that had been torn by war and social decadence throughout the third century of the Christian era. Soon after the murder of Commodus, the imperial throne had been seized by a rough soldier, Septimius Severus, who destroyed all rivals. In the year 211, after a successful military career, old Septimius lay dying at York, in Britain. To him came his two ruthless sons, asking how they should rule the Empire when he was gone. "Be of one mind," said the Emperor. "Enrich the soldiers; nothing else matters."

That had been the story of Rome in the third century—incessant marching and countermarching from the Tyne to the Euphrates, war after war for the throne, decay of classes and cities, exhaustion of mind and spirit within the Empire. The soldiers—peasants or barbarian mercenaries—had been paid, after a fashion; nothing else had mattered.

Diocletian's reorganization of imperial administration, a work continued by his successor Constantine, did save the Empire. The West would fall to barbarian invaders in the fifth century, but in the East that Empire—there more Greek and Asiatic than Roman—would survive for a thousand years longer. Yet this was salvation at the price of servitude, and what remained after Diocletian retired to his palace in Dalmatia was only the ghost of the Rome of the Republic, or of the Augustan Golden Age, or the Silver Age.

Today one may sit in a cafe in the piazza before the cathedral of Split, watching the tourists from West and East as they scurry past a black Egyptian sphinx that Diocletian brought to adorn his palace; that sphinx was as remote in time from Diocletian as Diocletian is from the tourists. The piazza was the peristyle, or central court, of Diocletian's enormous palace, and beneath it archeologists still are excavating his cellars. The cathedral was Diocletian's mausoleum, though the sarcophagus of the persecutor of Christians was violated ages ago. Another grim man, somewhat like Diocletian in character, is absolute master of Dalmatia today, and the creed of Marx and Lenin has supplanted pagan emperor-worship; otherwise, human life pullulates in Split much as it has for many centuries. (In modern Dalmatia, people no more believe in the infallibility of Marx than the Dalmatians of the fourth century believed, really, in Diocletian's divinity.) Human nature being a constant, the same virtues and the same vices appear in every era, though political forms fade away.

Rome was a thousand years old when Diocletian rose to power. Near the railway station in modern Rome, the colossal remains of the public baths that Diocletian gave to the city still strike the eye; those halls are churches and museums now. Roman art, in Diocletian's time, tottered on the edge of a collapse of style, but the engineering and the sculpture of these baths still have the marks of the Golden Age. Diocletian built this bewildering complex for a degraded population which was kept alive by doles and kept quiet by shows in the Colosseum and the Circus Maximus and the other circuses and theaters. Diocletian paid the soldiers, held the frontiers, and ruled as if he were a god, and still built as if Rome would endure forever. By that time, nothing else mattered.

How was it that Rome, though she gave law to the world, could not maintain her own civilization? The answers to that inquiry are too complicated for detailed analysis here; but one may suggest that the causes are to be found both in certain failings in the order of the commonwealth and in certain deficiencies of the inner order of the soul. For the barbarians' conquest of the Roman Empire was like air bursting into a vacuum: the Goths and Vandals and other invaders, at the end, penetrated a kind of hollow shell, within which they encountered little resistance.

Let us turn first to some social aspects of the decay of order. The political structure, the struggle among classes, and economic difficulties all are involved here.

1) Rome's political problem was quite the opposite of the failure of the Greek *polis*. The Greeks could not transcend the boundaries of the little city-state, and so fell because of dis-

unity: the word signifying such an obsession with local concerns is "particularism." But the Romans suffered from something very different—centralization or universalism.

True, the Romans did leave to the municipalities within the Empire a considerable degree of local autonomy. But the great provinces were ruled from the city of Rome; all real power was concentrated at the center, and no adequate system of representative government developed, except in the sense that a number of the senators and principal magistrates and generals might be drawn from Spain, Africa, or other regions. The diverse populations of the Empire, or the upper classes within those populations, might be thoroughly Romanized; yet with the decay of the non-Roman cultures and political systems, public concerns tended to descend into apathy and indifference. The whole imperial structure was grossly overcentralized, and when the center could hold no longer, the bough began to break. Within the Roman administration, the heavy and increasing concentration of power in the emperors loaded insufferable burdens upon a single individual; Diocletian, finding the load too painful even for his strength, divided imperial responsibilities among four commanders—the beginning of the dissolution of the Empire into fragments. The wonder is that the political structure endured so long as it did, considering the Empire's tremendous extent and the limited means of communication in those centuries.

2) The Romans never succeeded in reconciling the interests of social classes. Most of the free urban population of Rome itself became an unemployed and turbulent proletariat even in the late Republic; no means for regeneration ever were discovered. Between the senatorial and equestrian families on the one side, and the masses of free citizens in the cities on the other; between the freedmen and the native-born Roman citizens; between the citizens, urban or rural, and the millions of slaves; between the urban populations and the peasants—among all these social elements, little sympathy endured.

To obtain popular support, many of the emperors sided with the impoverished populace against the senatorial and equestrian classes; and equestrians (what we might call "upper middle class" or "bourgeois" people) had been virtually extinguished by the reign of Diocletian, indeed. Through insufferable taxation, levied to pay the soldiers and please the proletariat, the most industrious classes fell.

In the Rome of the fourth century, classes had vanished, supplanted by castes that were obligatory and hereditary. Political freedom had become inconceivable. "In this heritage there was almost nothing positive except the fact of the existence of the Empire with all its natural resources," Rostovtzeff writes. "The men who inhabited it had utterly lost their balance. Hatred and envy reigned everywhere: the peasants hated the landowners and the officials, the city proletariat hated the city bourgeoisie, the army was hated by everybody, even by the peasants. The Christians were abhorred and persecuted by the heathens, who regarded them as a gang of criminals bent on undermining the state."[12]

The only people relatively immune from central oppression, by the time of Constantine, were the great landed proprietors, who by bribery, influence, force, or remoteness sheltered their "clients" against taxgatherers and military recruiters. When the barbarian peoples overthrew the Roman state, many folk in city and countryside doubtless accepted the fall of central power as a relief.

3) In economic concerns, the disappearance of a free agricultural population—especially in Italy, Africa, and large regions of Asia—and the growth of tremendous estates tilled by slaves or serfs both transformed the social basis of Roman institutions and resulted in a decline of productivity. With the increase of apathy and despair, total population declined.

Taxation, and the growing bureaucracy, devoured prosperity. Through lack of imagination and need for public revenues, during the third and fourth centuries, commerce and manufacturing were burdened and regulated insufferably. Attempts to replace private undertakings with state industry did not prosper.

"The beneficent plutocrat of the past disappeared under lessening profits," Freya Stark observes of the social revolution in the third century. "Under an ever-increasing burden of coercion, the system of *liturgies*, by which public liabilities had been accepted by the wealthy in every state, was now tightened to suit the economic stress. Civic honors ceased to be voluntary; they became enforced and inescapable; gifts of corn, of oil for the gymnasia (a very big item in every city's expense), of transport for the restless armies—were gifts no longer but ever-growing governmental assessments; the man handling public money was required to pledge out of his own property and, if necessary, to meet any deficit out of his own pocket, and this transfer of collective to individual liability caused many of the taxable people from the third century onward to abandon their homes in despair."[13]

Fourth-century Rome, in short, had become an empire in which many felt that life no longer was worth living. Such were some, though by no means all, of the failings of the Roman social order. This decline was paralleled by a decay of the order of the soul, though from time to time—as under Augustus or under the Antonine emperors—some revival of moral purpose was attempted. We may set down here, very briefly, some phenomena of the decadence of the inner order.

1) The old Roman religion, deeply felt but simple and chiefly ceremonial, began to give way during the last two centuries of the Republic. The introduction of Greek religious concepts, especially during and shortly after the wars with Carthage, awoke no earnest popular response. Nor did the Stoic philosophy work upon the Roman masses effectually, even if it did energize some of the leaders of society.

2) The attempt to support the Roman imperial system by emperor-worship never really took root, being alien to the traditions of the West; indeed, it could not have been taken seriously, even in its most modest form, by such intelligent emperors as Hadrian and the Antonines. When, with Diocletian, the emperor's divinity was asserted more fully, with stern compulsion behind the claim, it must have provoked sardonic grins in secret: the Illyrian peasant who had risen by violence to supreme power might be awesome, but he could not be accepted, despite a certain natural dignity, as a supernatural being.

3) To fill the vacuum of faith, Oriental mystery cults —Syrian, Egyptian, Greek, Persian—flourished in imperial

Rome. But the very diversity of these exotic cults destroyed religious and ethical consensus among the Roman population, and terribly weakened the religious consecration of the Roman state. Moreover, although the early Roman religion had been more ethical than transcendent, many of the Oriental faiths scarcely were ethical or social at all: they offered no connection between personal salvation and public order.

In the fullness of time, the Christian religion would unite with belief in a transcendent truth certain strong principles of social community. But during the decisive third century, the Christians were a persecuted minority; and during that time irreparable damage was done to Roman society. When Constantine the Great decreed toleration for the Christians (313 A.D.), already it was too late for a new faith to buttress the whole social fabric of Rome; by the time Christianity was officially proclaimed the state religion, late in the fourth century, the Empire had fallen into two halves. The Christian Church indeed would preserve many aspects of Roman civilization through the Dark Ages, but in the West, meanwhile, the political order of Rome had dissolved almost totally.

The late Roman world, then, was a culture spiritually impoverished and disordered, lacking a common core of belief. It has been called a dead world: a time in which the old Roman virtues had been lost by the mass of men, but in which the Christian virtues had not yet come to dominate. It was a world spiritually and intellectually bored. Mankind can endure anything but boredom. Because men could not order their own despairing souls, the order of the commonwealth could not be saved.

What of those key words of Virgil—*labor, pietas, fatum?* They had sunk to literary tags only.

The decline of agriculture, and of the citizen-farmer's affection for the land, had commenced early, but had been accelerated by the violence and oppression of the third and fourth centuries. Commerce and crafts decayed, too, and shortly after the death of Diocletian, artistic and engineering talents dwindled swiftly.[14] A servile people labor only under hard necessity or compulsion. *Labor,* once deconsecrated, became tedium.

As for *pietas*, that sense of duty toward divine powers and toward one's ancestors, one's living community, and one's posterity—why, a people who have lost both their religious convictions and their freedom cannot feel it. Most people in the third and fourth centuries lived from day to day, as dogs do, without thought for anything but immediate physical survival. The Roman state, once the nexus of their affections, had become a taskmaster at best; the temples of Jupiter, Juno, and Minerva, on the Capitoline hill, no longer stirred the Roman soul. The "contract of eternal society" was forgotten.

And *fatum*—Rome's appointed mission? As population shrank, and as prosperity disappeared, as the barbarians defeated the legions, and as a sense of frustration crept over nearly everyone, so that hope and confidence trickled away. The emperors themselves no longer believed in *fatum*. On the eve of the fall of the West, it was a Greek philosopher from Cyrene, in Africa, who spoke best for Rome's greatness. Visiting Constantinople, he implored Arcadius, Emperor of the East, to put down Alaric's ravaging Visigoths and assert the ancient vigor of Roman order.

"The measures which Synesius recommends are the dictates of a bold and generous patriot," in Edward Gibbon's words. "He exhorts the emperor to revive the courage of his subjects by the example of manly virtue; to banish luxury from the court and from the camp; to substitute, in the place of the barbarian mercenaries, an army of men interested in the defense of their land and of their property; to force, in such a moment of public danger, the mechanic from his shop and the philosopher from his school; to rouse the indolent citizen from his dream of pleasure; and to arm, for the protection of agriculture, the hands of the laborious husbandmen."[15] The court politely applauded Synesius. But soon thereafter, Arcadius appointed the barbarian chief Alaric a master-general of the Empire.

Marching into Italy, Alaric and his barbarians took the city of Rome—the gates being opened to them by slaves in the night—in the year 410, and sacked the Eternal City. After that fall, no one believed in *fatum*, for the world had been turned upside down.

How had the grandeur that was Rome come to this ruin?

That question was asked by Saint Augustine in the year when Alaric sacked the city, and it was still being asked in the closing decades of the eighteenth century. Gibbon's history raised more inquiries than it answered. Americans of the formative years paid close attention to the subject—and not to Gibbon only, for there were published about that time several other influential studies of the crash of civilizations.*

The Roman experience was mentioned repeatedly in the constitutional debates at Philadelphia. The consequences of Roman centralization had their part in discouraging schemes for a central, rather than a federal, government in America —quite as the Greek disunity had a part in the arguments against a mere loose confederation. The Roman social struggles reminded American leaders of the need for recognizing and harmonizing the claims of different classes in their own society. And in the eighteenth-century climate of rationalism, American knowledge of the effects of Rome's religious and ethical decline upon the social order did something to secure American attachment to the free exercise of religion.

So Rome's example of decadence was a cautionary lesson to Americans. But also Rome's legacy of law was part of the American inheritance. And the Roman administrative genius, the insights of Cicero and Virgil, the heroic examples of Roman republicans and emperors, all went into the institutions and the cast of mind of the early Americans.† All American factions then took for granted what an American poet, Eliot, would write in the twentieth century—that so far as we inherit the civilization of Europe, we remain citizens of the Roman Empire. They had no intention of abandoning that patrimony.

---

* For instance, Count Volney's *Ruins, or Considerations on the Revolutions of Empires* (1791). Volney travelled in America.

† George Washington, though no classical scholar, was much affected by Joseph Addison's tragedy *Cato*, which represents the last days of the stubborn republican friend of Cicero. Cato killed himself at Utica, rather than accept Caesar's offer of friendship if he would surrender; he did not desire to survive the Republic. With almost no exception, the Americans of Revolutionary and Constitutional times were admirers of Cato and Cicero, not of Caesar.

For a thousand years more, the Empire of the East would maintain its capital at Constantinople; while even in the West, much of what was finest in Roman culture was preserved by the Church, if half unconsciously. The body of Roman law endured in the East, and centuries later took root again in the West. More than a hundred and thirty years after Alaric took Rome, the Emperor Justinian published in the East the *Corpus juris civilis*, his elaborate consolidation of Roman law, incorporating the natural-law doctrines of such famous Roman jurisconsults as Gaius and Ulpian. That monumental work still is the foundation of modern law in western Europe, and has influenced, if less directly, the laws of England and the United States.

In the twelfth century, through the doctors of law at the Italian university of Bologna, the Roman law as codified by Justinian made its triumphant way back into the medieval West. "The Roman law," H. A. L. Fisher puts it, "expressed the ideas of a society more civilized and more mature than the western Europe of the early middle ages. It was a society which had evolved certain clear-cut ideas about private property and possession, family rights and the sanctity of contract, and had come to regard law as a reasoned and intelligible system adapted to the needs of humanity as a whole. A great state with commercial dealings all over the world evolves a law capable of meeting the manifold occasions of its life. The Roman law though influenced by philosophy was close to reality. It was built up not so much by legislation as by custom and by the answers of jurisconsults upon the cases real and imaginary which were submitted to them. And so as western Europe emerged from medieval darkness it found in the Corpus Juris of Justinian a revelation of the great thing which European civilization had once been and might again become."[16]

In its law and in other concerns, the Roman commonwealth held more meaning for the new United States than did any other civilization and political community except the British and their own colonial society. And twentieth-century America, its ascendancy comparable to Rome's, confronts the old ideas of *labor, pietas,* and *fatum,* in a society increasingly urbanized and centralized, in a universal time of troubles, when power often acknowledges no virtue. What was the Roman tension is today America's tension.

Notes

[1] John Henry Newman, "The Patristical Idea of Antichrist", in *Discussions and Arguments on Various Subjects* (London: Longmans, Green, 1891), p. 51.

[2] *The General History of Polybius*, translated by James Hampton (fifth edition, 2 vols., Oxford: W. Baxter, 1823), Vol. II, pp. 177-78.

[3] Cicero, *De Re Publica* (translated by Clinton Walker Keyes; Cambridge, Mass.: Harvard University Press, 1928), III, xxii.

[4] Sir Henry Maine, *Ancient Law: its Connection with the Early History of Society and its Relation to Modern Ideas* (sixteenth edition, London: Oxford University Press, 1897), pp. 44-45, 78.

[5] Cicero, *De Legibus* (translated by Keyes; Cambridge, Mass.: Harvard University Press, 1928), I, v, vi.

[6] Cicero, *De Re Publica, op. cit.*, VI, i, vi.

[7] See Klemens von Klemperer, *Germany's New Conservatism: its History and Dilemma in the Twentieth Century* (Princeton: Princeton University Press, 1957); and Hans Rothfels, *The German Opposition to Hitler* (revised edition, Chicago: Henry Regnery, 1962).

[8] A. P. D'Entrèves, *Natural Law: an Introduction to Legal Philosophy* (London: Hutchinson's University Library, 1951), p. 13.

[9] T. S. Eliot, "Virgil and the Christian World", in Eliot, *On Poetry and Poets* (New York: Farrar, Strauss, 1957), pp. 135-48. (Despite common usage, "Vergil" is a more correct spelling than "Virgil".) For another informative essay on that poet, see "Vergil and Augustan Poetry", in H. J. Rose, *A Handbook of Latin Literature* (second edition, London: Methuen, 1947), pp. 233-94.

[10] For a good study of Seneca, see Richard M. Gummere, *Seneca the Philosopher, and His Modern Message* (New York: Cooper Square Publishers, 1963), pp. 44-45

[11] Ernest Renan, *Marcus Aurelius*, translated by William C. Hutchinson (London: Walter Scott, 1903), pp. xiii, 3-4, 15-16.

[12] M. Rostovtzeff, *The Social and Economic History of the Roman Empire* (Oxford: Oxford University Press, 1926), p. 453.

[13] Freya Stark, *Rome on the Euphrates: the Story of a Frontier* (London: John Murray, 1966), pp. 270-271.

[14] For the decay of the arts, see Bernard Berenson, *The Arch of Constantine: the Decline of Form* (London: Chapman and Hall, 1954); and Jacob Burckhardt, *The Age of Constantine the Great*, translated by Moses Hadas (New York: Pantheon Books, 1949), particularly Chapter VII.

[15] Edward Gibbon, *The Decline and Fall of the Roman Empire* (citations from Modern Library edition, 2 vols., New York), Vol. I, p. 1053.

[16] H. A. L. Fisher, *A History of Europe* (London: Eyre and Spottiswoode, 1935, 3 vols.), Vol. I, pp. 133-134.

CHAPTER V
THE GENIUS
OF CHRISTIANITY

The Suffering Servant Comes

In the year 713 from the founding of Rome, four decades before the birth of Jesus of Nazareth, Virgil wrote his Fourth Eclogue. The last age of the world was at hand, the poet proclaimed: a new cycle of generations would begin. Justice, the Virgin, would return, and the god Saturn—overthrown at the beginning of things terrestrial—would reign anew. From heaven a worthier race of men would descend. For a boy would be born who would efface the Age of Iron and restore the Age of Gold. All guilt and fear would be washed away. The boy, a living god, would rule over a world to which his father had given peace.

In later times, Christians would take this to be a poem prophetic of the coming of the Messiah. The latter half of the first century before Christ was stirred by many rumors of the approach of a Savior, a Redeemer, a divine being who would bring a new order to mankind. In the church of Santa Maria Aracoeli, on the Capitoline, visitors still are shown the remains of an altar said to have been erected by Augustus in celebration of that Unknown God destined to be born in his reign. The tradition of the Three Wise Men who made their way to Bethlehem is one representation of how tidings of a Redeemer's imminent advent had spread from land to land.

In all the classical world, the bloody chaos during the last century *ante Christum* had compelled mankind to long for divine intervention in history, for some supernatural savior of order in the soul and in the commonwealth. And as Plato had written centuries before, there can be no human desire that has not the possibility of fulfillment.

Among the Jews, such prophecies had been uttered for centuries. One of the more striking passages of this character occurs in the fifty-third chapter of Isaiah II: the description of the Suffering Servant whom the Lord would send. "He is despised and rejected of men, a man of sorrows, and acquainted with grief: and we hid as it were our faces from him; he was despised, and we esteemed him not." (Although these verses are in the past tense, they are represented as the speech of someone in the future, looking backward—an instance of the Hebraic idea of "psychic" time, mentioned in an earlier chapter.) He would be brought as a lamb to the slaughter. "And he made his grave with the wicked, and with the rich in his death, because he had done no violence, neither was any deceit in his mouth." So it is put in the King James version of the Bible. "But he was wounded for our transgressions, he was bruised for our iniquities: the chastisement of our peace was upon him, and with his stripes we are healed."

These verses from the greatest of the prophets are parallel-ed in Psalm 22 (here quoted in the translation of the Jerusalem Bible):

> My God, my God, why have you deserted me?
> How far from saving me, the words I groan? . . .
> I can count every one of my bones,
>   and there they glare at me, gloating;
>   they divide my garments among them,
>   and cast lots for my clothes.

Giving himself for the redemption of mankind, the Suffering Servant would pass through the jaws of death. In these particular prophecies of the Old Testament, though not in all such prophecies, the Suffering Servant or Messiah is a victim who sacrifices himself that God may forgive the people; like many of the earlier prophets, he is persecuted and done to death. The late apocryphal books of the Jews, too, contained such prophecies of a Redeemer.

But the Jewish populace supposed that the promised Messiah would be a king, restoring the glories of David and Solomon. He was to redeem them from alien rule and to triumph over their enemies: to save them collectively, as a people, in this world. Moral regeneration was implicit in the prophecies; the Messiah would intercede with Jehovah for the Jews; yet doubtless the common hope was that this Savior would be glorious in his coming, perhaps with an armed host at his back.

In the prophecies of the Old Testament, this coming Redeemer is variously referred to as the Messiah, the Suffering Servant, the Son of Man, and the Original Man; it is not clear whether all these titles referred to the same awaited person. The word "Christ" comes from the Greek, and means One anointed by God—the Messiah. The Christ whom the first Christians recognized as the Messiah did not much resemble the popular Jewish conception of their Redeemer.

Historical evidence concerning the earthly life of Jesus of Nazareth is limited; still, it is more detailed than the information we possess about most great figures of the ancient world. Our principal sources of knowledge are the Synoptic Gospels of his disciples Matthew, Mark, and Luke, together with the Gospel of John, though there is much additional detail elsewhere in the New Testament (especially in the Epistles of Paul), in lesser gospels that the early Christians found not so reliable as the four great gospels, and in traditions recorded by Eusebius and other church historians in the early centuries of Christianity. Although the Jewish historian Josephus mentions Jesus only briefly, some Greek and Roman writers of the period refer to Jesus and his followers. Probably Jesus' brief life was regarded by most of his contemporaries, if they had heard of him at all, as an episode of small importance, amidst the terrible troubles of the time; to them it seemed as if the movement that Jesus led had fallen to ruin after his death upon the cross.

His kingdom was not of this world, Jesus said. Yet within a few generations of his crucifixion, faith in Jesus as the Christ would spread throughout the known world and would begin to transform both the Roman Empire and peoples who knew next to nothing of Rome. Although the life of Jesus is the most famous story ever told, New Testament scholarship is so complex that almost all of Jesus' acts, and even the purpose of his mission, still are debated in theological schools.

Jesus was born to a Jewish mother in Galilee, then a kind of isolated outpost of Judaism. In that remote northern region of Palestine, Jesus would perform most of his "Great Works." His legal father was a carpenter, but Christian dogma holds that his true father was God and that he was born of a virgin, Mary. Except for a precocious wisdom, Jesus went unremarked for the first three decades of his life, laboring with Joseph.

But then the young carpenter went out to join John the Baptist, an ascetic who dwelt in wild places, foretelling the approach of God's final judgment. By some, John was believed to be a prophet—possibly even the ancient prophet Elias (Elijah) returned to earth, as later Jesus himself would be asked if *he* were Elias; others took John for the Messiah. John baptized Jesus: at that moment, according to Christian teaching, the Holy Spirit descended upon the young man.

Once baptized, Jesus spent forty solitary days in the wilderness, wrestling against the spirit of evil, Satan. Setting Jesus in a high place, Satan offered him domination over the kingdoms of the earth, as if the Messiah would desire to rule an earthly realm. This and other temptations Jesus rejected, and Satan (the "Opposer" or "Obstructer" of mankind, in the sacred writings of the Jews) retired until a more opportune time.

From the wilderness, Jesus went forth to the people of Galilee, preaching as the prophets of old had preached. There gathered round him crowds of followers, most of them men and women of humble origin; he accepted twelve (or, in some accounts, fourteen) close disciples. To his followers he declared that the reign of God was at hand, and that mankind would be redeemed from sin; he called everyone to repentance. He contended against the invisible power of Satan.

Jesus exorcised, casting out devils. To the devils who possessed men, he spoke sternly as one having authority, endowed with divine power. His followers testified that he worked miracles: he cured lepers, paralytics, the blind, the deaf and the mute; he fed multitudes, and was seen walking on the Sea of Galilee; he even restored to life three dead people.

Many acknowledged him as a prophet, and something more than a prophet. Might he be the Son of God, the Messiah of prophecy? He forbade his followers to proclaim him as the Messiah. (In Christian orthodoxy, Jesus became the Messiah only after he had risen from the dead.) The principal Jewish factions of the time, the Pharisees and the Sadducees, knew not what to make of him; even his disciples were uncertain what he might be. One of them, Simon Peter, asked by Jesus to say what he took him for, replied that Jesus was the Son of the living God. Then Christ told him that upon him, Peter, he would build his church: "And I will give unto thee the keys of the kingdom of heaven; and whatsoever thou shalt bind on earth shall be bound in heaven and whatsoever thou shalt loose on earth shall be loosed in heaven." Even had not Jesus healed the seemingly incurable and raised the dead, could a being who spoke thus be man merely?

At last he made his way to Jerusalem, a multitude of Galileans and others following him. Jerusalem and what remained of ancient Judah then lay under the power of Rome, as represented by a procurator or governor, but in most matters the city was regulated by the Sanhedrin, or court of Jewish religious elders. To the dominant faction among the Jews, Jesus' movement seemed heretical and dangerous, destructive of established Judaism.

Seized after he had been betrayed by the only one among his immediate disciples who was not a Galilean, Jesus was brought before the High Priest and a number of the elders, and was accused of blasphemy. The High Priest demanded of Jesus whether he were the Son of the Blessed—the Son of God, the Christ. "Thou hast said it," Jesus replied. "I am. Nevertheless I say to you: Hereafter you shall see the Son of Man seated at the right hand of the Power and coming upon the clouds of heaven."

Surely the Messiah could not be such a one as this Jesus, the Sanhedrin believed: he must be either blaspheming charlatan or madman, this preacher from Nazareth, and should be put to death. But punishment for capital crimes was reserved to the Roman authority. Before the Roman governor they brought Jesus, declaring him a dangerous revolutionary, intent upon making himself king of the

Jews—for in the eyes of Roman law, mere dissent from Jewish orthodoxy was no crime.

Examining this prisoner, the procurator Pontius Pilate must have been perplexed. The charge of rebellion that had been brought against Jesus was unconvincing. Perhaps Pilate, who had no sympathy for the Jews, regarded Jesus as an ethical teacher, not unlike the Greek philosophers with their bands of disciples; he found no fault in this man. "What is truth?" Pilate inquired of Jesus; he may have meant, "To what truth do you refer?"—the truth according to the Jews, or of the Roman state cult, or of Hellenic philosophy, or of some other body of doctrine.

Despite his misgivings, the clamor of the Jews intimidated the procurator into passing sentence of death upon the prisoner, lest a violent uprising of the turbulent people of Jerusalem be provoked. In a last attempt to save Jesus, Pilate offered the mob a choice: he would pardon one of two condemned men, either Jesus or a strong bandit and revolutionary, Barabbas. "Give us Barabbas!" the crowd cried.

So Jesus was crucified between two thieves, and in that hideous agony he promised one of his fellows in suffering that he should be with him that night in Paradise. The body of the dead Master was laid in a tomb, and to the Sanhedrin and the Roman power it appeared that all was over. Yet from the tomb rose the Christ, the Messiah, the Redeemer of mankind.

Here we turn to the teachings of Jesus of Nazareth during his three years of prophesying, exorcising, and healing. "I am the Way, the Truth, and the Life," Jesus had told his doubting disciple Thomas. "No one comes to my Father except through me. If you knew me, you would also know my Father. And henceforth you know him, and you have seen him." This was a declaration of divinity: the man who spoke so had asserted his godhood. Until very late in his life, even Jesus' disciples had been uncertain of the nature of the being they followed, except that he was more than a prophet. But after his death, Christ appeared to many of his followers, and spoke to some—"last of all to me," wrote Saint Paul. The risen Christ indeed was the Son of Man, the Son of God, God himself, the first Christians proclaimed. In the three years when he walked among men, what had he taught them?

There have come down to us only fragments of Jesus' discourses, for he wrote nothing. Of those fragments, the longest and most moving is the Sermon on the Mount—which, even in the version preserved by Saint Matthew, could have been spoken in twenty minutes. Yet Jesus' message was clothed in imagery, and has been interpreted a thousand different ways since that death upon Golgotha, the Hill of the Skull.

First of all, Jesus preached the great tidings that the kingdom of God was at hand. This news had two aspects. It meant that the people soon would have no king but God: that mankind would be redeemed from sin, that justice would triumph everywhere, that the old order of things was ended. Men then living would see God face to face, and know His perfect love. The reign of God would not be merely a new kingdom of this world, but the perfecting of the soul of the person and the perfecting of the community. To establish this kingdom, Jesus would come again, "as a thief in the night," when least expected; let all the faithful watch with hope.

Also this kingdom of God already was present: "the kingdom of God is within you," in the words of the Jacobean translation. That is, the community of true Christians, living as brothers in Christ under the New Dispensation, already could know the order that God had designed for them, even though the world seemed untransformed.

Christ would come again in glory at any moment, the first Christians expected; they waited eagerly, but the years passed, and the generations, and still (though the number of believers increased rapidly) Christ did not return as King. Gradually the Christians came to understand Jesus' promise as referring to the life eternal in Christ, after the end of earthly dominations—and so spoke less frequently of the literal establishment of the reign of God upon earth in the near future. Those who joyfully accepted Christ as their Savior would enter into Paradise now: for to God, past and present and future are as one.

How, then, should disciples of Christ live in this fallen world? Christ had pointed out to them a Way. He had come not to annul the Law and the Prophets, Jesus had said, but to fulfill them. His followers were to live in this world under a New Covenant, a New Dispensation, a covenant of brotherly love. But though they were absolved from obedience to some of the letter of the Law of the Jews, in much they must abide by the Old Covenant. And in some respects, the injunctions that Jesus put upon them were more exacting than the commandments promulgated by Moses.

At the heart of Jesus' ethical teaching stands the Great Commandment: "Thou shalt love the Lord with thy whole heart, with thy whole soul, with thy whole strength, with thy whole mind, and thy neighbor as thyself." So it had been written in the Law of the Jews, and every devout Jew repeated twice daily this precept. But by "neighbor," the Jews understood their immediate associates—at most, the community of Jews; while by that word neighbor, Jesus meant all mankind.

"Do unto others as you would have others do unto you": this "Golden Rule" enunciated by Jesus is the spirit in which Christians are to fulfill that commandment to love neighbors. In its negative form, the same precept was stated by Hillel, the great Jewish teacher who lived about Jesus' time: "Do not do unto others what you would not wish others to do unto you." It appears thus in other sacred writings of the Jews, and in other religions; in this negative expression, it was a saying of Confucius.

But the positive injunction of Jesus is more compelling, and requires higher sacrifice. In this, as in much else, the teaching of Christ urges men to be active in the service of God. The Jewish belief of his time was that Jews must obey the Law strictly—doing their duties under the Law, but not being expected to exceed the letter of the Law. To follow in the steps of Jesus of Nazareth required courage, and stern rejection of much that the average sensual man held dear. Far more must Christ's followers give than Jews gave under the Law. Sincere disciples of Jesus must forsake worldly possessions; they must forsake even father and mother, if need be, to follow the Way.

The Law of Love is this way. Jesus enjoined compassion: "I tell you to forgive seventy times seven." Yet the Christ was no preacher of an indiscriminate toleration of all human frailties: let man forgive his neighbor, but let all men tremble at the prospect of divine judgment. The uncharitable rich, he said, should enter Heaven no more easily than a camel might pass through the eye of a needle. When Jesus scourged the money-changers out of the courts of the Temple, because they profaned holy places, he was not the "gentle Jesus" of nineteenth-century sentimentality. When he cursed the barren fig-tree, he condemned those whose professions of faith in God bring forth no fruit. As for those who corrupt children, he declared, it would be better for such a one if a millstone should be tied round his neck and he should be cast into the deepest abyss of the sea.

Jesus' preaching of love, then, cannot be separated from his preaching of justice. He spoke in the tradition of the major prophets, exhorting the unjust to repentance. But he expected of his followers more than the formal justice required by the Law. His Sermon on the Mount was addressed primarily to the large band of his disciples out of whom the closer Twelve Disciples had been chosen: they who believed in him, Jesus made clear, must purge themselves of selfishness, in their love of God.

The Decalogue, said Jesus, prohibited murder; but his disciples must also keep themselves from anger, contempt, and reproaches, if they would escape the fires of Gehenna, the place of burning. The Law prohibited adultery; the New Dispensation also forbade looking upon a woman with lust. The Old Commandments prohibited light or false taking of oaths; the way of Christ told men to swear no oaths at all, but always to speak the truth and to fulfill all promises.

The Mosaic code exacted an eye for an eye and a tooth for a tooth; but the followers of Christ must turn the other cheek to the evildoer, and give to any man more than he demands. The Jews of old had been told to love neighbors and hate enemies; the Christians must love enemies also, and pray for their persecutors. The Law permitted a man to divorce his wife under certain circumstances; the teachings of Jesus, affirming the sanctity of marriage, spoke of that union as an indissoluble bond.

This path for the followers of Christ, then, was a stonier road than ever men had been told to follow before. Its principles demanded a new sort of heroism, more severe than that of the Law of the Jews, more sacrificing of self than the old Roman virtue. Out of this teaching there would rise what were to be called the Christian "theological virtues" of faith, hope, and charity.

To have faith is to respond morally, through an act of will, to God's love and wisdom: to trust in "the Father of our Lord Jesus Christ." To have hope is to rejoice in the reality of the Lord, patient and confident. To have charity is to fulfill the Great Commandment, in act and in spirit, loving God and loving all men. When to these are added the four virtues of the ancient philosophers—justice, prudence, fortitude, and temperance—the sincere Christian may be a hero, and a martyr. Thousands such died in the persecutions that began soon after the crucifixion of Jesus and that recurred from time to time until the age of Constantine.

But not enough men and women followed in the steps of Jesus to bring about the reign of God upon earth. Christianity has not failed, G. K. Chesterton would write in the twentieth century: it has not been tried. Christ's precepts, expressed often in parable, from the first were imperfectly understood by many; for those who did apprehend the teaching, still the way was hard. When at last the persecutions of the "Nazarenes" or Christians were ended by imperial edict, the Christian Church itself often had come to honor the letter of Jesus' precepts more than the spirit. It is not suprising, however, that Christian teaching did not succeed in erasing human vices; the surprising thing is the degree to which that faith did enable many people to order their souls, and so to improve the order of the commonwealth.

The kingdom of which Christ spoke was the kingdom of love, not of a different political structure. Jesus accepted the existing political dominations of the world, saying that men should render unto Caesar what was Caesar's, and to God what was God's. In all his preaching there was no advocacy of a political and social revolution, nor any plan for new social organization. He said nothing about war; he did not denounce slavery. The establishment of justice must come through the waking of minds and souls, not through armed force. Christ came to save sinners: to rouse them to the reality of the Father, and to lead them to righteousness through the example of the Son. He worked upon consciences, and those consciences worked as best they could to redeem society from its vices and brutalities. The Suffering Servant, God in the flesh of man, atoned for man's sinfulness by perishing in agony upon the Cross. By loving atonement, the world might be redeemed.

How was it that a religion so austere and exacting, so insistent upon charity and chastity, so contemptuous of worldly goods, seemingly so impractical, won over the masses of the ancient world? While everything else was falling into ruin, the Christian Church rose up. Many other religions, asking less of their votaries and apparently offering more to human appetites, competed with Christianity at its beginning; yet Christian faith increased among all social classes, while the other forms of worship withered away.

One reason for this triumph was Jesus' burning concern for the poor. By that word he did not mean the destitute, but rather the humble, the meek, the powerless, the oppressed—those who submitted themselves to the will of God. In that sense, the vast majority of people in the Roman imperial system were poor. They heard the words that were preached for them—at first in the cities, presently in the countryside.

Another cause of Christianity's success was that its appeal, unconnected with political systems, became universal. "Indeed," Jacob Burckhardt writes, "the great advantage of the religion whose kingdom was not of this world was that it did not set itself the task of directing and guaranteeing any definite state and any definite culture, as the religions of paganism had done, and that it was rather in a position to reconcile with one another and mediate between diverse people and centuries, states and cultural stages. It was not Christianity, then, that could bestow a second youth upon the senescent Roman Empire; but it could so far prepare the Empire's Germanic conquerors that they did not wholly tread its culture underfoot."[1]

Most of all, the new faith taught people how to restore

harmony in their souls, in this earthly life; and it offered them the promise of the Life Eternal. What shall a man do to be saved from sin and death, in a world of inner and outer disorder? The life eternal in Christ, as preached through the world by Jesus' apostles, seemed to many more real than the decaying society about them. What had begun among a handful of poor Jews in Galilee became the consolation and the amazing hope for the many millions of the Empire.

Four decades after the crucifixion of Jesus, the Jews rose against Roman mastery. The Zealots fought suicidally until they were extirpated, believing that total destruction would bring on the end of the world according to prophecy, with the coming at last of a Messiah very different from Jesus. Ruined by a hideous civil war within its walls, Jerusalem fell to the Roman legions, who slaughtered or enslaved the population and left the place wholly uninhabited. The earthly kingdom was ashes.

But in the forty years between the death of Jesus on Calvary and the death of the holy city, the tidings had spread from Nazareth to Antioch and Thessalonica and Corinth and Carthage and Alexandria and Rome itself. Early in the fifth century after the birth of Christ, Rome would fall as Jerusalem had fallen. In those four intervening centuries, the Gentiles would embrace what the Jews had rejected.

We Are God's Utopia

There was an energetic and ardent Jew called Saul of Tarsus, of the strict sect of the Pharisees, who had been Jesus' enemies. Without Saul's labors, what we call Christianity might not have spread beyond the little communities of Jewish Christians in Jerusalem and elsewhere in Palestine.

The city of Tarsus, in Asia Minor, had obtained for its citizens the privileges of full Roman citizenship. Because born in Tarsus, Saul was counted as a Roman, though a Jew in faith. He had been well educated, both in Greek and in Jewish learning, and had been a pupil of the famous scholar

Gamaliel. Zealous to put down dissent from the Law, this Saul or Paul (his name among the Greeks) made himself one of the most active persecutors of the infant Christian communities in the Levant. On such business he was engaged as he rode to Damascus. What happened to Paul then is recorded in the New Testament's Acts of the Apostles. Later, imprisoned, Paul described his vision to Agrippa, the Hellenized Jewish prince of that portion of Judea.

"At midday, O king, I saw in the way a light from heaven, above the brightness of the sun, shining round about me, and them which journeyed with me.

"And when we were all fallen to the earth, I heard a voice speaking unto me, and saying in the Hebrew tongue, Saul, Saul, why persecutest thou Me? It is hard for thee to kick against the pricks.

"And I said, Who are thou, Lord? And he said, I am Jesus whom thou persecutest.

"But rise, and stand upon thy feet; for I have appeared unto thee for this purpose, to make thee a minister and a witness both of these things which thou hast seen, and of those things in the which I will appear unto thee;

"Delivering thee from the people, and from the Gentiles, unto whom now I send thee;

"To open their eyes, and to turn them from darkness to light, and from the power of Satan to God, that they may receive forgiveness of sins, and inheritance among them which are sanctified by faith that is in me."

Having seen and heard and believed, the regenerate Paul took up the cross, and became the Apostle to the Gentiles. Jesus had gone forth from the wilderness telling men to repent of their sins; now Paul would carry that message, and proclaim the news of the divinity of Christ, throughout the Mediterranean world.

Although often sick, meagre of body, and poor enough, Paul was endowed with high gifts of preaching and writing. Sometimes flogged, sometimes stoned, contending sometimes figuratively and perhaps literally against wild beasts, Paul spread the message of Jesus of Nazareth to the cities of Asia Minor and of Greece, heedless of fatigue and peril. His letters, which make up a large part of the New Testament, only hint at the vastness of this undertaking. To many of the Jews, Paul was a heretic and a rebel, though throughout he professed himself a Jew, doing the work that the Messiah had commanded.

On his returning to Jerusalem, in the Temple he was seized by his enemies, who would have slain him, had not Roman soldiers carried him off. His Roman citizenship saved him from a scourging, but not from prolonged imprisonment while Roman governors deliberated what to do about this man, almost as embarrassing to them as Jesus had been. At last he was sent by sea to be judged at Rome on the charge of sedition that had been laid against him by the Sanhedrin; as a Roman citizen, he had appealed to the Roman authority. So commenced his labors as an apostle in the West, among Gentiles who never had heard of Jesus—or perhaps of sin, either.

In Rome, below the modern ground-level, one can see today the house where Paul is believed to have lodged. Probably he was acquitted of the Jews' accusations, after a long residence in the capital—during which he was free to live and act as he chose. He seems to have left the city after judgment had been rendered by Caesar, but to have returned later, and to have been seized there during Nero's infamous persecution of the Christian sect. Tradition says that he was flung into the Mamertine prisons, the last lodging of so many enemies of the Roman commonwealth. "For I am now ready to be offered," said Paul, "and the time of my departure is at hand. I have fought a good fight, I have finished my course, I have kept the faith."

Saint Peter, the "rock" upon whom Christ would build his Church, was put to death about this time, too, the persecutors crucifying him upside down. Saint Paul was spared that agony and dishonor, he being a Roman citizen. They beheaded him; but his words they could not undo.

"We are God's Utopia," says a modern German writer, Stefan Andres. It was the accomplishment of Paul of Tarsus to tell the Gentiles—that is, most of the civilized world—of how sinful man might be perfected through grace in death. Man suffers hideously from the corrupting power of sin, Paul taught; yet God, loving His people, makes possible the restoration of the soul in beauty. Knowing the rhetoric and the philosophy of the Greeks, Paul made intelligible to the Gentiles what otherwise might have remained to them an obscure Jewish cult. And in that process, Paul gave fullness to the truths that Jesus had put into parable.

To the Romans, Paul described the righteous God, Father and Son, operating invisibly upon souls through the Holy Spirit. God is a loving father of all; only through Him may man be saved from the wages of sin. But man has alienated himself from God by idolatry, by forbidden sensuality, by injustice. Through repentance and obedience, and the operation of God's grace, redemption is possible.

As Paul describes it, sin is man's vaingloriousness: man's ignoring of God, man's presumption, man's failure to become what God means man to be—we may almost say, man's refusal to become God's Utopia. In his pride and his loneliness, man falls into despair, if his eyes are opened to the terror of existence without God. Only by confessing that he is, after all, the child of God may man be redeemed from the body of this death. Christ, atoning for the sins of all men by dying upon the Cross, invites man to become once more a creature of God. Unless we accept Christ as our Redeemer, Paul cries, we are isolated, lost, slaves to time and the flesh.

These Pauline insights come down undiminished to some in the twentieth century. In T. S. Eliot's play *The Cocktail Party*, young Celia—who, in the end, will suffer martyrdom—is oppressed by the loneliness and sense of guilt that Paul had found common among intelligent people who have tried to live as if they were autonomous:

> It's not the feeling of anything I've ever *done*,
> Which I might get away from, or of anything in me
> I could get rid of—but of emptiness, of failure
> Towards someone, or something, outside of myself;
> And I feel I must . . . *atone*—is that the word?

As Celia discovers, it is indeed the word. But man by himself, said Paul, is too feeble to offer atonement for sin: it is Christ's strength that enables man to escape from a state of sin. Physical lusts are bound up with this power of sin, yet they are only consequences of man's separating himself from God. "The love of money is the root of all evil," Paul declares; but he means by this that avarice is the source of a wide variety of evils. The real root of sin is what we now call egoism: the desire of the individual man to usurp the throne of God, to defy the Father, to pretend that the Father does not exist.

How may a man be saved? Through faith in Christ Jesus, who descended from on high to suffer the deepest humiliation and pain for the sake of sinners. The Law reveals to man the character of sin, but only Christ can wash away sin's marks. We must be born again, through baptism, cleansed in the blood of the Lamb. No man is worthy of God's grace, yet God extends that grace. To have faith in Christ is to obey Christ—to endeavor to walk in his steps. Reborn in and through the Spirit, which is a power that comes from without to give man strength, a man truly may ask, "O Death, where is thy sting? O grave, where is thy victory?"

In Christ, we find our immortality; and this is no vague merging of the person into a World Soul. The life eternal means that the human person continues to exist as a soul, in harmony with God but not absorbed; beyond the jaws of death, indeed, we are promised the resurrection of the body. Were it not true that he should escape from death and live forever in Christ, said Paul, he would be the most miserable of men. For at the end of history, when Christ comes again in glory to judge the quick and the dead, all those who have kept faith in Christ will rise again. Meanwhile, we must live as if we were colonists from heaven, moved by the Holy Spirit. We must not fear to die for our faith. Christ liberates man from time and circumstances, at the final judgment rewarding by the gift of the life eternal those souls who have accepted His grace.

This new life of the Christian is not a solitary existence, Paul argues, either here and now or after the Second Coming. Walking by the Holy Ghost, Christians exist in fraternal love, comforting one another. The Church will endure to the end of time; and its members, invigorated by divine grace, will do eagerly more than the Law requires.

The power of Paul's Epistles is such that one is tempted to quote them at length, rather than compressing them into this bald summary. Wherever Paul went, the "colonies of heaven", the little churches, sprang up. Paul's death by the sword watered the faith almost as his Master's death on the cross had done. Some of the rich and powerful began to take the cross, despite the menaces of the Roman state. Soldiers were baptized, presently in thousands.

To embrace Christian teaching wholeheartedly meant that the person reborn in Christ must make moral choices every day of his life. No moral choice could be revoked: for good or ill, it would endure forever. But the enthusiastic Christians gladly accepted this burden, believing that the Spirit would guide them, and that the law of love would suffice them. For centuries, this choice might mean death, for those who would refuse to pay even token homage to the state cult of the Empire. That death, in the most horrible forms, would be encountered fearlessly, even joyfully, by some of the Christian martyrs: it was their opportunity to give the testimony of blood in witness of Christ. "Almost thou persuadest me to become a Christian," Agrippa had told Paul, when interrogating him near the end of Paul's imprisonment at Jerusalem. The heroism of believers, from the persecution by Nero to the persecution by Diocletian, converted to Christian faith many pagans whom mere words could not move.

So there rose up the Church—withdrawing to the catacombs beneath the cities in times of persecution, but emerging undaunted afterward. Gradually, despite the ferocity of the wars of those times and the degeneration of other social institutions, Christian teaching and example made their mark upon the public order. Material charities flourished more than ever—bringing with them converts more interested in the material benefactions of the Church than in salvation from sin: these were the sort of converts who would be called long later, in China, "rice Christians." Still the martyrs were found. The gladiators' combats in the Colosseum were ended forever, in 404 A.D., by the sacrifice of a monk who flung himself down to death in the arena, to prevent the slaughter of human beings.* The Spirit had begun to transform society.

Of the millions of people, within and beyond the Roman frontiers, who were baptized in that age, some were moved chiefly by the story of Jesus' redeeming sacrifice. Yet the most powerful attraction of the new faith, it appears, was the promise of the life eternal. The mystery cult of Mithras—a strong rival of Christianity, in the early centuries—offered immortality to its initiates; so did several other Eastern religions that had grown in power during imperial times. The thought of life beyond the grave remained terrifying to some, or else an impossible dream: the Epicureans rejected it, and so did the Sadducee party among the Jews. But the yearning for immortality grew in proportion as the vigor of the classical social order declined.

When Paul had been questioned by the Sanhedrin after his arrest (or rescue, rather) by the Roman garrison, he had professed his belief in the hope of resurrection of the dead. The Sadducees denied this hope. "And there arose a great cry: and the scribes that were of the Pharisees part arose, and strove, saying, We find no evil in this man: but if a spirit or an angel hath spoken to him, let us not fight against God." That belief of the Pharisees in a final judgment by God and in the resurrection thereafter of all men, both just and unjust, became the most powerful promise of Christian teaching.

Paul, and others before him, had seen Christ risen from the dead. As He had risen, so might all who had faith in Him and had followed in His way. The pagan mystery cults could not appeal for authority to a god made man who had risen from the dead; nor could those classical philosophers who had glimpsed the possibility of immortality. "In the person of Jesus, the *logos*—the divine Word of Law, which is Love—is made flesh," Dorothea Krook writes, "the infinite *logical*

---

* This martyr during the reign of the Emperor Honorius was an Asiatic monk, Telemachus. He is said to have been stoned to death by the Roman spectators, who were infuriated by his interrupting the gladiators' fight. The sacrifice of animals at pagan altars had been forbidden a few years earlier.

possibility of truth and goodness is rendered actual and concrete; contracted, as it were, into a single human soul and human body at a particular point in time; and thereby rendered accessible to all men for their salvation. And this again, the experience of an intimate, personal participation in the divine nature, is something that Plato had no knowledge of. Plato could conceive of the Form of the Good as that which transcends even pure being in dignity and power; but he could not conceive of it as incarnate."[2]

What Platonism could not provide, Christian belief did: an incarnate model of the way that man should live, and a mode of participating in the life eternal. As Jesus had been resurrected, so would all those faithful to Him, raised in spirit at the Last Judgment; they would attain the crown of life, with new spiritual bodies. "In a moment," Paul wrote in his first letter to the Corinthians, "in the twinkling of an eye, at the last trump," the dead shall be raised to live forever in Christ; "for the trumpet shall sound, and the dead shall be raised incorruptible, and we shall be changed."

What among the philosophers had been only a dim surmise and longing, became in Christianity a confident dogma. And so it was that to the Christian Church came, eventually, most of those who abjured the world, the flesh, and the devil, seeking a victory over the grave.

At the end of the third century after Christ, the Christians still were a minority in the Empire, greatly outnumbered by the pagan citizens. But they had grown to a powerful and coherent minority, with members in high office. Near the end of his reign, Diocletian ordered a systematic persecution of the Christians—perhaps because he had wind of a conspiracy of certain court officials, professed Christians, to snatch imperial power. That fierce persecution failed; it was the last forcible attempt of the imperial authority to crush Christianity. Constantine the Great, seizing power in the years that followed Diocletian's abdication, saw in the Christians an instrument by which he might hold the Empire together: since they could not be destroyed, they must be employed.

Declaring himself protector of the Christians, Constantine issued two edicts of toleration to shelter them; soon he heaped upon them exemptions, privileges, and powers. Although never baptized, he spoke as if he were a bishop. In the year 325, he dominated a convocation of churchmen, the Council of Nicaea, which was to settle upon a common confession of faith for all Christians—the Nicene Creed, which, along with the somewhat shorter Apostles' Creed, is still recited in most Christian churches today.

Constantine was "a great bad man" (Edmund Burke's description of Oliver Cromwell). Crafty, unprincipled, and merciless, he destroyed all rivals to his might, among them such members of his own family as made him uneasy. Having triumphed over most of his adversaries, Constantine sent menacing letters to old Diocletian, inactive in his palace near Salona: he meant that the retired emperor must die. Too tired to struggle, Diocletian took his own life; the Senate declared the dead ruler to be a god—the last emperor so honored. Constantine's colleague, earlier, had beheaded Diocletian's widow and daughter.

Now the family of Constantine had owed everything, including the Empire's preservation, to Diocletian. These needless acts of ferocity and ingratitude were typical enough of Constantine the Great. He lusted for total power; he obtained his heart's desire. There could have been no more incongruous patron of the visible Church of Christ. Thereafter the affairs of church and of state would be deeply entangled, so long as the Empire endured—and in the East, with its new capital at Constantinople, the Empire would last in one form or another for eleven centuries longer.

As a state religion, Christianity supplanted the old Roman state cult just when real power departed from the Eternal City on the Tiber and was concentrated instead at Constantinople. (In 380, Theodosius the Great, the last emperor to rule both East and West, would decree that Catholic Christianity must be the faith of all citizens of the whole Empire.) Because of this, the Christian bishops of Rome came to enjoy a relative independence from state domination. The comparative freedom of the "Latin Church" resulted from that shifting of the center of political power. At Nicaea, in the year 325, however, the assembled bishops dared not defy Constantine in anything. Happily for Christian doctrine, that emperor felt no true interest in the creed, and interfered only to compel some sort of consensus.

On what dogmas should Christians speak with one voice? The Nicene Creed of that Council ran as follows: "We believe in one God, Father Almighty, maker of all things visible and invisible; and in one Lord Jesus Christ the Son of God, begotten of the Father, only-begotten, that is from the substance of the Father, God from God, Light from Light, true God from true God, begotten, not made, of one substance with the Father, through whom all things were made, both the things in heaven and the things on earth; who for us men and for our salvation came down and was made flesh, was made man, suffered, and rose again on the third day, ascended into heaven, and cometh to judge quick and dead; and in the Holy Spirit. But those who say 'There was once when he was not,' and 'Before his generation he was not,' and 'He was made out of nothing'; or pretend that the Son of God is of another subsistence or substance, or created or alterable or mutable, the Catholic church anathematizes."

Other creeds had been uttered earlier, and yet others would appear.* But the creed of Nicaea served to define the Catholic (meaning "world-wide") faith in the time when it triumphed over Roman paganism. As Paul Elmer More writes, this Nicene Creed is the charter of the Church, "a bare and sharp statement of the one indispensable fact to which assent should be demanded of all Christians, a military oath of union, so to speak, stripped of emotional accessories and directed to the negative attention of defending the final citadel of faith against any possible perversion by heresy or diminution by incredulity."[3]

The Nicene Creed affirmed that God was one, and yet

---

* What is now often called the Nicene Creed is not identical with the document printed above; rather, the "Nicene" Creed as it generally is recited today appears to have been the baptismal symbol of the church at Jerusalem, with clauses from the creed adopted at Nicaea added to it, and with those additions presented to the Council of Constantinople in 381. See Arthur Cushman McGiffert, *A History of Christian Thought* (New York: Scribners, 1932), Vol. I, pp. 262-63, 272-74.

three: Father, Son, and Holy Ghost. It declared that Jesus Christ was God, not something less; that He had suffered to atone for the sins of man, and that He would sit in judgment upon the living and the dead. But this confession of faith in the divinity of Christ did not tell Christians how they should live in a dying social order, nor did it touch upon the immense moral and metaphysical questions that the Christians must confront. Those labors were undertaken by the Fathers of the Church, the powerful enlargers and apologists of Christian teaching during the Church's early centuries.

Of those Fathers, writing after Constantine and Theodosius had established Christianity as the state religion, the scholar whose influence upon civilized order looms largest was Saint Augustine, bishop of Hippo, in Africa. In a world of sin, will man ever become God's Utopia? Augustine, schooled in classical philosophy and literature, a man of the old Roman culture, applied to the dawning age the teachings of the carpenter of Nazareth and the tent-maker of Tarsus.

Living in a Sinful Order

Nearly thirty years after the Council of Nicaea, Augustine was born in Roman Africa—then one of the most prosperous and densely-populated regions of the world. It was an age in which the old pagan religions still stood in competition with the new Christian edifice: Augustine's mother, Monica, was a Christian, his father a kindly pagan. Of the many cities of Proconsular Africa, Numidia, and Mauretania, Carthage was the chief: a metropolis of half a million people, Roman in civilization, though in much of Africa between the Atlas range and the sea a considerable part of the inhabitants continued to speak the ancient Punic tongue.

At Augustine's birth, the Empire still seemed destined to endure forever, whatever its afflictions. Barbarian raids along the European and Asiatic frontiers did not injure the African provinces, nor was Italy in peril. All the outward trappings of classical civilization still shone in Rome and Milan, where

Augustine would spend years in study. Yet this was a house of cards, and it would collapse in Augustine's lifetime.

To posterity, Augustine left the only thorough autobiography of ancient times, his *Confessions*: not out of vanity, but because he felt impelled to tell others how he had been won to the love of God. In youth, he yielded to the lusts of the flesh that later he would despise so passionately: "Behold with what companions I walked the streets of Babylon, and wallowed in the mire thereof, as if in a bed of spices and precious ointments. And that I might cleave the faster to its very center, the invisible enemy trod me down, and seduced me, for that I was easy to be seduced."

Carthage, where he commenced his higher studies at the age of seventeen, was "a cauldron of unholy loves." Yet in later years it was not so much yielding to sensual temptations of which he repented, as of sinning for sin's sake. When he was a boy, with some companions he robbed an orchard of pears, "and took huge loads, not for our eating, but to fling to the very hogs. . . . " He knew the act was wrong: that was why he committed it. "For I stole that, of which I had enough, and much better. Nor cared I to enjoy what I stole, but joyed in the theft and sin itself."

Upon this turbulent young man, nevertheless, there operated the grace of God. Seeking some source of truth, Augustine investigated the fashionable cults and philosophies of the time—Neo-Platonism, the Manichean religion, Skepticism; none satisfied him. He came to loathe his own carnal appetites, and yet could not escape them; he prayed to the Lord that he might be made chaste—but not quite yet. In time, however, he came under the influence of Saint Ambrose of Milan (who, like Augustine, later would be designated one of the four Latin Doctors of the Church), and presently there came upon him the certitude for which he had sought so long. One day as he struggled to convince himself that he must enter upon a new life of spirit, he heard a child repeating *tolle lege, tolle lege*—pick it up, read it, pick it up, read it. Opening the Epistles of Saint Paul at random, he encountered this passage: "Not in reveling and drunkenness, not in debauchery and licentiousness, not in quarreling and jealousy. But put on the Lord Jesus Christ, and make no provision for the flesh, to gratify its desires." He obeyed.

Returning to Africa, Augustine founded a monastery, became a priest, and then bishop of the coastal city of Hippo Regius. The rest of his life would be spent in shepherding his flock, contending against the heresy of the fanatic Donatists of Africa, and incessantly preaching and writing: hundreds of his sermons and letters survive, in addition to his many treatises.

In the year 410, when Augustine was fifty-six years old, there occurred the catastrophic event that signified the beginning of the end of classical civilization: the city of Rome, almost unresisting, fell to Alaric the Goth. For nearly eight centuries, Rome had not known a foreign invader; now belief in the city's destiny was undone. Though Alaric plundered the Eternal City, outwardly the capital was not much harmed, and after Alaric's departure the old ways of life were resumed, for the most part. But it was clear that the world had been turned upside down, and everywhere in the Empire occurred a failure of nerve. Augustine himself did not despair altogether for the Roman system: the city might revive, and indeed the Empire at large possibly might be reinvigorated.

Yet should any man put his trust in creations merely human—in great cities and great states? Between the years 413 and 426, the Bishop of Hippo wrote and published his major treatise on political order, *The City of God*. Scarcely anything of Hippo is visible above ground nowadays, and Carthage is a heap of ruins overlooked by modern villas, in a Moslem land. But *The City of God* speaks to some twentieth-century minds and consciences with a power that the disasters of our own time augment.

Nearly four centuries after the Resurrection, it could not be denied that the kingdom of God upon earth seemed more remote than ever. Half the population of the Empire professed Christianity by that time, and other faiths were forbidden, and yet the Roman civilization was unregenerate. Pagan writers declared that the fall of Rome was a judgment upon the people for their desertion of the older religion; while Christian teaching, they said, had weakened ancient loyalties to the state, and so left the Eternal City naked unto her enemies. This argument *The City of God* was written to refute. Augustine's rejoinder, transcending the circumstances of the time, is an analysis of the human predicament as it must be faced until the end of history.

It was not the coming of Christianity, Augustine replies, that has brought afflictions upon Roman civilization: for from Adam's fall, before cities existed, man has been corrupt. Every age, suffering from violence and fraud, complains of its tribulations; but if we read history, we perceive that the human adventure is a chronicle of disasters. In every age, society has been relieved only by the endeavors of a few people moved by the grace of God, and has been made tolerable and constrained to relative peace from time to time only by the compulsions of the state—though the state itself shares in the general corruption.

Rome had fallen, Augustine says, for want of order in the soul. By their nature, men seek for order: not the unconscious order of swallows or bees, but an order which human intelligence understands. For men, their acts must have significance. Men are miserable unless they find "a disposition or arrangement of equal and unequal things in such a way as to allocate each to its own place." They must have purpose in their existence. And what is that purpose? Why, to glorify God, to know Him and enjoy Him forever.

Despite their yearning after order, the vast majority of human beings go astray in this quest. Until Adam and Eve sinned, they enjoyed perfect freedom. After the Fall, people still possess freedom—though ordinarily only the freedom to choose among sins. The power of sin is so mighty that it triumphs over man's rationality and man's will. And what is the essence of this Original Sin by which we are corrupted? With Saint Paul, Augustine replies that it is pride: the desire of the human creature to make himself the center of the universe. In this bondage to sin, the body commands the soul; the order that God had designed for man is inverted.

In the sinful condition that always has been the lot of the mass of mankind in every age, love lies subordinate to lust, or *libido*. In the clutch of lust, man prefers worldly things, the devil's bargains, to the things eternal, the gifts of God. Lust has three chief forms. There is cupidity, the lust for material possessions, heaping wealth on wealth, rousing envy and fraud and violence, setting man against man. There is the lust for power, the *libido dominandi*, the desire to be absolute as God, or rather in place of God: the appetite for subduing other human beings. And there is sexual lust, the abuse of the gift of procreation, a burning unclean desire that defies reason, conscience, and the higher will.

These lusts afflict all human beings, even infants: one need only observe those about him, and himself. Since Adam, man has not been able to restrain by reason or will these frightful appetites. The most learned man may be vicious as the most ignorant. It is these lusts, warring within every person, that bring about crimes, public disorders, and aggressive wars.

Then have we no help? Only from God. The soul may be restored to order through divine grace. Yet even the atonement by Christ, it could be seen four centuries later, had not opened the eyes of most men to their fallen condition, or reanimated their will to righteousness. The City of This Earth stands unredeemed; it was disordered from the first, and will be disordered to the last.

Truly, Christ's kingdom is not of this world. Then what hope remains? Why, hope of the eternal City of God, where order prevails always. This is the city of spirit during our mundane existence, and the city of heaven after the Last Judgment. That city is not crowded: many are called, but few are chosen. The individual man being too weak to choose the way of Christ, God must choose him. Those whom God redeems are the "elect," brands snatched from the fires of lust for reasons only God knows. Out of His compassion, God saves some, by His grace leading their steps aright.

We cannot guess who those elect are. Worldly success is no sign of a man's having been chosen by God, and those who think themselves righteous may be self-deceived. It is not good works that will save a man (though if a man loves God, charity and justice should flow from his faith): only divine intervention redeems him. Yet seek the city of God, through faith and prayer; repent; follow in Christ's steps. Then perhaps to you, all unworthy, grace may be given.

From their beginnings, all human institutions have in them the seeds of corruption. Though in a believing community of Christians there should endure more love and loyalty than in the world at large, and though therefore the Church is a feeble copy of God's city, still corruption afflicts the Church. Augustine had seen how professed Christians often preferred some fantastic sect or partial truth to the Gospels; he had contended strenuously against the heresy of the Donatists, whose armed bands of fanatics had threatened to overwhelm the Catholic Church in Africa; and in his closing years he would behold his diocese ravaged by barbarians who had embraced another heresy, Arianism. Doubtless he thought, too, of the self-seeking ecclesiastics gathered round the feeble Emperor Arcadius in the fortress-city of Ravenna, preferring court life to a cure of souls. The visible Church is not a community of saints, really: it is some refuge from the world, but it also knows sin.

If the Church is imperfect, what of the state? Plato had thought of the ideal state as a partnership in wisdom and virtue, the center of all human aspiration, governed by the idea of the Good. Aristotle had hoped for a state that would be a community of friendship, through moderation and balance reconciling classes and private interests. But Augustine rejects these notions. The state is governed by men, subject to sinful appetites—enslaved especially by the lust for power. On looking at the history of any people, one perceives how, despite heroic endeavors by some few good and strong men, any state soon is riddled with corruption. Put no faith in salvation through the political order.

Nevertheless the state is necessary—a necessary evil, if you will. For the state restrains men from the ruinous indulgence of their appetites and passions: the only alternative to the state is anarchy, which would bring destruction swiftly upon the whole race. Originating in force, the state inevitably exerts force so that men may live together at all. It limits violence and fraud as best it can, if primarily for the benefit of the possessors of power. The function of the state is this: to keep the peace. Repelling foreign enemies and withstanding or punishing criminals at home, the state makes it possible for men to be something better than so many Cains, with every man's hand against every other man's.

Therefore the Christian renders unto Caesar what is Caesar's, that the peace may be kept. Far from subverting the Roman order, the Christian citizens had obeyed the laws, recognized the authority of constituted magistrates, paid their taxes, and served in the legions. The Christian fulfills all his duties to the state, offering no resistance to its decrees, except in one possible contingency: if the state commands him to worship false gods, and to act as if he were a creature of Satan rather than of God, then the Christian must disobey, and follow instead the law of God.

Augustine was a Christian realist. What we find in this world is not a straight path to an unqualified Good, he perceived, but instead a choice among evils—of which we should choose the least, for the love of God and for our own survival. The world was created by God for man's happiness: life itself is good, and not to be thrown away. Yet how do we survive at all? It is necessary, for instance, to resist the violent and the ravenously unjust, if we are to live. Thus war is evil; but doctrinaire pacifism may be more evil, and a just war is conceivable. (If we apply no rules of justice to the conduct of wars, those wars become the more frightful and destructive.) "The real evils in war," he argued in his treatise *Contra Faustum*, "are the love of violence, revengeful cruelty, fierce and implacable enmity, wild resistance, the lust of power, and such like; and it is generally to punish these things, when force is required to inflict the punishment, that, in obedience to God or some lawful authority, good men undertake wars, when they find themselves in such a position as regards the conduct of human affairs, that right conduct requires them to act, or to make others act in this way."

Were there no state, with force at its command, there would be no civilized existence—indeed, no human existence at all, except on the most primitive and bestial level. "The advice of Augustine is therefore not to put your trust either in princes or in peoples, in kingdoms or in commonwealths,"

Charles Norris Cochrane writes, summarizing Augustine's political argument in *The City of God*. "Of kingdoms and kings he observes that they estimate their achievement in terms, not of the righteousness but of the servility, of their subjects. The vice of the commonwealth, on the other hand, lies in its ideal of merely economic and political (utilitarian) justice with which is bound up the equally vicious ideal of conformity or, as we should say, social adjustment. 'Like the Athenian woman,' he says, 'you can by a series of small doses accustom yourself to poison.' Yet such is the pressure to conform that recusancy means nothing less than social ostracism and 'he is a public enemy to whom this ideal of happiness does not appeal.' But it is an illusion to suppose that there can be any escape from the evils of organized society through a return to primitivism, since this involves the fallacy that 'nature' is intrinsically virtuous and 'law' the mark of degeneracy."[4]

So the City of This Earth is necessary for survival in this world. Although all states are corrupt in some degree, it does not follow that every political structure is as bad as every other. It does not follow that because laws are badly executed, or perhaps badly framed, mere lawlessness would be preferable. Because many men in political life are captive to their lusts, it does not follow that divine grace is denied to all rulers or leaders of men. In the City of This Earth, we must not expect perfection. A twentieth-century professor of politics, Michael Oakeshott, echoes Augustine's understanding when he writes of "the illusion that in politics there is anywhere a safe harbor, a destination to be reached or even a detectable strand of progress."[5]

How do we live in this world, then? We endure, trusting in God, and hoping to attain beyond time and death to the City of God. We dwell, if we can, in community, associating with those who seek to govern themselves by the New Dispensation, and endeavoring to help others to withstand trial and temptation. We exist here as pilgrims, travellers, knowing that beyond our present weariness and danger is an eternal destination. And we are not lost here upon earth: for God's providence governs all things. It is as if we were put into an arena to do battle for the truth. In mysterious ways, God moves every one of us, Augustine says: our sufferings are means for chastening and disciplining us, so that God's will may be executed in history.

For the Christian, as Herbert Deane comments on Augustine's view of history, "the end of the drama is not death or futility, but the perfect peace and felicity of eternal life with God. Sufferings and temptations are an absolutely necessary element in the earthly life of the pilgrim who seeks to reach the heavenly city. Without the experience of strife, pain, and temptation, there can be no advance in self-knowledge, no development of spiritual and natural strength."[6]

It is not a secular "progress" that Augustine discerns in the history of the City of This Earth; but neither is the significance of history a mere repetition of cycles, as many of the old Greeks had fancied. Genuine change and genuine movement exist in history: the character of the world after the coming of Christ is quite different from the character of the world before that central event. Yet we must entertain no expectation that the condition of mankind will improve steadily: on the contrary, we are told in the Revelations of Saint John the Divine that in the fullness of time (no man knowing how soon) there will emerge the Antichrist, the deluding impostor; that most professed Christians will mistake this creature from the abyss for the Savior, or will be seduced or terrified by him; that ruin far worse than the sack of Rome will fall upon the City of This Earth.

Men of Augustine's time, seeing the Empire dissolve before their eyes, found it quite possible to believe Augustine's vision of the future of the City of This Earth. People of the twentieth century, understanding that for the first time in history men possess the technological power to efface civilization and perhaps to destroy the great globe itself, may apprehend Augustine's forebodings better than could most people of the optimistic eighteenth and nineteenth centuries.

But at the end of history, Augustine insisted, the forces of destruction will not triumph. At the last, the Antichrist will be overthrown; Christ will come again; and beyond the City of This Earth, beyond the fallen world that we know, those who are chosen by God and who live in Christ will enter upon a perfection that the words of this earthly city—words being tools that break in the hand—cannot even express.

Saint Augustine has been called the philosopher of freedom. So he is, in a sense, and the philosopher of realism, and the philosopher of hope. True, we are enslaved by our lusts, which are produced by our false worship of ourselves; but beyond lust, there is true love, *agape*. Acting in charity and moved by grace, we may make ourselves citizens of the heavenly city. Our will, after all, is free in this important sense: we retain freedom either to accept God's grace, or else to reject it. Order your soul; reduce your wants; live in charity; associate in Christian community; obey the laws; trust in Providence—so will we find order, Augustine told his generation, and so will we come to know that service of God which is perfect freedom.

He was heard. Throughout medieval times, the authority of Saint Augustine's writings kept quick in the Church a consciousness of the principles of order, a harmony of spirit, despite the political disunity of that age. In the Reformation of the sixteenth century, the Protestant Reformers—Luther, Calvin, Zwingli—would turn to Augustine for renewal. Upon American religious faith, and indeed upon the ideas underlying American political principles, the treatises of Augustine of Hippo would exert an influence not yet exhausted. Believing in the reality of Providence, Augustine became a providential instrument.

In the year 430, at the age of seventy-six, the great Father of the Church lay dying in besieged Hippo. The barbarian Vandals under their King Gaiseric, converts to the Arian heresy, had crossed from Spain into Africa, sweeping all before them. Augustine refused to desert his flock. He consoled himself with "the maxim of a wise man" that has a Stoic ring: "No great man will think it a great matter when sticks and stones fall and mortals die."

Of the many hundreds of churches in Roman Africa, only three survived at that hour—those of Carthage, Cirta, and Hippo; everything else had fallen to the rapacious Vandals. "Those days, therefore, that he lived through, or endured, almost at the very end of his life, were the bitterest and most mournful of all his old age," Augustine's friend Bishop Possidius tells us. "A man such as he had to see cities overthrown and destroyed and, with them, their citizens and inhabitants and the buildings on their estates wiped out by a murderous enemy, and others put to flight and scattered. He saw churches denuded of priests and ministers; holy virgins and others vowed to chastity dispersed, some among them succumbing to tortures, others taken captive and losing innocence of soul and body, and faith itself, in evil and cruel slavery to their foes.'"[7]

Surrounded by destruction, Augustine put his trust in Providence, praying that Hippo might be liberated; or, if God should will it otherwise, that His servants might be given strength to endure what He willed for them; as for himself, Augustine entreated that "He will take me from this world." Though he could not rise from his bed, madmen were brought to him there, that he might cast out devils. A sick man experienced a vision in which it was revealed that the Bishop could heal him by the laying on of hands; Augustine said that if he had possessed any powers of that kind, he would have used them on himself; but he yielded to the sufferer's beseeching and touched him: to Augustine's own surprise, the man went away well. Then, in the third month of the siege of his city, Augustine passed into the City of God.

Though he had died, his prayers were answered in another fashion: to the astonishment of the citizens, Gaiseric lifted the siege of Hippo the next year. It was a brief respite only. Augustine's friend Boniface, Count of Africa, in the year 432 fought his last battle against the Vandals, and then fled by sea to Italy, taking with him most of Hippo's citizens—Boniface's army of Goths having 'been nearly annihilated, so that there was room in his ships for the townspeople.

With them they carried Augustine's library, including the impressive mass of his own writings, which he had bequeathed to the Church. Gaiseric's Vandals burnt Hippo then, and took Carthage in 439, making the splendid city into a pirates' lair. Gaiseric would raid Rome in 455, looting the fallen capital. But the writings of Augustine lay secure for the time at Ravenna. From that Roman twilight in the Adriatic marshes, those books would pass into the general possession of later ages; and the City of God would endure when the Roman city had bled to death.

Two There Are by Whom This World Is Ruled

A century and a half after Augustine's death, what men long had called the Eternal City still stood in its physical fabric. But the place was powerless and almost in anarchy. The Senate had ceased even to meet. The last emperor of the West, Augustulus, had abdicated in 476. Barbarian kings ruled most of Italy, and barbarian peoples, chiefly the Lombards, had occupied much of the Italian peninsula. At Constantinople, the emperors of the East still claimed sovereignty over the West as well, governing remnants of Italy through exarchs (viceroys) at Ravenna; but over the "duchy of Rome," ancient Latium around the Eternal City, their authority was tenuous.

During the last Gothic siege of Rome, in the middle of the sixth century, the besiegers had cut the aqueducts, and the defending commander had driven outside the walls all the civilian inhabitants. What people had returned to Rome occupied only a third of the area within the walls—shifting down to the Tiber, where they still could obtain water. A solitary monument from this age stands today in the Forum, the last thing ever erected there: the column of Phocas, honoring a brutish and incompetent emperor of the East. Rome would have expired altogether, had not the Papacy arisen on the ashes of empire.

Because Saint Peter had been the apostle to the Romans, because Saints Peter and Paul had been martyred at Rome, and because of the classical world's habit of looking to Rome for direction, the bishops of Rome, the Popes, came during this age to enjoy a certain independence from the distant emperors' authority, where concerns of the Church were in question. The primacy of the bishops of Rome over all other bishops was somewhat vague in the fifth century and much of the sixth: so long as the Eastern Empire held any real power in Italy, the bishops of Rome found it prudent to proclaim no formal claim of absolute superiority over the great sees of Jerusalem, Antioch, Alexandria, and Constantinople. Yet Pope Gelasius I, reigning from 492 to 496, declared firmly that "Two there are by whom this world is ruled"—by Church, by State, the doctrine of the "two swords." The drift of events soon made it possible for the Papacy to assert its authority more vigorously.

What we call the Middle Ages, between classical times and modern times, soon would swallow up the old order of things. The bridge between the ancient and the medieval worlds was Gregory the Great, pope and saint, last of the Latin Doctors of the Church. Within the Church, and to some extent outside it, he maintained a continuity of order during that historic transformation.

Gregory was born about the year 540, the son of a senatorial house with vast estates in Italy and Sicily. Like his ancestors before him, in youth he was intended for a public career, and indeed he was made urban prefect of Rome—the decayed city's governor, in effect. But being deeply religious, and much read in the writings of Saint Augustine, he left office in 574, became a monk, founded six monasteries in Sicily, converted his family palace at Rome into another monastery, and soon was appointed (after ordination as an archdeacon) the pope's ambassador to Constantinople. He had inherited his ancestors' talent for public service, yet he much preferred the life of contemplation, and became an abbot in Rome about 586. He would not be left in peace.

Pope Pelagius II, with many other Romans, died of the plague in 590. The clergy and people of the city unanimously chose Gregory as the new pope. That stern abbot begged the emperor at Constantinople not to ratify the election; he thought of fleeing from this elevation, but he was literally dragged to St. Peter's basilica and consecrated bishop of Rome, in 590. Like the magistrates of the Roman Republic, this last exemplar of the high old Roman virtue became a "conscript father."

Gregory's strong reluctance to sit in the seat of Saint Peter may not have been in consequence merely of a taste for religious contemplation. For Rome in that year seemed beyond human help. The Eastern emperor's exarch, "more depraved than the Lombards," had abandoned the city to its own resources; Lombard dukes menaced the Roman duchy from south and north. "Italy was in the grip of pillage," Daniel-Rops comments, "torn by a savage violence which was practised not only by the Lombards: each year more towns went up in flames; the highways were unsafe for travellers; the bands of prisoners reduced to slavery walked the streets, ropes round their necks as if they were teams of dogs."[8] Gregory had been prefect; now, though his health always was feeble, he must be pontiff. "In this epoch I wonder if to be pope is to be a spiritual leader or a temporal king!" he would say, grimly.

Because no secular power remained at Rome, Gregory of necessity became almost a secular prince also. Deserted by the Byzantine forces, he found it necessary to negotiate an independent peace with the Lombard dukes—and to give commands to armies. That he might maintain public order and feed the starving poor of Rome (for the state no longer could supply them with either bread or circuses), he must act as supreme magistrate. He organized the "Patrimony of Peter," the spreading estates of the papacy around Rome, elsewhere in Italy, and overseas, into what in time would become the States of the Church.

Still recognizing the sovereignty of the distant emperor, he made no formal assertion of ecclesiastical supremacy. Yet when the bishop of Constantinople, with the Emperor Maurice's encouragement, tried to style himself "Universal Patriarch," Gregory (who signed himself merely as bishop) successfully objected. Pope Gregory commonly used the style of "Servant of the Servants of God," but his policies changed the world as much as any emperor's.

In effect, Gregory's leadership severed what political links remained between West and East, and spread Christian faith and culture northward to the Teutonic peoples. Sent to Britain by Gregory, Saint Augustine of Canterbury converted the pagan Angles and Saxons. Gregory's dispatch of other missionaries soon would bear fruit in widespread conversions in German lands. The western Europe of medieval times began to take form, and Rome would be its spiritual center.

Under Gregory, as H.A.L. Fisher puts it, "the see of St. Peter stood out in western Europe like a lighthouse in a storm."⁹ Gregory possessed the old Roman genius for practical administration, and his social principles, like his theology, were drawn from Saint Augustine of Hippo. He endeavored to make the Church as near an approximation of the City of God as may be realized in this world; had he not made that attempt, dispatching missionaries to many lands, establishing regular relations with the barbarian monarchs, and building monasteries wherever he could—why, the continuity of culture and institutions between the classical age and the emergent West might have been broken altogether. His sermons still are models of practical Christian teaching, and his book on *Pastoral Rule* contains many aphorisms on the art of governing men that have not lost their point. He was the last man of order of the ancient mold.

Gregory knew that the classical frame of things could not be preserved. "See how the world now withers in itself; yet still flowers in our heart," he said in a sermon at the catacomb-basilica dedicated to the martyrs Nereus and Achilleus. "Everywhere is death, everywhere sorrow, everywhere desolation and sadness; we are struck from every side, from every side we are filled with bitterness. And yet, with minds blinded by carnal desires, we love this very bitterness; as the world leaves us, we pursue it; as it collapses, we cling to it. And since we cannot uphold it, as it falls we fall with it; we fall with that to which as it falls we cling."

His Roman congregation, there underground, as if buried already, still felt bound to the looted and crumbling City of This Earth, Rome, above their heads. Choose rather the things eternal, Gregory exhorted them:

"Once the world held us fast in its delight. Now it is filled with so many afflictions, that now it is the world itself that sends us to God: reflect therefore on how all that now runs past us in time is as nothing. The end of earthly things shows us the nothingness of that which can fade and pass away. The ruin of things declares to us, that this fleeting thing was then close to nothingness while it yet seemed to stand firm."[10]

Yet the divine order endures: the order of Heaven, and of Hell, and of Purgatory (this last a concept in considerable part developed by Gregory). Let us purge ourselves as best we can in this present life, Gregory preaches; our life should be one long penitence and penance. The Middle Ages, the Ages of Faith, loom before him.

Had all Saint Gregory's successors in the chair of Saint Peter been comparable to Gregory, the medieval order of society might have been more just than any order which had preceded it. The medieval Church did maintain a pattern of order, as it maintained a pattern of learning. But it did not grow into the City of God. In the nineteenth century, Lord Acton would write that indeed the Church must be divinely ordained: for no institution merely human could have survived so many crimes and blunders. However that may be, Gregory I transmitted to the barbarized West a concept of moral order, and a hard-pressed legacy of culture, that would survive even the terrestrial hell of the Dark Ages.

That order of which Gregory was steward would endure through the centuries, and would enter into the foundation of American society. The American order of the soul would be Christian: the responsible freedom of Americans, as Tocqueville would perceive in the nineteenth century, would develop from Christian "mores"—from those habits of thought and action by which men regulate their conduct. And the political order of America, though pluralistic and in part secularized, also would owe much to Christian teaching.

In the twentieth century, many people do not find it easy to understand how all aspects of a culture grow out of the cult—out of common religious convictions. Yet the Hebrew and Greek and Roman civilizations all had arisen from the soil of religion; and when the power of the cult had declined, those cultures had begun to decay. In the medieval age, to which the labors of Gregory the Great formed a bridge, once more a high culture would be produced by a common faith. The architecture of the Middle Ages, obviously enough, still to be seen in Gothic and Romanesque churches, was religious in inspiration; so were all the other arts. The very economy developed under the Church's shadow, from the agricultural estates of the monasteries to the craft guilds that began as Christian confraternities. And the medieval political order was chastened and often guided by the Church; emperors and kings were compelled to acknowledge the Church's moral authority; most of the practical business of political administration was executed by "clerks," or clerics.

At the end of the Middle Ages, changes of religious forms would be reflected in changes of political forms; still, the Christian patrimony would endure. So it is that a Christian understanding of the human condition, transmitted for the most part through Britain, still gives coherence to America's political order. American politics is not a matter of national party conventions or of presidential elections merely: rather, those conventions and elections and all the other contrivances of American practical politics are means for implementing a body of beliefs about the human condition. Those beliefs are not Christian only, but they are Christian in very large part.

This point is well expressed by John Hallowell, writing about modern democracies. "The peace and justice at which earthly kingdoms aim are good but only relatively good," Hallowell says, "for the peace and justice at which they aim, while essential to the attainment of everlasting peace and perfect justice, are not identical with them. Men owe allegiance to civil society; but, because they have an ultimate destiny that transcends life on earth, they have a greater obligation and a greater allegiance, namely, an allegiance to God.

"The effect of this teaching is not only to distinguish the secular from the spiritual spheres but to place the secular authority under the sanction of a higher authority. And the life of wisdom and virtue, which Plato thought possible only for a few, is now conceived as being available through the grace of God to all men equally. And this has important consequences in politics. For if there is an authority higher than the authority of any particular state, then no state can demand our absolute obedience or attempt to control every aspect of our lives. . . . That recognition has its roots, when it is recognized, in the teachings of the Christian religion."[11]

Christianity prescribes no especial form of politics. The Church has co-existed with monarchies, autocracies, aristocracies, oligarchies, republics, democracies, and even some of the twentieth-century totalist regimes. Yet if Christian belief be general among a people, then any political domination is affected by Christian teachings about the moral order. That moral order works upon the political order. Christian concepts of justice, charity, community, and duty may transform a society without any abrupt alteration of governmental framework. The worth of the person, the equality of all men before the judgment-seat of God, the limitations upon all earthly authority—such Christian convictions as these would shape the American Republic.

Notes

[1] Jacob Burckhardt, *The Age of Constantine* (New York: Pantheon Books, 1949), p. 216.

[2] Dorothea Krook, *Three Traditions of Moral Thought* (Cambridge: Cambridge University Press, 1959), pp. 143-44.

[3] Paul Elmer More, *The Catholic Faith* (Princeton: Princeton University Press, 1931), p. 76.

[4] Charles Norris Cochrane, *Christianity and Classical Culture* (Oxford: Oxford University Press, 1944), pp. 493-94.

[5] Michael Oakeshott, *Rationalism in Politics* (New York: Basic Books, 1962), p. 133.

[6] Herbert A. Deane, *The Political and Social Ideas of St. Augustine* (New York: Columbia University Press, 1963), p. 67.

[7] Possidius, "The Life of Saint Augustine", in F. R. Hoare (ed.), *The Western Fathers* (New York: Sheed and Ward, 1954), p. 229.

[8] H. Daniel-Rops, *The Church in the Dark Ages* (London: J. M. Dent, 1960), p. 223.

[9] H. A. L. Fisher, *A History of Europe* (London: Eyre and Spottiswoode, 1935), Vol. I, p. 173.

[10] Gregory I, "Pride Rebuked", in F. M. Toal (ed.), *The Sunday Sermons of the Great Fathers* (Chicago: Henry Regnery, 1963), Vol. IV, p. 262.

[11] John H. Hallowell, *The Moral Foundation of Democracy* (Chicago: University of Chicago Press, 1954), pp. 116-17.

CHAPTER VI
THE LIGHT
OF THE MIDDLE AGES

A Neglected Inheritance

Now there emerges before us the youngest of the four cities from which American order is drawn: London, on the Thames, a capital that would reach the height of its power nineteen centuries after the coming of Christ. Before the Romans conquered Britain, a British village or town probably stood on that low marshy site by the river. The administrative capital of Roman Britain was established there, and fortified; by the reign of the Emperor Hadrian, Roman Londinium was a considerable place, though humble enough by the side of the rich cities of the Mediterranean world.

Britain remained a Roman province for nearly five hundred years. Yet England, and Wales, and the portions of Scotland held from time to time by the Roman legions, were too rural and too distant from the centers of classical civilization to retain any continuity with Roman culture, once the Roman legions had withdrawn from Great Britain to defend more vital frontiers. The Angles and Saxons and Jutes, untouched by civilization, conquered most of Britain during the fifth century after Christ. Nearly two hundred years after the legions had departed, Gregory the Great sent his missionary Augustine of Canterbury into what had become England, and Latin Christianity began to reassert the culture of Rome in these remote northern islands. From that time forward, despite conquest by the Danes and later by the Normans, despite the English Reformation of the sixteenth century and the Civil Wars of the seventeenth century, one may trace the development of English law, English political institutions, and English civilization—a continuity that would spread to America in the seventeenth century and would provide fertile soil in which the American culture could take root.

Knowledge of medieval England and Scotland is essential to a decent understanding of American order. During those nine hundred years between the coming of Saint Augustine of Canterbury and the triumph of Renaissance and Reformation at the beginning of the sixteenth century, there developed in Britain the general system of law that we inherit; the essentials of representative government; the very language that we speak and the early greatness of English literature; the social patterns that still affect American society; rudimentary industry and commerce that remain basic to our modern economy; the schools and universities which were emulated in America; the Norman and English Gothic architecture that are part of our material inheritance; and the idea of a gentleman that still may be discerned in the American democracy. This medieval patrimony was so much taken for granted by the men who founded the American Republic that they did not even trouble themselves to praise it so much as they should have done.

America's independence came to pass in an age of revived classicism, when things Roman and Greek were rated very high indeed, and things medieval were rated low. Thus most of the Founding Fathers doubtless tended to think of the Middle Ages as the Dark Ages—the obscure time, a period of violence and superstition—and often failed to distinguish the anarchy and ignorance of the ninth and tenth centuries (the true "Dark Ages") from the splendid cultural achievements of medieval civilization, reaching culmination in England during the thirteenth century.

Besides, early America being Protestant, there existed a general inclination to think of the medieval centuries, the "Ages of Faith", as the era of the Roman Catholic Church's supremacy, somewhat alien to Americans' inheritance. Yet lack of interest in the Middle Ages during the last quarter of the eighteenth century does not signify that the Americans drew little from medieval civilization. That patrimony in its British form, and to some extent in its European form, is more immediately related to American institutions and even to American thought than is the legacy of Greece and Rome.

When American public men of the formative years did turn to the Middle Ages for instruction, sometimes they overvalued early medieval contributions and undervalued medieval culture at its zenith. Thomas Jefferson idealized Anglo-Saxon institutions before the Norman conquest of 1066, subscribing to the historical fallacy that England had suffered under the Normans a loss of liberty from which the nation had recovered only very slowly and painfully. (In this theory, Jefferson anticipated such Victorian historians of England as Freeman and Stubbs; but in the twentieth century, a more accurate assessment has been made by historians like Maitland and Stenton.) Jefferson wished to require all Virginian schoolboys to study the Anglo-Saxon language (deficient though it is in great literature) so that they might read constitutional and legal documents of that people in the original; he thought of feudalism as a grinding imposition by the Norman conquerors, supplanting the old freedoms of the Anglo-Saxons.

But in fact the American inheritance from Dark Age England, or even from the more enlightened Anglo-Saxon England during and after the reign of King Alfred, is slight enough. Only one enduring book was written during that time, the Venerable Bede's *Ecclesiastical History of the English Nation,* early in the eighth century—and that in Latin, though King Alfred had it translated into Anglo-Saxon, together with Gregory the Great's *Letters.* This work of the learned monk of Jarrow, on the Viking-ravaged North Sea coast of Northumbria, indeed is a high achievement; but it stands almost solitary as an intellectual accomplishment, except for a few poems of the Anglo-Saxon centuries. When the Germanic tribes took England, they were almost brutish, and only the introduction of Latin Christianity improved them, chiefly through the monasteries that were founded everywhere.

Nor were the Anglo-Saxon political and legal institutions

more praiseworthy. Life in the little barbarous kingdoms, eventually united into one England, was insecure and poverty-stricken. The Roman towns of Britain had been destroyed, and the new settlements grew slowly, always much inferior to the early medieval towns of France and Italy and Spain.

Of Anglo-Saxon legal practices, only fragments are embedded in English (and American) law today. Even trial by jury is Norman, derived from the inquest developed by the Frankish kings in the Continent—although in early Norman England a jury was composed of persons closely acquainted with the accused or with the circumstances of the case, just the opposite of present jury-selection.

Very little in the way of Anglo-Saxon customs remains in the common law of England. In medieval times, it was alleged that the common law incorporated various "old laws" passed down from Anglo-Saxon times. But in truth, nearly all those asserted "old laws" were invented (or else much distorted) by the Norman and Plantagenet kings; those monarchs merely placated the Anglo-Saxons among their subjects by alleging that such laws had existed before the year 1066. Thomas Jefferson and other American admirers of Anglo-Saxon institutions would have been painfully disillusioned, had they actually found themselves living under the barbarous and ill-enforced laws of the Anglo-Saxon society.

Yet it must be said that the Anglo-Saxon realm was made up predominantly of small freeholders and their dependents, or of people relatively free: slavery was rare, and the hard serfdom of the nations of the Continent was not prevalent generally. The Norman conquest did not substantially alter this social character, for the Normans neither butchered nor enslaved the Anglo-Saxons, who remained by far the larger part of the English population. In that sense, Jefferson's ideal of a society in which most men would enjoy economic and political independence, as free farmers, was historically rooted in the English experience from quite early times. American social and political institutions do reflect the English inheritance of widespread household and village liberties, under the king's laws for the most part, as contrasted with the rule of petty princes and barons in the Continent—where in many countries most of the medieval inhabitants were serfs who possessed no rights that they might assert against the will of their immediate masters.

This relative local freedom aside, little can be said for the Anglo-Saxon order in England. The relative freedom itself resulted from the lack of sound general government. As it is put by a twentieth-century English historian, Douglas Jerrold, "the only instrument of national government evolved by the Anglo-Saxons was a personal and irresponsible monarchy." The kings' agent in the shires (counties) was the shire-reeve, the sheriff—and that office is the only one which has descended to us from Anglo-Saxon times, and even that in a form much changed. Anglo-Saxon England lacked even a national army.

With so irregular a freedom, the other side of the coin is disorder. In effect, the real masters of England during that time were rough earls, often at feud one with another. The enforcement of justice was rude, when justice could be enforced at all; the weak might go to the wall. Under such conditions, there developed only a simple architecture, little literature or learning, and urban life (on a very limited scale) only at London and York. For centuries, the Anglo-Saxons suffered the torment of Viking raids; even without the menace of the Norsemen, life was insecure and impoverished.

"The social structure of the kingdom before and after the Conquest was, of course, essentially aristocratic," Jerrold continues. "Every man must have a lord. That is only to say, however, that in the early centuries of our history just as much as today every one was under government. . . . Nevertheless, the 'landlord' was the lord *on* the land, not lord *over* the land. Even in the village court the lord could only preside; he could not dictate. The court could only interpret and enforce the custom of the hundred or the manor, and the verdict was given by suitors; there was no judge. Custom could only be changed by consent."[1] This was no very reliable system for maintaining peace and order, but it did sustain local rights and personal freedom, and out of it grew, in time, the "common law" or "case law" of medieval England, much improved with the passage of the centuries, and still underlying much of American law.

It is not to the Anglo-Saxon era, however, that we can look for either the origins of representative government or the effective rule of law. The "witan," the council of the Anglo-Saxon and Danish kings of England, bore no resemblance to the modern Parliament of England, or to the many other representative assemblies (including the Congress of the United States) that have been strongly influenced by that "Mother of Parliaments" at Westminster. The Anglo-Saxon judgments by compurgation (collective oath-taking) or by trial of battle are infinitely removed from American ways of justice; and the payment of wergild, or blood-money, to compensate for crimes of violence scarcely resembles modern principles of criminal law. Only after the Norman conquest did England emerge from Dark Age political and legal simplicity.

William the Conqueror built the Tower of London to secure his hold upon the little city and the spreading country he had taken—built it upon the high ground where Julius Caesar, they say, had planted a fortress. Two influences would restrain the power of the Norman kings and their successors: St. Paul's Cathedral, rising near the other end of the old city, and the Parliament that in future times would meet in the precincts of Westminster Abbey, a little higher up the Thames. Tower, cathedral, and parliament-house still stand, though suffering change over the centuries.

Of medieval London, few traces remain today: most of its fabric vanished in the Great Fire of the seventeenth century, and remnants were demolished after the First World War or effaced by German bombs in the Second World War. Even St. Paul's is a neo-classical building on the medieval site of Ludgate Hill; even the famous river-profile of the Parliament Houses is nineteenth-century Gothic. But the invisible London, the city of the rule of law, the city of enterprise and cultural diffusion, still overshadows New York and Washington.

Situated upon a large navigable river, with easy access to the ocean, London would become far greater as a center of commerce than ever Jerusalem or Athens or Rome had been; by the end of the eighteenth century, England's adversaries would call her "a nation of shopkeepers." Also England would be a nation of lawgivers, poets, sailors, and soldiers.

With the exceptions of Louisiana and the old Spanish Southwest, English culture and institutions would come to dominate the whole of what is now the United States; even in the former French and Spanish territories of America, England's language and England's ways would engulf the culture of the original European settlers. America's classical heritage, and in some sense even America's Christian and Jewish heritage, crossed the Atlantic only after being transmuted by Britain's historical experience. So it is that the medieval civilization of Britain animated the founders of the American Republic even as they fancied that they were repudiating the Middle Ages.

The canvas of British medieval experience, from the eleventh century through the fifteenth, is too vast for us to describe here much of that picture. In this chapter we can sketch merely the outlines of the growth of laws; of representative government taking form; of chivalry and the idea of a gentleman; of Scholastic thought and the universities. For the most part, we deal here with the Middle Ages as those centuries passed in England and Scotland. For the medieval period, the focus of order thus is shifted all the way from Jerusalem to London—from a city set upon a stony hill to a city washed by the Atlantic tide. Yet London took from Jerusalem and Athens and Rome what was best in their cultures, and carried that best to continents of which Hebrew prophets and Greek philosophers and Roman emperors had known nothing.

The Reign of Law

The law, which is no respecter of persons, stands supreme: that is the essence of British legal theory and legal practice, and it passed into America from the first colonial settlements onward. The king himself is under the law; should he break it, his subjects would be absolved from their allegiance. And the law is not merely the creation of kings and parliaments, but rather the source of their authority. At heart, the law is the expression of natural justice and the ancient ways of a people.

From its Norman beginnings, English law had two aspects, and two systems of courts: common law, and equity. Both came to be administered by the king's judges. As the juridical structure developed, the common law was represented at its highest by the old courts of Common Pleas, King's Bench, and the Exchequer; equity by the court of Chancery, the lord chancellor's court (although Chancery, in one of its two tribunals, also was a court of common law). These distinctions endured in England from Norman times down to 1873. We turn first, and at greater length, to the common law.

The common law is quite different from statutory law—that is, different from the written statutes issued by the sovereign political authority. The common law is founded upon custom and precedent, although upon *national* customs and usages, rather than upon local. This common law is an "organic" development, arising out of centuries of judges' decisions upon the basis of what the people believed to be just. It is "prescriptive" law, derived from the man-to-man experience of people in community over a very long period of time; it is "customary" or "traditional" law. It is the fundamental body of law in England and in the countries that have received it from England: all other forms of law, in England and those other countries, have been developed later, in part to deal with cases for which the common law seemed inadequate.

The common law has been called "unwritten law," and so it probably was, in the very beginning. But soon the decisions of common-law judges began to be written down, and so there accumulated a mass of records of judgments, from which written precedents covering new cases of a similar character could be ascertained. Thus the common law is "case law," or a complex body of legal precedents upon which all judges are supposed to base their present and future decisions: to rule on a present case, they must consult the body of established precedents in earlier analogous cases. Or, to put this more accurately, the common-law judge is expected to hear the arguments of opposing litigants, both of whom will cite precedents favoring his own claim; and the judge is to decide in favor of the claimant whose lawyer has most convincingly demonstrated that precedent stands on his side.

Rather than "unwritten law," really, common law may be described as non-codified law. Formal statutes of a state ordinarily are embodied in a formal legal code; but common law is a different system, more complex, based on a multitude of precedents rather than upon a systematic compilation. To put matters in another fashion, the common law is not a corpus of acts passed by a legislature or a parliament, or of decrees issued by a sovereign; it is the "people's law," so to speak, for it has grown out of practical cases of actual contest at law, over centuries, and is sanctioned by popular assent to its fairness. There is no need for ratification of the common law by the Crown in Parliament or by some comparable political authority.

The central distinction of the common law, then, is the rule of *stare decisis,* "to stand by decided cases": all judges are supposed to be bound by previous decisions, that is (a principle which, in theory, still governs the judiciary in the United States, most of the time). The purpose of *stare decisis* is to ensure that evenhanded justice will be administered from one year to another, one decade to another, one century to another; that judges will not be permitted to create laws or to decide cases arbitrarily, or to favor particular persons in particular circumstances. They must abide by the accumulated experience of legal custom, so that the law will be no respecter of persons, and so that people may be able to act in the certitude that the law does not alter capriciously.

Another distinguishing feature of the common law is its employment of a jury of twelve good men and true; for in general the decisions of other courts, operating on other juridical principles, are handed down by a judge or a panel of judges. This fact-finding jury is peculiar, in modern times, to England and those countries that have emulated the English common-law system. Guilt or innocence must be determined in open court, by free men whose determination the judge cannot reverse. Whatever the deficiencies of the jury method, serving on juries became a powerful instrument for instructing the public in the nature of law. Jury service, besides, is a form of popular representation in public affairs: one important reason, this, why representative government arose first in England, for participation in common-law juries taught free men to assert a share in public concerns.

The "adversary" method of legal proceedings also distinguished the common-law courts from the civil-law jurisprudence of those countries in which the Roman law had been revived. In Europe generally, as systems of law developed in early medieval times, the judge determined the issue to be settled in a case at law, and in such a European court, to this day, the accused person is presumed to be guilty unless he can prove himself innocent; the authorities hold him to inquire sternly into his behavior. But under the common law of England, the plaintiff and the defendant, or the prosecutor and the defendant, are regarded as adversaries, on an equal footing. Their lawyers define the issue to be settled, while the judge remains neutral. A defendant is presumed to be innocent unless the evidence proves him guilty beyond any reasonable doubt.

In this and many other matters, the common law gives those who come to it privileges unknown in "Roman" courts, where generally the interest of the state stands first. Under the common law, for instance, a defendant cannot be compelled to testify, if he chooses to stand silent: he is saved from self-incrimination. A complex system of writs, under common law, makes access to justice relatively easy for the individual. No man may be imprisoned without a warrant, and he must be tried speedily. Civil rights are protected by the jury, in the sense that a state-appointed judge cannot enforce the policies of the political establishment without the sanction of twelve independent citizens. Even the king's officers, if they interfere unlawfully with subjects' rights, may be sued for damages under common law, or perhaps charged in a common-law court with criminal actions. In all this, the "private law" called "common law" secures the private person against arbitrary actions by the possessors of power.

In the United States, many of the civil liberties originally guarded by the common law were incorporated into the "Bill of Rights," the first ten amendments to the federal Constitution. One reason for this was that Thomas Jefferson and his allies declared that the common law of England did not run in the new Republic. American advocates of the common law, on the other hand, generally opposed the first ten amendments, on the ground that the common law did and must prevail in America also, that the common law already extended such protections to citizens, and that to enumerate some civil liberties in the Constitution might endanger civil rights not there specified. However this may be, the Jeffersonian Bill of Rights amendments were simply a reassertion of common-law principles. In its origin, American personal liberty perhaps owes more to the common law than to any other single source.

Despite these virtues, the common law of medieval times presently tended to become inflexible and sometimes harsh, demanding the letter of the document rather than recognizing the spirit of fairness. In theory, the common law would not take into account extenuating circumstances or consequences of decisions that seemed contrary to natural justice; sometimes it was hidebound. Therefore the kings developed a remedy for this unyielding attachment to strict precedent: to "ease the king's conscience," they turned to "equity," or fairness, expressed through the lord chancellor's court. If the common law seemed not to cover some new sort of case, or if the common law as applied rigorously seemed to deny reasonable remedies to litigants, then the court of Chancery would take up a case, or a category of cases, as a matter of equity. For centuries, many litigants enjoyed a choice: cases might be tried either in a common-law court or in a court of equity, depending upon the remedy sought. Nowadays the same judges deal with both common law and equity.

In practice, the common-law courts often were not so utterly bound by precedent as they professed to be. Actually, judges might interpret precedents in the light of altered social circumstances, and so in effect establish fresh precedents more suited to a different era. But the general principle was maintained, and is maintained in common law today, that the common law is a continuity, opposed to innovation, adjudicating suits at law upon the basis of enduring norms that for a long while have been recognized as just and binding. The common law is empirical law: that is, it is based upon men's experience over many generations, a good test of practicality.

But can simple experience, no matter how far back in a people's history it extends, be a sufficient guide to justice? Must there not be some theological or philosophical sanction that gives meaning to collective experience? Did wisdom begin with the common-law judges?

In medieval England, both courts of common law and courts of equity claimed that they derived their sanction from the established customs or the ethical beliefs of the realm, and not from Roman law; for a time, even the study of Roman law was forbidden in England. Hebrew law and Christian morals were recognized as part of the common law, but not so the Roman, or quasi-Roman, law that was revived in the Continent and in Scotland.

In reality, nevertheless, principles of Roman law formed an element in the common law, and more conspicuously in equity. The English first became acquainted with Roman ideas of law through the canon law, the law of the Church courts; and as more direct knowledge of Roman law was obtained at the Italian universities of Bologna, Padua, and Mantua, gradually that understanding filtered into medieval English jurisprudence, though never acknowledged formally. Natural-law concepts, owing much to Cicero, came to be a mainstay of both common law and equity. Besides, the opinions of the Roman jurisconsults, as collected in Justinian's code, increasingly served English judges as a basis for decision of puzzling cases. In theory, the common law offered a remedy for every complaint at law; privately, many common law judges seem to have found remedy and precedent by consulting Roman theory.

Sir Henry Maine, the most lively of English legal historians, declares that Henry de Bracton (often called "the father of English law"), in the reign of Henry III, borrowed from the Roman *Corpus Juris* the whole form of his own book on the common law, *De Legibus Angliae,* published about 1260; and a third of the contents of his book, too. Although later legal scholars have argued that Maine goes too far in this assertion, clearly Bracton and the other champions of the common law were much influenced by what they knew of Roman law.[2] In the time of the Norman and Plantagenet kings, judges ordinarily were men in holy orders—some of them bishops; and naturally enough such judges' familiarity with canon law, rooted in Roman law, had its part in the early shaping of the common law. Anyone who had read the works of Gregory the Great and of Augustine of Hippo could not ignore the strength of natural-law doctrine and the whole Roman understanding of justice.

To have acknowledged being moved by Roman law would have made an English judge suspect both to his king and to the English people: that was something foreign, and possibly perilous to the "old laws" of England. For all that, the common law does combine English customary usage with some Roman principles—or rather, the Roman principles give order to English legal custom. Far from being subversive of English liberties, the Roman tinge to the common law helped to make possible the emergence of judges' independence and of representative government.

Why is the common law so important? In part, because it was the foundation of good order in England, so that upon it rose the whole fabric of a free society, the model for other free societies. For a body of law to be really enforceable, it must receive the willing assent of the mass of people, living under such a law. Stable government grows out of law, not law out of government. If the political power decrees positive laws without reference to general consent, those laws will be evaded or defied, and respect for law will diminish, so that force must be substituted for justice: precisely that resistance to statutory law occurred in some European countries, over the centuries.

Now the English people looked upon the common law as *their* law, the product of their historical experience; it was not something imposed upon them from above. That being so, most of them willingly abided by the law, and so down to our own time the English have been the most law-abiding people, generally, among the major nations. This voluntary obedience to law made it possible, despite intervals of civil strife, for the English to unite against foreign enemies, to reconcile old ways with prudent change, and to prosper materially. Not least among the benefits of general respect for common law was the regular enforcement of contracts, which mightily assisted the growth of English domestic and foreign commerce.

And if the common law was the foundation of order, also it was the foundation of freedom. The high claim of the old commentators on the common law was this: no man, not even the king, was above or beyond the law. "The king himself," Bracton wrote, "ought not to be under man but under God, and under the Law, because the Law makes the king. Therefore, let the king render back to the Law what the Law gives to him, namely, dominion and power; for there is no king where will, and not Law, wields dominion." The Law is a bridle upon the king. Though the king may not be sued, he may be petitioned; if he will not do justice upon receiving a reasonable petition, the king's own Great Council, or the barons and the people, then may restrain his power. Just that had been done to King John, less than half a century before Bracton wrote, and would be done to later kings who tried to set themselves above the Law. Here are the beginnings of the principle of a government of laws, not of men.

By the reign of Edward I, in the last quarter of the thirteenth century, the common law was so well entrenched that no king could defy it, whatever else he might aspire to. Edward I cast out corrupt or incompetent judges, but left the common law itself strong, and indeed extended its functions. Soon the Inns of Court, the lawyers' guilds of London, would take form, improving the practice of both common law and equity. The development and refinement of the common law, and the better education of its judges, would continue as the

Middle Ages merged into what we call the Renaissance and the Reformation.

Even the Tudors, monarchs virtually absolute otherwise in the sixteenth century, would not think of tampering banefully with the common law; indeed, Henry VIII would profess himself the champion of the common law against Roman and canon law. By such jurists as Sir Edward Coke and Sir Matthew Hale, in the seventeenth century, the common law would be exalted still higher. And in the eighteenth century, Sir William Blackstone's *Commentaries on the Laws of England,* permeated with common-law doctrine, would exert a stronger attraction in America than in England.

As chastened and corrected by equity, the common law of medieval times was an instrument for social improvement, as well as for the conserving of old rights. It maintained the continuity of law, while itself amenable to correction by appeal to Chancery or to clarification by parliamentary statute. More than any juridical system on the Continent, it protected the subject from oppression by powerful individuals, through its writs, its court procedures, and its national enforcement. Its high value would not be seriously challenged until early in the nineteenth century, when Jeremy Bentham and his disciples would attempt to overthrow the common law for the sake of codified statutory law, on abstract principles of justice.

In America, common-law principles would work upon public affairs more powerfully than any other influences except Protestant Christianity and the colonial social experience itself. Into every colony, the common law would be introduced by colonial charter. The leading American public men of the last quarter of the eighteenth century—and especially the many practising lawyers among them—and their successors in the first quarter of the nineteenth century, from Republicans like Jefferson and Madison to Federalists like Fisher Ames and Joseph Story, would be thoroughly read in the common-law exponents of medieval times and the Renaissance; they would know their Glanville, their Bracton, their Coke, and others. (John Adams was one of the few Americans to make a careful study also of canon law.) Best of all, the Americans knew their Blackstone's *Commen-*

taries—even though Blackstone himself strenuously opposed American independence.

With the Revolution, true, would come opposition to the common law, as to nearly everything else English; but the American advocates of the common law would win the struggle in the nineteenth century. It is difficult, for that matter, to conceive how American society could have cohered at all, in the early decades of the Republic, had not the common law been adapted to American circumstances: there had been no preparation in America for administration of justice by state or federal statutory codes, and President Madison rejected Bentham's offer to write a code for the infant United States.

In the twentieth century, the common law of England, of the United States, and indeed of every country that has adapted English common law to its needs, steadily gives ground before the advance of statutory law. Some legislators scarcely seem aware that the common law still exists, and they succeed in enacting statutes which deal in less satisfactory fashion with subjects already adequately covered by common law.

Yet had it not been for the work of the old common law, those representative assemblies which today pour out new statutes might never have come into existence. For the common law of medieval England did much to give stability first to one nation, and then to others; at the same time, the common law maintained the principle of the supremacy of law, and the practice of forms of self-government.

The Frame of the English Constitution

It is an error to think of the Middle Ages as one long period of tyranny. Much violence was suffered in those centuries, and much ferocity; but political absolutism was the exception, rather than the rule, until the Renaissance. The police powers of modern "totalism" did not exist, and the strong Church often restrained kings and barons from assuming greater secular power. Ordinarily the medieval king was "first among equals," the greatest baron among many barons; if he desired unitary might, still he lacked the money and the professional army that could have brought him such arbitrary authority. The Holy Roman Emperor himself, dominating as best he could the Germans and much of Italy, held nothing like the *imperium* of the old Roman emperors. Within the feudal "system," vast diversity was possible, and even considerable liberty—though freedom of a kind different from the liberty of modern times.

Feudalism, a means of military government, made it possible for Europe to resist its Moslem enemies of Spain, Africa, and the Levant, and its Mongol enemies of the Russian steppes. Also feudalism maintained order of a sort within the Christian lands of Europe. By the "feudal contract," a baron or a knight held tenure of land in exchange for military service in time of need: he would serve his lord in defense of the lord's larger holdings, or in defense of the whole realm if the king should summon his vassals-in-chief and they in turn should summon their own vassals. The barons' jealousy of royal prerogatives, and the kings' perennial suspicion of unruly barons, generally maintained a tolerable balance of power.

Outside this feudal structure, though not unconnected with it, lay the Church (the greatest of landholders); and the boroughs or burgs, the walled towns of the merchants and craft-guilds, holding charters from a king or some princely noble. Beneath this feudal structure lay the mass of medieval people, cultivators of the soil, some of them serfs or villeins, others relatively free peasants. What with the influence of Christian teachings and of large economic changes, slavery was extinct: a serf might be bound to the soil, but he was a member of the social community, and of the spiritual community of the Church. A common religious faith and a need for protection against terrible adversaries held loosely together this medieval Europe.

Medieval society was a complex of personal loyalties and obligations, not much resembling modern political states. Because of her geographic isolation and the central authority asserted after the Norman conquest by the kings, England was nearer to being a coherent state than any other medieval realm. Within the realm of England, relatively secure, there began to grow certain political institutions which became the progenitors of American political order. The laws of England aside, the chief of these institutions is representative government.

According to Montesquieu, writing about the middle of the eighteenth century, the only grand change in the art of government which has come about since Aristotle's day is representative government. Nearly all of Europe, and indeed nearly all of the "free world," owes modern representative institutions to the English example. Were it not for representative government, either great modern states would be, at best, imperial structures like the Roman Empire, or else they would dissolve once more into city-states and cantons, in which the typical citizen could make his voice heard directly. Even though the Americans would throw off the nominal authority of the English king and the real authority of Parliament, American government (despite some borrowings from classical sources) in essence would be the English development of representation of the people in a deliberative assembly.

For the first stirrings of representation in national politics, we turn to the Great Charter, Magna Carta, extracted from King John by the barons of his realm, in the year 1215. John, though clever and an able soldier, was so grasping and evil a monarch that no later English king took the name of John. The king had arbitrarily imprisoned barons, knights, and burgesses, to extort large sums of money from them for carrying on his wars. With most of the barons in arms against him, and the menace of a French invasion imminent, John was forced to grant a guarantee of royal good conduct, which he signed at Runnymede, between London and Windsor. This we call Magna Carta.

Most of the many articles of this Great Charter have lost their significance with the passing of the feudal age. But a fundamental principle of Magna Carta, though not expressed in so many words in that document itself, endures to our day. This principle entered into the developing common law of the thirteenth century, and appeared in later royal charters and statutes. It became the rock upon which the English constitution was built. It is the principle of the supremacy of law: the idea that an enduring law exists, which all men must obey. The king himself is one of those men under the law. Along with this principle ran a corollary principle—that if the king breaks the law, and invades the rights of his vassals, then barons and people may deprive him of his powers.

From this principle the whole English constitution—an "unwritten" constitution in the sense that it can be found in no single document—developed in time. This principle would be asserted by the Americans in the last quarter of the eighteenth century; it is the root of the Declaration of Independence.

John's successor on the throne, too feeble to undo the concessions of Runnymede, left the machinery of government in the hands of the barons of his Great Council. That Council was not a representative institution, because the barons, as individuals, represented no one but themselves. But if the king is not absolute, and if barons rule in his name, surely both king and barons must derive their authority from some source greater than themselves. Down almost to the end of medieval times, all the kings of England were required to confirm afresh the Great Charter—some of them to confirm it several times over. The king is bound by the law: it became impossible to deny this principle. Yet if the king should break the law, who can restrain him without civil war? The answer to that question was found in the development of a representative assembly, Parliament.

Here we can only mention the principal stages in the medieval growth of Parliament. In the recurring contests between king and barons, both sides found it necessary to seek for support beyond the chief barons who sat in the Great Council—indeed, beyond the whole order of barons. To obtain such help, representatives of other orders, or estates, must be taken into consultation. If money was to be found, one must look beyond the baronial party.

Now in medieval Europe generally, three estates, or great social orders, were recognized: the clergy, the barons, and the commons. (By the "commons" was meant not the mass of peasants, but men of property and some standing who belonged neither to the clergy nor to the estate of baron; most of these "commons" were the free citizens or burgesses of the chartered cities and towns, together with such freeholders in the countryside as did not hold by feudal tenures.) In England, the sons of barons, and the knights—these latter originally tenants who owed military service to barons—also were ranked as commoners. To clergy and commons, then, the king must turn for support against the barons; and to clergy and commons, sometimes, the barons could turn for support against the king.

First the baronial party, and then the king, invited representatives of the commons to take part in deliberations of the realm. The Great Council, in the latter half of the thirteenth century, began to yield some of its powers to a more general parliament. By 1295, a "Model Parliament," representing all estates, was summoned by Edward I, a strong king who required help against the French and the Scots. This consisted of the great ecclesiastics (bishops and abbots) and the chief vassals of the old Great Council, but also of two knights from each county, two burgesses from each burgh, and representatives of the lower clergy. In this "model" parliament, the clergy still formed a separate estate, and the knights sat with the barons, leaving the burgesses to form the third estate (an arrangement which endured in France down to the Revolution in 1789).

But as the pattern of parliaments (a word that signifies "speaking") took form, the English clergy preferred not to be involved directly in political processes—lest they lose their old right to be taxed only by their own assessment. This meant that as the English parliament grew in power, it would consist of two houses only—the Lords Spiritual and Temporal (or great ecclesiastics and barons), and the Commons, composed chiefly of burgesses and knights. Social distinctions in medieval England being less rigid than those of the Continent, the knights found themselves more comfortable with the prosperous burgesses of the towns than with the grand barons, and so came to sit in the parliaments as representatives of the Commons, several knights being elected from every shire (county). The House of Lords was not a representative body, and for the most part is not a representative body today: peers sit in that house in their own right. But of course the burgesses and the knights were too numerous to be assembled collectively in a house of parliament, and so the election of members of parliament commenced, necessarily. Because elected to represent, in theory, the whole people of England, and because only from the commons could the kings obtain the money they needed, the House of Commons would grow to loom larger than the House of Lords, in later times. The bulk of the clergy, separating themselves from parliaments, were content to hold their own distinct Convocation of the Clergy at intervals.

The significant fact about the "model" parliament of 1295, then, was not its organization (which soon changed), but the writs sent out by the king's men of law to summon its members. *Quod omnes tangit ab omnibus approbetur*—so ran a phrase in those writs: what concerns all, should be approved by all. This principle was drawn from Roman jurisprudence. Taxation to support Edward's wars concerned all, and the Model Parliament granted him that monetary aid. But this appropriation did not suffice for long, and Edward levied fresh taxes without parliamentary assent. The barons protesting, Edward was compelled in 1297 to grant his "Confirmation of the Charters," in which the king affirmed that, conforming to old custon, he would levy no extraordinary tax, beyond feudal dues, without the consent of his realm's estates. What concerned all, must be approved by all.

Thus the power of the purse passed into the hands of what already was becoming a body recognizably similar to the modern House of Commons. Only a general representative body may approve of revenue-raising: this would become a primary feature of the emerging English constitution and of all constitutions later modelled upon it. This permitted parliaments to exert some control upon the crown's actions; or, to employ American terms today, this function would give to the Congress, or to the state legislatures, an effective check upon the powers of the executive branch of government. Lacking funds, a government can accomplish nothing—not even pay its troops. In all modern representative government, control of the purse therefore is placed in the representative assembly.

This Confirmation of the Charters was merely the beginning of parliamentary authority; in hard fact, the kings would continue to dispute with the Commons the exercise of the power of the purse, far down into the seventeenth century. But the principle had been established; and the form of Parliament, by the reign of Edward III, would be more or less settled, too, with the peers sitting in the House of Lords (nobles now, rather than quasi-independent barons of the old sort), and the burgesses and knights sitting in the House of Commons, and the bulk of the clergy withdrawn from parliamentary disputes.

The fourteenth-century Parliament could petition the king, and declare that its grant of funds might be contingent on whether the king should receive such petitions favorably; but that Parliament was permitted to initiate nothing. (In theory, even today the House of Commons is "a body of critics" rather than an assembly of law-makers.) Short of cutting off all supplies of money to the Crown, how might Parliament bridle the king in his actions?

The most effective check upon royal power which the medieval Parliament devised, aside from control over the purse, was impeachment. To have removed kings from the throne would have left the state powerless, and would have brought on civil war, ordinarily. But the king's servants might be held responsible for arbitrary actions. Thus the theory that the king can do no wrong was enunciated—meaning not that the king is perfectly virtuous, but rather that if Parliament must hold someone accountable for wrongdoing, it will seize upon the king's ministers. The process of impeachment commenced in the last quarter of the fourteenth century; and since impeachment might mean that the offending official would be beheaded, it had a chastening effect upon royal actions.

Richard II, at the very end of the fourteenth century, endeavored to shake free of all parliamentary controls and to return to absolutism. He was overthrown by Henry of Bolingbroke, who had the nation's support, and who was crowned Henry IV. In assenting to the coronation of Henry, Parliament in effect asserted its power to dethrone and to elevate another to kingship—even, as with Henry, a successor who was not in the direct line of primogeniture. This "revolution of 1399" would be a precedent for the Americans in the eighteenth century.

By the year 1430, an act of Parliament established permanent qualifications for county electors—that is, persons granted the franchise to choose members of the House of Commons. The fundamental qualification was one of property—possessing a freehold worth at least forty shillings a year in rent, "above all charges." This measure seems to have been intended to keep the ignorant and disorderly from disturbing elections. (The boroughs, down to the nineteenth century, could set their own requirements for the franchise, but most of them also established some property qualification.) Property qualifications for voting passed into the American colonies from the beginning, and were effective in the several states of the Union until the 1820's or later.

About the middle of the fifteenth century, then, something like representative government could be discerned in England. In theory, at least, the law was supreme. The king was bound by oath to respect the laws; he might not change the laws or impose new taxes without parliamentary consent. The people, through elections held in county courts and boroughs, chose from their own number members to represent them in the House of Commons, and those members were privileged against interference or even ordinary arrest. The power of impeachment prevented, or at least curbed, arbitrary acts or corrupt practices among the king's servants. Taxation could not be levied without the consent of the people's representatives, and this meant that petitions of grievance must be seriously considered by the king and his ministers. No hostility then subsisted between the Lords and the Commons. As the end of medieval times approached, England knew more of order and justice and freedom than did any other nation.

Or so the English constitution stood. But the medieval world was falling apart; and despite these aspects of representative government, the dynastic struggle of the Wars of the Roses, the house of York against the house of Lancaster, was ravaging the country. Peace would be restored only after both houses were destroyed, and Henry Tudor, crowned Henry VII, stood triumphant upon the ruins of the feudal structure. The house of Tudor, though preserving constitutional forms, would dominate Parliament by manipulation of elections and by potential force. The Renaissance, the Reformation, and England's approaching expansion overseas would cast into shadow the reality of representative government, so slowly and painfully achieved. Early in the seventeenth century, after a century and more of rule by strong-willed monarchs, England would know again the struggle between king and parliament. Yet the constitution's essential features were clear enough at the end of the Middle Ages, and those chartered rights of Englishmen, those institutions of ordered freedom, would spring up also along the Atlantic seaboard of America.

The Sword of Faith

The time of the growth of common law and of parliaments was also the time of the Crusades. Two types of humanity were the wonder of medieval Europe: the great saint and the great knight. In later ages, their descendants would be the scholar and the gentleman. We have said something of saints already; now we look at one famous knight.

From the closing years of the eleventh century to the end of the thirteenth century, the feudal West engaged in that enormous adventure and tragedy called the Crusades. At the beginning of those two centuries of warfare in the East, the objects of the Christian kings and barons, or at least the objects of the popes, were to rescue the holy city of Jerusalem from the Moslems, and to aid the Eastern Empire of Constantinople against its Moslem foes. In the former object, the Crusaders succeeded—for eighty-eight years. In the latter object, they destroyed the Byzantine system instead of saving it, for the Latin Crusaders stormed Constantinople in 1204 and chose one of their own princes as emperor, and then carved the Byzantine territories into feudal fiefs.

By the year 1187, Jerusalem had fallen back into the hands of the Moslems, and the Latin Christians of *Outremer* (the overseas stronghold of Christendom) held little more than a strip of land along the Palestinian coast, with the fortress-town of Acre as their actual capital—though they still called their state the Kingdom of Jerusalem. By 1208, the European colonists of *Outremer* lacked even a king, though they had a girl-queen, Maria, seventeen years old. They besought the king of France to find them a husband for Maria: such a husband, such a king, as could withstand the outnumbering enemy and restore to them Jerusalem.

King Philip Augustus of France, who had been a Crusader himself, chose for their king a landless knight, sixty years old. This was such a knight-errant as wandered through the pages of medieval romances, who might have jousted with Gawain or Lancelot. Yet he was flesh and blood—very much flesh and blood, because gigantic in stature. John of Brienne, soon to be King of Jerusalem, came from Champagne, and had been reared for a priest, but liked the sword better. His brother, through marriage to a forsaken heiress to the overthrown Norman rulers of the South, vainly asserted a forlorn claim to the throne of Sicily. For forty years and more this John of Brienne had been a gallant squire of dames, a champion at tournaments, and a valiant commander in the French king's armies. This huge scarred veteran was married to the girl-queen of Jerusalem; and perhaps she loved him, which was infrequent in the noble marriages of medieval times. Ordinarily he was as gentle with women as he was heavy-handed with armed men; indeed, the only charge that could be brought against him as king and emperor was his excessive indulgence of wives and daughters. The king of France gave him forty thousand silver pounds because John had nothing of his own, and Pope Innocent gave him another forty thousand. In the stronghold of Acre, King John bided his time until he should have force enough to take the field against the sultans.

Maria of Jerusalem bore him a daughter, Yolande, and

then died. The people of *Outremer* admired and obeyed him, for he was a man of political knowledge as well as a man of battle. By 1218, he was ready to lead the Fifth Crusade, and he meant to strike first at Egypt, the center of Moslem power. Pope Innocent III strained every nerve for this effort, and a hundred thousand armed men were gathered in Palestine for the undoing of Egypt and the recovery of Jerusalem: the king of Hungary, the duke of Austria, a fleet from the Frisian islands, the king of Cyprus, and crusaders from many other lands joined King John, who already had the three military orders of monks and the levies of *Outremer*. They marched into Egypt.

John of Brienne beat the sultan's hosts and took the port of Damietta; the Sultan of Egypt offered the Crusaders Jerusalem and more besides if they would withdraw from his domains; that was enough to satisfy John. But the new pope, Honorius III, had dispatched to Egypt a Spanish cardinal, Pelagius, as papal legate. Although he had neither diplomatic skill nor military experience, Pelagius asserted command over John, and with that the opportunity was lost.

There came to Egypt at this time, too, the strangest and most holy man of that age, Saint Francis of Assisi. In his youth, Francis had fought in the war between Assisi and Perugia, and had been taken prisoner; now he was the fearless peacemaker. Following more boldly in Christ's steps than perhaps any men before or since the thirteenth century, Francis and his friars lived in extreme poverty and simplicity. He was the humblest and most successful of all the reformers who from time to time renewed the medieval Church. His love extended to all animate creation—even to "Brother Wolf."

What could the saintly enthusiast and the grand knight-errant have said to each other? We have no record of their talk. Yet John of Brienne, a cleric in his youth, was so won by the ascetic of Assisi that he became a Franciscan of sorts himself; long later, he would be buried in the gray gown of Francis' begging friars.

Saint Francis crossed over to the Saracen lines and charmed the Sultan of Egypt. He asked the Moslem monarch that he might be permitted to walk barefoot on hot coals to testify to his faith in Christ. The Sultan al-Kamil spared Francis that test, but he did discourse on religion with the gentle hero from Umbria. "The Moslem guards were suspicious at first," a twentieth-century historian of the Crusades writes, "but soon decided that anyone so simple, so gentle, and so dirty must be mad, and treated him with the respect due to a man who has been touched by God."[3] The mystic of Assisi could not persuade the two armies to the peace of God, nevertheless: once he was gone from the camp, they took again to the sword.

By Pelagius' meddling, John's campaign was undone. The Crusaders were defeated with tremendous loss, and John of Brienne withdrew to Acre. He had married again, this time an Armenian princess, Stephanie; but she tried to poison his baby daughter Yolande, so John beat his Armenian wife, and later she died of that thrashing, rumor said—for John was accustomed to striking hard.

Although the Fifth Crusade had failed, John still held his scrap of a kingdom, and must find aid in the West for his people; he must find, too, a strong husband for Yolande, she being eleven years old, he far into his seventies. In 1222, he sailed with Yolande to Italy, and sought out Pope Honorius at Rome. The pope arranged that Yolande should marry the greatest sovereign in Christendom, Frederick II, Holy Roman Emperor—able, skeptical, licentious: then Frederick himself might go on crusade, and Jerusalem be delivered again. John hesitated; but the splendor of this match was too much for even the proudest knight-errant to resist.

While the marriage-treaty was being drawn up, John proceeded into France, seeking help for *Outremer*, and then into Spain. There he married another young bride, Berengaria, sister to the King of Castile. After grand ceremonies in Italy and *Outremer*, Yolande was married to Frederick at Brindisi, late in 1225. Frederick was masterful, learned, and the next thing to an atheist; also he was merciless and treacherous: the other side of the chivalric coin from John of Brienne.

No sooner had Frederick married Yolande—and debauched her cousin, a bridesmaid—than he deposed old John from the kingship of Jerusalem, assuming the throne himself on the strength of being now the husband of the young Queen Yolande. He deprived John even of fifty thousand marks that the dying King of France had given him for *Outremer*. Enraged, John of Brienne went to the pope at Rome; Yolande was dispatched to Frederick's harem in Sicily, where she died after bearing the emperor a son. Like Shakespeare's Lear, King John was desolate in his old age—or so it seemed.

Unlike Lear, however, John of Brienne was far from his dotage. Pope and emperor fell out; at last, in 1228, the excommunicated Frederick II sailed for Palestine on a crusade of sorts. Poor Yolande was dead and buried in Sicily now; John owed Frederick no love. With papal troops at his back, John marched into the absent emperor's Italian domains, taking towns and castles on behalf of the pope. John was nearly eighty years old in his hour of vengeance, and some thought he should be crowned king of England, that land then needing a king of might.

But then there came to John the offer of a more exotic throne. The Latin Empire of Constantinople, grandest of medieval cities, lacked a strong ruler. Who could defend that beleaguered realm better than John of Brienne? Berengaria had a little daughter by John, Maria, four years old: it was arranged that the baby Maria should be betrothed to Baldwin II, the boy-emperor of Constantinople, and that John himself should be emperor, as well as regent, until his death.

So to the palace on the Golden Horn John sailed, to become in title the successor of Constantine the Great. There he arrived in 1231, an emperor more than eighty-three years of age. For the time being, the terror of his name kept off the enemies to the north and the enemies to the east. John disbanded the armies and lived at ease with wife and daughter: his fire, it appeared, was extinguished at last.

So thought the Greek emperor of Nicaea and the formidable king of Bulgaria. In concert, they marched against Constantinople with a tremendous host and a large fleet, in 1235. At his immediate command, Emperor John had only a hundred and sixty knights, and a small force of sergeants and archers.

Constantinople was surrounded by the strongest fortifications in the world, but John of Brienne disdained them. Taking horse, he charged the enemy at the head of his chivalry; panic seized the Greeks and the Bulgars, and they broke; John's men gained much of their fleet. Then John sent messages to the vassal principalities of the Latin Empire, gathered the Westerners who held fiefs in what had been old Greece, and beat the Greeks and the Bulgars again in 1236.

That done, no one ventured to disturb him. At the age of ninety, full of glory but empty (as always) of pocket, John died peacefully in his imperial palace. By his command, he was buried in the habit of a Franciscan friar; at heart, this hero of the sword was brother to the mendicant of Assisi.

The age of chivalry was an age of wonders. Where did the actual begin and the imaginary end? No man knew. John of Brienne had done deeds marvellous as any knight's of romance. "Chivalry was the fine flower of honor growing from this soil," Henry Osborn Taylor comments, "embosomed in an abundant leafage of imagination. . . . For final exemplification of the actual and the ideally real in chivalry, the reader may look within himself, and observe the inextricable mingling of the imaginative and the real. He will recognize that what at one time seems part of his imagination, at another will prove itself the veriest reality of his life. Even such wavering verity of spirit was chivalry."[4]

The knights-errant of medieval times, most of them, were burly armored men who went about seeking causes to champion—widows' and orphans', sometimes—but usually for a price. From their number could emerge such a one as John of Brienne, and in time from the ideals of chivalry emerged the idea of a gentleman. The civilization of Europe has been maintained by two powers, Edmund Burke would say in the eighteenth century: the Christian religion, and the spirit of a gentleman. By the time of Miguel de Cervantes, in the sixteenth century, the old knight-errant would have vanished, and his last emulator, Don Quixote de la Mancha, would appear absurd. Yet Don Quixote, venerating such heroes as John of Brienne and John's peers of the medieval romances, stands up a true gentleman, loftier far in spirit than those who mock him. "A lean and foolish knight forever rides in vain," in G. K. Chesterton's lines: but not altogether in vain. For the sense of honor and of duty, and the sword of faith, passed in some degree from the medieval world to later times.

In the English Renaissance, the courtier and the gentleman would take the knight-errant's place. They would be as quick to love and to hate as the old knight had been, but their graces would be more polished. Sir Walter Raleigh, having planted the first settlement in Virginia, would be flung into London Tower on a trumped-up charge of treason; there he would write his immense *History of the World*, and invent medicines. At last he would go to the block, King James wishing to please the Spanish ambassador by Raleigh's death; and as a gentleman he would die.

The poet Sir Philip Sidney, mortally wounded in the Low Countries, would give his cup of water to a dying common soldier: "Thy need is greater than mine." In this fashion, the chivalric ideal of the Middle Ages endured after the feudal institutions had been swept away.

America was no aristocratic land, but such examples were not lost on the men of colonial times and later days. Captain John Smith, commanding what force the early Virginian settlement could muster, was a kind of latter-day paladin, full of tales—half fanciful, perhaps, half genuine—of his wars against the Turks. America would have no nobles, but it would have gentlemen. And they would dare much. One of these, not fearing to take the sword, was George Washington; another would be a later Virginian, Robert E. Lee. It is well that war is so terrible, said General Lee, for otherwise we should grow to love it.

It has been said that a gentleman is a person who never calls himself one. Certainly few Americans lay claim to gentility nowadays. And yet the heavy-handed champion of medieval times bequeathed to later centuries a spirit of valor and honor and fortitude, and sometimes of generosity, that has not lost all its value. The communication of medieval saints echoes down to us, and so does the communication of medieval knights. As the poet-adventurer Roy Campbell said to me once, "If you are Don Quixote, all your windmills will be giants; but then, all your giants will be windmills." Francis of Assisi, born a person of quality, was fearless in one fashion, John of Brienne in another; faith sustained them both. Their light, blending, still illuminates our own century, which confronts its own windmills and its own giants.

Schoolmen and Universities

Knights have vanished almost, but scholars have multiplied. From medieval times, one inheritance comes down to us uninterrupted: the universities. The work of a university is the ordering and integrating of knowledge. That work began systematically in the twelfth century, and without it modern civilization would founder.

Although Americans in the formative years of this country were influenced indirectly by medieval thought, few of them understood how much they owed to that source. With few exceptions, they tended to think of the Middle Ages as barbarous. Yet in essence their own schooling, at every level, was developed out of medieval education.

The Schoolmen, the Christian philosophers of the medieval universities, transcended the barriers of nationality and language. For the language of the universities was Latin, not vernacular tongues; and both professors and students shifted without much impediment from country to country, teaching and studying with small regard for political loyalties. The very word "university" implies the universal, the general—something more than local and private; the universities' degrees were recognized as valid throughout Christendom.

And the Schoolmen were in search of universal truths. At the height of their intellectual power, in the thirteenth century, they developed an elaborate structure of philosophy, the purpose of which was to prove that reason is not contrary to Christian faith. The greatest of them, Thomas Aquinas, reconciled the writings of Aristotle with Christian doctrine. The Schoolmen of that age, the Realists, perceived the universe as ordered by divine wisdom and love. True reality, they declared, is found in "universals"—that is, in general laws of being, somewhat like Plato's "ideas."

In politics, as in metaphysics and ethics, the Schoolmen of the thirteenth century sought for "universals." The state should be guided by universal principles of justice. Saint Augustine, centuries earlier, had written that the state was a necessary evil, resulting from man's sinfulness. But Saint Thomas Aquinas saw the political state as natural and beneficial: even had mankind been innocent of sin, government would have been desirable, as a means for attaining the common good. In this, as in much else, Aquinas restored the authority of Aristotle.

Where the civil social order was concerned, the Schoolmen's principal problem was to describe the proper relation between Church and State: how to balance the "two swords," or two powers by whom this world is ruled, that Saint Gelasius had defined when the Church was rising upon the ruins of the Roman imperial structure. How should pope and emperor share authority? At a time of crisis, should men be loyal to Church, rather than to State? Was the canon law of the Church independent of imperial or royal laws? These were immediately practical questions in medieval times, so that now and again they were tested by the witness of blood—as in the martyrdom of Thomas à Becket, archbishop of Canterbury, who by his death became the most popular of English saints.

One is tempted to discuss these questions in some detail here, for they have an enduring relevance to the problems of order. Yet Scholastic debates were not much heeded by the Americans who established a new nation in the eighteenth century: the Reformation would form a towering barrier between the "Papist" philosophers of medieval times and the settlers in British North America. At best, the concepts of Aquinas and other Schoolmen of the thirteenth and fourteenth centuries would pass to some Americans only at second-hand, through the books of Richard Hooker and some other Anglican divines of the Reformation. The Schoolmen of the Continent were sealed away from Englishmen and therefore Americans, once the medieval Church dissolved in the sixteenth century.

Many of the more eminent medieval scholars, nevertheless, were Englishmen or Scots, and in some degree their writings passed into the intellectual consciousness that was the seed-bed of American culture. The earliest of these English thinkers was Saint Anselm, archbishop of Canterbury in Norman England: a native of Italy, but the intellectual and practical architect of the medieval Church in England. The better-schooled among the American leaders would know something of Anselm's powerful proofs of the existence and perfection of the revealed God.

There were other English and Scottish Schoolmen famous throughout Christendom: in the thirteenth century, the Franciscan Alexander of Hales; Robert Grosseteste, bishop of Lincoln; and Roger Bacon, whose ideas anticipated modern scientific method. In the first half of the fourteenth century, the subtle John Duns Scotus set himself against the system of Thomas Aquinas; and there rose up in England the formidable William of Ockham, the Nominalist.

That Englishman William of Ockham, indeed, undid the earlier Realism of the universities—and so, if unintentionally, helped to clear the way for Renaissance and Reformation. The mode of thought called "Nominalism" denied the existence of "universals": that is, the Nominalists held that only names are general, and only individuals exist. There is no universal "horse," for instance: "horse" is merely a word which we apply, for convenience, to certain creatures of a particular species that resemble one another. This nominalist concept would lead on to a personal and social individualism that opposed the medieval ideal of universality; practically, it would work to break down the "medieval synthesis" of authority in church and state, and would be a factor in the personal individualism of the Renaissance and the religious individualism of the Reformation.

A contemporary of William of Ockham, in the first half of the fourteenth century, was Marsilius of Padua, a Schoolman more radical than the English Nominalist. Marsilius, at the University of Paris, argued that the Church must be subordinated to the State: even though divine law is superior to human law, it is the State that must decide the interpretation of divine law. Thus Marsilius carried Aristotle's politics—the politics of the *polis*, the autonomous city-state—farther than did Aquinas. In effect, the principles of Marsilius reduced papal authority and made conceivable the governing of churches by kings and princes—which would come to pass, in some countries, during the Reformation.

But for our purposes in this book, it will not do to go deeply into the debates of the Schoolmen, important though they were. For the majestic Schoolmen of the Continent—Albertus Magnus, Abelard, Hugh of St. Victor, even Aquinas—were little better than names even to the learned in eighteenth-century America. Only when Roman Catholic colleges and universities began to be founded in the United States, chiefly late in the nineteenth century, would the old Schoolmen's intellectual power be recognized in this country. Anglican and Presbyterian and Puritan divines, rather than the medieval philosophers, nurtured American faith and reason.

Despite that, the Schoolmen's medieval universities in Britain and northern Europe, converted into strongholds of Protestantism at the Reformation, have exercised a large influence upon American order, both in themselves and through the American colleges that in the beginning were modelled modestly upon them. The foundations which today are called Harvard, William and Mary, Yale, Princeton, and Columbia all were intended to carry into the colonies the English and Scottish patterns of higher learning. Even the state universities established early in the nineteenth century took "Oxbridge" or the Scottish universities for models, though later they would be much altered by emulation of German universities and by utilitarian aims.

The medieval university was an independent corporation of scholars, a body of schools of general studies, commonly with colleges of arts that prepared young men for the bachelor's or the master's degree, and also higher schools of theology, law, and medicine. The university arose out of the Church's monastic schools and cathedral schools, usually, in response to a thirst for higher learning.

In Britain and northern Europe, although not always in Italy or elsewhere in the South, these universities were dominated by the Church, and the students were clerks, or clerics, either in minor orders or about to take orders—some of those students very young indeed. At the University of Bologna, the students controlled everything—until the towns-folk of Bologna, objecting to the students' arrogant ways, contrived to end that. But the English and Scottish universities stood nominally under the direction of ecclesiastics, and were governed practically by their professors, who were priests, monks, and friars. Their first object was to pursue truth for the glory of God. Beyond that, they were meant to educate young men to become clergymen, to prepare some of those for prospective service with the State as well as with the Church, and to develop the other learned professions of law and medicine. In these universities, theology was queen of the sciences.

Thomas Aquinas, in the thirteenth century, held that there was no wall of separation between theology and philosophy: those studies differed merely in method. But William of Ockham, in the fourteenth century, divorced philosophy from theology, maintaining that he thereby freed Christian dogmas from the influence of pagan speculations. That divorce would lead to other speculations in the universities, however, and so toward the Reformation. Yet in their early centuries, Europe's universities were centers for the intellectual reinforcement of authority and tradition—even if professors quarreled passionately and students seemed lawless.

"They had no antique prototype," Henry Osborn Taylor writes of these medieval foundations: "nothing either in Athens or Rome ever resembled these corporations of masters and students, with their authoritative privileges, their fixed curriculum, and their grades of formally certified attainment. Even the Alexandria of the Ptolemies, with all the pedantry of its learned litterateurs and their minute study of the past, had nothing to offer like the scholastic obsequiousness of the medieval University, which sought to set upon one throne the antique philosophy and the Christian revelation, that it might with one and the same genuflection bow down before them both."[5]

The two English medieval universities, Oxford and Cambridge, had their origins near the end of the twelfth century and the beginning of the thirteenth, and so rank among the earliest of universities (as distinguished from monastic or cathedral schools). Both were unusual in that they did not grow out of old cathedral schools, but instead sprang up as guilds of teaching masters—though soon they would be endowed by great churchmen and by kings. The three medieval Scottish universities, on the other hand—St. Andrews, Glasgow, and Aberdeen—resembled most of the universities of northern Europe in being associated with cathedrals.

As a rather late specimen of the type and influence of medieval universities, we consider the oldest university of Scotland, St. Andrews. There are reasons for emphasizing here a Scottish university rather than Oxford or Cambridge. For one thing, by the eighteenth century Oxford and Cambridge would become aristocratic in character; but the Scottish universities would remain relatively democratic and popular foundations, and so their professors and students would more nearly resemble those of the early American colleges. Also the Scottish universities would be Calvinistic in their theology and pattern of church government, after the Reformation; while Oxford and Cambridge would be Anglican. And of the five early American colleges, Harvard, Yale, and the College of New Jersey (now Princeton) would be Calvinist.

Because the colonies were governed from London, sometimes Scottish contributions to young America are neglected by historians. But much of America's early energy, in politics, commerce, and on the frontier, was that of Scots—who would become more successful in America than any other ethnic group except the New England Puritans. James Wilson, signer of the Declaration of Independence, member of the Constitutional Convention, a principal author of the Constitution, and later an associate justice of the Supreme Court, was one of the more ardent advocates of popular sovereignty; he had been born and schooled at the Scottish university town of St. Andrews. Scottish Presbyterianism worked intricately upon American life and character.

So we turn for our representative university to a little

center of learning on the North Sea, St. Andrews—a place that had drawn pilgrims in the Dark Ages because in its cathedral rested an arm-bone and some finger-bones of Saint Andrew the Apostle. The bishops and archbishops of St. Andrews were Scotland's primates, and often the Scots kings' chancellors, too. As Scottish patriotism flourished in the century after Robert Bruce's defeat of the English at Bannockburn, the first university of that austere land was founded in a spirit of national independence.

Schools there had been in St. Andrews almost at the dawn of Scottish history: they had been conducted first by the Culdees, a Celtic Christian sect of Irish origin. At the beginning of the fifteenth century, a number of little schools under private masters were prospering in the town. But the time had come when schooling must be regularized and the higher learning dignified. A wise and strong bishop, Henry Wardlaw, was in St. Andrews; learned men among the clerics found him a patron competent to establish a university.

From its inception, this new university was intended to be a bulwark of orthodoxy. Lawrence of Lindores, Abbot of Scone and Inquisitor of Heretical Pravity for Scotland, appears to have been a master spirit in the undertaking, next to the bishop; and no man was more zealously orthodox. These ecclesiastics detected the first murmur of the storm that would be called the Reformation. They proceeded to buttress the wall of Faith with the prop of Reason.

It was a time troubled by heresy and schism. In the Great Schism of the medieval Church, Scotland adhered to the Avignon popes, while England supported the Roman claimants to the papacy. Thus the Scottish students who once would have walked south to Oxford and Cambridge now must risk falling into schism if they ventured over the Border. Ever since the Scottish wars of independence, Scottish clerks had crossed in increasing numbers to the Continent, especially to the Scots colleges at Paris and Orleans. But after 1408, France too forswore her allegiance to Benedict XIII, of the Avignon line of popes, and thus the whole of the Continent, except for Spain, was closed to Scots scholars. Besides, access to the English universities was impeded by the sore troubles of King Henry IV; while in France, civil war had hit the colleges at Paris and Orleans hard—it being perilous even to approach those cities.

Heresy was no less menacing than schism. The movement called Lollardry, bound up with the ideas of John Wycliffe (who had translated the Bible into English), seemed bent upon social revolution. The Lollards or Wycliffites declared that they would subject the Church to the authority of the Crown, confiscate and redistribute land, apply the laws of the Jews to England and Scotland, and sweep away the clergy together with their benefices. In 1407, John Resby, a Lollard preacher, had been burnt in Scotland, for he had denied that the pope was Christ's vicar, and had affirmed that bad character incapacitates priests from performing holy offices.

The late medieval Church in Scotland was tolerant of much, but these doctrines were perilous to its existence. The rising generation must be forewarned against these errors, before visionary reformers should seduce young men. With Lindores there joined other clergy, and they lectured in St. Andrews town upon theology, logic, the law of God, canon law, and civil law. In 1412, Bishop Wardlaw gave to these teachers a charter of incorporation, creating the University of St. Andrews.

But most medieval universities desired papal sanction. In 1413 there arrived from stern old Pope Benedict XIII, the last of the Avignon line, six papal bulls confirming the charter and authorizing faculties of theology, canon and civil law, arts, medicine, and other university subjects.

The new university had a chancellor, a grand personage intended to protect the foundation; and before the Reformation, the chancellor almost always was the bishop or archbishop of St. Andrews. From within the university was chosen a rector, who must be a graduate and a man in holy orders, and who exercised the university's wide civil and criminal jurisdiction, ordered its affairs, and prescribed its discipline: the first of these was Lawrence of Lindores, the Inquisitor. Scotland being thoroughly medieval still, no touch of the new humanism penetrated to the curriculum of St. Andrews. Lawrence of Lindores lectured on the *Sentences* of Peter Lombard, a textbook of the twelfth century; the scientific treatises of Aristotle, in their corrupt Latin version (for no teacher at St. Andrews knew Greek), provided the basis of philosophy; most of the masters were Nominalists.

Faculties at St. Andrews took the University of Paris for their model. *Bajans,* or entering students (most of whom were no more than fifteen years old, and many younger) were presumed to know grammar well enough; they were set to learning logic and rhetoric, and after those subjects, physics, metaphysics, and Aristotle's *Ethics.* A student might attain' the baccalaureate after eighteen months, be capped as a licentiate after four years, and become a master almost immediately thereafter. Eight more years of study were required if one would become a doctor of theology. Lecturers and regents all were clerics, most of tnem holding priests' livings but devoting their time to the college.

In medieval times, nearly all university students were very poor. At St. Andrews, they subsisted on porridge (the oats being fetched from their families' farms) and some fish. Then, as now, students' motives were mixed: some felt a thirst for learning, most desired advancement in society. To become a learned clerk was a way to preferment in Church and State, and humble birth was no obstacle, if one should become a good and useful scholar. Professors and students at the medieval universities came to form an order, or "estate", distinct from other social classes.

St. Andrews University grew. The original College of St. John was eclipsed by the new College of St. Salvator, founded by Bishop Kennedy in 1450. The powerful bishop built handsomely, almost on the scale of Oxford or Cambridge. And he provided for a hierarchy of theologians and artists: a doctor for provost of his college, a licentiate and a bachelor of theology, four priests who would be masters of arts and theological students, and six poor clerks, students of the arts and choristers. These thirteen members of the corporation would officiate at the collegiate church of the Holy Savior; also they would lecture and study. Thirty more chaplaincies were endowed by 1475. By the beginning of the sixteenth century, sixty to eighty undergraduates were studying at St. Salvator's.

Joining worship with the advancement of learning, St.

Salvator's became the model for all higher studies in Scotland. The sharp tower of St. Salvator still dominates the town of St. Andrews, and eighteen generations of scholars have passed through the archway at its foot.

One hundred years after the founding of the university, a third foundation arose: the College of Poor Clerks of the Church of St. Andrews. Its purpose was to educate novices of the Augustinian order, so that St. Andrews Priory might be served by men of learning. In its charter of 1512, establishing this College of Poor Clerks, the decay of the Church in Scotland is mentioned. That affliction could not be hid: for pilgrims no longer came to the shrine of St. Andrew. Rather uneasily, in the college charter this disappearance of pilgrims was attributed to the total triumph of Christian belief: God no longer needs to work miracles at saints' shrines, when all believe in Him.

But in truth, the Scottish Church was deep in disrepute by 1512, and the lack of pilgrims resulted from lack of belief in miraculous cures. From its beginnings, this new St. Leonard's College (as it came to be called) grew out of the decay of faith. It would not be long before this college, meant for a bastion of orthodoxy, would become a nest of Reformers. The phrase "to drink of St. Leonard's well" would signify contagion by Calvinism.

Patrick Hamilton, the first Scots Protestant martyr of the Reformation, was a St. Leonard's man; he was sent to the stake for heresy only sixteen years after the founding of the college. The greatest of Scottish humanists, George Buchanan, a stern Reformer, became principal of St. Leonard's and tutor to the young king. Before St. Leonard's well ran dry, every remnant of the old order that created St. Leonard's had been extirpated.

In 1537, just before the outbreak of the Reformation, Archbishop Beaton secured a papal bull for yet another college, which he built upon the site of the original St. John's. This "College of the Assumption of the Blessed Virgin Mary" remained rigorously scholastic, the Archbishop disregarding the entreaties of the principal, who would have commenced humane studies—Latin, Greek, and Hebrew. The last

Catholic primate of Scotland, Archbishop Hamilton, completed the college. Then the Reformation swept over the place, submerging St. Mary's College along with everything else. The archbishop who completed the building was taken in arms when the Reformers stormed Dumbarton Castle, and they hanged him in his canonical dress upon Stirling rock. After the triumph of the Reformers, the college was directed to the training of ministers, and it remains to this day the university's divinity school.

"The stones cry out to us as we pass," Sir D'Arcy Thompson writes of St. Andrews, "and tell us the story of our land, the chronicle of popes and kings, the history of the Old Church and the New."[6] Beside the University of Paris, he remarks, St. Andrews was a small foundation. Yet Scottish learning would be written large in America.

The northern universities had been created to serve the Church; soon, however, they would serve Renaissance and Reformation—and revolution. In the paving-stones of St. Andrews market place, a stone cross is traced. Here stood the medieval market-cross, and here Paul Craw was burnt in 1433.

Craw, a physician from Bohemia, had been sent by the Hussites of central Europe to disturb the Church in Scotland. The Hussites were social revolutionaries, as well as forerunners of the Protestant Reformers. Bishop Wardlaw, the university's founder, ran Craw to earth in the very year when teaching commenced at St. Andrews University. Urged on by two Schoolmen, the bishop sent Craw to the stake, where he died amidst the flames with a brass ball thrust into his mouth, that he might not harangue the crowd. But more men like Craw would come, as the university grew, and not all of them could be silenced.

In Scotland, as in Germany and other lands, the Reformation would rise out of the universities; so would the Renaissance, in most countries. Thus the Middle Ages' grand intellectual achievement, the universities, became the Middle Ages' undoing. Dante, near the end of medieval times, thought of the universities as a distinct estate equal in influence to State and Church. He called upon the universities to share in the restoration of the medieval order; but shortly after his time, they would turn instead to new modes of thought, soon producing new modes of action.

The half-dozen little American colleges of colonial times would be bare and narrow places, if contrasted with the medieval universities on which they were humbly modelled. Yet *veritas*, Truth, Harvard's motto, was a courageous echo of the high aspiration of the English and Scottish universities. There was more truth to be learned from medieval civilization, in its many aspects, than Harvard or William and Mary College knew at first. Even in its collapse, the medieval order passed on to America its vision of synthesis and harmony.

It is misleading to think chiefly of the Crusades, or of the Hundred Years' War, when one sees the words "Middle Ages." In medieval times, disorder broke out frequently, over that span of a thousand years; nevertheless there endured generally a concept of order that was a high vision, and sometimes the practical achievement of that long age was orderly. The attempt to achieve balance between the claims of Church and the claims of State; the development of civic liberties, of representative assemblies, and, in England, of the common law; the strong feeling of community in church, guild, town, and family—all these were the marks of a healthy culture, however rough its vigor. Renaissance and Reformation would not altogether deprive America of this medieval inheritance.

Notes

[1] Douglas Jerrold, *England: Past, Present, and Future* (London: J.M. Dent, 1950), pp. 23-25.

[2] Henry Maine, *Ancient Law* (London: John Murray, 1897), p. 82.

[3] Steven Runciman, *A History of the Crusades* (Cambridge: Cambridge University Press, 1954), Vol. III, p. 160.

[4] Henry Osborn Taylor, *The Medieval Mind* (fourth edition,

Cambridge, Mass.: Harvard University Press, 1950), Vol. II, pp. 536, 586n.

5 Taylor, *op. cit.*, II, p. 409.

6 D'Arcy Thompson, "St. Andrews", in *Science and the Classics* (Oxford: Oxford University Press, 1940), p. 240.

CHAPTER VII
THE REFORMERS'
DRUM

A Little Lower than the Angels

I n the fifteenth century commenced those sweeping intellectual and social changes which we call Renaissance and
Reformation. The medieval order crumbled, and gradually its
place was taken by a new order of things, which in part per-
sists down to our time.

Medieval civilization attained its highest expression in
Dante Alighieri, at the beginning of the fourteenth century;
for the rest of that century, especially in the south of Europe,
the Age of Faith would dissolve. Dante, the most nobly imaginative of poets since his exemplar Virgil, was an exile from
Florence for the last two decades of his life, seeing all about
him the flood of disorder rising in Italy. Yet knowing that
divine love had created the earth and all the stars, he trusted
in the City of God. Hell itself is necessary to the human condition, he saw in his "high dream"; most of us limp through
Purgatory, here and hereafter; though unworthy, the redeemed will win through to the blinding light of Paradise. Beyond
sin and time, divine order endures forever.*

In *The Divine Comedy* lie two meanings, Dante wrote to Can

---

* The doctrine of Purgatory, a purifying ordeal experienced by
the soul after death, would be rejected by the Protestant Reformers.

Grande della Scala, master of Verona, his protector: literally, its meaning is the state of souls after death; allegorically, the subject of that poem is man's free moral choice of good or evil. Scholastic philosophy and medieval imagery are joined in Dante. His great poem was a synthesis of knowledge, in that he drew his ideas and his images from the Hebrew prophets, the classical philosophers, the Roman jurists, the Schoolmen, even the Arab scholars. Half a century earlier, Saint Thomas Aquinas had given system to Christian and medieval thought: theology, metaphysics, morals, and politics all were summed up in Aquinas' powerful work. In Dante, that same synthesis—that ordering and harmonizing of knowledge and belief—is expressed through poetic insights and symbols. Truth was knowable; order was real. Truth was obscured by man's follies and passions, and order was broken by man's appetites and desire for power. Yet right reason might disclose truth to men's eyes again, and order might be regained by courageous acts of will. Such was the vision of *The Divine Comedy.*

For the most part, the order of the soul is the subject of Dante's tremendous poem. But Dante was a political thinker as well. How might the order of the commonwealth be regained, in the tormented Europe of the late Middle Ages? In his political treatise, *De Monarchia,* Dante sought for the restoration of social unity. The imperial power, the papacy, and the universities must join wholeheartedly in a common conservative undertaking to reaffirm law, truth, and grace. In the new Emperor Henry VII, Dante thought he saw the monarch who might bring about this synthesis in the world of men. But it did not come to pass. After initial successes in his progress through Italy, the German Emperor lost the support of the Pope, Clement V, and failed to pacify the Italian states; he died suddenly at Siena, in 1313. After that, the medieval order gave at the seams.

Social decadence beset fourteenth-century Europe. Nearly every country was ravaged by war, while the Black Death, the plague, depopulated towns and countryside. Public and private morality sank steadily. The feudal structure, that elaborate balance of loyalties, began to collapse between pressures from national monarchs and rising commercial interests, and in the old free cities of the South despots were arising upon the ruins of civic liberty. These things are described in the stanzas of Dante, and they would grow worse after Dante's death. The Age of Faith approached its close, and with it the sense of unity and spiritual community under the medieval ideal of Christendom. No longer would Europe be held together by a common Church, by the international character of its universities, and by a pattern of social ties that grew out of village communities and town guilds. Renaissance and Reformation would rush in to fill this moral and social vacuum left by the withering of medieval civilization.

As the ideal of the Holy Roman Empire, with its German sovereigns, faded in the West, the last vestige of the Byzantine Empire vanished in the East. In the year 1453, Constantinople fell to the Turks. At the end of the Crusades, Greek emperors had regained possession of the scraps of the Byzantine territories. But the stump of the Roman Empire of the East was hacked by the ambitions of the Italian merchant-cities from one side and by the ambitions of the Turkish sultans from the other; Constantine's capital fell at last. The wonder was that it had endured so long—the bastion of classical and Christian civilization for eleven imperial centuries.

As this disaster approached, Byzantine scholars and nobles fled into Italy. There, especially in Florence, they waked the West to a fuller interest in Plato and in the whole heritage of the vanished classical civilization. Philosophy, theology, the arts, and presently politics were deeply affected by this new "humanism" of the Renaissance. This Renaissance—this conscious rebirth of ancient culture—had commenced earlier, but was now accelerated by catastrophic events in the East. Courts, universities, and the papacy itself began to cast aside the medieval synthesis and medieval institutions, that they might enjoy the things of this world.

For although this word "humanism" originally signified an earnest devotion to the Greek classics, as the revelation of ancient forgotten insights, presently the word came to imply a concern for the present and dawning Europe, by contrast with the other-worldliness of medieval philosophy and religion. The Renaissance became many things, but to the medieval order it was death.

In 1486, there arrived at Rome a strange glowing representative of the new humanism, Pico della Mirandola. A son of the princely house of Mirandola (which claimed descent from Constantine the Great), one of the most illustrious of the grand families of the Italian Renaissance, Pico challenged the doctors of the schools to dispute with him on nine hundred grave questions. He was only twenty-four years old, handsome and rich, and he invited all the scholars of the world to join with him in Rome, at his private expense, there to discuss ultimate questions. "By no man was the sublime ideal of humanity, superior to physical enjoyments and dignified by intellectual energy, that triumph of the thought of the Renaissance, more completely realized," John Addington Symonds writes of Pico.[1]

Out of the bulk of the works of Count Giovanni Pico della Mirandola, the only production widely read today is his brief discourse "The Dignity of Man," delivered by him when he came to Rome. This oration, like a glove dashed down in challenge to medieval authority, lives as the most succinct expression of the high dreams of the early Renaissance. The later consequences of his doctrines might have confounded Pico.

From the age of fourteen upward, Pico had studied at the universities of Bologna, Ferrara, Padua, and Paris, becoming immensely erudite, proficient in Greek, Latin, Hebrew, Chaldee, and Arabic—though perhaps more rhetorician than original thinker. Mystic, magician, and scholar, he combined in his character the Gothic complexity of the Middle Ages with the egoism and enlightenment of the Renaissance. He was the most romantic of all the humanists. His titanic intention it was to effect a synthesis of Hebrew, classical, and Christian learning. In this, he was like Dante before him; but the effect of his challenge was divisive rather than integrating. Though he did not repudiate altogether the Schoolmen—Thomas Aquinas, John Duns Scotus, and Albertus Magnus were among those he had studied—he yearned for insights more piercing than theirs.

Among Pico's nine hundred questions were some propositions that hung close upon the brink of heresy. He thought that the secrets of the magicians could confirm the divinity of Christ, and that the Cabala of the medieval Jews (for he had studied under Jewish teachers, too) would sustain the Christian mysteries. Thus haranguing, reading, wandering, preaching, commencing a vast work to confute the enemies of Christianity, he spent his life, dying of a fever when barely thirty-one—though by that time he had abjured the world and the flesh, and planned to roam barefoot as an evangelist.

Now this precocious genius' "Dignity of Man" is the manifesto of humanism. Man regenerate—"this, visibly," Egon Freidell says, "is the primary meaning of the Renaissance: the rebirth of man in the likeness of God." The man of the Middle Ages had been humble, conscious almost always of his fallen sinful nature, feeling himself watched by a wrathful God. Through pride fell the angels. But Pico and his brother-humanists declared that man was only a little lower than the angels, a being capable of descending to unclean depths, indeed, but also having it within his power to become godlike. How marvellous and splendid a creature is man! This is the theme of Pico's oration, elaborated with all the pomp and confidence that characterized theorizing humanist teachers. "In this idea," continues Freidell, "there lay a colossal *hybris* unknown to the Middle Ages, but also a tremendous spiritual impulse such as only modern times can show."[2]

Man might make himself almost the equal of the heavenly hosts, the cherubim and seraphim, Pico taught, should man cultivate ardently his intellectual faculty. It is the spirit, the spark of Godhood, that raises man above all the rest of creation and makes him distinct in kind from all other corporeal things. Yet for all his glorification of man, Pico had no touch of the modern notion that "man makes himself" wholly, or that an honest god's the noblest work of man. It is only because man has been created in the image of God that man can become almost angelic. In his generosity, God has said to man, "We have made thee neither of heaven nor of earth, neither mortal nor immortal, so that with freedom of choice

225

and with honor, as though the maker and moulder of thyself, thou mayest fashion thyself in whatever shape thou shalt prefer. Thou shalt have the power to degenerate into the lower forms of life, which are brutish. Thou shalt have the power, out of thy soul's judgment, to be reborn into the higher forms, which are divine."

This is the essence of Christian humanism, which spread out of Italy unto the whole of Europe, reaching its culmination in Erasmus of the Netherlands and Thomas More of England. God had given man immense powers, and with those powers, free will. Man might take pride rightfully in his higher nature, and turn his faculties to the praise and improvement of his own kind. A world of discovery lay before the Renaissance humanists. Yet all this dignity of human nature was the gift of God: if the spiritual and rational powers are neglected, Pico and those like him knew, man must sink to the level of the brutes. The humanist does not seek to dethrone God. Instead, through the moral disciplines of *humanitas,* the classical heritage of humane learning, he struggles upward toward the Godhead.

So a degree of humility chastened the pride of many humanists. But the seed of intellectual arrogance, overweening self-confidence, was sown. A time would come when man would take himself for the be-all and end-all. By "the dignity of man," Pico meant the high nobility of disciplined reason and imagination, human nature as redeemed by Christ, the uplifting of the truly human person through an exercise of soul and mind. He did not mean a sensate triumph or an egoistic materialism. Pico believed that no man can dignify himself, for dignity is a quality with which one is *invested*: it must be conferred. For human dignity to exist, there must be a Master who can raise man above the brute creation. If that Master is denied, then dignity for man is unattainable.

Platonist and Christian and sorcerer and rhetorician, Pico designed his nine hundred questions as an irrefragable proof of man's uniqueness. Emerson would echo him, five centuries later:

> There are two laws discrete
> Not reconciled—

Law for man, and law for thing;
The last builds town and fleet,
But it runs wild,
And doth the man unking.

To make man kingly, even angelic—this was Pico's hope, and
the hope of other humanists. If Things were to be thrust out of
the saddle, and man mounted (in Pico's phrase) to "join battle as to the sound of a trumpet of war" on behalf of man's
higher nature, then some must go barefoot through the
world, preaching against the vegetative and sensual errors of
the time. Of the saint and the knight, of Francis of Assisi and
John of Brienne, there is a strong echo in this exhortation.

But Pico was no pillar of orthodoxy. He declared that
crosses and images ought not to be venerated; on the doctrine
of sin, he tended more toward Saint Augustine's adversary
Pelagius than toward the approved teaching of the Church,
saying that sin is a force shaping human nature; he doubted
whether Christ had descended literally into Hell; and though
he argued that astrology was a false science, he believed in an
arcane magical knowledge. Near the end of his life, he would
join Savonarola, the fanatic preacher of repentance, a precur-
sor of the Reformation—and might have been burnt with
Savonarola, had he lived long enough.

Even as it was, the pope would not permit this bewildering
Count Mirandola to argue his nine hundred questions in the
Eternal City, and for seven years Pico was investigated for
heresy. In 1493, he was purged of this charge by a brief of
Pope Alexander VI. That Alexander VI—Roderigo Borgia, a
Spaniard, before he had obtained the papal throne by
bribery—should find Pico blameless was an irony of the
Renaissance.

For Pope Alexander was a monster of avarice, lust, and
cruelty. With him, the papacy had sunk to its nadir. He
gathered riches by selling church offices—and then slowly
poisoned the dignitaries he had appointed, that he might sell
the posts again. "Every night they find in Rome four or five
murdered men, bishops and prelates and so forth," the Venetian ambassador to the Holy See wrote home in the year 1500.

When Alexander had been elevated to the papacy, the

humanists had rejoiced: here was a pontiff who would patronize arts and learning, who would enjoy to the full the good things of this world. Indeed Alexander VI did enjoy the world and the flesh, after his fashion, even though in theology he remained orthodox enough.

This merciless pope was a product of the darkest corner of the Renaissance. He courted the alliance of the sultan of Turkey against Christian rulers; his passion it was to advance his bastard sons, by murder and slaughter; he was the father of Caesar Borgia, but he sat in judgment on the visionary Pico della Mirandola. Alexander VI was considerably lower than the angels: the Roman populace believed he had made a pact with Satan. Yet Alexander sat where Gregory the Great had sat once. It was no wonder that soon Martin Luther rose up against Rome and the Renaissance: Luther's one visit to Rome would make a world of difference.

Much of the hopefulness for man's improvement that Pico had expressed would enter into Americans' beliefs, three centuries later. But otherwise there is little connection between the Renaissance and American beginnings. Early America had neither the wealth nor the leisure for splendid cultivation of the arts or of letters—and no fine libraries, no monumental architecture, no churchly or noble patrons of culture. Rather, colonial America generally shared the Reformers' destestation of Renaissance notions and ways. The early Renaissance they rejected as the blending of a resurrection of licentious paganism with a corrupted Catholicism.

Dante had prayed for a reunion of the political power, the intellectual power, and the churchly power of the medieval order: his prayers had gone unanswered. Pico had designed that the *pax philosophica,* the peace of the lovers of wisdom, should succeed the *pax romana* of old Roman imperial times and the *pax Christi* of the early Church: the appetites of the Renaissance had undone him. Now in Germany, where the egoism and the innovation of the Renaissance only had begun to work, there would speak out a Christian reformer, very much a medieval man himself in the beginning, whose stand would bring on the final dissolution of the medieval world.

In 1503, Alexander VI died hideously—of poison that he

had intended for someone else, the story went; in Rome there was general rejoicing. When that event occurred, there was studying at the University of Erfurt an earnest young man from a German peasant family, Martin Luther; his father, expecting him to become a lawyer, soon would present him with a set of the *Corpus Juris.* "What shall a man do to be saved?" Luther was asking himself; he disdained membership in the circle of humanists at the university. To the sixteenth century, Luther would bring not peace, but a sword. Pico had put nine hundred questions to the old Church; they had gone unanswered. Luther would publish ninety-five reforming theses; those the Church could not ignore. They would be condemned, and then drums would begin to beat.

The Priesthood of All Believers

In the beginning, America was Protestant: that point has been emphasized by every historian of the United States. Therefore we turn to the doctrines and the mentality and the social characteristics of what we call Protestantism—or rather, of certain types of Reformers. But also we need to remind ourselves that when we call early America Protestant, we mean that America was Christian. The fundamental Christian convictions discussed in earlier chapters of this book were not undone at the Reformation. Instead, certain of those beliefs received a renewed emphasis from Luther, Calvin, Zwingli, and the other Reformers. Occasionally one finds American cultural historians declaring that the New England Puritans believed in the sinfulness of man—and so phrasing this sound statement that one might be led to think the doctrine of original sin somehow peculiar to early New England. But other Protestant sects took for granted the fact of man's proclivity to sin; so did the Roman Catholic Church of the Counter-Reformation; so did the medieval Church; so did the Fathers of the Church; so did Jesus; so did the Jews and the Hebrew prophets.

In this, as in other major doctrines, Protestantism was not

a new religion, but a very old one. The Protestant Reformers believed that they were reasserting and reviving the teachings of the early Church of Christ. Late in the twentieth century, the Christian understanding of order is challenged by ideas and forces that would have been anathema to both Protestants and Catholics of the Reformation and the Counter-Reformation; and some of the differences in doctrine between Catholics and Protestants of the sixteenth century, or the differences among various Protestant sects of that age, look small enough to twentieth-century eyes.

The vast majority of people in the Thirteen Colonies professed the Christian religion in one or another of its Protestant aspects—chiefly in Anglicanism, in Puritanism (an offshoot of Calvinism), or in Presbyterianism (another outgrowth of Calvinism). So we examine here some of the differences between Catholics and Protestants of the sixteenth century, and among various Protestant communions. This should be borne in mind: despite the ferocity of the Wars of Religion, the similarities among various Christian bodies are more important than their differences, where we have to do with questions of the order of the soul and of the commonwealth. Hideously though Catholics and Protestants often dealt with one another, still their understanding of man and of society had come from one Christian root.

The Protestant and Catholic Reformations of the sixteenth century both were reactions against the excesses of the Renaissance. For that intellectual and artistic and social movement called the Renaissance amounted, often, to a denial of the Christian understanding of the human condition. The Renaissance exalted man's egoism, in defiance of Christian teachings of humility, charity, and community. The Renaissance gloried in fleshly pleasures—in what Luther, like Saint Augustine and Saint Paul before him, called "concupiscence"—as against the old austere morality of sincere Christians. The Renaissance accepted the crafty "power politics" of Machiavelli, as distinguished from the Christian political theories of justice and freedom and order that had prevailed from the time of Gregory the Great to the time of Dante. The Renaissance, a conscious rediscovery of classical civilization, essentially was pagan in its view of human nature; and the Reformation (or Reformations), though curiously interwoven with the influences that brought on the Renaissance, essentially was the wrathful protest of Christians against the rise of an anti-Christian culture. This is true both of the Protestant Reformation that commenced with Luther's Theses in 1517 and of the Catholic Counter-Reformation that commenced institutionally with the Council of Trent in 1545.

With the Renaissance's triumphs and excesses, the visible Church had become closely connected. The popes of the early Renaissance, and many of the great ecclesiastics and the clergy throughout Christendom, far from offering coherent resistance to the Renaissance spirit, often had made themselves eager patrons of the new culture—and shared often in Renaissance pride and vice. Indeed, the most immediate cause of Luther's revolt against the papacy was the Renaissance luxuriousness of Pope Leo X, who required enormous sums of money, in part to pay for his grand patronage of the arts of the Renaissance. To obtain those funds, the papacy sold indulgences—"Papal Tickets," written pardons for sins—with scandalous eagerness. This wholesale misuse of the authority that Jesus had conferred upon Peter provoked the rigorous monk Luther, in 1517, to challenge papal policy with his Ninety-five Theses. Luther intended merely a scholastic debate, but he produced a revolution.

So it was that the Protestant Reformation came to pass when the visible Church lay in decadence. During the thousand years of medieval Christendom, the Church had decayed in morality and intellect from time to time, but repeatedly had been renewed from within by a series of austere inspired churchmen—most of them founders of new religious orders. By the beginning of the sixteenth century, however, a decline of ecclesiastical virtue coincided with other tremendous changes—with the Renaissance challenge to Christian faith and morals, with the beginning of the Commercial Revolution and the discovery of the New World, with the rise of nationalism and despotism in most of Europe. Had not the medieval social order itself been dissolving, Martin Luther might have become one more of those churchmen of genius who in earlier times had purged and reinvigorated the medieval Church. Instead, by design of providence or by historical accident, Luther and his followers were separated from Roman authority and produced the division of Christians into Protestant and Catholic camps—which promptly converted themselves into armed camps.

We cannot trace the course of the Reformation in these few pages; all we can do, with a view to suggesting the influence of Protestantism upon American order, is to sketch the principal doctrines of the Protestant Reformers, and later to describe the course of the Reformation in Britain through the lives of a few men of thought and action. What commenced as a debate about theological questions and church discipline soon made an open breach in Christendom; and there followed a century and a half of devastation, the Wars of Religion, Catholic against Protestant and one Protestant sect against another. In the name of the Son of Man, the Redeemer, zealots took the sword against other Christians, illustrating practically the Christian dogma that all men are sinners. Yet out of that long agony of religious fanaticism (mingled with national political rivalries, class warfare, and ruthless private ambitions) emerged the religious pluralism and toleration of the United States.

What were the knottiest questions dividing the Catholic establishment and the Reformers? The Protestant leaders, though they attacked the corruptions of the sixteenth-century Church, argued that the visible Church's moral decay was the result of theological errors into which the papacy and the hierarchy had fallen. Both Martin Luther and John Calvin declared that the most profound difference between Papists and Protestants was the question of freedom of the will. Luther debated this subject with the Dutch humanist Erasmus, in 1524. Is the will free or enslaved? This is "the essential thing, the real knotty problem," Luther said; "instead of . . . tiresome trifles about the papacy, purgatory, indulgences, and other futilities of the same order."

Now the medieval Church, with Aristotle as its classical

philosophical authority, gradually had modified Saint Augustine's doctrine that man is wholly corrupt—that so far as man has free will, this is opportunity only to choose among evil acts. Man is a creature of mingled good and evil impulses, the Church had come to teach: in the depths of the soul, there lingers an essence or spark of divine substance, potentially enabling man (if given grace) to exercise his will for good. This medieval teaching, which runs through Dante's great poem, the Reformers denied utterly; they returned to the stern teaching of Saint Augustine. "For man cannot but put self-seeking first, loving himself above everything else," said Luther: "this is the root of his sinning."

Because man is utterly corrupted by self-love, the Reformers reasoned, man enjoys no freedom to act for the good. He can be saved from his total depravity only by the arbitrary grace of God. Because the Church, or rather its hierarchy, had fallen away from this dogma, the Reformers continued, the Church had been corrupted: the notorious system of indulgences for money was merely one of many abuses resulting from abandonment of the pure doctrine of original sin. Therefore the Church might be purged of corruption only if its ancient dogmas should be restored.

In the Middle Ages, the Church had taught that man can be saved both by faith and by good works. That good works—charitable and self-sacrificing acts—can be a means to salvation of the soul, the Reformers denied also. True faith in God should produce obedience to the moral law, and should result in good works; yet good moral choices and works are merely by-products, so to speak, of grace and faith. So the reformers demanded that the Church abandon the elaborate structure of penances and good works and absolving of sins that had been built up during a thousand years.

This controversy over freedom of the will, and over faith and works, was fundamental to the contest between Catholics and Protestants; yet many other points of doctrine and liturgy were as hotly disputed. Back of all these doctrinal clashes of the sixteenth century, as seen in the perspective of the twentieth century, there lay a profound disagreement concerning the source of true Christian belief. For truth, the Catholics turned to Authority; for truth, the Protestants turned to Private Judgment.

By Authority, the Catholics meant the teaching authority of the whole Church, over the centuries, as expressed in Scripture, in tradition, in the works of the Fathers and Doctors of the Church, in the consensus of church councils, in the sayings and acts of saints, in papal decretals. By Private Judgment, the Protestants meant the individual Christian's interpretation of the Bible, in the light of conscience, for the guiding of his actions. Thus Protestantism was intensely Biblical, believing that every man must come to know fully the Old Testament and the New, for the tutoring of his conscience. So the tendency of Catholicism, as presently it would be formulated at the Council of Trent in denial of Protestant theses, was toward a tightly-structured authoritative church and a close-knit society; while the tendency of Protestantism was toward religious and social individualism.

To simplify and purify, to cast off the immense weight of the institutional Church and return to the teachings and practices of an earlier Christianity—this was the hope of the Protestant Reformers. Martin Luther gave vigor to the movement of reform, and John Calvin gave it system. In 1535, at Basel, in Switzerland, Calvin published his *Institutes of the Christian Religion,* which would become the Protestants' intellectual artillery. "If Luther stands with the giants of religious intuition—Paul, Augustine, Bernard of Clairvaux, George Fox—Calvin is in line with the great doctors and princes of the church—Tertullian, Athanasius, Gregory the Great, Thomas Aquinas, Hooker, Bellarmine," J. S. Whale writes. "Indeed, what Aquinas did for classic Catholicism in his *Summa,* Calvin did for classic Protestantism in his *Institutio.*"[3] From Germany and Switzerland, the passionate arguments of Luther and Calvin would spread speedily to France, to Britain, to Scandinavia; for some years, it seemed as if even the Mediterranean countries might be fertile ground for Protestant evangelism.

By 1536, already the Roman Church and the Holy Roman Emperor and the Catholic kings were striving to put down the Reformers; already the Protestant princes of the

Germanies had taken up arms on behalf of Reform. Already there had arisen Protestant sects, the Anabaptists especially, far more radical than the Lutherans and the Calvinists, and already Luther and Calvin had found it necessary to denounce reforming extremists. But the fierce intricate history of Reformation and Counter-Reformation in the Continent cannot be related here.

Within a few decades, papal authority would be overthrown totally throughout northern Europe. The Empire would be riven asunder. In the north, the monastic system, with its immense landholdings and organized charities, would be violently dissolved; in several countries, even the episcopal structure would vanish or be reduced to the shadow of a shade. Dante's aspiration for an harmonious universal order, with imperial and churchly power coordinate, would be effaced altogether. The fight between Protestant and Catholic would be waged in the New World, too; and in most of North America, with the eventual victory of the English, Protestantism would triumph.

From the sixteenth century onward, northern Europe would be dominated intellectually and morally by what has been called "the Protestant ethic"—which survives, however weakened, to our own time. This Protestant ethic, or "value-system", became intertwined with the expanding commercial economy of the north, and with the fast-growing middle classes of society, and with the emergent nationalism of the northern kingdoms and principalities. The Protestant ethic helped to form this new society, but it is more than the reflection of a new social order.

The Protestant ethic is rooted in what Luther called "the priesthood of all believers." Every man, if he has burning faith in Christ and is granted even one momentary experience of divine grace, may enjoy that communion with God which the medieval priesthood had restricted to its own numbers. Christians require pastors or ministers, indeed, to instruct and guide them—but not as a priestly class set apart, for sincere Christians, if they have faith, require no intermediary with God. As Dillenberger and Welch put this Lutheran concept, "The universal priesthood means that each man is a priest to every other; he can, in Luther's words, be a Christ to his neighbor."[4]

So the Protestant (or Evangelical) divines taught; and as they swept away monk and priest, so they abolished all the medieval sacraments but two—baptism and the Lord's Supper. Study the Scriptures; search your conscience; follow in the steps of Christ; pray earnestly that the grace of God may be extended unto you: so, God willing, may you be saved from the body of this death. "To believe in God is to go down on your knees," said Luther.

Out of such convictions developed what we may call a Protestant character. Self-reliance was encouraged, for in a sense every believer was compelled to judge of the Scriptures' meaning for himself, rather than looking to Authority. Self-examination and introspection developed, because every man should be perpetually searching his own conscience, for his soul's salvation; and this tendency often produced a certain censoriousness of other people's actions. Among Calvinists especially, indications that God had chosen a man to be saved were eagerly sought after; it was popularly supposed that one such indication might be a man's success in his worldly vocation, made possible providentially—so hard work and material accomplishment tended to be approved. The cloistered life of medieval times having been rejected, godly endeavor in the secular world was emphasized in its stead.

Politically, the tendency of Protestantism was toward democracy. Luther preached obedience to legitimate princes; Calvin established at Geneva a kind of aristocratic republic of virtue, governed in effect by presbyters (ministers and elders of the church). Yet the idea of the priesthood of all believers gradually would be transferred from the realm of religion to the realm of politics. The presbyterian form of Calvinism especially would become a forerunner of democratic institutions, even though in the beginning it had more nearly resembled the ancient Hebrew concept of theocracy.

This Protestant cast of mind and social view would dominate England's Thirteen Colonies. Did the Protestant spirit then create American civilization? One must beware of possible exaggeration. Had the bulk of the early settlers on

236

the Atlantic seaboard been Roman Catholics rather than Calvinists and Anglicans, would the shape of American society have been unrecognizably different? The Catholic minority in Maryland, or the French Catholics of Canada whom British victories brought within Britain's colonial structure, did not live an existence radically dissimilar from that of the dominant Protestant colonists.

Suppose that massive Catholic Irish migration to America had occurred in the seventeenth and eighteenth centuries, rather than in the nineteenth; suppose farther that this transplanting had been conducted under English law and within the frame of English political institutions, the Irish Catholics nevertheless being accorded complete religious toleration—as, after the English victory at Quebec, the British government would extend such toleration to the Catholic French of Canada. In such hypothetical circumstances, would not America then have developed socially much as it actually did develop with a Protestant population? Economic growth might have been somewhat slower in such conditions, and surely New England's republican tendencies would have been less pronounced; still, perhaps these hypothetical Catholic colonies, by 1775, would have become rather like the actual Protestant colonies in 1775.

So it is somewhat more true to say that the Christian spirit, rather than the Protestant spirit only, helped to create American civilization. Be that as it may, Edmund Burke was fairly accurate when he declared to the House of Commons that the Americans represented the Protestantism of the Protestant religion, and the dissidence of dissent. The jealousy for their civil liberties which the American colonial population displayed was bound up with their Protestant heritage, and the readiness of many of them to break with royal and parliamentary authority had its earlier counterpart in Protestant rejection of papal authority. In New England at least, the framework of local government had certain Calvinistic roots. Assiduous reading of the Bible cultivated a faculty of private judgment and self-reliance in colonial America. And the feebleness of the Church of England's establishment in America (partly because the bishops of Lon-

THE ROOTS OF AMERICAN ORDER

don, in whose spiritual charge the colonies lay, could not readily ordain colonials as Anglican clergymen) would leave America more dissenting in religion than otherwise the colonists might have been. All this being so, the events and ideas of the Reformation in the Old World remain relevant to our study of American order.

The Protestant Reformation occurred in the sixteenth century; something of the sort almost had happened a hundred years earlier, but then had been put down or restricted in its scope. In Britain, the Lollards, followers of John Wycliffe, had been suppressed only with much difficulty. In central Europe, the followers of John Huss (burnt as a heretic in 1415) had maintained their faith successfully against royal and papal forces. The Hussites' most talented general had been John Zizka, who had commanded in the field for three years after he had lost his eyesight. When their blind leader died of the plague in 1424, his followers used his skin to cover a drum, so that Zizka still would summon the Hussites to arms. Just a century after that skin drum was made, Protestant drums began to sound in the German states. From 1525 onward, Catholic and Protestant fifes and drums ecclesiastic would echo from the Alps to the bogs of Ireland, until general exhaustion and disillusion brought an end to the Wars of Religion.

Our immediate concern here is with the new churches that were established in England and Scotland, and with dissent from those churches: American thought and patterns of government took form amidst those church controversies. The English Reformation bears the stamp of Richard Hooker; the Scottish, of John Knox.

England's Middle Path

"Muddling through," it is said, has been England's method for meeting public difficulties. By comparison with the domestic struggles of other modern nations, surely, the English civil social order had been kept in tolerable balance through a principle called "moderation." The English talent for healing compromise, for avoiding extremes, for reconciling opposed factions, is not the least of England's contributions to American order. And Americans learned something of moderation not only from English political institutions, but also from the English national church that took form during the Reformation.

Yet moderation scarcely was a virtue of the belligerent king who overthrew papal authority and destroyed the English monasteries. Henry VIII was an able monarch of powerful appetites and a short way with dissenters. He was no Protestant: because of Henry's fierceness against Lutherans, the pope had styled him "Defender of the Faith"—until Henry's Spanish queen failed to bear him a male heir. To secure his dynasty, Henry demanded a divorce, for reasons of state; the pope could not grant it; then Henry broke with Rome, proclaiming himself supreme head of the Church in England, and dissolving the monasteries to seize their wealth.

In medieval times, the popes had found it possible to put down such defiance by excommunicating kings and imposing acts of interdict upon offending realms. But the medieval awe of papal authority was dissolving; the Tudor sovereigns of England were more strongly entrenched in power than any medieval king had been; and the spirit of Reform, already spread to England, reinforced Henry's assumption of churchly power. By the year 1534, Henry had separated the English Church altogether from Rome.

The old order of the Church did not lack for martyrs. Sir Thomas More, the wisest and best man in England, Henry's lord chancellor, refused to submit to the king's denial of papal authority: Henry sent him to the scaffold, where More died declaring himself the king's good servant—but God's first. In Yorkshire and Lancashire, clergy, nobles, gentry, and people rose against Henry's schism, in an armed protest called the Pilgrimage of Grace; Henry crushed them, at first by deceit, then by executions. The king would have his rough way, and the Church of England arose—though not at first a Protestant church.

The succeeding reign of Edward VI, Henry's son, controlled by Protestant noblemen, was indeed a triumph of Protestantism; but Edward died after only six years. There followed him Henry's Catholic daughter Mary, who for five years persecuted the Protestants. Then there came to the throne Henry's younger daughter, Elizabeth, and with her the pendulum swung back to Protestantism.

Under Elizabeth, the Church of England took permanent shape through the statement of belief called the Thirty-Nine Articles and through the Book of Common Prayer, a ritual prescribed for all churches. In the reign of Elizabeth's successor, James I, the Authorized Version of the English Bible, with its splendor of language, would extend its influence beyond Anglicans to the whole range of English-speaking Protestants. What had emerged was a national church differing from Rome and differing from Geneva, neither wholly Catholic nor wholly Protestant.

Despite repeated persecutions of one party or another, this English Reformation of the sixteenth century had been accomplished with less domestic violence than the religious struggles of the Continent had produced: the power of the Tudor sovereigns had postponed a total civil war, though that disruption would occur in the seventeenth century. Queen Elizabeth endeavored to hold to a middle path, granting something to Protestants and something to Catholic subjects; she succeeded through the intellect of Richard Hooker, a philosopher of moderation. It is Hooker, rather than Henry VIII, who deserves to be called the founder of the Church of England.

The divines of the Church of England, or Anglican theologians, affirmed the primacy of the Bible, but declared also that church tradition should be respected, when it did not conflict with Scripture. The central truth of Christianity, they agreed with Lutherans and Calvinists, was the Incarnation—that Christ was God made man; but they would not accept fully the Protestant concepts of justification by faith alone, of predestination, or other radical departures from medieval Christian teaching. The Church of England claimed to be the Catholic Church in its national English form, and in several respects it abided by ancient ways. The Anglicans distinguished between "fundamentals" and "accessories" in Christian worship—that is, between things necessary for salvation and things convenient in religious practice: they refused to join the Protestants of the Continent or of Scotland in making a clean sweep of the old ritual and liturgy, finding much that was convenient and valuable in the traditions and customs of the old Church.

Hooker and the Anglicans who followed him deliberately sought after moderation and balance—after what came to be called the *via media*, the middle way. For Hooker, this middle path was no mere splitting of the difference, no uneasy compromise of the moment: rather, it resembled Aristotle's golden mean, the prudent avoiding of extremes so that faith might be both strong and temperate. Queen Elizabeth and the Stuart kings of the seventeenth century would be severe enough from time to time upon Catholics and Dissenters, true; yet by comparison with the religious intolerance of the Continent, the Anglican establishment was relatively mild. The Anglican concept of moderation would contribute substantially, if in a subtle way, to practical religious toleration in eighteenth- and nineteenth-century America.

Richard Hooker deserves close study—in part because the Anglicans or Episcopalians (and the Methodists who in the eighteenth century branched off from Anglicanism) had much to do with the forming of American thought and custom, and in part because his principles retain enduring value in their own right. In the Christian humanist Hooker, the right reason of Thomas Aquinas was joined with the renewing vigor of the Reformation.

Very unlike Martin Luther and John Calvin and John Knox, the "judicious Hooker" was a mild scholar, withdrawn from public affairs while he wrote his powerful book; yet his understanding of the principles of a good society was clearer than that of any of his contemporaries. In Elizabeth's reign, strong peril existed that the infant Church of England might surrender to the "Geneva men," the English Presbyterians who had sought refuge in Calvin's Swiss city during their persecution by Mary Tudor. Calvin's English disciples would have abolished bishops and all "Romish" ceremonies; they would have set up in England the law of the Scriptures, through local courts composed of the devout—enforcing, incidentally, the Mosaic penalty of death for blasphemy, adultery, murder, and heresy. The Bible was the sole source of truth, the Geneva men proclaimed: all life, private and public, must be regulated by the Bible's ordinances. Whatever was prescribed in Scripture must be observed to the letter, and whatever was not mentioned in Holy Writ must be cast aside.

Half a century later, the Puritans of Massachusetts Bay would endeavor to establish a commonwealth almost identical with that advocated by Thomas Cartright and other Presbyterians or Puritans (those labels then being almost identical) during Elizabeth's reign. That American attempt would be abandoned after a short experience of its difficulties; a similar endeavor at Biblical rule by the Lord's elect failed in Scotland, too. Richard Hooker knew how impractical the Geneva scheme must be, if applied to the realm of England.

 He set himself, therefore, to writing a treatise in eight books, *Of the Laws of Ecclesiastical Polity*, of which he published the first four books in 1594. This is a work of religious philosophy, rather than of theology strictly; its political theories have outlasted the immediate controversies that brought forth the treatise. Hooker's arguments, like his prose style, came to permeate Anglican discourse from that time forward, and would be familiar—if only in paraphrase, sometimes—to nearly all educated men in eighteenth-century America. Here we discuss principally certain ideas of Hooker's that passed into American social assumptions. They are his concepts of law, of continuity, of constitutional liberty, and of tolerance.

All creation is governed by law, Hooker argued, implying clearly that a misapprehension of law had led the Geneva men into confusion and error. There exists Eternal Law, "that order by which God before all ages hath set down with Himself, for Himself to do all things by." There is the Law of "Natural Agents," which operates upon creatures that are not rational. There is the Law of God for angels—that is, for discarnate intelligences. And there is the Law of God for man, made known through Scripture, but not through Scripture only.

The Geneva men had maintained that God's law for man may be found only in the Bible: this argument Hooker demolishes so systematically that even the Puritan theologians and preachers made only feeble attempts to defend it thereafter. Drawing from Aristotle and from Aquinas, Hooker demonstrates that we may know the Law Rational—accessible to our natural reason. This reason enables us to discern certain ethical principles and to understand that God exists. The Law of Reason prevailed, indeed, before Revelation occurred.

Man is rational; but also man is rebellious and depraved, and his evil impulses cannot be controlled by the Law Rational alone. If men are to live in society, there must be provided checks upon their wills and appetites. Scripture, though unerring, does not furnish a complete set of rules by which men may govern themselves in all circumstances and ages. Therefore men have developed, and submitted themselves to, what Hooker calls the Law Positive—enacted law, that is, law enforced by the commonwealth. To set aside that positive law would be to ruin all civil social order.

Although the Law of Reason is universal, positive law—including church polity—varies from land to land and age to age. It would be a disastrous error to try to impose upon all people and eras some uniform set of legal imperatives: the kingdom of England is not the kingdom of Israel. And if all truth is supposed to be contained in Scripture—why, then there can have been no King Henry VIII, for he is not mentioned in Holy Writ.

This analysis of law leads Hooker to examine the origins of government. People combine to form a state, he reasons, from two motives: "to seek communion and fellowship with others"; and to restrain man's depravity, for "to take away all mutual grievances, injuries and wrongs there was no way but only by growing unto composition and agreement amongst themselves by ordaining some kind of government public and by yielding themselves subject thereunto." In general, submission to government is voluntary, and laws are valid only if the whole people assent to them; although some governments have originated in force, the civil social order is no conspiracy of the strong against the weak, but instead a willing cooperation. Here Hooker advances a kind of "social compact" theory, but it is not the same as John Locke's later idea of the social compact, and is very different indeed from the notion of the social contract that Jean Jacques Rousseau would present in the eighteenth century.

Before government existed, Hooker believes, men were not altogether anarchic, because even then they possessed the moral law, the Law Rational; but the political state offers mankind a far better security and comfort than primitive "freedom" without positive law could afford. It is impossible to know the terms of the original contract of society, Hooker continues; therefore we abide by written law and custom—by what Burke later would call "the chartered rights of Englishmen."

Once men have entered into a social compact, they are not at liberty to disobey the Law Positive or to dissolve the state at their pleasure. A people may, indeed, improve the positive law on the basis of their experience and their present need, for the Law Positive (unlike the moral law) is not immutable, nor should it be. But improvement of laws is very different from overturning the state. If a government is unjust or negligent, the people may petition and remonstrate, but to make a social revolution is extreme medicine.

"The general and perpetual voice of men is as the sentence of God himself," Hooker writes. This judgment is far from identical with the argument of some democrats that "the voice of the people is the voice of God." Rather, Hooker means that divine revelation works through the experience of mankind under God. Over thousands of years, a people learn certain truths about the personal and the public order: mankind forms a consensus of opinion on certain vital matters. It is not simply the people living in any one year whose opinions we must consult, but more amply the conclusions of all the generations that have preceded us in time—a kind of filtered wisdom of the human species. Here, as in much else, Hooker reasserts a conviction of the medieval Schoolman Bernard of Chartres, who declared that we moderns are dwarfs standing on the shoulders of giants: we can see farther than our ancestors did only because we have the vast advantage of their experience and their reflection. "The general and perpetual voice of men" signifies the common understanding of the human condition that men have derived from ages of existence in community; it is "common sense", the body of wisdom upon which all sensible people agree.

So Hooker is a convincing exponent of the idea of continuity—of the principle that in concerns of both church and state, we must seek to link generation with generation. Churches and states are immortal corporations: if we break down established laws, thriving customs, and beloved ceremonies, we rashly ignore the lessons of the past and endanger society's future. Our religion, our culture, and our political rights all are maintained by continuity: by our respect for the accomplishments of our forefathers, and by our concern for posterity's well-being. Just as the individual human body can survive only if its vital continuity is maintained during its processes of organic change, so the Church and the civil social order must perish unless law and custom remain the same from year to year, decade to decade, century to century. Any man is foolish who disregards the beneficent incorporation of society, which goes on though individuals perish; for it is not in the power of anyone to create a new church or a new society out of whole cloth.

Out of continuity grows the good political constitution. Here Hooker resists the demand of Presbyter and Puritan for a universal uniform pattern of politics. Kingship is not commanded in Scripture, Hooker points out; different forms of government may be beneficial in varying circumstances; but any tolerable government must be consonant with a nation's historical experience. He supports earnestly the constitutional monarchy of England, founded upon voluntary assent of the people to the laws; he re-expresses the venerable English juridical principle that the king is subordinate to the laws. Such a constitution does not diminish liberty, but protects it, for the power of the sovereign is limited by the constitutional framework.

Within the realm, Hooker would tolerate a considerable range of opinion and custom; within the Church of England, there is room for some divergence of practice. General peace and freedom are preserved by persuasion and discussion. As F. J. Foakes-Jackson observes, Hooker was "fighting the battle of toleration and progress, to which the assertion of infallibility (whether by Puritans or Papists) must oppose an insurmountable barrier. Circumstances tended, in after days, to cause posterity, rightly or wrongly, to identify puritanism with civil and religious liberty; but the demand for the establishment of a discipline, rigidly defined and sanctioned by the unerring voice of Scripture, must, if granted, have meant ecclesiastical stagnation and tyranny."[5]

Hooker's temperate and learned treatise averted for a time such stagnation and tyranny. "There will come a time," Hooker wrote, "when three words uttered with charity and meekness shall receive a far more blessed reward than three thousand volumes written with disdainful sharpness of wit." Few polemicists of the day except Hooker himself heeded that admonition. But Hooker won the intellectual battle of the sixteenth century in England, shy and retiring clergyman though he was.

His book so shored up the tottering new Church of England that it would endure through even the civil wars and revolutions of the next century: Hooker marked out the *via media*. Presbyterians and Puritans respected his power of mind, if grudgingly; and the pope himself was lost in admiration on reading *Of the Laws of Ecclesiastical Polity.* "There is no learning that this man hath not searched into," said Clement VIII, himself a moderate and reforming ecclesiastic. "This man indeed deserves the name of an author; his books will get reverence by age, for there is in them such seeds of eternity, that if the rest be like this, they shall last until the last fire shall consume all learning."

Hooker's understanding of the benign character of law, of historical and cultural continuity, of constitutional government, and of prudent toleration would persist even among most leaders of the American Revolution—whether or not they had been reared as Anglicans, for Hooker's arguments penetrated beyond the communion of the Church of England. Many Americans (though not most New Englanders) acquired their early concepts of human nature and of the civil social order from the Elizabethan Book of Common Prayer, which Hooker's defense of the *via media* secured as the basic ecclesiastical teaching of reformed England.

In an age of absolutism and fanaticism, Richard Hooker (that "poor obscure English priest," as Pope Clement called him) had expressed afresh the great tradition of things spiritual and things temporal, as earlier it had been developed by Plato and Aristotle, by Saint Paul and Saint Augustine, and by the Schoolmen: that knowledge of the relations between the soul's order and the community's order which saves man (in Hooker's phrase) from being "little better than a wild beast." He had published his treatise, Hooker wrote, so "that posterity might know that he had not loosely through silence, permitted things to pass away as in a dream." The sixteenth century was a nightmare for many, but Hooker opened eyes afresh to the vision of order.

Kirk and Covenant

Richard Hooker's moderation may make the Reformation seem almost gentle. But the process was rough in England, and harsher still in Scotland—where the principal founder of the reformed Kirk (or Church) of Scotland, John Knox, did not resemble the judicious Hooker. Through Knox, preacher and mover of multitudes, Calvinism triumphed over the decayed Catholic establishment.

To infertile Scotland, the Renaissance had only begun to penetrate when the storm of the Reformation burst upon the country. In Scotland, unlike most northern lands, the ruling house, the Stuarts, fought hard in defense of the Catholic faith. But once Henry VIII cast off the authority of the pope, the Tudor sovereigns of England encouraged and supported the Protestants of the northern kingdom. That intervention from the south was too much for the weakened Catholic hierarchy of Scotland.

During the first half of the sixteenth century, Scotland was allied with France against English power. James V, king of Scotland, strengthened this French connection by marrying the talented, energetic, and beautiful Mary of Guise (sometimes styled Mary of Lorraine), daughter to the Duke of Guise, the great champion of the Catholic party in France. The only child of this marriage would be Mary Stuart, later Queen of Scots, who would be put to death many years later by Queen Elizabeth of England.

On the eve of the Reformation, the Catholic establishment in Scotland was closely interwoven with the political fabric of the Stuart monarchy. The archbishops of St. Andrews, primates of Scotland, commonly were the king's chancellors. The Scottish Catholic establishment in that age was anything but bigoted: its vice, rather, was religious indifference or latitudinarianism. Archbishop James Beaton, soldier and politician, was the right hand of King James V. Beaton was cunning, tireless, and patriotic—but no saint. Where, indeed, in the Scottish Church then, could one find a wholly devout and righteous bishop or abbot? The dissolution of the Roman Church in Scotland commenced from within; Knox and his followers only accelerated the process.

As the Ages of Faith faded into the past, and pilgrims ceased to flock to the ancient shrine of Saint Andrew the Apostle, the great noble houses of Scotland competed for possession of abbeys and priories and the vast lands of the Church, making their younger sons into lay abbots. One of those noble lay abbots was Patrick Hamilton, to whom Ferne Abbey was given when he was but fourteen years old. This winning and fearless young man became a convert to Lutheranism; and after talking with Luther and Luther's learned friend Melancthon in Germany, he returned to Scotland, late in 1527, and began to preach Lutheran doctrines. So commenced the Scottish Reformation.

Archbishop James Beaton summoned Hamilton to St. Andrews for inquisition. It was found that Hamilton, once a member of the faculty at St. Andrews, had preached without a license, denied authority, held the sacraments to be suspect, urged the neglect of tithes, maintained the inefficacy of good works as a way to salvation, scoffed at purgatory and prayers for the dead, and slandered churchmen. In point of law, he was guilty.

Yet the archbishop, knowing it imprudent to make martyrs, seems to have been ready to connive at Hamilton's escape, so that the Church might rest content merely with a formal condemnation of the heretic. Hamilton, however, preferred truth to life, dying (somewhat paradoxically) in order to affirm that man does not possess free will, but is saved solely through faith and grace.

So the archbishop's men burnt Hamilton before the gate of St. Salvator's College. He was six hours in his dying. A professed well-wisher to the archbishop (according to John Knox's *History of the Reformation*) advised Beaton that he would destroy the Scottish hierarchy if he burnt more godly men like Hamilton: "Yf ye will burne them, let then be burnt in low cellaris: for the reik of Maister Patrik Hammyltoun hes infected as many as it blew upoun."

The reek of Hamilton's execution blew upon many Scots. But Scottish state and Scottish church kept Hamilton's disciples down for nearly two decades. James Beaton was succeeded as Scottish primate by his nephew, David Beaton—strong and grim and crafty as his uncle. So long as the Stuart sovereigns and the archbishops of St. Andrews were powerful, the old order endured. But then Henry VIII, aspiring to English domination over Scotland, changed the course of events.

Late in November, 1542, an English army under the Duke of Norfolk slaughtered the Scots forces at Solway Moss. A few days later, there was born to Scotland's French queen a daughter, Mary. But Scotland's King James V, only thirty years old, sickened at the dread news of Solway Moss; and he died, leaving to the proud Mary of Guise and the astute David Beaton (now made Scotland's first cardinal) the defense of church and state. Already the man who was to work their ruin had studied at St. Andrews under the great

Scholastic teacher John Major; and when Solway Moss was fought, this man was an unknown priest, notary, and tutor—John Knox.

In St. Andrews, Cardinal Beaton confidently resisted the rage of Henry VIII, who could ravage Scotland but not conquer the country. The king of England not succeeding in his attempt to take the cardinal by force, he turned to the method of private murder.

Henry's agents began to treat with various lords and desperate lairds (Scotland's squires) in Scotland, men at feud with Beaton, or violent Reformers, or wretches out of pocket. An intimate associate of these conspirators was a strange fanatic named George Wishart, a person of quality, possibly a mover in the plot against the cardinal, possibly no more than friend and spiritual guide to the conspirators, but certainly a bitter hater of Beaton and the Church establishment.

Wishart was a reformer more radical than Luther or Calvin. He himself was an inspired prophet, he proclaimed, God's appointed agent, and he went about preaching prophecies that worked their own fulfillment. All men were priests, Wishart declared, so that no preacher need be ordained or licensed. He had learned from a Rhineland Jew that all religious art is idolatrous; at one time, he had doubted whether Christ was the Redeemer.

Here Knox's story joins the cardinal's. For Wishart's most devoted personal follower was one John Knox of Haddington, a middle-aged man of some education, though (like Luther) a peasant's son. He would fulfill Wishart's prophecies.

Wishart's dubious renown sounded too loudly in Cardinal Beaton's ears. He ordered the arrest of the "prophet", and the rough Earl of Bothwell seized Wishart. (Knox tried to defend his leader with a two-handed sword, like Peter in the Garden of Gethsemane, but Wishart forbade him.) The cardinal promptly tried Wishart for heresy. On March 1, 1546, George Wishart was strangled and burnt before St. Andrews castle. The doomed man made his last fierce prophecy, staring at the primate: within a little space, the cardinal too would perish, he cried. Then the executioner drew tight the noose about the heretic's throat, and Wishart's body was burnt to powder.

Cardinal Beaton now stood at the summit of his power. Yet he fell less than two months after Wishart died upon the faggots. Some Fife lairds had a dispute with the cardinal, and in Renaissance fashion swore to take his heart's blood: little reverence for the hierarchy remained. With them joined partisans of the English faction, and some extreme Reformers. By a clever ruse, the rebels burst into St. Andrews castle and set upon the cardinal.

"All is gone," the dying cardinal gasped. They hanged the cardinal's corpse from a window, but later lapped the body in lead, and put it into a dungeon, for eventual burial. "These things we write merrily," John Knox reports in his *History*, "but we would that the reader should observe God's just judgments . . . these are the works of our God, whereby he would admonish the tyrants of this earth, that in the end he will be revenged of their cruelty, what strength soever they make in the contrary."[6]

John Knox himself, a hunted man, took refuge in St. Andrews castle with the cardinal's murderers. He preached to the Protestant garrison, but reproached them for their loose and impious ways. After a long siege, the regent of Scotland took the castle by storm, with the aid of a French fleet; and Knox, with other prisoners, was condemned to row in the French galleys. Near the end of the winter of 1549, he was set free, and made his way to England.

Meanwhile, Scotland burst into flame. The Protestant Lords of the Congregation took up arms; Mary of Guise, Queen-Regent, skirmished with them. Hamilton, the new archbishop, tried to persuade the Reformers to agree with him on a plan for purifying the Church—but too late. They had turned revolutionaries now, and John Knox's hour of mastery had arrived.

In May, 1559, Knox returned to Scotland. In Edinburgh he was declared an outlaw, but he eluded Mary of Guise, and made his way preaching along the eastern coast. When he came to Perth, a "rascal multitude"—so Knox himself described them—sacked St. John's Kirk and destroyed the monasteries. Like a conqueror, Knox entered Fife, and a crowd of Protestant fisher-folk trudged at his heels along the coastal road to St. Andrews; the archbishop and the queen-regent withdrew before the Reformers' strength.

On June 11, 1559, Knox commenced preaching in St. Andrews cathedral, grimly denouncing the wickedness of the Church establishment. Four days he preached; on the last day, the mob put a wild end to eight centuries of ecclesiastical history. They stripped the vast cathedral of all its treasures, leaving it an empty shell; they sacked the splendid priory of St. Andrews and the two friaries in the town. With hammers, the rioters defaced the Gothic sculptures over which their ancestors had labored lovingly.

As the dying Beaton had groaned, all was gone. The cathedral fabric still stood, after that ferocious day, but it was a mere desecrated shell; since they would have no bishops, the Calvinist Reformers wanted no cathedrals, but only parish churches. What Paul Craw's burning had foreshadowed, long before, and what Patrick Hamilton's burning had hastened, now was consummated. Mary of Guise, besieged by the Reformers, died of some sickness in June, 1560, heroic to the last. That August, the Three Estates, Scotland's parliament, met in Edinburgh, with Archbishop Hamilton and other ecclesiastics attending. The Three Estates made a formal end of the old Church, abolishing the pope's jurisdiction, condemning all practices contrary to Knox's new creed, and forbidding the celebration of the mass, on pain of death for a third offense. Only the young queen, Mary Stuart, stood between the Reformers and the remnants of the ancient system. And Knox would defeat her, too.

Even while Mary still held the throne, Protestant lords and lairds parcelled out among themselves the lands of the Church, except what fragments Knox could save for the support of the Kirk and the schools. Once Mary fled to England and was imprisoned there, the Scottish Catholic party was stamped out, Catholic "recusants" surviving only here and there in the Highlands and the Western Isles.

In his own *History of the Reformation*, the first important prose work of Scottish literature, Knox figures as no model of Christian charity or mercy. He was brave, personally incorruptible, and eloquent; and he was no respecter of persons, himself included. (Unlike most Scots, he did not pretend to gentility, saying that he was a man of base origin.) Through his preaching, an austere Calvinism was established in Scotland.

For Knox, the Bible was the sole source of authority. In his old age, younger ministers ventured to differ with Knox's interpretations of Scripture; and when he objected, they asked how, on his own principles, he could set himself up as an authority: they could read the Bible as well as he. Knox retorted dourly that he had read the Bible many more times than they had. But the younger Reformers' objection was a serious weakness in the Protestantism of Luther and Calvin: for if every man might interpret Scripture for himself, what if men should differ on the Bible's meaning? This difficulty would lead later to splitting of the Kirk of Scotland into sects, and would bring sharp division among English Protestants also.

The Kirk that Knox founded was rooted in two principal theological doctrines: Luther's doctrine of justification by faith, and Calvin's doctrine of predestination. "Justification by faith" signifies that a man may be made right and just before God only through total unquestioning faith in the word and the reality of Christ. Only God is righteous; all men are wholly corrupt; but through God's arbitrary mercy, God's grace, those may be saved who trust in the Lord—quite regardless of their actions in this life.

"Predestination" signifies that God, even before He created the world, decreed that certain people should be saved, and others damned. The "elect," those saved by God's decree, could not be surely distinguished: many are called, but few are chosen. No act of will in this life may secure a man's redemption from sin, for whatever occurs here below is God's intention, formed before Adam was put into Eden. Confession of sins is of no avail; absolution is impossible, for God's grace and God's wrath upon sinners have been decreed from the beginning.

These two rigorous doctrines were at the heart of Calvinistic belief. They were shared by the Dutch Reformed Calvinists of the Netherlands, by the French Hugenots, by many of the Swiss. The Presbyterians of England professed this creed, but were put down by Cromwell's Independents and later by the Anglican establishment. The Puritans of England and America subscribed to this theology, although not to the Presbyterian form of church-government that developed in Scotland.

From Scotland, Knox's Calvinism spread to the "Scotch-Irish" of Ulster, in the north of Ireland, and from both Scotland and Ulster to the New World. Scottish missionaries, as the British empire grew, would carry the teachings of the Kirk nearly everywhere in the world—even to the heart of Africa. Although the Church of England was established by law in most of the American colonies, and the Puritan variety of Calvinism dominated New England, what came to be called "Presbyterianism," the creation of Knox, became the profession of a multitude of Americans in the eighteenth century—especially along the western frontiers of the colonies.

"Presbyterianism", strictly speaking, means government of churches by presbyters, or ministers and elders meeting in session—as distinguished from the authority of bishops in Catholic, Anglican, and Lutheran churches. In that sense, Knox himself was not quite a Presbyterian: he would have tolerated bishops, if only they would have consented to preach. The first of the post-Reformation archbishops of St. Andrews, poor old John Douglas, died of stage-fright in the pulpit of Holy Trinity Kirk, St. Andrews, vainly endeavoring to comply with the demand of the Knoxites that he edify them with sermons. In the seventeenth century, the Scottish Calvinists would purge the Kirk of bishops altogether.

To supplant the old episcopal establishment in Scotland, there emerged the General Assembly of the Kirk, presided over by an elected "moderator." In organization, J. M. Reid writes, "the Scots Kirk was unbelievably democratic. It did not aim at political democracy, although there was a radical strain among the first Reformers. The object of the men who made it was to reproduce as far as possible the sort of Church they found in the Bible. But in doing this through ministers and elders elected (or at least approved) by each congregation, men who again appeared in the courts of the Kirk or sent their chosen representatives there, they produced General Assemblies which could speak for the whole nation with far more backing than any parliament of those days."[7]

After the crushing of Mary Stuart and the Catholics, the Kirk enjoyed virtual political supremacy—although the Kirk was not supposed to be a political body at all. In the Kirk's *Second Book of Discipline* (1578) there was developed the theory of the "Two Kingdoms"—the temporal kingdom and the kingdom of God. In the temporal kingdom, kings and magistrates possess the power of the Sword. But in the Church or Kirk, Christ's kingdom upon earth, there is no head but Christ himself; the Kirk possesses the power of Christ's Keys. (The medieval Church had maintained that the Keys were held by the popes, as successors to Saint Peter.) Ministers are subject to the secular jurisdiction of magistrates, but magistrates are subject to the spiritual discipline of the Kirk, in things of conscience and religion. This doctrine of the demarcation (rather than the separation) of Church and State was virtually ignored, nevertheless, during the seventeenth century: through its General Assembly, the Kirk tried to manage the Scottish State.

However that may be, the doctrine of the Two Kingdoms (very similar to Pope Gelasius' doctrine of the Two Swords, in the early centuries of the Church) led the Presbyterians of Scotland, in the seventeenth century, to proclaim their National Covenant, inspired by what they had read of the Hebrew covenants. This National Covenant was not an assertion of civil or religious liberty, but instead a kind of declaration or constitution meant to assure the Reformed Kirk's freedom from control by the king. What resulted from this proclamation of Presbyterian unity was something like the struggle between the kings and the prophets of Israel in Old Testament times.

Scotland's king, James VI, Mary Stuart's son, would become King James I of England also, after Queen Elizabeth's death. For eighty-five years (except for the interregnum of

Cromwell's Commonwealth) the Scottish house of Stuart would reign in both England and Scotland. During that time, in a kind of love-hate relationship with the Stuart monarchs, the Kirk would behave often as if it were also the Scottish State. The National Covenant became the symbol both of religious unity and of national independence. Only after the fall of the last of the Stuart kings, James II, in 1688, would the Kirk find it necessary to return to its own principle of the Two Kingdoms, giving up its political power.

The relatively democratic form of church government in Presbyterian Scotland passed over to Presbyterian churches in America, and presently began to influence the pattern of colonial politics. The idea of a Covenant, as declaration and frame of a common national purpose, would form part of the background of the Americans' Declaration of Independence and of the federal Constitution. And the theory of the Two Kingdoms would have some influence upon American concepts of the separation of Church and State.

No less important, as influence upon the roots of American order, was the character which Knox and his allies gave to the Scottish people. The typical Presbyerian Scot was earnestly religious, frugal, and enterprising: he drew strength from his austere creed. He tended to be independent in judgment and assertive of his rights. The doctrines of justification by faith and of predestination made him God-fearing and stern of purpose, often. These were people well framed for civilizing a new land, and they began to settle in large numbers in the American colonies even in the seventeenth century. When the Act of Union, at the beginning of the eighteenth century, united the Scottish and English crowns and settled all parliamentary authority at Westminster, Scots poured into the Thirteen Colonies; so did their cousins, by race and religion, of Ulster.

Throughout the empire that Britain created in the eighteenth and nineteenth centuries, Scots even more than Englishmen prospered as administrators, soldiers, and merchants. In America as elsewhere, Scottish settlers often had the advantage of a sound schooling; only the Puritans of New England exceeded them in emphasis upon learning.

Popular education, nationally authorized, from elementary schools through the four Scottish universities, was Knox's aspiration, second only to his passion for establishing a religious faith drawn directly from the Bible. Such schooling was necessary, if the people were to be sufficiently literate to understand the Scriptures well.

For the support of Kirk and schools, Knox extracted from the Scottish state only a small portion of the revenues that had belonged to the pre-Reformation Church. Still, he was able to make a sound beginning in his scheme of national education. (Until well into the twentieth century, parish ministers were *ex officio* members of Scottish school boards.) The parish schools imparted pure Calvinist doctrine; the universities became centers of Reformed theology. In secular studies, Scottish schools became renowned, so that the popular level of learning was higher in Scotland of the seventeenth and eighteenth centuries than in any other nation. That literacy and respect for learning, founded upon Bible study, also passed into America.

Much though he had accomplished, both creatively and destructively, John Knox was little satisfied with the turbulent and grasping Scotland from which he had driven the Catholic prelates and the Catholic queen. Among magnates who professed zeal for the Reformed Kirk, he found as much corruption as he had denounced in the times of popery. Only here and there, as he lay dying in 1571, did he discern sparks of regeneracy. He approved a sermon by a Fife minister that described the Kirk's poverty and ignorance: "John Knox, with my dead hand, but glad heart, praising God that, of his mercy, he leaves such light to his Kirk in this desolation."

They buried him in what was then the kirkyard of St. Giles, at the heart of stony Edinburgh, and today the city's traffic rumbles over his grave. Out of Scotland and northern Ireland, to fight the Indians and the French along the American colonies' frontiers and to settle a wilderness, would pour many thousands of hardy men of Knox's persuasion, in the succeeding two centuries.

Lutheran in conception, Anglican or Calvinist in development, the Reformation took possession of all British America, if one excepts the little Catholic minority in Maryland and elsewhere, the handful of colonial Jews, and later the conquered French-Canadians; for of course the Baptists, Quakers, and other dissenting sects came out of the Reformation's cauldron too. Up from the Old World's religious ferment bubbled the energy and the individualism of the nascent American order.

Notes

[1] John Addington Symonds, *Renaissance in Italy: the Revival of Learning* (second edition, London: Smith, Elder, 1882), p. 330.

[2] Egon Freidell, *A Cultural History of the Modern Age* (translated by C. F. Atkinson; New York: Knopf, 1930), Vol. I, p. 154.

[3] J. S. Whale, *The Protestant Tradition: an Essay in Interpretation* (Cambridge: Cambridge University Press, 1959), p. 121.

[4] John Dillenberger and Claude Welch, *Protestant Christianity, Interpreted through its Development* (New York: Scribner's, 1954), p. 320.

[5] F. J. Foakes-Jackson, "Of the Laws of Ecclesiastical Polity", in *The Cambridge History of English Literature* (Cambridge: Cambridge University Press, 1949), Vol. III, p. 411.

[6] John Knox, *The History of the Reformation of Religion in Scotland* (Glasgow: J. Galbraith, 1761), pp. 98-100.

[7] J. M. Reid, *Kirk and Nation: the Story of the Reformed Church of Scotland* (London: Skeffington, 1960), p. 53.

CHAPTER VIII
THE CONSTITUTION
OF CHURCH AND STATE

Civil War and Recovery of Order

Some three hundred years ago, Britain was tormented by the clash of hostile religious persuasions, political theories, and material interests. Out of those civil wars of the seventeenth century there emerged at the end much of the constitutional pattern and the religious toleration that America knows today. From our twentieth-century perspective in time, those who fought so bitterly—Royalists and Parliament men, Anglicans, Presbyterians, Independents, martyrs and fanatics—"are folded in a single party." All those who died in such contests were contributors, in their fashion, to the society in which we now exist. Here we outline the chief events of that religious and political struggle, and then single out some of the men of ideas and faith who shaped the constitutions of church and state.

In one aspect, all this is the story of the Stuarts, kings of England, Scotland, and Ireland. James I of England, "the wisest fool in Christendom," may have succeeded in little else, but he kept the peace in Britain during his reign, from 1603 to 1625. During those years, permanent English settlements were established in Massachusetts and Virginia; during those years, antagonism between the Crown and the House of Commons, and hostility among Anglicans, Independents, and Presbyterians, grew hotter.

James declared that he ruled by divine right; but some powerful voices in Parliament would have reduced royal authority to a shadow. James maintained the principle of "no bishop, no king"—that is, the Episcopalian establishment was essential to the security of the throne; but Presbyterians and the growing sects called "Separatists" would have it otherwise. The seventeenth century has been described as the century of genius. But also it was a century of immoderate zeal for religious and political causes. Although courageous and high-principled, King Charles I, James' son, was not the man to achieve such compromises as might have averted a political explosion.

At first, in Charles' reign, political questions loomed larger than religious differences. England was involved in the religious and dynastic wars of the Continent, and Charles required money for forces on land and sea. Like other kings before him, he tried to obtain those funds by whatever means he could, and so came into conflict with Parliament. In his difficulties, Charles resorted to taxation without Parliament's assent, to forced loans, to martial law, to billeting of troops, to imprisonment without warrant. Still he could not raise money enough: concessions must be made to Parliament, if the King were even to defend the realm. So in 1628, angrily and grudgingly, Charles accepted the parliamentary "Petition of Right," a stern protest against those arbitrary measures which Charles had employed for finding revenue. Although not a statute, in effect the Petition of Right took the force of law.

This Petition's acceptance meant merely that Parliament had secured the king's promise not to resort again to what Parliament opposed as unlawful measures. Parliament made no theoretical claim to possess authority larger than the king's: the argument of the Petition was simply that the king's servants had entered upon courses conflicting with the long-established rights of Englishmen, and that the king should amend those courses. Yet with the Petition of Right, real sovereignty began to slip from the hands of the monarch to the hands of Parliament, as representing the people. (Charles I believed firmly that the common folk of England were more truly protected by himself than by the Parliament, which tended to represent wealth rather than numbers.) It was to the precedent of the Petition of Right, among other constitutional precedents, that American Patriots would look in the 1760's and 1770's, and many of the grievances listed in the Petition would reappear in the American Declaration of Independence.

Nevertheless, the Petition of Right did not suffice to satisfy the House of Commons that they had nothing to dread from Charles I, or to restrain the king from asserting his prerogatives in church and state. Out of this confrontation arose a series of civil struggles, and the attempt of the Stuarts to rule as Elizabeth had ruled would not be crushed finally until the year 1745. It would be pointless here to assign to one side or the other the blame for that fierce struggle: there were arrogance and self-interest on both sides, and in either party there were men of strong devotion and courage.

Charles, and his Royalists or "Cavaliers," saw themselves as defenders of the laws and customs of old England against men eager for power and wealth, and against fanatic religious visionaries; the majority in the House of Commons, and the Presbyterians and Independents, saw themselves as the champions of the people's rights and of Protestant truth. London, the mercantile class, and some of the great landed proprietors stood by the claims of the House of Commons; the backbone of the royalist party was made up of squires and of the bulk of the rural interest. But there were many exceptions to these generalizations; moreover, some Puritans joined the Cavaliers, and some gallant gentlemen were leagued with the parliamentary forces (which came to be called the "Roundheads"). Except for some noblemen in the House of Lords, mediators were few and feeble.

Usually we describe the forces that defeated Charles I as "Puritans"—although not all were Calvinist in profession. At first the Puritans had no intention of separating themselves from the Church of England; they meant instead to "purify" or reform that church from within, on Calvin's model. These

Puritans were people strong in their individualistic faith, highly moralistic, setting their austere forms of worship above the claim of the throne to obedience and church unity. In the beginning, both Presbyterians and Independents (or Congregationalists) were labelled as Puritans; they shared Calvinistic theology and a detestation of anything that "smacked of Rome"; both demanded thorough simplicity in church liturgy, and both scowled upon bishops.

But the Presbyterians adhered to the form of church government that gives them their name, while the Independents—and the more radical sects of Protestants who made even the typical Independent uneasy—insisted upon more democratic forms in the church, congregations undirected by any general church authority. When presently some Independent congregations fell away totally from communion with the Church by law established, they were described as Separatists. Charles I and William Laud, Archbishop of Canterbury, resolved to prevent the disintegration of the Church of England by bringing these Dissenters to heel.

But first Charles had to confront another breed of Calvinists. To compel the defiant Scottish Presbyterians to conform to the Prayer Book and the episcopal establishment, he marched north in 1639. Once more the old difficulty about money beset the king: the Commons would not pay his troops nor supply them, and the expedition failed; indeed, the Scots army invaded England. On November 3, there met what would be called the Long Parliament, its large majority bitterly hostile to Charles' measures and to Archbishop Laud's high-handed ecclesiastical ways. Parliament impeached the Earl of Strafford, Charles' ablest great servant, found Strafford guilty of treason, and sent him to the block on Tower Hill; Archbishop Laud, too, soon was condemned and made to pay for his ritualism with his head.

When the House of Commons moved to deprive the king of command over the militia, and threatened to impeach the Queen (who was a Catholic), Charles in person attempted to arrest for treason five of the Puritan leaders in Parliament. He was baffled in this, and left London, soon setting up the royal standard at Nottingham. The Civil War had begun.

We cannot trace in detail here the fierce intricate story of the Civil Wars. Revolutions have a way of devouring their own children, it is said, and so it came to pass in seventeenth-century Britain. By 1644, the Royalists had been beaten in the field. But by that time, the Puritans had split into two opposed factions, in Parliament and in Britain generally: the Presbyterians of England, allied with the Presbyterian Scots, on the one hand; and on the other side, the Independents or Congregationalists, more radical in church government and in secular politics. The Presbyterians dominated Parliament, but the Roundhead army, commanded by Oliver Cromwell, adhered to the Independents.

In these circumstances, Charles came to an understanding with the Presbyterians and Scots, and Britain was racked by a second Civil War. Cromwell, the Independents, and the smaller Protestant sects expelled the Presbyterians from Parliament, setting up a "Rump" Parliament that consisted of only one-eighth of the former members. Once again the Roundheads triumphed in their campaigns, against Cavaliers, Scots, and Presbyterians. Charles was taken prisoner, and Cromwell determined that he must die. The Rump Parliament established a special "high court of justice" to try him for treason; and in January, 1649, the king was beheaded.

By this act of blood, it seemed that the revolution had succeeded totally. But now that the Independents had destroyed the old order, on what basis could Britain be governed? In the month when the king was put to death, the more extreme Independents proposed to the House of Commons an "Agreement of the People," a written constitution purporting to be the common will of Englishmen, establishing a democratic republic with universal suffrage, religious toleration (at least of Christians who did not differ fundamentally from the Independents and their allies), and rights of liberty and safety that could not be impaired by Parliament. Here was one of the forerunners of the Constitution of the United States.

This Agreement, however, was rejected as too radical. Between February and May, 1649, the Rump appointed a council of state to govern Britain, abolished the monarchy and the House of Lords, and established a "Commonwealth and Free State." In practice, this meant that Britain would become a military oligarchy, with Oliver Cromwell as a master more absolute than ever Charles had been.

Violent political revolutions commonly follow a discernible pattern—though in part the American Revolution would not conform to that pattern. A revolution begins with relatively moderate objectives, led by men not altogether radical; but as blood is shed and hatred increases, the early leaders of the struggle give way to men more extreme and violent. The old order dissolves in anarchy, but no tolerable new order emerges. Presently confusion becomes so terrible that the recovery of peace matters more to the people than does anything else. And then there appears a "man on horseback," a talented military commander often, who restores order at the price of freedom. This revolutionary progression may be traced from the ancient Greek states to very recent examples in Africa.

Oliver Cromwell was England's man on horseback in the seventeenth century. Monarchy and Church had been swept away; someone must fill the vacuum of authority. Once in power, Cromwell the Independent proceeded ruthlessly to put down all actual or potential opposition. This was a grim necessity, for Cromwell confronted fanatic idealists who, though capable of overthrowing a domination, had not the practicality to frame and maintain a new government—let alone a new social order. The most formidable of these extremists, during England's seventeenth-century troubles, were called the Levellers.

Some parallels may be drawn between the Levellers and the Lollards of late medieval times. The English Levellers emerged about 1646, during the Long Parliament, while Charles I was held in an easy captivity. These political and religious sectaries were particularly strong in the army, and stood hostile toward the Presbyterian majority in Parliament. The Levellers demanded the creation of a democratic republic, founded upon universal suffrage, the people sovereign, with guarantees of complete religious toleration. They meant to level all ranks and to establish equality of titles and estates; in much, they anticipated certain French revolutionary factions of a century and a half later. What they sought was quite inconceivable, practically, in the circumstances of seventeenth-century England.

Many of the Levellers advocated the literal levelling of hedges, fences, walls, and ditches, as barriers to equality in the possession of land. They sought to restore to common use the "common lands," which had been enclosed, over a long period of time, by private proprietors. The "meanest of the people," they argued, should be eligible for the highest state offices. Some of their principles were expressed in James Harrington's treatise *Oceana*, published nearly a decade after the Leveller movement had reached its height. Cromwell detested the Levellers, saying that their theories were no more than "overturn" and that they were "little better than beasts."

By 1648, the Levellers were surpassed in radicalism by the "Diggers," a group calling themselves the "True Levellers." This sect found an able pamphleteer in Gerrard Winstanley, the author of *The Law of Freedom*. In April, 1649, a number of Diggers began to cultivate in common St. George's Hill, in Surrey, defying Parliament; they were dispersed by troops.

As represented by Winstanley, the Diggers intended to alter completely the structure of English society, seizing common lands and waste lands, which they would cultivate communally. In Winstanley's words, "We may work in righteousness, and lay the foundations of making the earth a common treasury for all, both rich and poor, that everyone that is born in the land may be fed by the earth his mother that brought him forth, according to the reason that rules in the creation."

Even more than the original Levellers from whom they issued, the Diggers or True Levellers were also innovators in religion. Winstanley rejected belief in a personal God, at one time proposed to substitute the word "Reason" for "God," called Christ "a true and faithful Leveller," and considered Jesus not an historical figure, but "the spreading power of light." He denied the reality of miracles and of heaven or hell, rejected the doctrine of original sin, and doubted the immortality of the soul. True freedom, he declared, cannot exist while private property endures. All officers of the commonwealth must be elected, annually.

To Cromwell, such notions were detestable and ruinous. To save Britain from anarchy, the general who had put his king to death now swept away the old form of representative government. In 1653, he dissolved the Rump by force, and presently created a "Little" or "Barebone's" Parliament, which dissolved itself in the same year. Thereafter Cromwell ruled according to an "Instrument of Government" drawn up by military men—which, like the earlier Agreement of the People, would be one of the models of constitutions known to the framers of the American Constitution.

Under the Instrument, all legislative authority was vested in a Lord Protector (Cromwell) and in a new Parliament drawn from among the Puritans. Upon that Parliament, the Lord Protector was given strong checks. Religious toleration would be extended to all Christians except Catholics and Episcopalians. In theory, this Instrument transferred all sovereignty to the people. Actually, the two Puritan Parliaments that were chosen under this Instrument spent so much time in fruitless debate that they were ineffectual, and the able Cromwell governed without them as he found best.

This "rule of the Saints" soon was desperately unpopular with the mass of the people—especially with some of Cromwell's earlier associates, whom he imprisoned. Dictatorships have the disadvantage that when a strong master dies, only rarely is a competent successor to be found. At Cromwell's death, the Protectorate collapsed. Charles II, son of Charles I, returned to England with the support of an overwhelming majority, including the aid of some of the generals who had dethroned his father. The monarchy and the episcopal establishment were restored in 1660, although never thereafter would royal authority be so formidable as it had been in Tudor times, and the Church of England would find it necessary to enlarge the scope of its toleration. In little more than three decades, Britain had swung almost full cycle.

Across the Atlantic, England's little American colonies had been powerless to influence events in the mother country, throughout those three decades. Almost all New Englanders had favored the Puritan cause, and most colonists in Virginia and Maryland had sympathized with the Cavaliers. Both factions in the colonies submitted to the Restoration, as they had submitted to the Protectorate. But the lessons of the English Civil Wars were not lost upon the American settlers. They perceived that royal power might be overthrown; they perceived also that royal power might be succeeded by a more arbitrary regime.

They acquired from the passionate debating and pamphleteering of the English Revolution a knowledge of innovating political theories, and the concept of written instruments of government; also they came to be wary of utopian proposals, violent change, and military commanders with political ambitions. This influence of England's seventeenth-century struggle upon American thought and institutions is well expressed by George Burton Adams:

"Nearly everything for which the revolution strove is now a part of the English constitution, but not as a result of its endeavor. Rather as a result of the slower and more normal process of growth, out of which in a sense the revolution indeed came, but which it for a moment interrupted. In the Puritan and Quaker colonies of America the ideas of this revolution created the .natural political atmosphere. There they were not revolutionary, but became the material from which the normal constitutional life of these little states drew its strength. Their natural political development began with these ideas and led, as their population and needs increased, to more and more extensive realization of them in practice, until at the last they had large share, with other influences, in shaping the institutions of the second great Anglo-Saxon nation."[1]

The return of a Stuart king did not put an end to violent political contests in seventeenth-century England: risings against James II, Charles' successor, would occur—and would end in the "Glorious Revolution" of 1688, with practical consequences far more enduring than those of the Puritans' overthrow of the monarchy. Religious struggles, too, would break out sporadically in England and Scotland

267

down almost to the middle of the eighteenth century—and in Ireland, down to the present day. A turbulent age often produces political and religious writers of genius, who seek for principles upon which a tolerable order may be built or restored. Of such thinkers in the seventeenth century, we will examine here four who illustrate as many aspects of the influence that English thought had upon the developing American order: Thomas Hobbes, Sir Thomas Browne, John Bunyan, and John Locke.

The Face of Leviathan

How may men be kept from such explosive violence as tore Britain apart during the Civil Wars? What are the origins of government, and why must men obey the law? Such questions were in the forefront of thinking men's minds about the middle of the seventeenth century, most naturally, and the most systematic treatise on this question was written by Thomas Hobbes.

Hobbes' view of human nature brings to mind the definition of realism that Ambrose Bierce gives in his *Devil's Dictionary:* "The art of depicting nature as it is seen by toads." Yet Thomas Hobbes himself was no toad.

In his diverting *Brief Lives*, Hobbes' contemporary John Aubrey describes that formidable philosopher as a witty and even whimsical man, much affrighted by darkness and ghosts, not much given to book-reading, fond of argument, song, and tennis. Born in 1588, Hobbes lived prosperously through a desperate time, despite a skill in making enemies that amounted to a science, or perhaps a fine art; he expired in the fullness of his reputation at the age of ninety-two.

Hobbes seemed capable of doing everything under the sun: he translated Thucydides, in his youth, better than anyone has since; he was tutor to two Earls of Devonshire, and to the exiled Prince of Wales, later Charles II; he carried on fierce mathematical controversies, and discussed nearly every major scientific topic of his age; when he was eighty-seven, he published his translation of Homer, in a homely English style, of which the following address of Zeus to the Olympians may be a sufficient specimen: "Hallo, you gods, and all you goddesses; give ear!"

This man possessed the commanding intellect of England in his age, though it may have been a malicious intellect, and his works went against the grain of all factions. He left few avowed disciples. Leo Strauss describes Hobbes as "that imprudent, impish, and iconoclastic extremist, that first plebian philosopher, who is so enjoyable a writer because of his almost boyish straightforwardness, his never-failing humanity, and his marvellous clarity and force."[2] In Hobbes' political treatise *Leviathan* we see at work, for good or ill, a mind of the first order, and there are contained in the book certain incisive truths that will bear repeating today.

Leviathan, or most of it, was written just before the Civil Wars; and in 1640, when Strafford was sent to the Tower by the Long Parliament, Hobbes foresaw the coming wrath and hastened off to Paris, "the first of all that fled," as he wrote of himself. During those terrible years which intervened between his flight and the publication (in 1651) of *Leviathan*, Hobbes altered the manuscript somewhat, after a fashion that might make possible his return to England, then under Cromwell: he took a bolder stand against religious orthodoxy than he had ventured to make public previously.

Though *Leviathan* professedly is a defense of monarchy, Lord Clarendon and other Cavalier exiles perceived it to be a denial of the principles they held dear. Much chagrined at the Royalists' hostility, Hobbes made his way back from Paris to London, fearing Cavaliers more than Roundheads, and dwelt in England under the Commonwealth until Charles II ascended the throne and received his former tutor into favor.

To Clarendon and other Royalist political thinkers, influenced as they were by Richard Hooker's *Laws of Ecclesiastical Polity* and by their respect for the English tradition of liberty under law, the state was a voluntary community, under God, and under the king—the king himself being governed by divine and natural law, and by the laws of the realm. To Hobbes, the state was a vast necessary beast, Leviathan. In truth, Hobbes' book assaulted the very foundations of the old English monarchy and of the Anglican establishment; it was an attack upon that "loyalty to persons" which later would be called Toryism. Hobbes' argument denied those ancient bonds of love and duty that connect sovereign and subject. For those ties, Hobbes would have substituted a practical despotism founded upon fear and the law of the sword. The Royalists believed in a community of souls, owing loyalty to God and loyalty to a Christian king; but Hobbes believed that only individuals really exist, and that the individual's motives in society are not love and loyalty, but self-interest and fear.

Although much of Hobbes' argument seemed repellent to the English colonists in America, almost from the first a strong individualism prevailed in the colonies. The absence of monuments of a visible past, the feebleness of the Church of England's structure there, the smallness of the colonial towns, the remoteness of the king and the great English families, the lure of cheap land along the frontier—these and other influences tended to make individualists out of Americans, except in the early close-knit townships of the New England Puritans to some extent. So the individualistic teachings of Hobbes worked upon the colonial mind, even though few American leaders cared to acknowledge that subtle contagion.

George Sabine expresses Hobbes' individualism succinctly: "This individualism is the thoroughly modern element in Hobbes, and the respect in which he caught most clearly the note of the coming age. For two centuries after him, self-interest seemed to most thinkers a more obvious motive than disinterestedness, and enlightened self-interest a more applicable remedy for social ills than any form of collective action."[3]

An absolute central authority, a "sand-heap" of individuals: that is Hobbes' social pattern. It was at the opposite pole from the proliferating variety of the Middle Ages, with the medieval complexity of social organizations and self-governing corporations and communities. Hobbes' system offered freedom from Church, town, guild, and local authorities—but in exchange for servitude to Leviathan.

These ideas are more easily understood in the twentieth century than they were in the seventeenth.

Indeed, Hobbes has been called the founder of modern political philosophy. Hobbes divorced politics from religion, and did his best to reduce religion to "the kingdom of the fairies." He converted the classical and Christian theory of natural law, as expounded by Aquinas and Hooker, into a mere statement of the general rules by which men have found it convenient to live together. He substituted for the principle of honor, or Aristotle's "magnanimity," the principle of "commodious living": thus, according to Hobbes, the aim of politics is not the elevation of a nation, but instead material aggrandizement for the individual.

Hobbes replaced the idea of society as a providentially-ordained covenant, governed by love, with the idea of society as a collection of selfish individuals, kept from one another's throats by the sword of an absolute monarch. He introduced into philosophical speculation the grand question of Sovereignty. He influenced profoundly even the thinkers who endeavored to refute him, Locke in particular. And the total state of the twentieth century is Leviathan given flesh and blood; for Hobbes made it clear that this absolute sovereignty does not really require a Christian king.

What strikes some readers with especial force, in this cold and relentless book of Hobbes', is the almost diabolical truth (if only a partial truth) in Hobbes' interpretation of human nature. One perceives as if by a flash of lightning in the night why, in the twentieth century, the Nazi and Communist tyrannies could snatch power from the nerveless hand of the old order. Hobbes wrote that the life of the savage, the man in a state of nature, is "solitary, poor, nasty, brutish, and short." Therefore, seeking safety and creature-comforts, men submit themselves absolutely to the power of the state. Indeed, the life of many people in all ages is little better than that of man in a state of nature. Only centralized force keeps such people from destroying their neighbors and themselves. Leviathan, the absolute authority of the state, is preferable to anarchy. Man has the right to refuse to obey only one command of the state: the command that he kill himself, or that he be killed.

Between Leviathan and savagery, Hobbes reasoned, there lies no middle ground.

It scarcely is possible to love Hobbes' system, which appeals to no loyalties of the heart. Men unite in society, says Hobbes, only because they rightly fear one another more than they fear Leviathan. The reason for their violence is "a general inclination of all mankind, a perpetual and restless desire after power, that ceaseth only in death." This power which men seek for themselves really is the power to go on living, to obtain security and physical well-being, to dominate others: it is a lust. In the world of Hobbes, as in Alice's Looking-Glass Land, one must run as fast as he can in order to stand in the same place: men engage in a ceaseless competition for power and for "good things conducive to delectation." In a state of nature, then, all men live in fear of one another. Thus has it ever been, Hobbes tells us, and ever shall be, world without end. Only Leviathan, the rule of sword, absolute power concentrated in central government, can restrain individuals' lust for power and relieve fear; only Leviathan makes existence tolerable for the voracious individual that man is.

We recognize nowadays the measure of truth in these mordant sentences. Some people in the twentieth century have come to understand afresh how the lust for power is rooted in the corrupt nature of mankind. If that lust is not restrained by religious sanctions for morality, then it will be kept in bounds only by force and a master. Hobbes, who lived with the Cavendishes and other noble families, would have despised the squalid oligarchs of the twentieth century; but those oligarchs are proof of Hobbes' thesis. Seventy years ago, it was far less clear that Hobbes wrote about conditions which afflict mankind repeatedly, throughout history. In the optimistic years of the first quarter of the twentieth century, some scholars suggested that Hobbes' doctrines had ceased to be relevant to the circumstances and convictions of modern society.

"If history has taught anything about war in the past," E.L. Woodward wrote then, "it is that victory does not belong to despots and that free men uncoerced make the best soldiers. As for the future, war will not be ended, because men are become more fearful of death—through their very fearlessness is the spring gone out of the year for our time—but because of the desire for a more 'commodious' life and because the force of things, the accidents of economic need, the blind destructiveness of our weapons, have made victory scarcely less a calamity than defeat. The forts of which Hobbes wrote are becoming cumbersome ruins, and the frontiers old boundary-marks. There can no longer be a song of the sword.

"So remote, then, and so antique is become the scheme of Thomas Hobbes that I can end with the thought of men going out to find fear which has been lost from the world."[4]

Since Woodward wrote, however, wars have grown more frequent and more terrible, and the secular ideologies behind those wars have been even more merciless than were the religious hatreds behind the wars of the seventeenth century. The Biblical Four Horsemen of the Apocalypse ride again—war, famine, death, and revolution. Hobbes, assisted by history, defeats his optimistic critics. The scheme of Hobbes is far from remote: it is as close to us as Orwell's fantasy *Nineteen Eighty-Four*. In much of the twentieth-century world, total states with far greater powers of compulsion than Charles' or Cromwell's fulfill the image of Leviathan.

Hobbes' low view of human nature and absolutist theory of politics did not go unchallenged in his own day. In effect, Hobbes was an atheist; he denied that man possessed any freedom of the will, believed that all man's actions were determined by appetites and forces beyond his rational control, and tried to secularize the Christian concept of the Mystical Body of Christ. In Christian theology, all baptized human souls are particles, so to speak, of the Redeemer's mystical body, which is not of this world: human beings are immortal only because they live in Christ. Hobbes cleverly substituted for the image of the Mystical Body his image of Leviathan, the monstrous social creature which includes all human beings—and distinctly *is* of this world: only Leviathan, the state, is immortal.

John Bramhall, Anglican Bishop of Derry in Ireland, made the most effective of the several contemporary replies to Hobbes' theory that human beings are no more than atoms—and very selfish atoms, at that—in the body social. Bramhall had no difficulty in demonstrating that Hobbes' psychology and politics could not be reconciled with Christian teaching. Moreover, if we accept Hobbes' arguments, said Bramhall, we are left with no standard for good conduct; it will be vain to praise or blame anyone for anything. We praise or blame persons on the assumption that they possess, through the grace of God, some freedom of moral choice: "If a man be born blind or with one eye, we do not blame him for it; but if a man have lost his sight by his intemperance, we blame him justly," Bramhall puts it.

For Bramhall and the other Anglican divines, the purpose of human existence is to know God and enjoy Him forever; for Hobbes, that purpose is only material success and safety, and the enjoyment of fleshly rewards. For Bramhall, though the king is sovereign, the king is God's steward in the world; for Hobbes, the ruler is absolute altogether, and may do absolutely as he pleases, if he holds the power. Clearly, Hobbes was as radical, though in a different fashion, as were Winstanley and the Diggers. Both forms of radicalism—the radicalism of the total state and the radicalism of utopian ventures—descend to our own time.

In general, the Americans would reject both these types of metaphysical and political radicalism. Certainly the forms of government which the Americans adopted after their Revolution were in earnest opposition to Hobbes' theory of absolute unitary political power. The materialism and the egoistic individualism in Hobbes' system, nevertheless, would make themselves increasingly felt in the age that followed Hobbes'; they would be at least as powerful in America as in the Old World.

Yet from the seventeenth century America inherited more than selfishness and violence. To redress the balance, we look at two religious writers of that age. First we turn to Sir Thomas Browne, then to John Bunyan.

An Anglican Doctor and a Puritan Lay Preacher

Much of this book about the origins of American order has been concerned, necessarily, with violent conflict and social failure. In the history of ideas and institutions, one learns no less from disasters than from successes. With some relief, nevertheless, one digresses from the hard political and military events of the seventeenth century, and from the stony system of Hobbes, to examine briefly two good men without worldly ambition. One was a learned physician, the other a half-schooled tinker and lay-preacher.

In America, by the end of the seventeenth century, Christian belief would have a fairly tolerant character, differing from both the inflexible High Churchmanship of Laud and his allies, and the militant self-righteousness of the Independent "saints," Pharisees in major-generals' uniforms, of the Protectorate. The Anglican *via media*, well represented by Sir Thomas Browne, became the religious persuasion of most of the leading men in the southern colonies. The earnest and humble self-searching of John Bunyan was a direct influence in New England and elsewhere.

The inimitable Sir Thomas Browne—physician, philosopher, and master of a complex literary style—was born in London in 1605. He attended Winchester school, one of the two grandest medieval public-school foundations, and was graduated bachelor and master of Broadgates Hall (now Pembroke College), Oxford; he studied also in France, Italy, and Holland, becoming a doctor of medicine of the University of Leyden in 1633. Most of his life was spent at the cathedral city of Norwich. It was a placid life, despite a certain constitutional melancholy reflected in Browne's books.

The Civil War passes quite unnoticed in Browne's writings, though he was a Royalist. *Religio Medici*, his most enduring book, a doctor's reconciliation of faith and science, was written (so Browne told Sir Kenelm Digby) "as an exercise unto myself . . . contrived in my private Study." It was not published until 1643, the year in which the Civil War commenced. His *Hydriotaphia,* a glowingly melancholy discourse on the brevity of human life, appeared in 1658, on the eve of the Restoration that terminated the fanaticism of those dark years. His *Christian Morals,* though nearly as masterful in style as his earlier works, was not published until 1716, thirty years after his death.

A Platonic conviction that this material world is only an imperfect reflection of a world of essences—this pervades all Browne's writings. Everything on earth is significant to him only so far as it affords a subject for contemplation. Although, like Hobbes, Browne diligently studied the innovating physical sciences of the seventeenth century, his deductions from those sciences were vastly different from Hobbes' deductions. Hobbes' interpretation of natural science reduced the stature of man; but Browne's interpretation of those same scientific speculations made man and nature more complex, more moved by spirit. "I love to lose myself in a mystery," Browne says, "to pursue my reason to an 'O Altitudo!'"

In an intolerant age, Browne was temperate. "Every man is not a proper champion for truth," he wrote in the first part of his *Religio Medici,* "nor fit to take up the gauntlet in the cause of verity; many, from ignorance of these maxims, and an inconsiderate zeal unto truth, have too rashly charged the troops of error and remain as trophies unto the enemies of truth."

Feeling some sympathy with all theological systems, he respected the traditions of every people and every age. Common opinion and tradition, Browne holds, are entitled to a legitimate presumption in their favor: if a thing has been long believed or practiced, we ought not to discard it unless we obtain clear evidence that it is mistaken or outworn. Some of the most important aspects of human existence, he continued, are not open to experiment. In those concerns, we rely upon revelation, authority, and the wisdom of our ancestors.

He protested on principle against the word "Protestant"—a courageous protest, considering his times and his situation in a district commited to the Parliamentary cause. A truly enlightened skepticism taught him to smile at the vanities of the Hot Gospeller, the religious enthusiast; for the truth is not simple, nor easily come by. This double skepticism of Browne's—his doubting that all things have been settled by authority, and his doubting that new-fangled schemes can overthrow all authority—is one of the chief attractions of his mind for modern readers.

Within every soul, Browne wrote, Reason, Faith, and Passion are forever disputing. He foresaw that in future, the real danger to order would come not from the differences among Christian sects, but from atheism: human reason would try to take total control of the soul—at the devil's urging. "Thus the Devil played at Chess with me, and yielding a Pawn, thought to gain a Queen of me, taking advantage of my honest endeavours; and whilst I labored to raise the structure of my Reason, he strived to undermine the edifice of my Faith."

Though a sincere member of the Church of England, he had no hatred or fear of the "Old Profession," the Roman Catholic Church:

"We stand reformed from them, not against them . . . There is between us one common Name and Appellation, one Faith and necessary body of Principles common to us both; and therefore I am not scrupulous to converse and live with them, to enter their Churches in defect of ours, and either pray with them, or for them. . . . I should violate my own arm rather than a Church; nor willingly deface the name of Saint or Martyr."

The vanity of human wishes, and the mysteries of death, always fascinated Browne, even when he was humorously examining trivialities. Sometimes, Browne wrote, he felt a hell within himself, the forewarning of a hell hereafter; and one of his famous lines is this, "There is a man within me that's angry with me." But Browne himself was angry with no one, in that passionate age; he preached complete forgiving of enemies.

After the restoration of the Stuarts, when Anglican worship was made possible again in those colonies where it had been repressed or knocked about during the period of the Civil Wars, the Church of England overseas generally reflected the tolerant spirit which Browne expressed. When the American Revolution came, it would not be a revolution against a church by law established, or against Christian teaching—in this very unlike the French Revolution. In America, Browne was read only by the well educated; his Anglican learning and his Christian aphorisms reached the mass of people only slowly and indirectly. A large proportion of the leading classes in America were Anglican, nevertheless, and the Christianity of gentlemen like George Washington was very like the Christianity of Sir Thomas Browne.

One English writer of the seventeenth century did reach directly the majority of people in the colonies: John Bunyan. His allegory *The Pilgrim's Progress* has been immensely popular from the year of its publication (1678) to the present, wherever the English language has penetrated. Only a few years ago, wandering through South Africa, I saw little Xhosa boys and girls of the Transkei running to school, books and slates under their arms. When I inquired of the Transkei's minister of education what they studied, I learned that their basic books were the King James Version and *The Pilgrim's Progress*. It was not very different in eighteenth-century America. Being brought up on Bunyan was some protection against being swallowed by Hobbes' Leviathan.

The Pilgrim's Progress has been called the first English novel; conceivably it may outlast all the many thousands of novels that have poured from the presses since then. It was even more generally read in America than in England, and so became a formative influence upon America's early important writers, notably Washington Irving and Nathaniel Hawthorne. Out of Puritanism came one other great writer—John Milton, Cromwell's Latin secretary, the magnificent poet and the prose champion of civil liberties. But Bunyan's allegory worked more strongly than did *Paradise Lost* upon men's minds and consciences—even upon the minds and consciences of philosophers. Samuel Taylor Coleridge, early in the nineteenth century, would find that *The Pilgrim's Progress* was incomparably the best work of evangelical theology "ever produced by a writer not miraculously inspired."

In style and in background, the author of *Pilgrim's Progress* was remote from the author of *Religio Medici*. John Bunyan was born in 1628, near the town of Bedford, in a mean cottage. He was a tinker's son, and was reared to the tinker's wandering trade, going about from door to door mending pots and pans. Except for criminals and possibly gypsies, then or now, no class in English society has been lower than the tinkers. According to Bunyan's own account, his early life was infinitely wicked—though his sins appear to have consisted simply of bad language, dancing, ringing the bells of the parish church, and reading one knightly romance.

In 1645, when young Bunyan was serving as a soldier, a comrade who had taken his place in the siege of a town was killed in action. Bunyan took it that he had been providentially spared, and on returning home he assumed a mode of life that was Puritanism in its most austere form. All his life he was poor, involuntarily as well as voluntarily.

He joined a Separatist community, and in time became an eloquent lay preacher; later he could be most nearly classified as a Baptist, though his writings moved Christians in general. "I would be, as I hope I am, a Christian," he wrote. "But for those factious titles of Anabaptist, Independent, Presbyterian, and the like, I conclude that they come neither from Jerusalem nor from Antioch, but from Hell or Babylon."

Tormented by fears that he might be damned, Bunyan sought in prayer and soul-searching and study of the Bible the path to salvation. *The Pilgrim's Progress* is Bunyan's own progress toward reconciliation of his imperfect soul with the design of God.

Many lay preachers like Bunyan were suspect during Cromwell's domination, and Bunyan was watched lest he work subversion, but was not imprisoned. With the restoration of the Stuarts, however, misfortune fell upon this evangelical tinker. Puritanism then was in the sere and yellow leaf, detested by the large majority of Englishmen because of the Puritans' repression of old English ways during the Commonwealth. Besides, the more extreme Separatist sects, like the Fifth Monarchy Men, remained a potential danger to the restored monarchy and Anglican establishment. In the mistaken belief that Bunyan was a seditious person, possibly harboring and encouraging armed sectaries who refused to conform to the Book of Common Prayer, a magistrate sent Bunyan to jail. Having leisure in prison, he began to write. He was released when Charles II, in 1671, temporarily (and unconstitutionally) annulled the penal statutes against Catholics and Noncomformists. In 1675, Bunyan again was imprisoned, briefly, and while in jail at that time he wrote *The Pilgrim's Progress*. Other works followed, in the liberty he enjoyed until his death in 1688, but none was so striking and conscience-moving as *Pilgrim's Progress*.

The best way to understand Puritanism is to read that allegory. The Puritans have been called a "spiritual aristocracy," although the immense majority of them were anything but aristocratic in social station. Also they have been called seventeenth-century Pharisees, in the unpleasant sense of thinking themselves holier than all others. Often, whether in England or America, the Puritans were narrow and joyless. Yet their faith was deep, their motives were high, and sometimes their intellectual power was amazing. Until recent decades, generally the Puritans were praised in histories of American life and thought. Today, however, a reaction has set in, and frequently Puritanism is treated with an uncritical contempt at least as delusory as the earlier uncritical applause. Both the virtues and the failings of the Puritan mind and conscience entered deeply into the character of many Americans of later times: without the Puritan intellectual and moral strain in this country, the American experience might have been unrecognizably different.

At their best, as in Bunyan, the Puritans were a breed who subdued will and appetite, sought the Celestial City steadfastly, and (despite their frequent intolerance) planted in America a moral and political order that was an endeavor to reconcile the claims of authority and the claims of freedom. At their best, the Puritans were faithful to a high vision of the community of souls and the community of this earth.

Like other famous allegories of the human condition, *The Pilgrim's Progress* should be read through, if its homely power is to be communicated. An allegory is a description of one thing under the image of another, in C.S. Lewis' definition, "to represent what is immaterial in picturable terms." *The Pilgrim's Progress* is an allegory of a man's striving after the salvation of his soul, under the image of a perilous long journey from his condemned home to the heavenly Jerusalem, the Celestial City. John Bunyan knew scarcely any English literature besides the Scriptures and Foxe's *Book of Martyrs*, but his moral imagination created out of simple experiences and inner tribulations one of the seminal books of modern times.

At the devil's booth in Vanity Fair, all things are sold. Because Christian, the Pilgrim of this Progress, rejects Vanity Fair's "shows, jugglings, cheats, games, plays, fools, apes, knaves, and rogues, and that of every kind"—why, he and his companion Faithful are tried by Lord Hate-Good, testified against by those false witnesses Envy, Superstition, and Pickthank, and flung into prison. Faithful is tormented to death hideously, but Christian escapes, and comes after many temptations and combats to the Celestial City, and is admitted.

Even within sight of that City is a door in the hillside, opening to Hell, and through that door is cast a very different pilgrim, Ignorance. Abjure vanity, linger not in ignorance, be faithful unto death: so may many a pilgrim be saved, through God's grace, from the corruption of his nature and his time. This is the preaching tinker's message to his age and to ours.

The imagery of Bunyan's passionate exhortation took hold upon the American mind and the American conscience, and not in New England only. So it is that modern scholars who try to trace the Puritan shaping of American order through political tracts—through books like James Harrington's *Oceana*, say—have taken a misleading path, if they are looking for major influences. Imagination, not dialectic, rules the world. For every American who read *Oceana* once, ten thousand Americans read *The Pilgrim's Progress*.

Had it not been for the influence of such Christian writers, indeed life in raw America might have become nothing better than Hobbes' universal and perpetual lust for power and possession. Though the American colonies had been affected strongly by the religious and social thought of seventeenth-century England, they had been touched only glancingly by the military and political events of the Civil Wars. The English internal contest for power came to an end, with some reconciling of factions and sects, in 1688—well before the American colonies were rich or populous enough to afford the luxury of prolonged civil hostilities. But the western frontiers were savage and brutal enough: existence there would have been almost at an animal level, had not Christian teaching in its Protestant forms provided the rudiments of a moral order.

For nearly a century, American civilization would develop under the protection of a stable Britain and through a colonial policy of "salutary neglect." So we come to the time of John Locke and the Whig ascendancy.

A Note on John Locke

Three months after John Bunyan died, the house of Stuart lost the throne for a second time. James II, second surviving son of Charles I and brother of Charles II, was a convert to Roman Catholicism. In a Protestant country, he was so injudicious as to advance Catholics in high military and civil posts. In 1687, he published a Declaration of Indulgence, relieving Catholics and Dissenters from the penal statutes against them. He ordered the Church of England's bishops to read his Declaration in the churches; when seven of them refused, James brought them to trial.

Then the Protestant nobles combined against James, and invited William of Orange, ruler of the Netherlands, to land in England and dethrone his father-in-law—for William was married to Mary, James' daughter. James fled; though he would raise an army in Ireland, he would be beaten there. The "Jacobites", or supporters of the claims of James and his descendants, would struggle for fifty-six years to restore the Stuarts; they would lose. With the accession of William and Mary as king and queen of Great Britain and Ireland, Protestantism was secured. Also the possibility of arbitrary rule by a king was much reduced. The triumph of William of Orange, William III of England, was the victory of Parliament and of the great Protestant families called Whig.

In February, 1689, a scholar and sometime physician named John Locke, active in Whig politics, returned to England after nearly six years' exile in Holland. He sailed in the ship that carried the Princess Mary to her English throne, wrested from her father by her husband.

Locke, the son of a Puritan attorney, had been an undergraduate at Oxford when *Leviathan* was published. He would endeavor to undo that book—though in some ways, unintentionally, he would extend rather than reduce its influence. He had reacted against Presbyterians' intolerance and against Independents' fanaticism, and he came to find himself comfortable with the liberal Anglicans called the "Cambridge Platonists." His close association with Protestant politicians, during the intrigues of James II's reign, had made it well for him to take refuge in Holland. Now he could return to England—though soon he was not very well satisfied with the settlement after the "Glorious Revolution" of 1688. At the age of fifty-eight, Locke entered upon a career as a philosophical man of letters, and for fifteen years he would dominate England intellectually.

His two *Treatises of Civil Government,* written in large part twenty years earlier, were published a few months after his return to London, and his *Essay Concerning Human Understanding* appeared in 1690. These books still work among us. Though they were designed to conserve English religious and social institutions, in the next century they became weapons for American and French revolutionaries.

Surely no political philosopher is more generally mentioned in America today, but less carefully read, than John Locke. Locke's name has become almost a synonym for virtue, toleration, and representative government. We are even told by some scholars that until the present, Locke's ideas have been virtually identical, for good or ill, with the American way of life.

Locke has an eminent part in the American political mind, true, but he is no monarch in that realm. It is desirable to review what Locke actually wrote and advocated, if we wish to judge the extent of Locke's influence over the Americans of 1776 and the Americans of our own time.

Although Locke's treatises purported to be abstract discourses on the origin and character of society, in truth they amounted to an explanation of the English political experience over many centuries. *Civil Government* was a kind of anticipatory apology for the Revolution of 1688—although much more than that.

Locke's objectives in the practical politics of the seventeenth century may be stated simply. Political sovereignty belongs to the people, he argues—and not, by implication, to the king. The people delegate their power to a legislative body, Parliament, but they may withdraw that power on occasion. The executive authority, derived from the legislative, is dependent upon Parliament. That ought to be the constitution of England, Locke believed; and the powerful men with whom he was allied gave flesh to his theories.

Despite Locke's conformity to the Church of England, these ideas resemble the theories of certain Puritan writers and politicians: In New England, between 1642 and 1660, the Puritan settlers had governed themselves on such principles—though they had found it necessary to submit to Stuart authority at the Restoration. Under Locke's system, the king would hold next to no personal power, except as defender of the realm and guardian of the laws. (Actually, the strong new King William III would exert practical power exceeding that assigned to the Crown in Locke's treatises.) Such was the immediate purpose and significance of Locke's political tracts; but in them are larger and more enduring meanings, worth examination.

Locke's *Second Treatise of Government,* one of the cardinal works of English political theory, really is an attack upon Hobbes' Leviathan, published forty years earlier—although Locke seldom mentions by name his clever adversary. Locke intends to prove that government is agreed upon by free contract; that governors hold their authority only as a trust from the people; and that when this trust is violated, a people may use their strength rightfully to undo tyranny—although only under heavy provocation. These arguments explain and defend the Revolution of 1688, but also they explain the nature of a long struggle for balanced government in England, from the thirteenth century onward. And they lay down principles, in Locke's opinion, by which an enlightened nation may achieve the "law of nature" in politics.

To understand Locke's arguments—especially Locke's emphasis upon the "natural rights" of life, liberty, and property—it is well to recollect the ideas of Hobbes, discussed earlier in this chapter. John Locke endeavors to find an alternative principle of order, something better than Hobbes' law of sword. In his own time, most educated people believed Locke to have succeeded in this attempt.

Locke's work ran contrary to the strong tendency of power and policy in the Continent, during his time. But John Locke defied the Age of Absolutism. During the eighteenth century, Locke's political ideas would penetrate into the Continent, helping there to overthrow the paternal despotisms that had seemed destined to carry everything before them. Whether his principles are equally strong in the twentieth century remains open to question.

In most matters, Locke was not an original thinker, but rather a synthesizer or popularizer. In moral philosophy, he endeavored to harmonize the findings of seventeenth-century science with the Christian heritage. Similarly, in politics he sought to work the opinions of earlier philosophers into a system consonant with the historical experience and the new needs of his country.

Society is the product of a voluntary contract among men equal in a state of nature, Locke writes, to secure better the rights which are theirs by nature—life, liberty, and property. (Usually Locke employs the word "estate", meaning real property or property in land, rather than the word "property.") He has much more to say about estate, or property, than he does about life and liberty. Several times he declares that "the reason why men enter into society is the preservation of their property." This argument was especially appealing in colonial America, where a very high proportion of the white inhabitants owned some sort of real property.

But can Locke's idea of the social compact be taken seriously in the twentieth century? Did men in a state of nature ever enter into such a compact voluntarily, as a whole people? Indeed, how much "estate" do primitive people have to protect? Locke's contract theory is one of several postulates that he fails to establish satisfactorily. As a reply to Hobbes, it now seems inadequate.[5]

Only sixty years later, David Hume would make mincemeat of Locke's theory that men, at any remote period, ever joined themselves into a formal compact for their common welfare. The historical origins of the state, Hume would point out, are nothing like Locke's primitive voluntary union: in England as elsewhere, force and conquest have occurred sometime, to form a state—even though states are not held together by force alone.

So, too, Edmund Burke implied when, a century after Locke, he advised his generation to "draw a sacred veil" over the remote origins of the state. An historian of political thought, C.E. Vaughan, criticizing Locke's notion that the law of nature ordains free consent and mutual assistance, observes that "all human excellence is based upon conflict; and, much as we may shrink from owning it, without the combative qualities, there is little virtue and no such thing as progress."[6] Perhaps Locke's "law of nature" does not apply to primitive men, really, but rather to civilized Englishmen whose impulses have been chastened by Christian teaching.

Actually, Locke's references to the "state of nature," to Biblical verses, and to self-evident truths were little more than half-conscious concessions to the climate of opinion in 1689: everyone was using such terms then. With no element of hypocrisy, Locke adapted those terms to his thesis. What he really was after, at the heart of the matter, was not metaphysical apprehension, but rather a passable symbolic explanation—perhaps we may call it a myth—to account for the existence of Englishmen's rights.

Possibly Locke did not succeed in refuting Hobbes very successfully—precisely because Locke, as much as Hobbes, was a philosopher of individualism. He had no deep affection for the Christian concept of a "community of souls." No doubt Locke would have been surprised at certain late developments from his theories—as when, in the next century, Jean Jacques Rousseau would erect Locke's praise of submission to the political majority into a misty doctrine of the sovereign General Will. Locke would have been more chagrined when Karl Marx, in the nineteenth century, would develop his socialist theory of value out of the argument of Locke (and later, of Ricardo) that the value of property comes from the labor expended upon it.

For Locke intended, by his arguments, to restrain government to the smallest possible compass, lest government interfere with the right to estate, from which comes the common welfare. In the earlier years of this century, critics were hard upon Locke for his preoccupation with the right to property—and not without some justification. Yet in our time more people are coming to understand, as Paul Elmer More wrote, that so far as civilization is concerned, the right to property may be even more important than the right to life. Freedom of every sort is linked with security of private property—a truth which Locke took for granted.

This said, nevertheless it remains true that Locke's emphasis upon primitive freedom endangers that spiritual continuity which we call human society. Except for some references to "tacit consent" by later generations to the social compact, Locke has nothing to say about the Christian view of society as a bond between God and man, and among the dead, the living, and those yet unborn. There is no warmth in Locke, and no sense of consecration. His social compact is a far cry from the words in Genesis, "I do set my bow in the cloud, and it shall be for a token of a covenant between me and the earth." Utility, not love, is the motive of Locke's individualism. Locke's isolated individual, a kind of social atom, has the possibility of life, of liberty, of property. But what sort of life, and liberty for what?

Locke was the first great Whig thinker, and Burke was the last. During the French Revolution, a century later, Edmund Burke found it necessary, if disagreeable, to examine the idea of the abstract social compact or contract. Replying to Rousseau's followers, in his *Reflections on the Revolution in*

France, Burke said that there exist genuine natural rights and a genuine social contract; but they are not the rights and the contract expounded by Rousseau. Had it not been politically awkward for him, because of his links with the Whigs, Burke might have added that those true rights and that true contract were not the ones expounded by Locke, either.

Society, Burke said, indeed is a contract, a partnership; but it is not a mere commercial concern to ensure private profit, nor yet expressed in the unlimited General Will of Rousseau. Indeed men do have rights by virtue of their human nature; but these rights are not bloodless abstractions, nor are they limited to mere guarantees against governments. To narrow natural rights to such neat slogans as "liberty, equality, fraternity" or "life, liberty, property", Burke knew, was to ignore the complexity of public affairs and to leave out of consideration most moral relationships. One of the most important of the rights which men possess in society, Burke remarked, is the right to be restrained from actions which will destroy their neighbors and themselves—the right to have some control put upon their impulses and appetites.

"If civil society be made for the advantage of man," Burke wrote in 1789, "all the advantages for which it is made become his right. It is an institution of beneficence; and law itself is only beneficence acting by rule. Men have a right to live by that rule; they have a right to do justice, as between their fellows, whether their fellows are in public function or in ordinary occupation. They have a right to the fruits of their industry, and to the means of making their industry fruitful. They have a right to the acquisitions of their parents; to the nourishment and improvement of their offspring; to instruction in life, and to consolation in death. Whatever each man can separately do, without trespassing upon others, he has a right to do for himself; and he has a right to all which society, with all its combinations of skill and force, can do in his favor. In this partnership all men have equal rights; but not to equal things."

Some of the flavor of the *Second Treatise* lingers in these sentences of Burke, but there are stronger touches of Richard Hooker and the Schoolmen. Burke had appealed back beyond

Locke to an idea of community far warmer and richer than Locke's or Hobbes' aggregation of individuals. The true compact of society, Burke continued, is eternal: it joins the dead, the living, the unborn, and we all participate in this spiritual and social partnership, because it is ordained of God.

In defense of social harmony, here (in his *Reflections on the Revolution in France*) Burke appealed to what Locke had ignored. For by the time of the French Revolution, John Locke's argument in the *Second Treatise* already had grown too weak to sustain a tolerable social order. John Locke, that is, had relied upon the principle of self-interest, chiefly. But Burke reminded the Englishmen of his time of the love of neighbor and the sense of duty.

Locke's other principal work, his powerful *Essay Concerning Human Understanding,* was four times revised by its author. Locke's reputation, already high throughout Europe, was so enhanced by this book that he eclipsed every rival for the intellectual leadership of his time. In France, Condillac declared that between Aristotle and Locke there had lived no true philosophers.

Locke reasoned in this lengthy essay that the whole of our knowledge is derived from the experience of the individual's five senses. We see, hear, touch, taste, smell: these are our sole sources of information, of knowledge, of wisdom, Locke declares. This theory burst like a bomb upon his generation. The theory involves, says Paul Hazard, "a complete revolution in the hitherto universally accepted hierarchy of values. The noblest, the fairest, the purest of ideas; moral teaching, the promptings of the spirit—all derived from the senses! Our mind, which functions at the call of sensation, is merely a servant, a laborer."[7]

In this famous book, the thesis of Locke is that the mind of every human individual, at birth, resembles a blank tablet, on which experience marks a series of impressions. These impressions gradually are formed into general ideas. No innate ideas exist, says Locke: all that a baby inherits from his forefathers, or receives from God, is the *means* of giving significance to separate impressions.

The infant, according to Locke, does not apprehend intuitively or instinctively the idea of infinity, or the idea of eternity, or the idea of continuity, or the idea of worship, or even the idea of God. All these concepts he acquires through experience, and that experience reaches him through his five senses—through the process of sensation. Moral beliefs are not implanted in human individuals, Locke argues, by any agency superior to the flesh; no, they are learnt through experience of pleasure and pain, so that we shun as evil whatever harms us, and embrace as good whatever benefits us. All that the untutored human mind possesses is the power of comparing, distinguishing, judging, and willing. In his *Civil Government*, Locke had maintained that the feeling for human equality, and the desire for life, liberty, and property, were innate qualities of man; but in this later *Essay*, he repudiates (though only implicitly) the earlier doctrine. Merely the capacity for acquiring ideas is left to the human person.

Civil Government was meant to demonstrate the sufficiency of individual interest and private judgment in politics; *Human Understanding* was intended to establish an individualism of the mind. The *Essay* accorded with the ardent desire of Locke's age, opening the way for the rationalism of the eighteenth century. Everything in heaven and earth must come under the critical scrutiny of private judgment. It was easy for the Deists, and for skeptics who went beyond Deism, to apply the philosophy of Locke to their own innovating concepts. Locke was neither Deist nor skeptic, but he did intend *Human Understanding* to be a weapon, especially against the Catholics, whose fortresses of Authority and Tradition must tremble now.

Large though the influence of this *Essay* has been for more than two hundred and eighty years, there remain today few people who would defend the whole of the book. Some would go beyond Locke, all the way to untrammelled mechanism, denying that even the capabilities for comparing, distinguishing, judging, and willing are innate. Others, pointing to the wealth of inquiry into the mysteries of human nature since the end of the seventeenth century, would remark that Locke does not take into account those operations of the mind which lie below the level of consciousness; nor those which lift man, by mystical ways or by poetic and mathematical insights, to a condition that transcends the limits of pure reason. Yet other critics would remark that Locke could know nothing about genetic inheritance, the science of genetics not having been dreamed about in Locke's time.

Locke does not deny the existence of God. But he argues that God has not imparted any innate truths to mankind generally. Rather, God has given individual human beings powers of sensation and reflection, through which people can discover what they need to know in this world. As Basil Willey summarizes Locke's position, "We should seek our knowledge, then, in the consideration of 'things themselves' (our minds are themselves included amongst these 'things') and use our own, not other men's thoughts."[8] Locke was confident that a thorough intellectual individualism, very reasonable, would secure mankind against the violence of Unreason. Formal schooling, Locke thought, would suffice to keep human beings reasonable.

In part, Locke's theory of knowledge was a reaction against the religious fanaticism of seventeenth-century Britain. Turn away from religious dogmatism, Locke is saying, in effect: hereafter base your actions upon sweet reason, as ascertained by the individual's five senses. But Locke did not foresee the coming, a century later, of fanatic political ideology; still less did he foresee that there would develop a fanatic cult of Reason, beginning in France.

Now how far did Locke's politics and Locke's psychology affect American beliefs in the latter half of the eighteenth century? From studies of Americans' reading during that period, the answer seems to be that educated Americans often mentioned Locke on the eve of the Revolution, but seldom read his books at first hand.

The Americans would make use of Locke, but they would not worship him. In general, American leaders accepted neither the determinism and absolute sovereignty of Hobbes, nor yet the whole doctrine of the origins of society and of the human understanding as put forward by Locke.

This was true even of the more innovating Americans, among them Thomas Jefferson. As Gilbert Chinard writes,

"The Jeffersonian philosophy was born under the sign of Hengist and Horsa, not of the Goddess Reason."[9] That is, Jefferson was more influenced by his understanding of English history (especially of the Anglo-Saxon period, beginning with the landing in Britain of the Teutonic chieftains Hengist and Horsa) than he was influenced by the rationalism of the Enlightenment. Jefferson knew his Locke, and praised him highly; but in his Commonplace Book and his public papers, Jefferson cited more frequently such juridical authorities as Coke and Kames. And Jefferson denied that he had copied the Declaration of Independence from Locke's *Second Treatise*.

Or consider John Adams, the most learned of the Federalists. In the ten fat volumes of Adams' works, references to Locke are relatively few. Adams' *Thoughts on Government*, written in 1776, does contain praise of Locke; and in his *Novanglus*, written two years earlier, Adams quotes Locke at some length. Yet Adams treats Locke merely as one of several commendable English friends to liberty—"Sidney, Harrington, Locke, Milton, Neville, Burnet, Hoadly . . ." Montesquieu, to name only one major author, seems to have made a stronger impression upon Adams than did Locke.

Adams, Jefferson, and other reflective Americans made use of Locke, because they found themselves in circumstances similar to those of English Whigs in Locke's day, and because he was the first philosopher of the Whig party. In terms of English politics, the American Patriot leaders were Whigs, to a man; for that matter, so were nearly all the American Loyalists, miscalled "Tories." Genuine Toryism scarcely existed in the American colonies: political factions, on the eve of the Revolution and during that Revolution, actually were factions of radical Whigs (Patriots) on the one side and moderate Whigs (Loyalists) on the other. Therefore, if only out of partisanship, almost all American politicians paid their respects to Locke.

At bottom, the thinking Americans of that day found their principles of order in no single political philosopher, but rather in what has been called the "Great Tradition," drawn from Hebrew and classical and Christian teaching, and tested by the personal and national experience of their British ancestors and their own colonial life. Those Americans who had read Sir Thomas Browne might have found in one passage of Browne's *Christian Morals* a sufficient expression of their own fundamental assumptions:

"Live by old Ethicks and the classical Rules of Honesty. Put no new names or notions upon Authentick Virtues and Vices. Think not that Morality is Ambulatory; that Vices in one age are not Vices in another; or that Virtues, which are under the everlasting Seal of right Reason, may be Stamped by Opinion. And therefore though vicious times invert the opinion of things, and set up a new Ethicks against Virtue, yet hold thou unto old Morality; and rather than follow a multitude to do evil, stand like *Pompey's* pillar conspicuous by thyself, and single in Examples of Virtue; since no Deluge of Vice is like to be so general but more than eight will escape; Eye well those Heroes who have held their Heads above Water, who have touched Pitch, and not been defiled, and in the common Contagion have remained uncorrupted."

The Politics of Whigs

When James II fled from England, the peers and members of the House of Commons who had opposed him called together a new parliament, the "Convention Parliament," that met at the beginning of 1689. This body drew up a Bill of Rights—which, on acceptance by King William and Queen Mary, became a Declaration of Rights. This is the most important of English constitutional documents. A century later, its general character and many of its provisions would be incorporated into the first ten amendments to the new Constitution of the United States. Because it was the triumph of the political party called the Whigs which produced the Bill of Rights, we digress here briefly to glance at the two factions which contended for power in Britain from the reign of Charles II until well into the nineteenth century: the Tory and Whig parties.

293

"Toryism" means the principles and practices of Tories, or champions of the established order in church and state. Like its opposite term "Whiggism" or "Whiggery", Toryism first was employed as a term of abuse, but near the end of the seventeenth century it was embraced by the faction to whom it had been applied as an epithet.

The word "Tory" is derived from an Irish Gaelic expression meaning "Come, O king!" Late in the sixteenth century, in Ireland, this term acquired the implication of searcher or plunderer; it was used by the English and Anglo-Irish masters of Ireland as an epithet against outlawed men who were Roman Catholics and defied the government. Yet a century later, this word "Tory" was pinned to Englishmen, Scots, and Irish who heartily supported the monarchy, the Church of England and its offshoots, and things established in Britain.

John Henry Newman, in the nineteenth century, would call Toryism "loyalty to persons." He meant that the Tories of the eighteenth and nineteenth centuries thought of society as a network of personal attachments—rather than as a concern stuck together by what Thomas Carlyle called "the nexus of cash payment." Loyalty to Church and Crown was the distinguishing mark of the Tory party from the Restoration onward: the Tories were heirs to the Cavaliers of Civil War times.

Throughout the seventeenth and eighteenth centuries, the Tories (whose backbone consisted of the "squirearchy," or smaller landed proprietors, and of the Anglican clergy outside London) upheld the claims of the monarchy and the Anglican establishment against the aspirations of Whigs and Dissenters. Also Tories generally stood for the rural interest, as opposed to commercial and industrial interests. The Jacobite rebellions against England's Hanoverian kings, ending in 1745, were supported by the extreme wing of the Tory interest, loyal to the Stuarts. From the accession of William III to the French Revolution, the Tories usually stood in opposition to Whig governments, although occasionally the Tories would command a majority in the House of Commons, and never ceased to be fairly strong in the House of Lords.

In the American colonies, on the eve of the Revolution that broke out in 1775, the word "Tory" was flung contemptuously at those Americans who remained loyal to George III and Parliament. Actually, genuine Tories were rare in North America, either before or after the Revolution: most men so labelled really were conservatively-inclined Whigs, sympathetic to the Shelburne or the Rockingham Whigs in England.

The word "Whig" also was a term of abuse originally, derived from a Scots Gaelic term meaning a thief of horses and cattle; it first was applied to the "wild western Whigs", the Scottish Convenanters, stern Calvinists, who took up arms against the Anglican establishment. During the reign of Charles II, "Whig" came to mean those who advocated parliamentary authority, as against the king's, and who favored a policy of toleration toward religious Dissenters. Leslie Stephen writes that the Whigs "were invincibly suspicious of parsons"—meaning that the Whigs were no strong friends to the established Church (though most Whigs themselves remained in the Anglican communion), and therefore in some degree were the heirs of the Roundheads.

By the time of the Glorious Revolution, the Whig party was dominated by great landed proprietors; these, including some families that had come over from the Continent with William and Mary, obtained through their wealth an effective control over many seats in the House of Commons. With them were allied most of the merchants and manufacturers. Of the two parties, the Whigs were more aristocratic than the Tories.

These Whigs opposed arbitrary monarchical power, were dubious of many of England's ventures overseas, and often were advocates of the internal reform of governmental administration. "Even in those affairs of state which took up most of the Whigs' time," Lord David Cecil writes, "they troubled little with dry details of economic theory or administrative practice. Politics to them meant first of all personalities, and secondly general principles. And general principles were to them an occasion for expression rather than thought. They did not dream of questioning the fundamental canons of Whig orthodoxy. All believed in ordered liberty, low taxation and the enclosure of land; all disbelieved in despotism and democracy. Their only concern was to restate these indisputable truths in a fresh and effective fashion."[10]

This Whig orthodoxy came to power through the Revolution of 1688. The last Stuart king was overthrown, without bloodshed, by what has been called a "Venetian oligarchy" of England—by the combined strength of the great Whig families. This bloodless revolution did not affect England's social foundations; instead, it shored up the position of the aristocratic families and of the prosperous merchants.

Edmund Burke would write that the Glorious Revolution was a "revolution not made, but prevented." He meant that in the Whigs' eyes, James II had been the real revolutionary, what with his attempts to increase royal prerogatives. By preventing the intended revolution of James II, the Whigs believed, they had fulfilled the English constitution: they had upheld the chartered rights of Englishmen against a monarch who would have reduced those rights. The Bill of Rights of 1689, drawn up by the Whigs, nevertheless was revolutionary in that it established the supremacy of Parliament from that day to this.

Like the later Constitution of the United States, the Bill of Rights, on the face of it, is not theoretical at all; it is a practical statute dealing with constitutional procedures. The new rulers, William and Mary, are expected to be bound by this Bill. Parliament, rather than king and queen, determines the nature of the English constitution. The Bill lists grievances, and specifies permanent remedies for those grievances, but it does not set forth any abstract principles of politics. The assumption behind the Bill of Rights is that here Parliament simply reaffirms certain old rights of Englishmen that had been guaranteed earlier in royal charters. Actually, the Bill is the fruition of English constitutional development during the four preceding centuries.

In 1689, the primary concern of the triumphant Whigs was religious: the Bill of Rights insists that William and Mary, and all their successors on the throne, must be Protestant, and must swear to uphold the Protestant religion. If a king or a queen "shall profess the popish religion, or shall marry a papist," then "the people of these realms shall be and are hereby absolved of their allegiance." In addition to their own Protestant convictions, the great proprietors were haunted even in 1689 by the dread that a Catholic king might return the old monastic lands to a restored Catholic Church; those lands, for the most part, had been granted to Whig noble families. Fear of "popery," even more than concern for the powers of Parliament, had brought on the Glorious Revolution.

The rest of the Bill of Rights has to do with restrictions upon the power of the throne. James II, said the Convention Parliament, had endeavored "to subvert and extirpate the Protestant religion and the laws and liberties of this kingdom by assuming and exercising a power of dispensing with and suspending of laws and the execution of laws without consent of Parliament. . . ." The dethroned king was accused of having prosecuted bishops for resisting his Catholic ambition, of levying money without consent of Parliament, of raising an army without parliamentary approval and of quartering soldiers unlawfully, of disarming some Protestants at a time of peril, of violating the freedom of parliamentary elections, of prosecuting in court certain matters rightfully in the cognizance of Parliament, of choosing unqualified jurors, of requiring excessive bail, of imposing excessive fines, of decreeing cruel and unusual punishments, and of threatening unlawful fines and forfeitures.

By way of remedy, the Bill of Rights reiterated these grievances in the form of a declaration that all these specific abuses of regal authority were illegal. The crown was conferred upon William and Mary in the understanding that the new king and queen fully accepted every item in this declaration of the nation's "undoubted rights and liberties." Parliaments ought to be held frequently, the Bill specified. The implication was clear that should any king thereafter infringe upon these rights and liberties, Parliament might deal with such a royal transgressor as the Whig interest had dealt with James II.

Nothing was said in the Bill about Locke's theory of the social compact, but the document itself is a form of compact between the new rulers and the nation. Nothing was said about natural rights of life, liberty, and estate: Parliament appealed not to abstractions, but to precedents in law—to "the known laws and statutes, and the freedom of this realm," to what Edmund Burke later called "the chartered rights of Englishmen." Nothing was said about the century-long struggle between royal prerogative and parliamentary claims: the Bill referred only to recent grievances against James II. The authors of the Bill wrote as if nothing had been changed: it was only that old rights had been reaffirmed by Parliament and expressly recognized by William and Mary.

Yet out of the Bill of Rights, in the eighteenth century, would grow the cabinet system of government, with a prime minister responsible to Parliament and representing the dominant party or faction—or coalition of parties and factions—in the House of Commons. Increasingly the king would be excluded from partisan politics; although from time to time until the reign of Queen Victoria, in the middle of the nineteenth century, the sovereign might endeavor to manipulate Parliament through his personal influence and the wealth at his disposal. When George III, in the age of the American Revolution, would try to rule as a "patriot king," and to direct the course of events, he would not venture to resort to the heavy-handed methods of the Stuarts; chiefly he relied upon the patronage powers of the Crown. And he would be baffled by Whigs even in that attempt.

What occurred in 1689, then, was the recognition that sovereignty had passed from king to Parliament. This transfer, accomplished by a practical statute rather than by appeals to abstract rights, would avert for Britain the wave of violent revolution that swept over the Old Regime at the end of the eighteenth century. (At least the general impression that the British people, through Parliament, held the sovereignty served to diminish the sort of resentment against monarchy which burst out in France.) The Bill of Rights established representative government firmly—even though, in 1689, the large majority of British subjects were not admitted to the franchise. In practical effect, power had passed from the king and his court to the grand landed families and the successful merchants. In Parliament, the only effective check upon Whig domination remained the "squirearchy" of smaller landed proprietors, together with such of the chief noble families and the commercial classes as considered themselves Tories.

The monarchy was preserved, but at the price of surrendering its executive authority, theoretically, in many concerns. (Actually, by using the Crown's patronage and other devices, a king still would be able to manage Parliament much of the time, down to the beginning of the nineteenth century.)

The American colonies grew to maturity after the acceptance of the Bill of Rights. During the reign of Charles II, the English had taken New Netherland from the Dutch and had made that colony into New York; they had chartered William Penn to undertake his "Holy Experiment" in Pennsylvania; Carolina had been granted to eight English proprietors; New Jersey had begun to take form. New England, Virginia, and Maryland already were English possessions. So before the Glorious Revolution, the Atlantic seaboard, from Maine to what is now northern Georgia, had become British territory. But the rapid growth of population and relative prosperity in the North American colonies came to pass after the Bill of Rights was accepted. Thus America grew up with the Bill of Rights, taking for granted its provisions. The American colonists assumed that they participated in the liberties of free-born Englishmen, and that freedom was guaranteed through certain specific chartered rights, with appropriate remedies at law for infringement upon those charters.

These ideas and conditions lie back of the Declaration of Independence and the American Constitution. In the first ten amendments to that Constitution, much of the language of the English Bill of Rights reappears. Similarly, the American understanding of effective representative government was derived from the English Parliament—whose supremacy the Americans would deny in 1776.

A few quaint old houses in eastern New England or along the shores of the Chesapeake are the only visible memorials of the seventeenth century that remain to our time in the United

States. But American patterns of government still bear substantially the mark of the seventeenth century, and the "Protestant ethic" which took form then is not yet extinct.

Notes

[1] George Burton Adams, *Constitutional History of England* (revised by Robert L. Schuyler; New York: Henry Holt, 1936), p. 333.

[2] Leo Strauss, *Natural Right and History* (Chicago: University of Chicago Press, 1953), p. 166.

[3] George H. Sabine, *A History of Political Theory* (London: Harrap, 1937), p. 403.

[4] E. L. Woodward, "Thomas Hobbes", in F. J. C. Hearnshaw (ed.), *Social and Political Ideas of the Sixteenth and Seventeenth Centuries* (New York: Barnes and Noble, 1949), p. 153.

[5] See the chapter "The Basis of Authority", in Russell Kirk's *John Randolph of Roanoke: a Study in American Politics* (Chicago: Henry Regnery, 1964); also H. V. S. Ogden, "The Decline of Lockian Political Authority in England", *American Historical Review*, Vol. XLVI (October, 1940).

[6] C. E. Vaughan, *Studies in the History of Political Philosophy* (London: Longmans, Green, 1925), Vol. I, p. 159.

[7] Paul Hazard, *The European Mind (1680—1715)* (London: Hollis and Carter, 1953), p. 400.

[8] Basil Willey, *The Seventeenth Century Background* (London: Chatto and Windus, 1949), p. 274.

[9] Gilbert Chinard, *Thomas Jefferson: the Apostle of Americanism* (Boston: Little, Brown, 1928), p. 87.

[10] Lord David Cecil, *The Young Melbourne* (London: Constable, 1939), p. 20.

CHAPTER IX
SALUTARY NEGLECT:
THE COLONIAL ORDER

Austerity, Isolation, and Freedom

To see the Thirteen Colonies through the eyes of the settlers whom England planted there, one ought to approach America from the sea. For those were maritime colonies, narrow ribbons of settlement along the Atlantic shore; nearly all their considerable towns were ports. The colonies' communication with one another, and even within their own borders, was by sailing-vessel chiefly. Westminster and Whitehall were many weeks distant across the ocean, and out of that fact grew in time the distinct American society and America's political independence.

Until the Revolution, the vast majority of Americans looked eastward, and their economy was intricately connected with the Atlantic and the broad rivers that flowed from the Appalachian Mountains down to the ocean. Especially the Old Dominion, Virginia, never could have grown grand without the sheltered waterways along which its first tobacco plantations nestled.

For understanding a nation's history, it is well to look closely at the land and at the surviving monuments. This still is possible along much of the Atlantic seaboard. Even today, if one sails up the broad James River from Hampton Roads, the shores of Virginia are not unlike the land seen by the adventurous souls aboard the three vessels sent out by the Virginia Company of London in 1606. One can anchor off Jamestown Island, where those hundred men went ashore on May 13, 1607, to build a fort that would be the first permanent English settlement in the New World.

Lower down, nowadays, there are anchored in the James hundreds of "mothballed" warships and transports and cargo vessels left over from the Second World War, most of them. The smallest of these ghostly ships could have carried many times over the cargo and the men that the Virginia Company's three vessels brought to America. What was commenced at Jamestown would grow into the richest and most powerful of nations: quite beyond the dreams of any of the adventurers who landed in 1607, for they sought only to enrich themselves by discovering gold and precious stones—and soon were undeceived. A single one of those mothballed twentieth-century ships represents a capital investment greater than the combined resources of all the English chartered commercial companies that commenced the settlement of North America in the seventeenth century. English beginnings on the mainland were meagre, less important seemingly to the homeland than the English stake in the little luxuriant island of Barbados. But the consequences of the landing at Jamestown Island in 1607, and at Plymouth on Cape Cod Bay thirteen years later, would be greater than all other colonial ventures by the European states.

At Jamestown today there remains little but a ruined church and a graveyard full of Founding Families' bones. A few miles inland, on that long peninsula between the James and the York rivers, there stands the old Virginian village-capital of Williamsburg, elegantly restored: English culture transplanted to what had been Powhatan's country. And on the York shore of that peninsula is Yorktown, where in 1781 Cornwallis would surrender to Washington while a band played "The World Turned Upside Down." Nearly as many years elapsed between the settlement of Jamestown and the triumph of the American Patriots as between that Yorktown victory and our own day.

"Salutary neglect": that happy phrase of Edmund Burke

was the history of the English colonies down to the reign of George III. Even after the whole of the seaboard from stony Maine down to the swampy Florida frontier had been occupied by the British, the North American colonies would be of small value to Britain except as suppliers of tobacco, furs, naval stores, some dyestuffs and foodstuffs, and a few other products of no great consequence. Barbados or Jamaica alone—or, for that matter, some other islands in the West Indies—seemed worth more to London than all the thirteen mainland colonies put together.

True, the North American colonies served in some degree to hold in check England's French and Spanish rivals in the New World, and therefore they were worth defending in time of crisis. In general, nevertheless, those North American territories were disappointing to the British trading companies that made the early settlements; they were disappointing to the great English proprietors—some, noblemen; others, commoners—who for decades controlled the vast empty lands; they were sufficiently disappointing even to the English kings who eventually asserted direct sovereignty over the Thirteen Colonies. The trade of the West Indies and the East Indies, of India, of China, even of Africa, was more rewarding.

So the Thirteen Colonies, only of minor significance in England's growing political and mercantile ascendancy throughout the world, were left to their own devices ordinarily. Accustomed from the first to virtual autonomy, the colonists developed their character as a people and their social institutions under England's protection, but without England's express direction. Some of them would resent even the protection, when occasionally it meant that they were restrained by Crown and Parliament and royal governors from pushing the Indian tribes farther westward.

Plymouth Colony was founded in 1620, Massachusetts Bay Colony in 1628; Calvert established a refuge for English Catholics in Maryland in 1634; the Puritans arrived in Connecticut, and Roger Williams founded Rhode Island, in 1636; the settlement of North Carolina (from Virginia) commenced in 1653; the English took New Amsterdam from the

Dutch in 1664, making it New York, and in the same year New Jersey's settlement began; Charleston, in South Carolina, was founded in 1670; Maine was added to Massachusetts in 1677; New Hampshire became a royal province in 1679; William Penn was granted Pennsylvania and Delaware in 1681, and founded Philadelphia the next year; Georgia, last of the Thirteen Colonies, was a wilderness until General Oglethorpe built his fort at Savannah in 1733. Almost in a fit of absence of mind, Britain had brought into being a power that would grow stronger than Britain itself.

By the standards of seventeenth-century England, and even by the standards of western Europe generally, the Thirteen Colonies were poor lands—poor as Ulster, or as the Scottish Highlands. Except for some of the Puritans and Quakers, who came to America for religious freedom, and some lesser sects, nearly all the permanent settlers began as relatively or absolutely poor emigrants from Britain or Europe who hoped to do better in the New World, materially, than they had done in the Old. Economic advantage, rather than political freedom, was their first object. Freedom, nevertheless, grew out of Britain's "salutary neglect" of those hard-scrabble territories.

Although the colonists generally were poor enough—in Georgia, least successful of the Thirteen, many of the early settlers were paupers—they possessed great expectations. Also they possessed remarkable vigor. To the challenge of the harsh environment, they responded courageously: American health and longevity soon exceeded English health and longevity. Their birth-rate became phenomenal, higher than any rate ever before attained by any European people, so that they doubled their numbers (not counting later immigration) every quarter-century. The life of the large majority of Americans remained austere until well after the Revolution, and even the upper classes usually worked hard and rarely accumulated fortunes that would have made much show in Britain.

The Indian tribes of the seaboard, ravaged by disease or forcibly expelled, dwindled at the coming of the Europeans—though little pockets of Indians survive to this day in

Cape Cod, in Long Island, and here and there near the southern coasts. European and Indian ways of life could not survive side by side, on any considerable scale: the Quakers' generous Indian policy in Pennsylvania soon fell into ruin. A modified version of English society came to predominate in all Thirteen Colonies, absorbing or containing the Dutch, Germans, Swedes, and French Huguenots who also had arrived in the seventeenth century.

Soon the white man brought in the black man. Manual labor was in short supply from the first, especially on the southern plantations of tobacco, rice, and indigo. Indentured servants from England, Scotland, Ireland, Wales, and the European continent soon worked off their obligations, achieved civil freedom, and acquired land or a trade for themselves; the Indians of North America, unlike the semi-civilized agricultural Indian peoples of Latin America, could not be persuaded or compelled to cultivate the lands of the European settlers. So increasingly America looked to Africa, and to the slave trade, for hands. The first black slaves were sold to Virginians in 1619, though mass importation of blacks did not occur until the eighteenth century; by 1709, a public slave market was established in New York City, and the first repression of an abortive Negro rising occurred in that city two years later. Thus began the troubling paradox of chattel slavery in a land politically free as England, and in most ways closer to social equality than any European country of those times.

Inheriting English liberty under law, the colonists soon found themselves possessed of even greater freedom of choices than Englishmen or Scots knew. The king and his ministers, and Parliament, were too distant and too much occupied with more pressing concerns to trouble themselves greatly about the governing of the colonies. America had no noblemen (not even one peer settling permanently in the colonies), no bishops, no ancient families of rural magnates on the English pattern, no generals, no admirals (except when London dispatched military and naval men for the defense of the colonies against French or Spanish forces). America had no rich manufacturers, few grand traders on the scale of the London or Bristol or Glasgow merchants, not even an affluent clergy. Everywhere in America, then, there existed room at the top for the enterprising, and the developing institutions of self-government encountered little opposition—they merely filled a vacuum.

In every colony, cheapness of land was a mighty factor in the growth of individual freedom. Almost any man might acquire his own farm, if he had energy enough to clear and improve the land. With no capital at all, for that matter, he might become a tenant farmer on the Hudson, a squatter on the vast western tracts of some eastern proprietor, or a lawless harvester of someone else's forest. Almost from the first, land speculation became an American passion. It would nurture hardy frontiersmen; also it would produce the "poor whites," like the Lubbers of "Lubberland," the shiftless folk along North Carolina's colonial border with Virginia. The ambitious or the discontented could carve out from the wilderness not only private estates, but whole new communities—as did Roger Williams and his followers in Rhode Island, as did the Quakers in Pennsylvania, as in Pennsylvania or elsewhere did the German Amish, Mennonites, and other sects.

This ready availability of land worked against the growth of cities, or even of large towns—except for the principal seaports—in seventeenth- and eighteenth-century America. The individual farm and the hamlet became the common pattern of early American society. In Puritan Massachusetts, this dispersing of population was regarded with suspicion, for it might break down the moral and social ties of community; yet even there, the attractions of cheap land were too strong to resist, so that the English pattern of the close-knit village (dominated by landed families, by magistrates, and by clergy) gave way to the proliferation of many new "townships" without proper towns. In every colony, before long, virtually every "freeholder" of land obtained a vote in the political order. Freeholders being far more numerous proportionately than they were in Britain, this meant that a practical political democracy of sorts prevailed in British America well before anyone but extreme radicals ventured to expound democratic theories in Europe.

Few effective restraints endured in early America, then, upon internal political and economic freedoms. Freedom of religion, too, was larger than in Britain or Europe—though it had a stonier path to tread than did other American forms of liberty. New England's orthodox Puritans, though they had sought freedom of conscience for themselves, had no intention of indulging others in what Puritanism believed to be heresy and folly. Antinomians, Anabaptists, Quakers, and other sects they expelled and prosecuted, even unto death; Catholics they dealt with ruthlessly; merrymaking Anglicans they thrust out of their territories, when they had the power. Only when compelled to conform to the English policies of toleration adopted after 1688, and only when Puritanism had softened into eighteenth-century Congregationalism, did New England abandon its short way with dissenters.

In Pennsylvania, all Quakers had a secure refuge, because William Penn acquired by his charter from Charles II the proprietorship of a whole colony as an asylum for his fellows in the Society of Friends: there, until 1756, the Quakers dominated the colonial government, and fully tolerated other dissenters. The sanctuary for Catholics in Maryland soon collapsed, however, and throughout most of the colonies Roman Catholics labored under disabilities, and sometimes stood in peril, during the seventeenth century.

In those colonies where the Church of England was established by law, and most notably in Virginia, toleration of dissent was the general rule. In America, the mode of Anglicanism tended to be "broad church" and "low church"; the bishops of London, under whose jurisdiction lay all the colonial Anglican parishes, had neither the ability nor the desire to enforce strict conformity to the Thirty-Nine Articles of the Anglican establishment. In Virginia, a man was regarded as conforming to religious obligations if he attended any church; some dissenting congregations even were assisted financially by the dominant Anglicans.

Throughout the colonies, Scotch-Irish and Scottish Presbyterians, Dutch Reformed communicants, German Lutherans, French Huguenots, and other denominations of Lutheran or Calvinistic roots seldom encountered difficulties.

307

If colonial toleration was imperfect, still it was more generous than anything known in Europe at the time, or in England before 1688.

By the general standards of the seventeenth and eighteenth centuries, certainly, British North America was almost uniquely free. Was this an ordered freedom, or an anarchic freedom? In recent years, we have been told by various publicists and political figures—and even by some historians—that violence has plagued American society from its beginnings. That is true enough, in the sense that violence lies just under the veneer of civilization in all societies. Also it is true that often it became difficult to enforce writs at law along the rough frontier, or in the back-country remote from colonial capitals: it hardly could have been otherwise, in a new and sparsely-settled land without swift means of communication and law-enforcement. There occurred several violent risings against constituted colonial authority—most notably, Bacon's Rebellion in Virginia (1676) and the late-colonial "Regulators' War" in North Carolina (1771). These were small and brief affairs, however, if set beside British domestic troubles down to 1745 or even the Gordon Riots and other anti-Catholic disturbances in Britain late in the eighteenth century.

Questions of law and order ought to be seen in the perspective of an age, not judged in the abstract. By comparison with Europe and even Britain, the American colonies were reasonably tranquil and law-abiding. In any American town, crimes against persons and property were far less common than in London or Edinburgh. When religious and political passions reached their grim height in seventeenth-century Britain, they did not burn so fiercely in the colonies. There occured a short miniature civil war in Maryland, while in Puritan Massachusetts and in Cavalier Virginia the possessors of power were compelled to abdicate, temporarily, by an English government's intervention. Yet these affairs were mild and trivial, if contrasted with the political violence of Britain and Europe during those years. Somewhere in America, during the darkest times, fugitives (of whatever faction) from the English troubles could find refuge.

The Indian wars were another matter. If there were red savages, so were there white savages, merciless as their adversaries: treachery and massacre were committed repeatedly by both Europeans and Indians. But so it went, in those times, in India, Africa, and wherever else two radically different cultures fell into conflict; so it goes in much of the world today, man's inhumanity to man being suspended only at relatively brief intervals in the course of human events. The Puritans slaughtered the Pequots in 1637; no less terribly, Cromwell slaughtered the Irish at Drogheda and elsewhere, in 1649. Relatively speaking, most of colonial America within a hundred miles of the Atlantic shore was one of the more peaceful and secure regions of the world, for a century before the American Revolution.

Full civil liberty, even-handed justice, and broad toleration are the exception, rather than the rule, in human societies: earlier chapters of this book may have made that point sufficiently. Colonial America needs to be judged by its successes, rather than its failures, in these concerns. If one has little historical perspective, the infamous witchcraft trials at Salem, in 1692, seem evidence of New England's bigotry and superstition. But fierce persecutions of witches occurred frequently throughout northern Europe in the seventeenth century; in Scotland, alleged witches were lynched well into the eighteenth century. (Though, incidentally, it is common enough to talk of "witch-burning" in Puritan Massachusetts, actually no convicted witch was burnt in British America: the score who suffered death in Massachusetts were hanged, and one pressed to death.) In cases not concerned with heresy or witchcraft, New England's justice during that century was fair enough, the world at that time considered; certainly it was honestly administered.

So the colonial society was neither a particularly harsh nor a particularly violent society, in the light of seventeenth- and eighteenth-century practice. Learned men of law were somewhat scarce in early America, as were well-qualified physicians; but the desire to live by the rule of law was genuine. The settlers repeatedly referred to their rights as "free-born Englishmen," and took for granted the benefits of the English constitution and of the English juridical system, as those institutions had developed in the mother-country over the centuries.

No very innovating political theorists arose independently in colonial America. Puritan political ideas were the reflection of the contemporary English political controversy; and Virginian champions of liberty, down to Patrick Henry, appealed to the English Whig concepts of freedom. Certain colonial governors might be desperately unpopular, and opposed by petition or positive resistance; yet there was little deep-felt dissent from the distant general authority of Crown and Parliament, down to the eve of the Revolution. This colonial acquiescence in prescriptive English political usages and ideas is the more remarkable when one remembers that a considerable part of the colonial population was not English by descent, and when one takes into account the fact that America had been a refuge for the partisans of more than one cause which had been lost in Britain.

So long as British military and naval forces protected the Thirteen Colonies against the ambitions of France and Spain, loyalty to the homeland was an obvious necessity. Throughout the "Old French Wars" (1689 to 1763), as they would be called by later Americans, the colonies stood in peril of foreign conquest. King William's War, Queen Anne's War, King George's War, and the French and Indian War (all of these being American parallels of simultaneous military struggles in Europe and elsewhere) broke the power of the French in Canada. Britain bore the principal cost of military operations in America all that while. When George III, in a time of peace, would ask the Americans to pay in part for their own defense through taxation, many Americans grew indignant at this innovation.

Both Bacon's Rebellion and the Regulators' War had been attempts not to overthrow royal authority, but instead vehement demands that the royal governors should act more decisively against Indians on the frontiers. Most American men, unlike Europeans, were armed and accustomed to the use of firearms for hunting or defense of the household: they saw no need for standing armies after the French and the Indians had been broken. American trust in a militia was connected with American opposition to Europe's dynastic wars, rather than with a popular bellicosity: as Daniel Boorstin writes, "Americans would long find it hard to understand the military games played by kings, ministers, and generals who used uniformed pawns on distant battlefields, or the diplomatic games in which such wars were only interludes."[1] But the colonial militia fought well against French and Indians, perceiving that in America those struggles saved their own firesides.

In essence, then, colonial America was a poorer and more individualistic English society, transplanted—looking to Britain for ideas, for literature and the arts, for constitutional and legal precedents, for protection in time of need, yet content with British suzerainty most of the time. Because Parliament scarcely intervened at all in American affairs, Parliament's sovereignty went unchallenged until late colonial times.

The various Navigation Acts, by which Britain incorporated American commerce and manufactures into her economic scheme of mercantilism, actually gave the colonies more advantages than disadvantages. Only the requirement that all exported American tobacco must go to England, rather than being sold on the general European market, was much resented. Such other British regulations of American trade as seemed disadvantageous might be circumvented easily enough. Until George III's reign, the British government did not attempt to impose taxes upon the Americans, and left their domestic political concerns to their own management, through the several colonial assemblies. The authority of the royal governors was limited, because the colonial assemblies retained the power of the purse.

As for religion, the Church of England made no attempt to dictate to American consciences. In England, the Church was a great landowner, richly endowed even after the Reformation; but the Anglican parishes in America were poorly funded and lacked much connection with one another. The only important link between the parent Church of England and the colonial parishes—even in those colonies where Anglicanism was nominally the established faith—was the circumstance that nearly all parsons came out to the colonies from England. (No clergymen were ordained in America, and few young Americans studied in England with the hope of being ordained.) After 1688, no religious controversies seriously troubled relations between England and America—except (after 1774) New England's resentment of the Quebec Act, by which Parliament had conceded religious toleration to the Catholic French-Canadians. In church concerns, as in state concerns, salutary neglect had its rewards, even if that policy grew out of English indifference.

Although very English in culture, the Thirteen Colonies gradually developed a public order, and a type of character, that differed from their English models in important respects. We need to consider here the sort of leadership that arose in America; the patterns of self-government; and the cast of American religious belief.

American Gentlemen

Democracy in America was made possible by the growth of a colonial aristocracy. That is not really a paradox, for (as Solon knew, and Aristotle) no democracy can achieve much, or even survive long, without a body of able leaders.

"By aristocracy," John Adams would write to John Taylor of Caroline, in 1814, "I understand all those men who can command, influence, or procure more than an average of votes; by an aristocrat every man who can and will influence one man to vote besides himself. Few men will deny that there is a natural aristocracy of virtues and talents in every nation and in every party, in every city and village."[2] Adams and Taylor both were members of that colonial aristocracy of talents, which became a republican aristocracy.

Such an aristocracy of virtues and talents began to make itself felt in the earliest American settlements; and once some Americans had acquired large tracts of land, or wealth from commerce—or both—there developed a class of American gentlemen. That class would dominate American politics, through colonial assemblies and local governments, and through the standards it set. That class would sign the Declaration of Independence and write the Constitution of the United States.

Very few of the early settlers in America were gentlemen by birth—despite the appetite of twentieth-century American families for acquiring doubtful ancestral coats of arms. The Winthrops and Saltonstalls of Massachusetts, the Washingtons and Randolphs of Virginia, could claim English pedigrees as gentlefolk; but aside from such rare exceptions, the early Americans were the sons of small merchants or yeomen at best—and commonly of artisans or obscure rural folk. John Adams had no notion even of from what place in England his grandfather came; Benjamin Franklin's father, though he had emigrated from England, presently forgot all about his own connections there. Those early American families which did preserve some record of their British origins seldom could boast of descent from a squire, let alone a lord: the Eliots of Massachusetts, soon eminent in the peculiar aristocracy of New England and still a prominent family today (T.S. Eliot having been one of them), were descended from a humble cordwainer of the Somerset village of East Coker, who came over to Massachusetts Bay in 1667.

But, as John Adams wrote to John Taylor, the possession of lands and other wealth, and good family connections, presently establish an aristocracy in every society. "Would Washington have ever been commander of the revolutionary army or president of the United States, if he had not married the rich widow of Mr. Custis? Would Jefferson ever have been president of the United States if he had not married the daughter of Mr. Wales?" Talent tends to join itself to property, and out of that union comes aristocracy, which tends to perpetuate itself.

Successful Americans had before them the model of the English gentleman—who in some sense was the institutional descendant of the Renaissance courtier and, more remotely, of the medieval knight. The landed gentry of England during colonial times, and for long after, set the tone of English society and governed its politics through their parliamentary seats and their control of local government. The rising men of the colonies knew these living exemplars; also they were familiar with various manuals on the duties and education of gentlemen, among them Sir Thomas Elyot's *Boke Named the Governour,* written in Tudor times. The ideal of the gentleman was much discussed about the middle of the seventeenth century, when England was torn by civil war and the colonists of Virginia, Maryland, and Massachusetts were cast upon their own resources. In 1648, that witty English clergyman Thomas Fuller published his popular book *The Holy State and the Profane State,* which contains descriptions of "The True Gentleman" (with supplementary essays on his hospitality, dress, travelling, company, recreations, and marriage) and of "The Degenerous Gentleman."

A gentleman either comes of "ancient and worshipful parentage," Fuller wrote, or else "if his birth be not, at least his qualities are generous. . . .Thus valour makes him son to Caesar, learning entitles him kinsman to Tully, and piety reports him nephew to godly Constantine. It graceth a gentleman of low descent and high desert, when he will own the meanness of his parentage. How ridiculous is it when many men brag, that their families are more ancient than the Moon, which all know are later than the star which some seventy years since shined in Cassiopea."[3]

The leading men of the Thirteen Colonies could not honestly brag of genealogies "more ancient than the Moon," but they could develop generous qualities. The English gentleman, first of all, was a man of good breeding—that is, of courteous and graceful manners. He was a man of honor, who would not lie or cheat; he was a man of valor, who would not flee before enemies; a man of duty, who would serve king and country as magistrate or member of a representative assembly; a man of practical charity, a steward under God of what wealth he might have inherited or acquired, for the common good. (As for the Degenerous Gentleman, "vacation is his vocation," in Fuller's description.) The gentleman is not puffed up with pride at his inheritance, Fuller declares; he is a diligent university student; he acquires a knowledge of the laws; he rides his horse well; he accepts public office if it is given to him; he is severe but just; he judges of any matter meditatively, but acts swiftly when the right of the matter is clear. "He furnisheth and prepareth himself in peace against time of war." He will be known by his openhandedness, his dress, his companions. "He is courteous and affable to his neighbors. As the sword of the best tempered metal is most flexible, so the truly generous are the most pliant and courteous in their behavior to their inferiors."[3]

Such characteristics the colonial men of property and education aspired to develop in themselves. Many succeeded in becoming gentlemen as true as their English counterparts with the long pedigrees, even if few reached the perfection of the type sketched by Thomas Fuller. Without their leadership and example, the moral and social order of the raw new America might have become as brutal throughout as life on the frontier frequently became.

These early American gentlemen, planters or merchants or clergymen or lawyers, never received patents of nobility from Windsor, though a very few Americans were knighted in colonial times. They formed an aristocracy of talents, which presently became also an aristocracy of birth (though usually a hard-working and public-spirited aristocracy), as certain families in every colony achieved eminence and intermarried one with another.

"By *natural aristocracy*, in general, may be understood those superiorities of influence in society which grow out of the constitution of human nature," Adams told Taylor. "By *artificial aristocracy*, those inequalities of right and superiorities of influence which are created and established by civil laws." The American gentlemen, like the common people of the colonies, desired no superimposed artificial aristocracy.

What happened in Carolina emphasizes this point. Charles II granted all Carolina (later divided into North and South Carolina) to a group of eight proprietors, Lord Ashley most active among them. This Anthony Ashley Cooper, later the first Earl of Shaftesbury, was the cleverest of Whig politicians. Early in life, he had been much influenced by the theorist James Harrington; the close friend of his later years was John Locke. At Lord Ashley's request, and with his participation, Locke drew up an instrument of government for the colony, "The Fundamental Constitutions of Carolina." Neither Ashley Cooper nor John Locke ever had set foot in America, but they had every confidence in this "Grand Model" for a perfect society.

By the Fundamental Constitutions, an American nobility was decreed. The greatest noblemen in Carolina would be the lords proprietors, with their senior, the lord palatine, at their head. Then would come landgraves; after them, caciques. (Since only the king of England could confer the old English titles of nobility, Locke and his patron had to be content with borrowing titles from the Germans and the Indians.) All these nobles would hold immense tracts of land from the proprietors. Also there would be gentlemen commoners, lords of the manor, holding not more than twelve thousand acres—the squires of Carolina. Below them would be the yeomen, who would vote if they held at least fifty acres. The proprietors and the noblemen were to hold two-fifths of the lands of Carolina, and the commoners three-fifths.

This constitutional document, drawn in part from Harrington's theories but Locke's creation in essence, had other curiosities. No legislative act should endure more than sixty years, it was ordered: after that term, any law should become null and void. But this constitution itself must be immutable: "Since multiplicity of comments as well as of laws have great inconveniences, and serve only to obscure and perplex, all manner of comments and expositions on any part of these Fundamental Constitutions, or any part of the common or statute law of Carolina, are absolutely prohibited." Discussion brings change; the Fundamental Constitutions being perfect, any change must be for the worse.

But this fantastic constitution never took effect. Lord Ashley might be cunning; Harrington and Locke might be men of grand designs; still, the Carolina settlers rejected the Fundamental Constitutions, even when the document was modified. From the first, the colonists were suspicious of political abstractions. They governed themselves, instead, according to the practical circumstances in which they found themselves. Carolina's proprietors, indeed, had difficulty in maintaining their claims at all; and in 1719, a bloodless popular uprising overthrew the proprietary administration, so that thereafter South Carolina was a royal colony. This should be a chastening thought for those historians who argue that John Locke's writings formed the American political mind; for when colonists were confronted with Locke's one practical proposal for the colonies, they rejected it root and branch.

So although English culture and English law were transplanted to America, the English aristocracy was not. America's own early aristocracy, self-created, assumed leadership: an aristocracy without hereditary titles or formal privileges, an aristocracy made up of what Edmund Burke would call "men of actual virtue." In Carolina, with its capital Charleston on its narrow neck between the Ashley and Cooper rivers, arose a class of gentlemen who combined the large-scale planting of rice and indigo—and later cotton—with the development of seaborne commerce. They came to dominate the colony through the Carolina assembly. In all the other colonies, though with variations, some similar class composed eventually a natural aristocracy.

The Virginian gentleman-planter is best remembered as one type of this class of leaders—in part because the "Virginia Dynasty" of American presidents were members of that class. Some plantation houses, now open to the public, still stand to suggest the masterful Virginia gentleman's pattern of life: Carter's Grove on the James, Washington's Mount Vernon on the Potomac, Jefferson's Monticello far inland, several others. These were like the country houses of English squires or Scottish lairds, though the servants and the agricultural laborers of the plantations were black slaves, not freeborn Englishmen or Scots.

In 1814, when Jefferson's Embargo and the war with Britain had damaged severely the plantation-economy, a Virginian planter of the strong-willed old breed, John Randolph of Roanoke, described to his Massachusetts friend, Josiah Quincy, the old aristocracy of the Tidewater: "Before the Revolution the lower country of Virginia, pierced for more than a hundred miles from the seaboard by numerous bold and navigable rivers, was inhabited by a race of planters, of English descent, who dwelt on their principal estates on the borders of those noble streams. The proprietors were generally well educated,—some of them at the best schools of the mother country, the rest at William and Mary, then a seminary of *learning,* under classical masters. Their habitations and establishments, for the most part spacious and costly, in some instances displayed taste and elegance. They were the seats of hospitality. The possessors were gentlemen,—better-bred men were not to be found in the British dominions. As yet party spirit was not. This fruitful source of mischief had not then poisoned society. Every door was open to those who maintained the appearance of gentlemen. Each planter might be said, almost without exaggeration, to have a harbor at his door. . . ."[4]

As John Randolph declared of himself in the nineteenth century, so might those gentlemen-planters have said of themselves in the seventeenth and eighteenth centuries: "I am an aristocrat: I love liberty, I hate equality." Such men, when their liberty seemed in question, made a Revolution—on conservative principles. Their class dwindled steadily after the Revolution that began in 1775, and Randolph suggested to Quincy the reasons for decay: too generous a style of living and too large debts, often poor agricultural practices, destruction by force during the Revolution, and Jefferson's legal reforms—chief among those the abolishing of the statute of entail(by which landed property passed regularly from father to eldest son) and the new statute of distributions that gave all children an equal share of an estate. Yet for a century and a half, this planter-aristocracy ruled the Old Dominion.

In most of the Thirteen Colonies, possession of large tracts of land was the foundation of gentlemen's fortunes, though even in the southern colonies successful men of business, professional people, and holders of university degrees made up a part of this informal aristocracy. It was so with the "patroons," the grand landed proprietors (chiefly Dutch by descent) along the Hudson, in the colony of New York, who drew rents from the white farmers on their lands. It was true even of the "river gods," the planters or large farmers of the Narragansett Valley in New England, with their commercial and social center at Newport, Rhode Island. The gentlemen of Charleston, of Philadelphia, of Newport, of New York, and of other flourishing colonial towns (though not generally of Virginia) often were both landholders and men of commerce: they being industrious and shrewd, as well as endowed with manners and education, usually their ascendancy went unresented by the common people of colonial times.

In most of New England, however, the leading men were of a somewhat different cast. Though most of them owned land, often it was a single infertile farm, or a few such little farms. Clergymen, merchants, ship-owners, and (as the economy grew) bankers formed that northern aristocracy of talent and family; Harvard's and Yale's professors, too, exerted strong influence. At Boston, New Haven, Providence, and lesser towns, there grew up a body of sober gentlemen whose money came from trade, for the greater part, and from such manufactures as early New England produced. Like Virginia, New England lived by exports; those exports did not come mostly from New England's soil, nevertheless: they were rum, naval stores, wooden wares, timber, salt fish, train-oil, furs—together with some surplus foodstuffs. In New England, as a rule, the fine houses stood in the towns, not in the countryside, and communities were closer knit than elsewhere.

New England's Puritan patrimony, if seemingly more democratic in church-structure and in politics than the cultural inheritance of other colonies, did not exclude gentlemen. The stiff dignity of John Adams, a successful man of law, suggests the New England pattern. In the seventeenth century, there was observed a marked social distinction between the styles of "master" (or "Mr.") and of "goodman": the former was a gentleman, the latter an ordinary citizen. (Indeed, "Mr." then was a style commanding more respect than "honorable" might today.) No one would have ventured to address a Winthrop, a Mather, a Cotton, or a Saltonstall as "goodman."

Even more than in the colonies to the south, learning and

strict morality were the marks of a New England gentleman. Yet these New England leaders came from a variety of backgrounds. Money and daring, rather than devoutness, might make a grand gentleman: consider William Phips (1651-1695), born in Maine. He came upon a treasure-map; he sailed to the West Indies in search of sunken Spanish gold; he found it—three hundred thousand pounds' worth of it, of which sixteen thousand pounds sterling fell to his share. He was knighted; he led sea-expeditions against Canada; he became governor of Massachusetts. Piety counted for much in New England's society, but so did an eye for the main chance.

Or take the great family of Winthrop, in which the Puritan aristocracy of talents and the Puritan aristocracy of birth were united. The first John Winthrop (1588-1649) was the chief figure in the founding of Boston, the first governor of Massachusetts (elected to twelve terms), and a high exemplar of the Puritan life of spirit. His son, the second John Winthrop (1606-1676), also born in England, founded the New England towns that are now Ipswich, Saybrook, and New London; was several times governor of Connecticut; became deeply learned in science, and was the first American elected to membership in the Royal Society (of philosophy and science) in England; established iron-works.

Fitz-John Winthrop, the second John Winthrop's son (1638-1707) born in Massachusetts, was educated at Harvard, served against the Scots with the army of the English Parliament, commanded the expedition of the New York and Connecticut militia against Canada in 1690, fought the Dutch in Long Island, was Connecticut's agent in London for four years, and served several terms as governor of Connecticut. Two later John Winthrops of this line became eminent scientists, during colonial times; yet other descendants of the first John Winthrop would be eminent in politics, military affairs, and scholarship far into the nineteenth century. A score of other New England families illustrate the energetic character of the New England gentleman, passed down (along with their Puritan religious patrimony) from generation to generation.

Whatever differences existed between the gentry of one colony and another, in every colony, that class looked to Britain for standards. By the middle of the eighteenth century, hundreds of young men from the American gentry studied at the English and Scottish universities, or learnt law in London's Inns of Court. Nearly all books came from British booksellers, and British architectural styles were reflected, if with adaptations, in colonial architecture; so were fashions in the arts and in dress. British administrators and military officers sent out to America, and an occasional peer as royal governor—whatever their failings—were arbiters of colonial manners. The ties of every colonial capital to London were stronger than the ties of one colonial capital to another. So it was that the American gentleman, despite his lack of a pedigree extending back beyond the coming of his ancestor to American shores, tended to model himself upon the "true gentleman" of Thomas Fuller, and the living successors of that exemplar whom he might encounter, one side of the Atlantic or the other.

Americans saw one such gentleman in the last of the colonizers, General James Oglethorpe—Christian soldier and friend to the unfortunate, admired by Samuel Johnson, conspicuous in London clubs, founder of the fortress-town of Savannah, full of fortitude and ability until he died at the age of ninety. Perhaps the American gentleman idealized his English models; if so, that did him no mischief.

In considerable part, America's social order was guided by gentlemen down until the day when that conscience-searching little Massachusetts gentleman John Quincy Adams lost the presidency of the United States to the frontier-soldier Andrew Jackson. Yet even with that event, the influence of the American gentleman would not end. Jackson himself, though he had begun at the very bottom of American society, was a member in his prime of the plantation gentry, with his Tennessee mansion called The Hermitage. A young man once remarked to Josiah Quincy (the Federalist who was John Randolph's correspondent), "Of course, General Jackson is not what you would call a gentleman!" But Quincy would not agree to that disparagement. For Quincy had found, when Jackson visited Massachusetts (and Quincy was his official host) to receive an honorary degree from Harvard, that "the seventh President was, in essence, a knightly personage—prejudiced, narrow, mistaken upon many points, it might be, but vigorously a gentleman in his high sense of honor and in the natural straightforward courtesies which are easily to be distinguished from the veneer of policy . . . ."[5]

Nearly all presidents of the United States, whatever their antecedents, have been gentlemen. Much as the ideal of the high old Roman virtue could ennoble a rough peasant soldier like Diocletian, the ideal of the gentleman in America persisted beneficently into democratic times. American social and political changes, occurring conspicuously in the 1830's, would reduce the direct political influence of the heirs of the colonial gentry. But one still hears the commendatory phrase, "He's a real gentleman." While people still say that, honor and courtesy continue to work in the American order.

The American understanding of the word "gentleman" probably was best expressed by James Fenimore Cooper, in his forthright book *The American Democrat* (1838). "In most countries," this first important American novelist would write, "birth is a principal source of social distinction, society being divided into castes, the noble having an hereditary claim to be superior to the plebian. This is an unwise and an arbitrary distinction that has led to most of the social diseases of the old world, and from which America is happily exempt. . . . In a social sense, there are orders here, as in all other countries, but the classes run into each other more easily, the lines of separation are less strongly drawn, and their shadows are more intimately blended. . . . The word 'gentleman' has a positive and limited signification. It means one elevated above the mass of society by his birth, manners, attainments, character and social condition. As no civilized society can exist without these social differences, nothing is gained by denying the use of the term."[6]

Such an assumption is implicit, Cooper suggested —though it is not put into words—in the American political constitutions: one man is *not* as good as another, and a society without sound social distinctions is a miserable society, and a republic requires leaders with a sense of honor. The existence of a recognizable class of colonial gentlemen made possible the first great national democratic society: had they been lacking, or few in number, the American Republic might have fallen promptly into violence and corruption—if, indeed, it could have been erected at all.

Representative Assemblies and Local Autonomy

"Liberty!" was a rallying cry on the eve of the American Revolution precisely because the people of the Thirteen Colonies always had known a high degree of political freedom. They were not demanding new rights, but were protesting in defense of political customs long established and sanctioned. The Patriots turned to theorists' books only for philosophical confirmation of practices they had enjoyed in America from the beginning.

Because the British thought of their colonies as commercial investments almost exclusively, Crown and Parliament never established any regular and consistent system of administration for the far-flung eighteenth-century empire. The North American colonies—so far as they were controlled by any systematic London policy at all—lay under the jurisdiction of the Board of Trade and Plantations, established by William III in 1696. (Earlier, there had been an ineffectual standing committee of the king's Privy Council called the "Lords of Trade"; earlier still, the royal authority had operated only through those trading companies and those proprietors to whom royal charters had been granted.) Parliament left the Thirteen Colonies so much to their own contrivances that when the Revolution was at hand, the Patriots would argue that only the king, and never the British Parliament, had any claim to sovereignty over North America.

The Patriots' demand that there be no "taxation without

representation" would be founded upon usages that began with the first settlements in America.* For until the reign of George III, no British government had attempted to lay taxes upon the colonists. The colonies were valuable to Britain for their commerce and raw materials, not as sources of revenue for the British Exchequer. When large expenditures were required for defending the colonies, the British government would ask the colonial assemblies to vote grants for defraying part of the cost of military operations—which grants sometimes were made grudgingly or insufficiently. (Only under strong pressure from William III—to whom William Penn's loyalty was suspect—would Penn, as proprietor of Pennsylvania, agree to raise eighty soldiers to help defend his colony; during the wars with the French and Indians, the Quaker-dominated Pennsylvania assembly would appropriate only modest sums even to supply some food and clothing for distressed Indians allied with the British, let alone provide armed men or munitions.) Taxes for the internal administration of the colonies were levied by the colonial assemblies, as they pleased or did not please. This control of the public purse by the colonists' legislative bodies assured the Thirteen Colonies of virtual autonomy in domestic policy.

Representative government in America grew up early, on the model of English representative government. In some of the colonies, provision was made in their charters (whether corporate, proprietary, or royal charters) for a representative assembly; in other colonies, such assemblies began to be held by the colonists themselves, without express authorization from England, but even the Stuart kings found it prudent to

---

* Actually, the American opposition to George III would make no serious attempt to obtain the right to send representatives to the British House of Commons: they meant, in effect, "no taxation by Parliament." Even had the colonies been permitted to elect members to the House of Commons, that bloc of colonial members would have been in a hopeless minority if their interest had conflicted with that of the mother country; besides, there were no American peers to sit in the House of Lords. A conceivable alternative to representation at Westminster would have been a separate national American Parliament, including all Thirteen Colonies, comparable to the Irish Parliament of the eighteenth century; like the Irish Parliament, an American Parliament would have acknowledged the sovereignty of the Crown, and passed its own money-bills. But nothing of the sort was considered soberly on either side of the Atlantic.

recognize these assemblies—so obtaining the consent of the governed. (In 1619, says a colonial writer, "a House of Burgesses broke out in Virginia.") Although at first these assemblies were expected by the Crown or the proprietors to be mere ratifying and tax-granting bodies (as the medieval Parliaments had been originally), in short order the colonial assemblies successfully asserted their own power to pass their own colonial statutes. As the Westminster Parliament's powers grew during the seventeenth and eighteenth centuries, so in parallel fashion the powers of these colonial assemblies increased—though without authorization or direction from Westminster or Windsor.

To restrain the colonial assemblies' claims and to carry on executive tasks, there existed in every colony a governor—in some, appointed by the king; in others, by the proprietors (although only in Pennsylvania and Maryland did proprietary governors survive beyond the middle of the eighteenth century); in Connecticut and Rhode Island, the governors were elected by colonial freeholders. These governors were advised and supported by governors' councils, made up of eminent and wealthy colonials—in modest emulation of the king's Privy Council in England. These councils scarcely can be regarded as an upper legislative house, comparable to the House of Lords: for the colonial councillors all were appointed by the Crown, and in theory, at least, were dependent upon royal favor.

Struggles for power between a governor and his council on the one side, and an assembly on the other, occurred frequently. But the odds ordinarily ran against any arbitrary governor. Lacking funds except from assemblies' grants, distant from London, and not backed immediately by strong military forces, the governors fell into difficulties if assemblies should be hostile toward them. (In Massachusetts, when Governor Andros confronted a successful armed rising after news of the English Revolution of 1688 had reached Boston, he had only twelve soldiers under his command.) Effective representative government was better entrenched in North America, especially after 1688, than anywhere else in the world except Britain.

These colonial assemblies, nevertheless, were anything

but radical bodies. They were composed overwhelmingly of the colonial gentry: the most famous of them, Virginia's House of Burgesses, was the most aristocratic. Similarly, the wealthy Quakers of Philadelphia dominated the Pennsylvania assembly, the Low Country merchants and planters controlled South Carolina's, the New England assemblies were made up of those New England gentlemen described earlier in this chapter, and so it went in New York, Maryland, and everywhere else. The franchise differed somewhat from one colony to another, but in general most freeholders of land could vote for candidates for the assemblies. Because many of these freeholders had no very large amount of real property, a democratic element entered into the colonial constitutions. Even so, the reputation and wealth of the American gentry sufficed to secure the predominance of their class in every assembly.

This predominance of the gentry produced little class hostility; for ordinarily disputes in the assemblies were not along class lines, but between the governor and the assembly, or sometimes between the eastern region of a colony and the people toward its western frontier. The smaller freeholders seem ordinarily to have thought themselves sufficiently represented by the richer freeholders who made up the majority in every assembly.

Though under the Stuarts the assemblies might fear for their prerogatives from time to time, after the accession of William and Mary the colonial legislatures grew secure enough—a natural development paralleling the terms of the Act of Settlement in Britain. Although of course there was no general American assembly comparable to the Congress established under the Constitution of the United States, in every colony the habit of representative self-government was so firmly grounded by the 1760's that royal or parliamentary decisions contrary to an assembly's will could not be enforced without the dispatch of military or naval forces from England. And even that extreme measure, in the long run, would not defeat the assemblies' power.

If the colonial assemblies were led by the affluent and well-born, so were the various types of local government in

America. The forms of local administration varied widely: most colonies left local concerns to local authorities, although South Carolina's system was strictly centralized. For our present purpose, it is best to examine the institutions of local government in Virginia and Massachusetts, the two most populous and self-assertive colonies.

In the Old Dominion, county governments overshadowed towns; indeed, the typical county center was scarcely even a hamlet, but instead a court house in the countryside, with an inn, a grocery, and a few straggling houses nearby. Some good examples of the "court house" pattern survive in Virginia to this day—Charlotte Court House, where old Patrick Henry debated with young John Randolph, for one. The Virginian counties were controlled by the county courts—which were composed of a county's justices of the peace (perhaps eight to twelve of them), meeting as a body. These county courts amounted to benevolent oligarchies, powers unto themselves; even the House of Burgesses had to defer to them on occasion, and did not venture to interfere with their authority.

The justices of the peace who sat in the county court were appointed by the royal governor, in theory; actually, as the pattern of local government developed in Virginia, these justices became virtually a self-perpetuating body, for the governors found it unwise to appoint any new justices except those candidates on a list submitted by the county courts, or to interfere with what became life tenure of office. The justices (who received neither salary nor fees), and therefore the members of the county courts, were men of large landed properties, usually well educated, and sometimes trained in the law: Virginia gentlemen.

These county courts selected, indirectly or directly, all other county officials; they had jurisdiction over most criminal cases, as well as civil; they possessed in fact judicial, legislative, executive, and electoral powers in their counties. Thus most of the practical business of government in Virginia was carried on by men who were neither elected nor, in reality, appointed, but who chose their own successors. "Neither Williamsburg nor London controlled the government of the

Virginia counties," Charles Sydnor writes.[7] Such magistrates would not take kindly to any attempt of royal authority to interfere with colonial affairs; but neither would they be persuaded by radical theories of politics which would arise in France during the eighteenth century. In general, they were not men of theory at all, but of practical experience in governing. Being intimately acquainted with their neighbors in those sprawling rural counties, in a sense they represented public opinion and responded to it on occasion, even though they never had to submit their candidacies to a public vote.

"The semi-independent status of the counties had long-run effects on American history as well as immediate effects on the choice of political leadership in Virginia," Sydnor remarks. "Those Virginians who helped draft the Federal Constitution had lived under a quasi-federal system in colonial Virginia. They had seen the advantages of strongly-fortified local positions during conflicts with the king's representatives at Williamsburg. The experiences of these men in Virginian politics and government must not be forgotten when reflecting on the origins of the American federal system of government....The courts were undemocratic, but they served democracy well."[8]

Though in no other colony were there county courts powerful as Virginia's, the county tended to be the basic unit of government in the southern colonies and later in those states strongly influenced by the states of the southern seaboard. In New England, however, and later in those states where New Englanders settled and to which they transplanted their institutions, the basic unit of government became the "town"—or, more properly speaking, the township.

New England's town meetings often have been described as models of the later American democracy—although that praise is more applicable to the America of yesteryear than to twentieth-century urbanized America. Certainly the town meetings are an important aspect of what Orestes Brownson (a New Englander by birth) would call America's "territorial democracy." In the beginning, nevertheless, township government in the New England colonies was distinctly not democratic in structure.

By "town" (after New England's population began to spread beyond the early settlements, and especially once the pattern of detached farms came to prevail in New England, as in the other colonies) was generally meant a quasi-rural township, roughly six miles square. In New England, the counties had next to no political functions, practical authority being concentrated in these "towns." (The pattern soon spread to eastern Long Island, populated by New Englanders, where it still exists.)

Massachusetts' declaration of "Laws and Liberties" (1648) opened town meetings even to persons not classified as "freemen"—that is, to persons who were not members of the Puritan churches. These, though they could not vote at town meetings, could present petitions and complaints; so, from an early date, the meetings helped to train the whole population in participatory self-government. Township officers were elected annually, another practice that tended to relate local government directly to public opinion.

Yet only by slow stages did the town meetings become the schools for democracy that Alexis de Tocqueville would admire in the 1830's. At first, although in theory state and church were not identical in New England, only church members in the strictest sense were permitted to vote at these meetings—that is, godly folk who could testify to a direct personal experience of salvation. This being too exclusive, presently the privilege was extended to persons whose ancestors had known such a spiritual experience. Only these "freemen," too, could vote for deputies to the Massachusetts General Court, that colony's representative assembly.

In 1692, a new colonial charter for Massachusetts changed these provisions to make property-holders, rather than the religious elect, the political power in the colony. "It was not for the sake of majority rule," Rowland Berthoff comments, "but rather in order to maintain the Puritan moral community that the towns enlisted the 'prudent and amicable composition and agreement' of all independent men—of all those whose economic position gave them the freedom to exercise a will of their own in town affairs."[9]

At these monthly town meetings, proposed local ordinances were approved or disapproved by majority vote of the qualified freemen attending, and many questions could be discussed at some length; public opinion could make itself heard effectively. As the hold of Puritan belief weakened in the eighteenth century—many influential New Englanders going over to Episcopalianism or to other Christian denominations—the town meeting became less a place where consensus of the members of the church was obtained, and more purely a civic institution. In this later form, one finds the town meeting still a living political reality, at least in rural regions of states far to the west which have been powerfully influenced by the New England mind.

Both county and town governments—the one emphasized in certain colonies, the other in different colonies, but both embedded in the American political structure—were adaptations from British institutions of local government that extended far back to medieval times or even to Anglo-Saxon patterns. Because of the lack of any central British authority operating systematically upon all Thirteen Colonies from a center in North America, and because in the larger colonies even the colonial capitals could not hope to govern counties and towns directly, local government in British North America sometimes manifested a vigor and independence greater than had been known in the mother country. Thus Virginia's method of issuing commissions to justices of the peace, rather than electing them, was drawn from old English practice; but in Virginia those justices, acting as a body, acquired an ascendancy over all sorts of local affairs that in the mother country were reserved to other agencies of government. These modes of American local government persisted in part throughout the United States until very recent years, although nowadays they retreat before the growth of cities and suburbs, shifts in population, different ways of life, and positive governmental reorganization.

In the French and Spanish colonies, detailed supervision from Paris or Madrid was the rule; the authority of royal governors was far greater there than in the English colonies; colonial representative bodies of the French and Spanish settlements were correspondingly feebler than in British North America, and colonial local government less energetic.

The autonomous character of British colonies, produced by "salutary neglect," increased their power of self-defense and their desire to extend their boundaries far beyond their early frontiers. Also that autonomous character developed a proud spirit of provincial and local liberties that could not be put down, when the crisis came, by all the might of Britain.

Colonial America's freedom outwardly seemed the freedom of a peculiar colonial aristocracy, rather than a democratic condition. But there lay in it the seeds of a democratic society. Those seeds would begin to germinate as the center of population shifted westward after the Revolution. The people of the western territories, beyond the Appalachians, would defer less to distant British precedent, and would sweep away many of the cultural or institutional checks upon popular opinions and popular desires. Massachusetts and Virginia, though they sent out many thousands of their people to the western frontiers, and gave the West their general frame of political institutions, would come in time to count for less than they had in colonial days. As early as 1805, the Virginian planter-politician John Randolph of Roanoke would declare that "the Louisiana purchase was the greatest curse that ever befell us."[10] He meant that the ways of the old Thirteen Colonies would be engulfed by the western democracy. Yet the chief aspects of representative government and of local political institutions, taking form in the seaboard colonies, would be communicated to a national population a hundred times greater than that of the Thirteen Colonies in the middle of the eighteenth century.

Interesting and complex though the political history of colonial North America is, the central meaning of that history may be put quite simply, so far as the understanding of American order is concerned. It is this: American freedom and order grew "organically" in colonial times, out of the practical social experience of the colonial people, who adapted British political institutions to their American circumstances. The colonial leaders did not design their society upon any abstract plan; few of them were utopians. Beginning with British example and precedent, they accepted as good most of their political inheritance from England and

Scotland, and they put it into practice without more alterations than it needed. While adapting these transplanted political forms, nevertheless, America's economic and social circumstances produced an effectual political order considerably different from its British original.

Though many colonial gentlemen were well read in history, philosophy, and humane letters, they did not shape their order upon any political manual, ancient or modern. Their developing forms of civil government could be discerned well before John Locke published his Treatises. The members of Maryland's assembly, for instance, asserted as early as 1635 that the representatives of the people might make their own statutes, as well as ratify or disapprove the lord proprietor's laws. The New World's order was not consciously or defiantly new: it arose out of experience (including the experience of their ancestors in the Old World) and out of practical necessity.

The New World's Christianity

Most colonial people took their religious beliefs from Britain, much as they accepted the general form of English political institutions. Yet certain emphases and tendencies among American Christians were new to Europeans visiting the Thirteen Colonies.

Both the direct influence and the indirect influence of religion upon American society were incalculably strong, Alexis de Tocqueville would find in the 1830's; and the characteristics which he discovered in that decade had prevailed about the middle of the eighteenth century. "The sects that exist in the United States are innumerable," Tocqueville wrote. "They all differ in respect to the worship which is due to the Creator; but they all agree in respect to the duties which are due from man to man. Each sect adores the Deity in its own peculiar manner, but all sects preach the same moral law in the name of God. . . .Religion in America takes no direct part in the government of society, but it must be regarded as the first of their political institutions; for if it does not impart a taste for freedom, it facilitates the use of it. . . .How is it possible that society should escape destruction if the moral tie is not strengthened in proportion as the political tie is relaxed? And what can be done with a people who are their own masters if they are not submissive to the Deity?"[11]

It was not a mystical or a highly imaginative Christian belief that Tocqueville would find prevalent in America; nor was it strong in ritual and liturgy. "I have seen no country in which Christianity is clothed with fewer forms, figures, and observances than in the United States, or where it presents more distinct, simple, and general notions to the mind. Although the Christians of America are divided into a multitude of sects, they all look upon their religion in the same light." And there was in America little of medieval man's condemnation of this world here below: "The American ministers of the Gospel do not attempt to draw or to fix all the thoughts of man upon the life to come; they are willing to surrender a portion of his heart to the cares of the present, seeming to consider the goods of this world as important, though secondary, objects."[12]

Among the earnest Puritans and the grave Quakers, during most of the seventeenth century, salvation and immortality had been man's principal objects; yet even among those sects, too, hope of substantial success in this world had been powerful from the first—and generally had been gratified. Late in the seventeenth and early in the eighteenth century, until a tremendous evangelical revival commenced about 1734, the several Christian communions settled down to moralistic Christian routine. Christian moral teaching was so generally accepted that no one ventured to challenge it, but this mood was far removed from the religious passions of the sixteenth and seventeenth centuries.

The principal bodies of Christians within British North America already have been described: the Anglicans and the Calvinists. The latter included the Puritans or Congregationalists, the Presbyterians, and the Baptists. (Roger Williams, in Rhode Island, was the first American Baptist leader; the

Baptists' differences from other Calvinistic churches need not be analyzed here.) A fair number of Lutherans, a sprinkling of Catholics, a few Jews, and a variety of little pietistic sects also inhabited colonial America, but were not then influential upon society. One body of believers, however, deserves attention—though its working upon American order has been more subtle than popular: the Society of Friends, or Quakers.

In Pennsylvania and West Jersey, the Quakers exerted during the first half of the eighteenth century a predominance that they lost when hard political decisions were forced upon them. Going far beyond the Puritans in their quest for a Christian life of apostolic simplicity, the Quakers began as followers of George Fox (who travelled in America), about the middle of the seventeenth century. They rejected dogmas, creeds, rituals, liturgies, priests; they rejected even preaching ministers, in the usual Protestant sense of that term; they rejected sacramental practices, even baptism and the Lord's Supper; they rejected church buildings; they admitted women to equality in their meetings. These doctrines, or rather anti-doctrines, made them suspect to both Anglicans and Calvinists; and the eccentric ways of many early Quakers—who, seeming to desire martyrdom, deliberately affronted the established churches—brought fierce persecution upon the Society of Friends. Through the Inward Light, the Quakers proclaimed, any person might triumph wholly over sin, here on earth. They would "swear not at all," taking literally an injunction of Christ; rather than be violent in any circumstances, they would turn the other cheek. They seemed ill suited for the rough New World.

Nevertheless, they prospered mightily in Pennsylvania, which the kindly William Penn (whose father had been a famous English admiral) had obtained from Charles II as a refuge for them and for other persecuted sects. Their "Holy Experiment" created the biggest colonial town, Philadelphia, and a remarkable degree of security, prosperity, and freedom—so long as the hard-fighting Scotch-Irish and other frontiersmen of western Pennsylvania sheltered the Quakers of eastern Pennsylvania from the Indians and the French.

The Inward Light had its material reward. "Like the

ethical code of the Puritans, Quaker ethics were conducive to the growth of the capitalistic spirit and to the increasing commercial prosperity of Pennsylvania," Louis B. Wright points out. "The Puritan preachers of Boston never emphasized the virtues of thrift, diligence, and sobriety with greater earnestness than the Quaker merchants of Philadelphia. Mystics as they were, they never let the illumination of inward revelation blind them to the good things of this earth. Few traders had sharper eyes for a sixpence or showed greater care for the conservation of money than the Friends displayed. Though they rejected ostentation and extravagance, they loved no ascetic retirement from the world and made good use of their money."[13]

Even at the height of their ascendancy in that colony, the Quakers did not make up a majority of Pennsylvania's population; but their wealth and intelligence gave them effective control of the Pennsylvania assembly until 1756. Then their principles of the order of the soul became impossible to reconcile with order in the commonwealth—or even with survival of the commonwealth. In the American phase of the Seven Years' War, the French and Indians fell upon western Pennsylvania. As pacifists, the Quakers would not take up arms against the raiders, or help others to defend the frontier. Their established policy of generosity toward the Indians availed them nothing. The governor of Pennsylvania and his council declared war upon the Delaware and Shawnee Indians; the Pennsylvania assembly, with its majority of Quaker assemblymen, either must supply funds to carry on the war or else must seem treasonable and indifferent to the commonwealth's fate.

In that stern test, the leading Quakers resigned from the assembly, rather than assume responsibility, and Anglican assemblymen took their places. Never thereafter did the Quakers regain political supremacy. In the Revolution, twenty years later, they would stand neutral.

Whether or not all human beings may be redeemed from sin in this life, Quaker principles could not fend off tomahawk and scalping-knife. So, their personal order not consisting with a tolerable public order, the knotty old problems of defense of the realm undid the Quakers as a possible leading force in American society. Their numbers thereafter did not increase in proportion to the growth of American population, and today there are more Quakers in the African state of Kenya than in the whole of the United States.

In some respects, for all that, Quaker spirit has contributed to the American order. Their upholding of civil liberties, their toleration, and their charitable bent entered deeply into American institutions. Two members of the Society of Friends would be elected to the presidency of the United States, in the twentieth century. Though the Holy Experiment could not maintain itself in a violent world, the Quakers' brotherly love did something to restrain and modify the aggressive individualism of expanding America.

Far more than William Penn and his friends, a young Anglican clergyman reinvigorated Christian belief in the Thirteen Colonies—not so much through his own brief ministry there as through the followers he won. In the middle of Reynolds Square, Savannah, there stands today a statue of John Wesley, the founder of Methodism—who to his dying day considered himself a clergyman of the Church of England. Wesley went out to the young colony of Georgia for the Society for the Propagation of the Gospel, in 1735; made enemies in Savannah by his strict High Church ways; and was back in England by 1738. But at Savannah he had formed among his congregation a little circle that discussed the Christian life, prayed, and sang. "These were the first rudiments of the Methodist societies," he would write in 1781. Also these were the beginnings of what would be called, in America, the Great Awakening—the rousing of Christians of the Thirteen Colonies from the lethargy of spirit into which they had been sliding.

It has been said that the evangelical Christianity of the Wesley family was one of the chief influences which saved England from following eighteenth-century France into ruinous revolution. Probably it is true, too, that the indirect influence of Wesley helped to keep the American Revolution within bounds. Methodist communicants numbered only a few thousands on the eve of the American Revolution, but the evangelical revival set in motion by Wesley spread to every colony and affected profoundly hundreds of thousands of members of other denominations. Initially this Great Awakening divided Christian churches, as well as rousing them; yet in the long run, the evangelical movement would permeate American Christianity and give that religion in the United States a character which endures noticeably to the present.

Appealing to the emotions, Wesley's preaching was bound up with what was called "enthusiasm" in the eighteenth century—that is, conspicuous fervor of belief in the redeeming power of Christ, to be attained by faith, rather than by ritual observance. By the grace of God, said Wesley, every life may be transformed: we may grow in holiness and overcome sin. People of all classes listened to this eighteenth-century gentleman with the Oxford degree, but the working people of England and Wales were won by his sincerity and his power of expression.

Throughout Europe and even America, the disillusionment that followed upon the end of the Wars of Religion had brought some toleration with it—but also apathy or indifference of spirit. Scientific and metaphysical speculation, late in the seventeenth century and throughout the eighteenth, had weakened Christian belief among many of the educated. Christian churches often seemed dull and smug, and many clergymen were content to collect their stipends but not eager to perform their duties. In much of Europe, a confused popular resentment against established churches began to stir; quite as serious was the contempt for Christianity that grew among not a few members of the upper classes. Anti-Christian feeling was one of the forces that would explode in Paris in 1789, and thereafter would sweep across other European nations. Men must believe in something more than themselves; and if the Christian churches seemed whited sepulchres, men would seek another form of faith. So it was that during the first half of the eighteenth century, in England and America, the mode of thought called Deism made inroads upon the Christianity of the Apostles' Creed.

Deism was neither a Christian schism nor a systematic philosophy, but rather a way of looking at the human condition; the men called Deists differed among themselves on many points. (Thomas Paine often was called an atheist, but is more accurately described as a rather radical Deist.) Deism was an outgrowth of seventeenth- and eighteenth-century scientific speculation. The Deists professed belief in a single Supreme Being, but rejected a large part of Christian doctrine. Follow Nature, said the Deists (as the Stoics had said before them), not Revelation: all things must be tested by rational private judgment. The Deists relied especially upon mathematical approaches to reality, influenced in this by the thought of Sir Isaac Newton. For the Christian, the object of life was to know God and enjoy Him forever; for the Deist, the object of life was private happiness. For the Deists, the Supreme Being indeed was the creator of the universe, but He did not interfere with the functioning of His creation. The Deists denied that Old and New Testaments were divinely inspired; they doubted the reality of miracles; they held that Jesus of Nazareth was not the Redeemer, but a grand moral teacher merely. Thoroughly rationalistic, the Deists discarded all elements of mystery in religion, trying to reduce Christian teaching to a few simple truths. They, and the Unitarians who arose about the same time, declared that man was good by nature, not corrupt; they hoped to liberate mankind from superstition and fear.

John Wesley had to contend against both Deism and the complacency into which the Church of England and other Christian communions had fallen. His burning earnestness attracted to him vigorous evangelical followers—among them George Whitefield. By renewing the credibility of Christian teaching, by speaking once more in Christian terms to the mass of men, by passionately exhorting the people to believe in Christ and imitate Him, Wesley and his friends did much to renew the popular consciousness of the Christian life as means to redemption of the soul. Although their aim was the ordering of souls, rather than the ordering of the state, one effect of their preaching in Britain and America was to avert in those countries the rise of a kind of pseudo-religion of fanatic politics, which would occur in France near the end of the eighteenth century.

In the North American colonies, the work that Wesley barely had commenced was taken up by George Whitefield, a Calvinist preacher (though ordained in the Church of England) endowed with amazing eloquence and capable of rousing audiences to emotional intoxication. He went out from England to Georgia for three months, in 1737 and 1738, at Wesley's invitation—the first of several expeditions to America. In the colonies, as in England, Whitefield was rebuffed by many of the clergy, but he preached in the open air, winning over huge crowds. Many of those who heard him fell into extravagances and wild doctrines that equalled the religious excesses of a century earlier.

Yet if he sometimes attracted the neurotic and even the psychotic, Whitefield (who broke with the Wesley family in 1741) also moved to action the most important of American theologians. This was Jonathan Edwards, heir to the demanding creed of the old New England Puritans. The Great Awakening in New England would be chiefly Edwards' accomplishment, and it would spread to the other colonies, and would endure in its consequences after Deism had ceased to be a considerable movement.

In his last year of study at Yale College, the young Edwards had become convinced through a private experience that truly God is an absolute sovereign, not to be judged by men; he embraced the teaching that God saves some men (for reasons that are His, not ours) and condemns others to eternal suffering. In 1740, Whitefield came to Northampton, Massachusetts, where Edwards had become minister; his preaching led Edwards to evangelical dedication. Thereafter Edwards was bent upon waking men and women to awareness of the dread condition of sin in which they lay, upon exhorting them to repentance out of the fear of God, and upon showing them the burning need for conversion to faith in Christ. In his sermons and his books, Edwards revived Calvinism at its sternest, smiting hip and thigh the liberal clergy of latter-day New England.

With most of his congregation at Northampton, Edwards

grew desperately unpopular—in part because of the fantastic excesses of conduct by many of the "redeemed" enthusiasts who were converted by the Great Awakening. He was driven from his Northampton pulpit; he became a missionary to Mohawk Indians at Stockbridge, a dangerous frontier settlement in western Massachusetts. Near the end of his life, he was made president of the College of New Jersey (now Princeton University), for his influence had spread beyond the Congregationalists to the Presbyterians whose foundation Princeton was.

"You can't turn back the clock," we are told. Yet Edwards did just that. Although he seemed to have failed in his Massachusetts ministry, his logic and his imagination worked upon the rising men among the Congregational clergy and other denominations. The New England mind, which had been sliding into Deism, returned under Edwards' guidance to its old Puritan cast. For the rest of the eighteenth century, and for long thereafter, an evangelical Christian revival rooted in Calvinistic doctrines spread through New England and presently throughout the rest of America.

Directly or indirectly, most Americans were moved by Edwards' powerful intellectual defense of revealed religion. Although much of Edwards' labor was meant to counter the growth of Arminianism (Anglicanism, that is), its practical force was stronger against Deism and the rising sects of Unitarianism and Universalism. Most Americans were persuaded to reject the concept of an impersonal God who was Prime Mover merely—and to reject the argument that man is naturally good. They would say again, with Saint Paul, "Christ came to save sinners, of whom I am the chief."

It will not do to think of Jonathan Edwards merely as John Calvin raised from the dead. Despite his discourses on human depravity, on divine wrath, and on the necessity for an overwhelming personal experience of conversion if a man would be saved, Edwards was a thinker of his own time, and one of remarkable originality. He had become familiar early with the writings of Sir Isaac Newton and of John Locke; he made Locke's empiricism—that is, the use of mankind's experience as proof of propositions—one prop of his renewed but reinterpreted Calvinism. As a theologian and a philosopher of creative imagination, Edwards has been called the peer of Calvin, Fénelon, Aquinas, Spinoza, and Novalis.

"His power of subtle argument," Sir James Mackintosh would write early in the nineteenth century, "perhaps unmatched, certainly unsurpassed among men, was joined, as in some of the ancient Mystics, with a character which raised his piety to fervour."[14] All existence is mental, Edwards held—a concept which would work upon Ralph Waldo Emerson and the other American Transcendentalists, generations later. Certainly Edwards himself, the champion of Necessity and Revelation, was almost pure intellect.

God is the "being of beings," Edwards taught, the source of all benevolence. Virtue is the beauty of moral qualities, in harmony with the being of God. Goodness consists in subjugation of one's own will to God's good-will. Sinful though man is, God's design is benevolent: the misery and sinfulness that we behold about us are necessary for the contrasting existence of their opposites, happiness and virtue.

This world is a battle-ground, and we are put into it that we may contend for the good. In his most enduring work, his treatise on the Will, Edwards argued that even God is bound by God's own will to pursue the good; no man is free from constraint to obey the divine will. Sin is only a negative, a vacuum—in short, sin is the absence of God, from whom all goodness radiates. "True religion in a great measure consists in holy affections," Edwards wrote in his discourse on Religious Affections. "A love of divine things, for the beauty and sweetness of their moral excellency, is the spring of all holy affections."

Although the severe Puritan morality was undiminished in Edwards, and although he held with Calvin that our every act is determined by some inexorable Necessity, his system won Americans by its consistency, appealing to their inherited beliefs, but adding to those doctrines a fresh persuasiveness. "Clearing away the crust of ancient superstition," Leslie Stephen says, "we may still find in Edwards' writings a system of morality as ennobling, and a theory of the universe as elevated, as can be discovered in any theology. That the crust was thick and hard, and often revolting in its composition, is, indeed, undeniable; but the genuine metal is there, no less unmistakably than the refuse."[15] From a nineteenth-century rationalist like Stephen, this is very high praise.

"Unquestionably he was the biggest intellect in the history of American Christianity," one of Edwards' less friendly biographers declares. Edwards' poetic insights, expressed as logical propositions, captured both many of the learned and the mass of Americans, during the generation after his death. "His disciples crossed the mountains into western New York and into the Western Reserve of Ohio," Henry Bamford Parkes continues; "they swarmed into Michigan and Indiana; they spread themselves out across the prairies along the lonely trail to the Pacific. His books and his followers carried his doctrines into the Presbyterian churches of New Jersey and Pennsylvania; and thence, in ever-widening circles, into the Baptist and the Methodist churches."[16] The work of Gilbert Tennent among Scotch-Irish Presbyterians and of Bishop Asbury among the Methodists combined with Edwards' teaching to check the advance of Deism and other liberal theological and philosophical tendencies.

Although Deism in America would seem to be at flood-tide during the American Revolution, actually a revived Christian orthodoxy already was vigorous then—and would be stronger still by the time of the Constitutional Convention. The American people came to expect their public men to be Christians, or at least to give lip-service to Christianity. Aaron Burr, grandson of Jonathan Edwards (though a very different sort of man from his grandfather), would win the vice-presidency of the United States, and very nearly the presidency, because of public admiration for his grandfather the theologian—particularly in New England and the Middle Atlantic states. Thomas Jefferson, who did become President instead of Burr, would find it prudent to conceal his Deism as much as possible. While in the White House, Jefferson would write to Benjamin Rush that he would not publish his compilation *The Life and Morals of Jesus* (the "Jefferson Bible"), he being "averse to the communication of my religious tenets to the public, because it would countenance the presumption of those who have endeavoured to draw them before that tribunal, and to seduce public opinion to erect itself into that inquest over the rights of conscience, which the laws have so justly proscribed."

Here Jefferson meant that were his Deism (including his rejection of belief in Christ as supernatural Redeemer) fully known, he and his party would be in deep difficulty with popular opinion. As author of the Declaration of Independence, Jefferson had written of "Nature, and Nature's God"—with the concurrence of John Adams, at that time also a Deist. Benjamin Franklin, Richard Henry Lee, and other Revolutionary leaders were Deists. But it was not in "Nature's God" that the American people generally believed, by the end of the colonial period: they believed in Jonathan Edwards' absolute God, the source of all goodness, the being of beings. Later it would be said that Jonathan Edwards' philosophy was the foundation of the Democratic party—during the administration of President Jackson: Jeffersonian Deism was defeated even within the political organization that Jefferson had created. President Jefferson is said to have told the Dey of Tunis that America was not a Christian nation; but the American population thought otherwise.

In 1691, when Virginians had sought from the Lords of the Treasury, in London, a grant for building a college at Williamsburg to save the colonists' souls, they had been told by Sir Edward Seymour, "Damn your souls! Make tobacco!" The Americans had made tobacco, and much besides. But they had not neglected their souls altogether.

True, Americans' religious observance lacked the beauty and mystery and outward pomp of the Anglican establishment in the mother country, or of the Catholic regions of Europe. Yet it was a biblical Christianity, this American faith, securely rooted in popular conviction. Tocqueville would observe that democratic societies dislike the idea of spiritual intermediaries between God and man: American Christianity said little of angels, and neglected the calendar of saints, preferring the direct relationship of the individual to

343

the Lord. If the typical American at the end of the colonial era had nothing of the mystic in him, and was more urgently concerned, often, for practical success in this life than for a possible immortality—why, still he subscribed to Christian morals; still he took for certain the reality of the Father Almighty and of the Son, of one substance with the Father. Without these general convictions, as Tocqueville would perceive, the emerging American democracy would have been ungovernable and almost unthinkable.

Notes

[1] Daniel Boorstin, *The Americans: the Colonial Experience* (New York: Random House, 1958), p. 352.

[2] John Adams to John Taylor of Caroline, April 15, 1814, in Charles Francis Adams (ed.), *The Life and Works of John Adams* (Boston: Little, Brown, 1851), Vol. VI, pp. 451, 461-2.

[3] Thomas Fuller, *The Holy State and the Profane State* (Cambridge: Williams, 1648), pp. 138-41.

[4] John Randolph to Josiah Quincy, July 1, 1814, in Edmund Quincy, *Life of Josiah Quincy* (Boston: Little, Brown, 1867), pp. 353-55.

[5] Josiah Quincy, *Figures of the Past*, edited by M. A. DeWolfe Howe (Boston: Little, Brown, 1926), p. 296.

[6] James Fenimore Cooper, *The American Democrat*, with an introduction by H. L. Mencken (New York: Knopf, 1931), pp. 73, 76, 112.

[7] Charles S. Sydnor, *Gentlemen Freeholders: Political Practices in Washington's Virginia* (Chapel Hill: University of North Carolina Press, 1952), p. 82.

[8] *Ibid.*, pp. 125, 126.

[9] Rowland Berthoff, *An Unsettled People: Social Order and Disorder in American History* (New York: Harper and Row, 1971), p. 118.

[10] Speech of John Randolph in the House of Representatives, *The Annals of Congress*, Ninth Congress, first session, p. 928.

[11] Alexis de Tocqueville, *Democracy in America* (edited by Phillips

Bradley; New York: Knopf, 1948), Vol. I, pp. 303, 305, 307.

[12] *Ibid.*, Vol. II, p. 27.

[13] Louis B. Wright, *The Atlantic Frontier: Colonial American Civilization* (New York: Knopf, 1947), p. 242.

[14] Sir James Mackintosh, "Dissertation on the Progress of Ethical Philosophy", in *The Miscellaneous Works of the Right Honourable Sir James Mackintosh* (London: Longman, Brown and Green, 1846), Vol. I, p. 108.

[15] Leslie Stephen, *Hours in a Library* (London: Smith, Elder, 1899), Vol. I, p. 344.

[16] Henry Bamford Parkes, *Jonathan Edwards: the Fiery Puritan* (New York: Minton, Balch, 1930), p. 252.

CHAPTER X
EIGHTEENTH-CENTURY
INTELLECTS

Constitutional Order: Montesquieu

Although the eighteenth century's "Enlightenment" was full of would-be enlighteners, says Samuel Taylor Coleridge, it was singularly lacking in light. His stricture applies better to Europe than it does to America.

A legacy of social institutions and a legacy of thought were united in the development of American order: that point has been made in earlier chapters of this book. The preceding chapter has dealt chiefly with the institutions of colonial times; now we turn to certain eighteenth-century ideas that moved American minds during the late colonial period.

One ought not to exaggerate the power of abstract speculation in America. The American colonial people were eminently practical, and often suspicious of abstractions. Although most of them were religious, few of them were metaphysical. When educated Americans of that century approved a writer, commonly it was because his books confirmed well their American experience, justified their American institutions, appealed to convictions they had held already: with a few exceptions, the Americans were not fond of intellectual novelties. Nevertheless, several eighteenth-century men of ideas suited the colonial mind admirably, and four of these will be discussed in this chapter.

347

In any era, public opinion tends to heed especially those important writers who are contemporary with that particular age. Or, to speak more precisely, the leading public men of any age are influenced deeply by important books published during their own formative years. They read those books when they are young, not long after the books have been published; a generation later, the opinions expressed in such books often are reflected in the actions of leading men who had studied them closely when, aged fifteen to twenty-five years, they were seeking for first principles. In Britain and America especially, it is usual enough for some three decades to elapse before the ideas of a powerful writer result in changed public policy or altered consciences—though in some countries, notably France, well-expressed ideas may move society more quickly (not necessarily to society's unqualified advantage). It was so with the thought of Jonathan Edwards; it was so with the thought of Montesquieu, Hume, Blackstone, and Burke.

The closing years of the seventeenth century and the whole of the eighteenth century often are called the Age of Enlightenment. By this is meant the strong intellectual tendency toward doctrines of progress, rationality, secularism, and political reform. The Enlightenment's center was France, but in varying degrees the whole of western Europe—even Russia, for that matter—and Britain were suffused by the ideas of the *philosophes,* the Parisian intellectuals. The movement had begun with the mathematical philosophies of Descartes and other scholars, and was reinforced by scientific discoveries, notably those of Sir Isaac Newton. In popularized form, these ideas were applied to moral and social concerns, often extravagantly. The French *Encyclopedia,* edited by Diderot and published in 1751 and 1752, was the culmination of Enlightenment thought. Boldly anti-Christian, contemptuous of the Middle Ages, dedicated to speedy intellectual and social change, developing their own dogmas of the perfectibility of man and society, the *philosophes* of the Enlightenment expected the swift transformation of civilization on purely rational principles—and meant to assist powerfully in that transmutation.

At the heart of the "Enlightenment" mentality was an enormous confidence in the reason of the individual human being. Man's private intellectual faculties, if awakened, could suffice to dissolve all mysteries and solve all problems—so the Encyclopedists believed. Religion must be discarded as mere superstition, old political forms must be swept away as irrational and oppressive, the natural goodness of man must be enabled to prevail—through an appeal to Reason. If properly cultivated, every man's private rationality could emancipate him from the delusion of sin, from ways of violence and fraud, from confusion and fear. This dream ended in the French Revolution.

To America, the mentality of the Enlightenment scarcely penetrated. A few Americans of cosmopolitan experience, notably Benjamin Franklin, were affected by these doctrines—but even in them, the boundless optimism of the typical *philosophe* was chastened by direct experience of reality in practical America. A moderate Deism was the furthest advance of Enlightenment theories in the Thirteen Colonies. The eighteenth-century men of ideas whose direct influence upon Americans was strongest stood in partial or total opposition to the *philosophes* generally and the Encyclopedists particularly. Montesquieu, with his devotion to the hard lessons of historical knowledge; Hume, with his good-natured contempt for the cult of Reason; Blackstone, governed by legal precedent and prescription; Burke, appealing to the great traditions of medieval and Christian and classical belief—these were America's teachers in the latter half of the eighteenth century. If they enlightened, it was not with the torch of the French Enlightenment.

Those sixteenth- and seventeenth-century thinkers who have been discussed in earlier chapters lived and wrote in an era of fearful turbulence. It was otherwise with the authors—one of them French, one Scottish, one English, one Irish—to be dealt with in this present chapter. Montesquieu, Hume, Blackstone, and Burke existed in a time of relative security and tranquillity; of the four, only Burke had some experience of violence and foresaw the coming of more terrible troubles. Yet their ideas would be applied practically to re-establish order in a perplexed land, after America had endured more than a decade of war against a great power, civil strife, and political disruption.

At the Constitutional Convention in 1787, no man would be more frequently cited and quoted than Charles Louis de Secondat, Baron de Montesquieu (1689-1755). His *Persian Letters* had been published in 1721, his *Considerations on the Grandeur and Decadence of the Romans* in 1734, his major work *The Spirit of Laws* in 1748; all appeared in English translations not long after their publication in French. All of Montesquieu's writings were eagerly read, in youth, by many of the men who signed the Declaration of Independence and drew up the Constitution of the United States; others absorbed Montesquieu's ideas at second hand through Blackstone's *Commentaries on the Laws of England.* Even when done into English, Montesquieu's style is pithy and vigorous: most books that move public opinion achieve their purpose as much by their rhetoric as by their logic.

Montesquieu's works soon were to be found in every British country house; they were almost as frequently encountered on the library shelves of educated Americans. My own copy of the first English edition (1750) of *The Spirit of Laws,* picked up at a Scottish auction, bears the bookplate of a Lord Lyon (the chief heraldic office of Scotland, not an hereditary peerage). Montesquieu, eminently an urbane gentleman, became essential reading for all urbane gentlemen—or persons wishing to become urbane eighteenth-century gentlemen—on either side of the Atlantic.

Born in the closing third of the reign of Louis XIV, the "Sun King" whom Montesquieu would learn to detest, the author of *The Spirit of Laws* inherited large estates, was educated in the law, presided for twelve years over the ancient Parlement of Bordeaux, and traveled widely and discerningly in Europe. He was open-minded, amiable, temperate; his life was a series of successes. He possessed to the fullest that gift for brilliant generalization which is found more often among French men of letters than among any other people, a talent that Alexis de Tocqueville would apply to America in the next century. Montesquieu might almost be called the first sociologist. "Montesquieu's greatness," says Paul Hazard, "lay in his resolve to gain those lofty peaks whence he could look down and discern order in disorder, and all his life was one long upward climb towards those commanding heights."[1]

There are many aspects to Montesquieu's thought, but for our purposes in this book it is well to emphasize Montesquieu on the nature of law, on the influence of custom and habit (as opposed to the notion of a "social contract"), and on the separation of powers in government. These concepts of his were received so sympathetically in America (and in Britain) that to Montesquieu often has been attributed far more influence upon the Constitution of the United States than was exerted by any other political philosopher.

Montesquieu's ascendancy over English and American minds was not gained because he was a radical innovator: he was nothing of that sort. On the contrary, Montesquieu expressed better than could any Englishman or American of his day the very principles in which most thinking Englishmen and Americans already believed. He had resided for two years in England, and was an ardent admirer of the English constitution. His understanding of the nature of law confirmed Englishmen and Americans in their affection for their own jurisprudence and legal institutions; his discussion of the power of custom and habit in shaping society agreed with the prescriptive politics of the English-speaking peoples; his advocacy of the separation of powers sustained the political experience of Britain and the colonies. Upon Englishmen and Americans, his influence was conservative.

It would be somewhat otherwise in France, where Montesquieu's praise of the English constitution would produce demands for reconstruction of the French political structure upon the English model. Those who so read Montesquieu were disappointed in the event. For as Montesquieu himself made clear, one country's historic experience cannot be transported to a different land, and customs and habits cannot be altered by positive law—they can only be distorted. In France, the early ideals of many revolutionaries, Mirabeau among them, were connected with the English pattern of politics. But the Revolution, as it ran its course, redoubled the very defects—centralization especially—which Montesquieu had assailed obliquely in the France of the Old Regime; what emerged from the French Revolution did not resemble either the English constitution or Montesquieu's general model of a constitution with separation of powers and local liberties. Somewhat wistfully, Montesquieu had desired French reform—but no revolution. In America, his great book would help in the recovery of order after a revolution.

To live under law is natural for man, said Montesquieu, and reasonable. Although the mass of laws bewilders most people, actually laws form a pattern, relating to one another and connecting all the concerns of society. In essence, laws are relationships: the necessary bonds between man and man, among classes, joining communities in common interests. Laws relate men to the circumstances under which a society exists. True, all law has its root in general truths: "Law is human reason, inasmuch as it governs all the inhabitants of the earth; the political and civil laws of each nation ought to be only the particular cases in which this human reason is applied." But those particular cases vary in many ways.

Although law is reasonable, Montesquieu continues, we cannot expect it to assume a universal pattern. For men's circumstances vary mightily one from another—affected by climate, by soil, by extent of a country, by historic experience, by customs and habits, by strategic situation, by commerce and industry, by religion, by a multitude of other influences. Therefore every people develop their own particular laws, and rightly so. Montesquieu is a "relativist" in believing that there is no single "best" body of laws or pattern of politics.

Nevertheless, Montesquieu does not deny the existence of natural law; in effect, he affirms the concept of natural law that had come down from Plato and Cicero and Aquinas and Hooker. "Before laws were made, there were relations of possible justice. To say that there is nothing just or unjust but what is commanded or forbidden by positive laws, is the same as saying that before the describing of a circle all the radii were not equal." Positive law should conform to the principles of natural justice.

On those principles, Montesquieu was the first political philosopher to oppose human slavery, root and branch. He set his face against a different concept of "natural law"—against the seventeenth-century legal theories of the Dutch jurist Hugo Grotius, who had argued that one of the laws of nature is this: that a conqueror has the right to slaughter or perpetually enslave a whole people whose armies he has defeated. This would deny, said Montesquieu, the natural law of preservation of life; it would be contrary to the political law of the survival of communities; contrary, indeed, to even the conqueror's self-interest. What is ruinous to society cannot be natural law. Although Montesquieu was a witty critic of the Church in his age, at bottom his understanding of natural law is religious.

For Montesquieu, the highest achievement of any country's law is the enlargement of personal freedom. Law and freedom are not opposed; for there cannot be freedom without law, only violent anarchy; and without freedom, law is despotic, obeyed only out of fear. Law does restrain men from injuring others and themselves, but it did not come into existence merely to establish a despotic authority.

Here Montesquieu drubs Thomas Hobbes. "The natural impulse or desire which Hobbes attributes to mankind of subduing one another, is far from being well founded. The idea of empire and dominion is so complex, and depends so much on other notions, that it could never be the first that would occur to human understandings." Laws, rather, are the beneficial rules by which we contrive to live in community, the products of human wisdom to satisfy general human wants.

So Montesquieu rejects Hobbes' theory of a social compact formed out of fear, requiring total submission to Leviathan; also he rejects, less explicitly, John Locke's theory of a social compact formed to shelter life, liberty, and property. (Despite much writing about Locke's influence upon Montesquieu, actually Montesquieu disagrees with the great Whig more often than he agrees; he may have learned as much from the Tory Bolingbroke, with whom he was personally acquainted.) Montesquieu does not believe in the necessary existence of any social compact at all.

For political and civil laws are not abstractly ordained or agreed upon at any one moment in history: instead, laws slowly grow out of men's experience with one another—out of social customs and habits—as, one may add, the common law of England developed. "When a people have pure and regular manners, their laws become simple and natural." In this argument, Montesquieu draws extensively upon the laws of the Romans, as well as upon his own observations in his time.

It is not because of some conscious artificial early agreement that men live under law. Human communities, even on a tiny scale, cannot exist without at least rudimentary laws; man is not really man, not fully human, until he lives by law. Montesquieu, as the first historian of modern times to seek for philosophical meaning in the course of human events, cast the notion of the social compact into eclipse.

Let us look at laws, especially those fundamental laws called constitutions, more realistically. Forms of government arise out of complex combinations of circumstances and experiences; and governments are reflections of a nation's laws, rather than the source of laws. We can no more expect a universal pattern of government than we can expect identical positive laws in every country. Montesquieu discerns three general patterns of government, nevertheless: the republic, the monarchy, and the despotism. The republic is sustained by the citizens' virtue, the monarchy by the king's honor, and the despotism (like that of the Ottomans) by the subjects' fear. Ordinarily a people do not *choose* one constitutional form or another: they find themselves necessarily under the sort of government which is suited to their social circumstances. In a sense, any people obtain the kind of government they deserve—or, at any rate, the kind of government which their history and their conditions of existence have brought upon them.

Still, it does not follow that all governments are equal in merit. What governments most successfully reconcile the claims of order and the claims of freedom? Here Montesquieu admires the constitution of the Roman Republic, as described by Polybius, before foreign conquests and luxury worked corruption; and he finds the best government of his age in the constitutional monarchy of England, where the subject enjoyed personal and civic freedom. Once France, too, had been like England in some sort, a true monarchy balanced by a degree of representative government: but Louis XIII and his minister Cardinal Richelieu had ruined French freedom, so that in Montesquieu's time the French state was sinking toward despotism, a centralized state apparatus excluding from real participation the nobles, the clergy, and the people.

How did old Rome and modern England maintain an ordered freedom, liberty under law? Why, so far as institutions are concerned, by the devices of separation of powers and of checks and balances. Power can be restrained only by counterbalancing power, Montesquieu reasoned. No man, and no political body or office, ought to possess unchecked power. For the sake of personal liberty and free community, power ought to be divided and hedged. Might this slow the actions of the state? Well, be it so, Montesquieu thought: freedom is better than haste.

Although the concept of the separation of powers and the concept of checks and balances are related, they are not identical. By the separation of powers is meant the apportioning of authority to different branches of government: to the executive branch, to the legislative, to the judicial. Checks and balances to prevent the arbitrary employment of power may work *within* a government of separated powers, or they may be applied to a "mixed government" of classical times, or to some other form of government. Checks and balances upon power may be exerted by non-political bodies, among them the Church and the university. Montesquieu desired both separation of powers and the development of checks and balances. His plan is the precise opposite of Hobbes'. Representative parliaments, competent local governments with established usages, and the claims of conscious social classes all are restraints upon Leviathan.

In England, Montesquieu saw a successful separation of powers: the king as executive, the Parliament as representative assembly (incorporating check and balance through its two houses, Lords and Commons), the courts as an independent judiciary. (Although in theory modern Britain does not separate the executive power from the legislative, actually this separation still exists: the power formerly possessed by the king now is possessed by the cabinet, which is not simply a committee of Parliament.)

In France, an independent judiciary survived to Montesquieu's time; but from Louis XIV onward, and indeed earlier, executive and legislative had been merged in the French state, so that the Parlement of Paris and the lesser French *parlements* had ceased to function as representative assemblies. Even the independence of judges was more secure in England than in France, having been guaranteed by the Bill of Rights in 1689. In France, nearly all checks upon the power of king and court had vanished by the time Montesquieu wrote. That harsh concentration of power would be the primary cause of the French Revolution.

Even separation of powers and effective checks and balances, Montesquieu feared, might not suffice to ensure continuity of law and evenhanded justice. Somewhere there ought to exist a "depository" or guardian of laws, protecting the fundamental laws, the constitution of a country. He thought the nobility not intelligent enough for this function; he was not clear as to how any political body could undertake this task impartially. What Montesquieu desired would not take form until some decades after his death; and then it would be called the Supreme Court of the United States.

This has been only a summary description of the temperate wisdom of Montesquieu. Because his principles of politics found their best embodiment in eighteenth-century England, his reputation in that realm stood high. And it is not difficult to understand why Montesquieu was far more popular with Americans than he was either with the French masters of the Old Regime or with the rash French reformers who brought on the Revolution.

For Montesquieu's understanding of the nature of law was shared by the Americans. They recognized religious and moral sanctions behind positive law; they had been brought up in the English juridical principles and practices of common law and equity, which clearly had developed out of a people's experience in community; they looked upon law as the protector of freedom. The Americans knew that their own society was not the product of a single formal social compact; it was in part an inheritance from British social development, and in part the consequence of their own peculiar geographical, economic, and political circumstances; it had grown accidentally or providentially, rather than being created out of an abstract general agreement. They understood very well indeed the benefits of separation of powers and of checks and balances: in every colony, the governor held executive power, the assembly representing the freeholders controlled legislation, and the courts were independent. (In Virginia, the county courts even resembled Montesquieu's "depository of laws.")

Thus Montesquieu, who never saw America, provided philosophical and historical justifications for the framework of ordered liberty that the Thirteen Colonies experienced in the latter half of the eighteenth century. In effect, Montesquieu was America's apologist. His books acquired authority among Americans because his principles and deductions were sustained by American experience of political reality. Montesquieu's federalism, detesting centralization, struck a sympathetic chord; his warning against the decay of constitutional monarchy into despotism would furnish the American Patriots with arguments against the policies of George III.

Montesquieu's moderation did something to moderate the passions of the American Revolution. His exposition of the rule of law helped to point the way, for American leaders after the War of Independence, toward a frame of government which would be neither oppressively central nor weakly confederate, but something new (or at least eclectic) in political contrivances. More important still, his aphorisms directly assisted in the triumph of the separation of powers within both general and state governments, and in the reinforcement of elaborate checks and balances at every level of the American political structure. Montesquieu had little expectation of reforming or renewing the political forms of France under Louis XV; perhaps he would have been astounded to find that across the Atlantic his books had encouraged republican virtue. Political virtue, Montesquieu had written, is eagerness to serve the commonwealth. That eagerness in America had been augmented by much reading of Montesquieu.

France, through all its violent changes of regime after 1789, would grow steadily more arbitrary and centralized in government. England's separation of powers and political equilibrium were changing even as Montesquieu wrote. But in the Constitution of the United States there would be fulfilled practically the polity sketched by Montesquieu, with freedom and order balanced on the scales.

Skeptical Realism: Hume

"A writer equally solid and judicious": that is Alexander Hamilton's description of David Hume, in Number 85 of *The Federalist*. Other American leaders thought less well of Hume, though the popularity of his writings—particularly his *History of England*—confounded them. John Adams would write to Jefferson, in 1813, that Hume's *History* "had destroyed the best effects of the Revolution of 1688"; Jefferson would call Hume "a degenerate son of science," and would try to bring out an American edition of John Baxter's bowdlerized abridgement of Hume's historical work, so that students at the University of Virginia might be saved from Hume's Tory doctrines.

These remonstrances notwithstanding, Hume was read far more widely in America than was any other historian of that age, and made his mark in other ways. He was the friend, host, and correspondent of Benjamin Franklin, who convinced the Scottish philosopher of the future greatness of America. And much as the Americans liked Montesquieu's concept of law as "relation," so they tended to relish Hume's skeptical realism—this despite Hume's Toryism and his alleged atheism (though the Deist Franklin called Hume "a good Christian").

"A gloomy, hair-brained enthusiast," Hume observes in his *Enquiry Concerning the Principles of Morals*, "may have a place in the calendar; but will scarcely ever be admitted, when alive, into intimacy and society, except by those who are as delirious and dismal as himself." The words would have applied to many *philosophes* of the eighteenth century, but never to Hume himself.

Now Hume has a place in the calendar of philosophy, though not of saints; being a jolly, fat, witty, cosmopolitan gentleman, in character and accomplishments rather like his friend Franklin, he did well as respects intimacy and society. The ladies doted on Hume, though he was a confirmed bachelor who thought marriage too much of a luxury for a frugal Scot. Once, in a French tableau, he figured as a sultan between two *houris,* represented by Parisian beauties: thus, between conviviality and books, his life was spent. Adam Smith, his best friend, considered him "as approaching as nearly to the idea of a perfectly wise and virtuous man, as perhaps the nature of human frailty will admit."

Born in 1711, the second son of a Border laird, Hume made much money from his books (which no philosopher does nowadays), twice went on diplomatic missions, was an undersecretary of state for a time, served as Keeper of the Advocates' Library for years, lived on sixpence a day in his rooms in the towering pile of James' Court by the Lawnmarket of Edinburgh, and knew nearly everyone of the world of fashion and letters in Britain and France. If the mind and character of the eighteenth century may be represented by any one man, that man is Davie Hume.

He spent his days in dissipating philosophical illusions, and his influence is at work among us still. Thomas Henry Huxley would observe that "if you want to get a clear conception of the deepest problems set before the intellect of man, there is no need, so far as I can see, for you to go beyond the limits of the English tongue. Indeed, if you are pressed for time, three English authors will suffice, Berkeley, Hume, and Hobbes." However that may be, certainly Hume is one of the most powerful of modern thinkers, more influential than either Berkeley or Hobbes.

Dr. Samuel Johnson, who detested him, said that Hume was a Tory only by accident. He meant principally that

Hume's skepticism in religion made him a curious partisan of the faction of King and Church. An ardent High Tory David Hume was, for all that, venerating Charles I and Strafford in his *History*. Our impressions, morals, and tastes are the products of Nature, rather than of Reason, Hume argued in his books; there is not much accounting for them; and so, perhaps, it was with his own politics. A contemner of enthusiasm, a man possessed of scarcely a strong emotion of any sort, Hume nevertheless stood for the Old Cause against Whiggery, for Faith against Reason, for Nature against the Rights of Man. To understand his work properly, one needs to read *A Treatise of Human Nature* (written when he was twenty-four), *An Enquiry Concerning Human Understanding* (1748), and *An Enquiry Concerning the Principles of Morals* (1751). Of these, Hume himself believed *Human Understanding* to be the most valuable.

The chief philosophical systems are perennial. Hume stood in the line of the Greek Skeptics, or of the medieval Nominalists: his pleasure was to puncture balloons. The biggest balloon that came his way was John Locke, whom he undoes thoroughly in *Human Understanding*. Reason with a capital R, pure rationality as the guide to morals and politics, dominated the first half of the eighteenth century, and Locke was the grand champion and exponent of this system—though others carried it to extremes. Pure Reason never recovered from Hume's needle-prick, and Kant would carry on Hume's criticism. But philosophical systems last a long while, in the public consciousness, after they have been mortally wounded, so that journalists like Thomas Paine were crying up the Age of Reason well into the nineteenth century, and Reason has its worshippers still.

"Reason is irrational, theism is permissible only in utter attenuation: oh for a revelation! but not, if you please, the one we are supposed to have had already." So Basil Willey sums up Hume's theology.[2] The thread of Hume's discourse runs thus. Locke did not understand the nature of innate ideas. These innate ideas do exist; they form, indeed, our human nature, which we apprehend through the study of history; and it is these innate ideas, or impressions, which guide us through life.

The knowledge we pick up in our experience of life is fragmentary, and necessarily imperfect, because of the imperfection of our five senses. There are vast realms of being of which we can know nothing; and we do not form our judgments upon the basis of logically-arranged accumulations of experience, but rather attach those experiences of ours to general ideas. Those ideas are produced from "impressions"; but the origin of impressions is inexplicable. We cannot say whether they arise immediately from the object, or are produced by the creative power of the mind, or are derived from God. The imagination, not mere experience-knowledge, is the source of whatever wisdom we possess. And no one can account for the existence of the imagination in individuals: it is literally *genius,* though Hume does not say so.

What we learn in this world we learn through custom, repeated experiences, rather than through pure Reason. "Our reason never does, nor is it possible that it should upon any supposition, give us an assurance of the continued and distinct existence of body." Education really is the accumulated custom of the race. The ways of society are not the ways of reason, but of the customary experience of the species, beginning with small family-groups and growing upward into the state. It is perilous to meddle, on principles of pure rationality, with valuable social institutions that thus are natural developments, not logical schemes. (Here Hume agrees with Montesquieu.)

All religion is irrational; it is derived from Revelation and Faith; it cannot be sustained by logical argument, which only betrays Christianity to its enemies. (This had been the stand of the medieval Nominalists, and of others before them.) In nature are enormous mysteries which we cannot possibly fathom. There exist no metaphysical or supernatural sanctions—at any rate, not clear ones—for morality; reason reveals only a universe in which the mysterious powers have no regard for human good or evil. No, our morality—which Hume was sedulous to uphold—is obedience to the rules of approbation and disapprobation long accepted. The standard of morality is shown to us by the study of history, and its arbiters are men of strong sense and delicate sentiment, whose impressions force themselves upon the wills of their fellow-men.

A moderate skepticism of this sort, Hume declared, is the only effectual defense of Christianity, morality, and established social institutions. Follow Nature, not a vain illusory Reason; understand the nature of man, and be guided accordingly; we cannot know more, our intellects being puny. "Mankind are so much the same, in all times and places, that history informs us of nothing new or strange in this particular. Its chief use is only to discover the constant and universal principles of human nature." The chain of argument is forged with skill and power, and expressed with urbane good humor. The effect of Hume's books, joined to the general influence of similar reflections by other men of intellect, began to change the climate of opinion after the middle of the eighteenth century, so that the *philosophes*, or many of them, turned away from the cult of Reason and busied themselves with history, political reform, and scholarly concerns that did not aspire to perfect knowledge.

Thus Hume demolished Rationalism by rational argument. Similarly, he demolished the theory of the social compact (or contract), upon which Montesquieu had cast strong doubt, by his commonsensical powers. True, Locke's idea of the Compact would linger on—especially among the Jeffersonians and their heirs—long after Hume's death. And Jean Jacques Rousseau would publish, in 1762, his revolutionary *Social Contract*—quite ignoring the arguments of his sometime friend and host David Hume. (Hume had treated Rousseau with invariable kindness, but the Frenchman's eccentricities eventually led the canny Scot to conclude that Rousseau was little better than a madman—one of those gloomy, hair-brained enthusiasts.) Intellectually, nevertheless, Hume undid the compact theory in his *Treatise* and his *Morals*. The American Constitution would not be framed on the compact theory of Locke, really—and certainly not on that of Rousseau; though in the middle of the nineteenth century, some Southern secessionists would turn to the idea of social compact, as justifying secession from the Union.

Society does not commence with a deliberate compact of a

people previously living in anarchy, Hume reasoned. Instead, the first form of human association is the little family group. To defend themselves from enemies, such groups league together, and the political state grows slowly out of their military necessity: "camps are the true mothers of cities." (To some of Hume's readers, this point was easily illustrated by the living English cities of York and Chester, whose streets and walls follow the lines of the Roman camps that were the beginnings of those towns.)

At first, then, people are moved by self-interest to join in a larger community, obtaining the benefits of a rude government's protection—though not ordinarily as the act of desperate submission conjectured by Hobbes. Later, a sense of obligation arises among the members of a commonwealth, and habit accustoms them to loyal obedience to the laws.

Historically considered, Hume continues, the notion of a social compact cannot be substantiated. Governments, including Britain's, were founded upon force: so we find when we look at the history of modern states. The Normans, conquering Britain, neither obtained the voluntary assent of the Anglo-Saxon people, nor yet extracted from them a promise of total obedience: so much, respectively, for Locke and for Hobbes. Even among the states of eighteenth-century Europe, after centuries of civilization, how many governments could be said to rest upon the consent of the governed? Only the United Kingdom, the Dutch Republic, and some of the Swiss cantons, says Hume. Why should we indulge the political fantasies of Locke? So, in effect, Hume argues. The state never has been established by perfectly free contract among the majority of people—let alone unanimous consent.[3]

In 1787, the several states of the new American nation would establish "a more perfect union," founded upon the consent of the governed, through the labors of the Constitutional Convention, "a bundle of compromises." But the basis for that national political agreement would be more realistic than either Locke's or Hobbes' theory of compact. Hume, with Montesquieu, Blackstone, and Burke, contributed to this clearer understanding of the consent of the governed.

The framers of the American Constitution would be quite aware that their nation began in violence—in the sense that a War of Independence was fought and that the Loyalists (one third of the colonial population, according to John Adams' estimate) were either driven abroad or forced to submit. The advocates of American federalism would be quite aware that some of the states ratified the new Constitution only after much controversy and sometimes by slim majorities. And yet the American federal compact was neither the tyranny described by Hobbes nor the universal willing assent described by Locke. In the Constitution, as in the Declaration of Independence, there can indeed be found an idea of compact. But that idea is more nearly related to the Hebrew understanding of the Covenant than it is to Hobbes' or Locke's theories.

Hume himself certainly did not rejoice in the American Revolution. Destructive critic of conventional eighteenth-century theories though he was, Hume did not lust for innovation. He desired to preserve the tranquil society of Britain in his time—tranquil, at least, by comparison with the preceding century. He did not wish to alter the established morality of the age, nor to injure popular religious belief, nor to make sweeping changes in social institutions. Revolutionaries of every description, Hume said, the civil magistrate justly puts on the same footing with common robbers. He was aware that novel abstract concepts, safe-seeming when confined to the drawing-room or the coffee-house, nonetheless may burst suddenly and catastrophically like fire-bombs once they have been vulgarized, and said so. "Why rake into those corners of nature, which spread a nuisance all around?" The obsessions of *philosophes* with abstract reason, *a priori systems*, and unprofitable teachings tend toward injury to society. "Truths which are *pernicious* to society, if any such there are, will yield to errors, which are salutary and *advantageous*." It is quite possible to reason ourselves out of virtue and social enjoyment. "The passion for philosophy, like that for religion, seems liable to this inconvenience, that, though it aims at the correction of our manners, and extirpation of our vices, it may only serve, by imprudent management, to foster a predominant inclination, and push the mind, with more determined resolution, towards that side which already *draws* too much, by the bias and propensity of the natural temper." Philosophy, that is, can produce fanatics, as religion has done on occasion. Nor ought a man to let his speculations disturb the even tenor of his ways: Hume himself postponed the publication of his *Natural History of Religion* until his death, to spare himself the fury of outraged orthodoxy.

Like Montesquieu, Hume disliked revolutionary minds and revolutionary slogans. In the long run, nevertheless, Hume's ideas had their revolutionary consequences. It was sufficient unto his time that the gentleman and the scholar, like Hume himself, should set the standards of taste and morality; their approbation secured the substantial emulation of the mass of men. But when the gentleman and the scholar ceased to fix the tone of life, the fate of morality would be called into question. It was sufficient unto Hume's time that moderate skepticism should chasten the presumption of established churches: those churches then seemed secure indeed, with the mob on their side, so that when Hume died, in 1776, it was found prudent to set a watch by his grave on the Calton Hill for eight days, lest Edinburgh's Presbyterian zealots wreak their vengeance on the skeptic's corpse. But a time would come, in much of Europe, when faith would go out of the masses, and revelation would be forgotten. Then religion might need the Schoolmen's bulwark of reason.

And though Hume's books undid Locke and the French philosophers of pure rationality, philosophical systems and their refutations work their way only slowly to the cognizance of the large public. By the last decade of the eighteenth century, Reason was enthroned as a symbolic goddess (represented by a prostitute) in the cathedral of Notre Dame, at Paris; and *a priori* assumptions were applied to the governance of great states; and the Rights of Man triumphed over custom and prudence. That urbane, leisurely, orderly world of Hume was submerged in France and other lands.

With his dislike of all things vulgar, David Hume probably would have been uncomfortable in the twentieth century. And yet our era is of Hume's making, in part. In

France, d'Alembert and Turgot were Hume's intimates: the great rationalizer and the great centralizer, the advocates of radical social reform and democracy, who reaped the whirlwind—curious friends for the champion of customary ways and Stuart causes.

At home, Hume found for his disciple Adam Smith, the philosopher of the new industrial and commercial order that would give the quietus to the old rural Scotland of which Hume was patriotically proud. In England, Jeremy Bentham, the "great subversive," took his ethics straight from Hume—Bentham, whose jurisprudence and political utilitarianism helped open the way for a society that could have been more repugnant to Hume than the ascendancy of the Whigs whom he mauled so cavalierly.

It was in 1776, the year of *The Wealth of Nations* and of the Declaration of Independence, that Hume went to his grave on the Calton. In his will he left a sum for the repair of a bridge near Ninewells, specifying that the work must not injure the aspect of a charming old quarry which he had admired for years. Despite all his causticity, to the last Hume stood by ancient usage, prescription, old sights and ways, and refined taste. As the sardonic critic of fashionable delusions, and as the exemplar of scholarly candor, Hume won an enduring influence, not least in America. The Whigs, with their abundant preferment to bestow upon men of letters, he once wrote to the Earl of Balcarres, do not rest content with *small* lies. And Hume never condescended to tell any big lies. The Americans of 1776, and later, recognized in Hume an honest man.

How is it that Hume, with his Tory prejudices, obtained a considerable following in Whiggish America? For one thing, he took America seriously. He advised Edward Gibbon to write his *Decline and Fall* in English (rather than in French, then the language of polite learning, as Gibbon at first intended), because "Our solid and increasing establishments in America, where we needlessly dread the inundation of barbarians, promise a superior stability and duration to the English language." That was in 1767. Twenty years later, Hume's ideas on government would have a part in the drafting of the American Constitution—through the medium of the chief drafter of that instrument, James Madison. As Irving Brant notes, "From David Hume, who saw that social conflicts were infinitely more complex than Aristotle thought them to be, came the idea that stability could be attained by balancing class against class, interest against interest, wherefore a large republic should be more stable than a small one, though harder to organize."[4]

What Madison and other Americans found attractive in Hume was Hume's common sense—Hume's freedom from mystification, vulgar error, and fanatic conviction; Hume's powerful practical intellect, which settled for politics as the art of the possible. Though so effective a critic of abstract Reason, David Hume was conspicuously rational. He shunned the narrow zealot in politics—and so did most Americans, after the Revolution, as they do to this day.

As an historian, too, Hume worked upon the American mind. Despite errors of fact and partisan judgments in his *History*—items after which Jefferson and the English radicals of his day sought eagerly—Hume's several volumes, published between 1754 and 1761, gave to English history a significance and a drama that it had lacked before. And, whatever Hume's small blunders, by and large it was sound history. Hume maintained, for instance, that the English constitution and English liberty under law had their beginnings in Norman times, while Jefferson and the English Whigs argued passionately that there *must* have been an Anglo-Saxon constitution from which modern freedom is remotely derived—even though they were unable to find any documents in evidence. Almost to a man, serious twentieth-century historians have come round to Hume's stand in this matter, and the "Whig historians" lie in disrepute. Hume had the wisdom of imagination, and his adversaries among the historians of his era did not have it.

How was it that such a skeptic as Hume could be read attentively in an America that venerated Jonathan Edwards? In part, this is because there was not merely a monolithic American public: Hume tended to be read by people of Episcopalian and Deist background, Edwards by those of Calvinist persuasion. But also there was no necessary contradiction in reading both. Edwards defended Revelation and Faith; so, after his own fashion, did Hume. Both attacked the strutting Rationalism of the Enlightenment. It is no paradox that down to our time the American people continue to adhere to faith in their religion, but to skepticism in their politics. Skepticism is not disbelief; rather, it is rejection of simplistic approaches and passionate narrowness. So far as the political insights of Hume still affect American political attitudes, they are a healthy leaven.

The Laws of England: Blackstone

Colonial America had no regular schools of law, and lawyers educated in England were few. Just when the Stamp Act, in 1765, was rousing many Americans to oppose the imperial government, there was published in London Sir William Blackstone's *Commentaries on the Laws of England,* a book that would become more influential in America even than in Britain. As Burke would tell the House of Commons a decade later, nearly as many copies of Blackstone were sold in the Thirteen Colonies as in England, despite disparity in population.

England had the Inns of Court, the professors of law at Oxford and Cambridge, the learned judges; America had only lawyers without much formal instruction—and Blackstone as their manual. From Blackstone, most Americans with any interest in the law acquired their principal stock of knowledge of natural law, common law, equity, and "the chartered rights of Englishmen."

William Blackstone (1723-1780) was Oxford's first professor of English law (as distinguished from Roman law), and later a judge of Common Pleas. He wrote lucidly, and a number of his decisions on the bench are in the case-books. He was a Tory, opposing the American Revolution and asserting the supremacy of Parliament. No matter: his book was as popular in America after the Revolution as it had been before the War for Independence. Even Jefferson, though differing with Blackstone on some points and lamenting that the judge had made all England Tory, read Blackstone through and through, and was as much influenced by him as by Coke, Kames, and other juridical authorities whose passages Jefferson copied into his Commonplace Book.

In Blackstone's account of English law there is something of Locke, and something of Montesquieu, but chiefly the inheritance of common law and equity discussed in an earlier chapter of this book. Then as now, English law was not codified, unlike the law of the Continental nations; Blackstone's *Commentaries* served the highly useful purpose of making it possible for "the gentleman and the scholar" (Blackstone's own phrase), as well as the lawyer, to discern some order in the tremendous mass of precedents accumulated over seven centuries. In America, the educational function of the *Commentaries* loomed larger still, and Blackstone's reputation stood high in the United States well after it had been diminished in England by the attacks of Bentham and the Analytical Jurists. (After the middle of the nineteenth century, Blackstone's book began to regain stature in Britain, because approved by the newer school of Historical Jurists.)

In the United States, where no national legal code was promulgated nor any full-fledged state code but Louisiana's (a revision of the French Civil Code), Blackstone remained the standard manual of law until the publication (1826-30) of the *Commentaries on American Law* by Chancellor James Kent, of New York. Even after that, Blackstone was preferred for a time in some states and districts. The two principal writers on jurisprudence in the early Republic, Joseph Story and James Kent, owed much to Blackstone and repeatedly acknowledged their debt.

Blackstone commenced his *Commentaries* with an affirmation of the natural law—which confirmed Americans in their appeal to a justice beyond parliamentary statute, not altogether to Blackstone's relish. In Blackstone, two streams of "natural law" thought mingle: that of Cicero, the Schoolmen, and Richard Hooker, and that of the seventeenth-century scholars Grotius and Pufendorf and the eighteenth-century Swiss jurist Burlamaqui. These two schools do not always consist well together; but Blackstone himself, and the Americans whose legal concepts he helped to form, made few nice distinctions concerning the natural law.

"This law of nature," Blackstone writes, "being co-eval with mankind and dictated by God himself, is of course superior in obligation to any other. It is binding over all the globe, and all countries, and at all times; no human laws are of any validity if contrary to this; and such of them as are valid derive all their force, and all their authority, mediately or immediately from this original." Then he continues in tones like Montesquieu's to describe "recourse to reason" and "the particular exigencies of each individual" as modifying application of the natural law; he is not expounding the old Puritan notion of God's laws operating directly upon modern society. But the "law of nature" soon would become the American Patriots' sanction for an appeal to arms against the Crown in Parliament.

That half-accidental result aside, Blackstone's book tended to preserve the legacy of English law in America; as Daniel Boorstin observes, the *Commentaries* "deprived colonial lawyers of the dangerous temptation of making their own code."[5] Blackstone was a champion of ancient precedent and long-sanctioned usage; had the little-schooled American lawyers not been restrained by him, much of enduring value in the tested English rule of law might have been lost through ignorance or hasty improvisation.

The common law itself, even had Blackstone not been its expounder, is at once highly conservative (being founded on immemorial customs) and capable of growth and adaptation (not being confined by a written code). This fortunate conjunction was what America required, and the common law prevailed—if sometimes in a simplified or modified form—throughout the colonies until the Revolution. In every state of the original thirteen, and ultimately in all states but Louisiana (though in part, even there, too), this common law would endure: attempts would be made to codify American laws, in one state or another, but these attempts would fail or would linger in rudimentary form. Whether the Constitution of the United States was meant to include, or rest upon, the common law of England was a question warmly debated down through the 1830's, and not settled by scholars of the law even today. Yet it remains true that although most Americans nowadays think of law as an enactment of a legislature, actually the basis of American law, still applied in countless cases, is the common law which began to develop in England nine hundred years ago.

The natural law described by Blackstone was rooted in Christian ethics; and it declared "the absolute rights of man"—the natural liberty of mankind, consisting of three articles, "the right of personal security, the right of personal liberty, and the right of private property." Yet these rights were not absolute in the sense of having no limits: as Blackstone put it, "but every man, when he enters into society, gives up a part of his natural liberty, as the price of so valuable a purchase; and, in consideration of receiving the advantages of mutual commerce, obliges himself to conform to these laws which the community has thought proper to establish." There, more clearly expressed than by Locke, is a fundamental doctrine of American politics.

Man's modern laws are declaratory of natural laws: that teaching was affirmed repeatedly by Blackstone and by his American disciples Story and Kent. All looked upon the common law as the nearest approach (however imperfect) to natural law, because it had grown out of the experiences and observations and consensus of many generations of wise men, and had been tested repeatedly for its conformity to natural justice. To Jefferson and his followers, however, the common law was suspect precisely because it was ancient; preferring modernity, they tried in vain to develop an alternative body of peculiarly American laws.

Also the common law was assailed in America by its formidable English adversary, Jeremy Bentham—who would write to President Madison, to the governors of the several states, and even to the citizens of America in general, offering to draw up for them a perfect new code of laws, on utilitarian principles. (Bentham never had visited America; his closest

American friend was Aaron Burr, who lived with Bentham in London for a time while in exile, and whose daughter, Theodosia, undertook to translate some of Bentham's manuscripts from French into English.)

Madison, nevertheless, appreciated more than did Jefferson the virtues of the common law, and was taken aback by the incoherence of the eccentric Bentham's letter; he declined the proposal. (James Mill, Bentham's closest disciple, later declared that he could write a full-fledged code of laws for India—though he never had set foot in that land.) Not until the late 1830's was it quite certain that the common law would prevail in all of the states except French-founded Louisiana.

The doctrinal legal writings of Kent and Story, imbued with Blackstone's concepts, won the battle on behalf of the common law. Had it not been for their textbooks, Roscoe Pound says, "our American law might have lost its unity. Had it lost its unity the movement for a premature Benthamite code might well have swept the country as the French codes swept over Europe. If the flood of statutes which poured from our legislatures from the beginning had been turned upon a system of purely local rules, as the country became unified economically we should very likely be seeking relief in codes, if we had not done so long ago."[6] But American law remained uncodified, and therefore more flexible as well as more strongly connected with English precedents of private freedom and immunity. Otherwise, ill-instructed American state legislatures might have diminished the practical rights of Americans in the confused belief that they were cutting the people free from anachronistic medieval customs.

Along with the English common law there was established, in time, English equity as applicable to American courts. Equity was still more suspect to some Americans, particularly in New England and on the frontier, because it seemed to give judges discretionary power of an anti-democratic cast, and was merciful toward fools. But here again Justice Story triumphed, chiefly through his text on equity jurisprudence, and by the last quarter of the nineteenth century even the courts of Massachusetts would possess full equity jurisdiction.

Although Blackstone was not quite the Solon of America, probably no other new nation-state has been so much governed by a single legal authority from abroad. Until the middle of the nineteenth century, or even later, there were not a few American judges whose chief source of legal knowledge was a copy of Blackstone, possibly supplemented by Kent. (Some, indeed, thought they could dispense even with Blackstone—deciding cases by a kind of rule of thumb.) In the absence of such a manual as the *Commentaries,* justice would have been meted out far more rudely. And without the natural-law foundation of Blackstone's manual, the history of American jurisprudence during the nineteenth century might have been remarkably different.

When John Marshall was a boy in the Blue Ridge Mountains, on Virginia's frontier, his father subscribed for him to the first American edition of Blackstone, edited by St. George Tucker (who held that the common law was not made national through the Constitution of the United States). Father and son read those volumes together, the boy being intended for the bar. John Marshall would become the greatest of chief justices, though he never was a fine scholar in the law; his only other formal preparation for the practice of law was a series of lectures by George Wythe, at the College of William and Mary, while Marshall was on furlough during the Revolution. Like his more learned colleague Joseph Story, Marshall accepted Blackstone as the best of guides in the labyrinth of the law. And thus, in a sense, Sir William Blackstone came to preside over the Supreme Court of the United States during the period when the independent powers of that body were established.

In twentieth-century America, Blackstone still is studied. We have returned, says Sir William Holdsworth, the exhaustive historian of English law, "to a larger philosophy of law, which does not disdain the lessons of the past or the wisdom which can be extracted from old law. And so to us Blackstone is not, as Bentham pictures him, the enemy to all reformation, and the inaccurate thinker who used his literary gifts to bolster up established abuses. Rather, he is the literary artist, the historical scholar, and the accomplished lawyer, who has woven into a harmonious texture all the variegated strands which made up the fabric of that English law of the old regime, which, both in England and the United States, is the foundation of the law which governs us today."[7]

Alexis de Tocqueville, about the time when the common law was defeating its American adversaries, wrote that the American political structure is controlled by a kind of professional aristocracy of lawyers, respectful of precedent and long-established rights and customs, hostile toward rashness, who curb unruly democratic impulses. "If you ask me where the American aristocracy is to be found, I have no hesitation in answering that it is not among the rich, who have no common link uniting them. It is at the bar or the bench that the American aristocracy is found. . . . An American judge, armed with the right to declare laws unconstitutional, is constantly intervening in political affairs. He cannot compel the people to make laws, but at least he can constrain them to be faithful to their own laws and remain in harmony with themselves."[8]

Those American lawyers and those American judges were Sir William Blackstone's heritors.

The Politics of Prudence: Burke

Edmund Burke (1729-1797), an Irishman who would become the most eloquent defender of the English constitution, was a man of many aspects, all of them brilliant. "Burke, sir," said Dr. Samuel Johnson (who almost forgave Burke his Whiggery, though Johnson was the staunchest of Tories), "is such a man, that, if you met him for the first time in the street where you were stopped by a drove of oxen, and you and he stepped aside to take shelter but for a few minutes, he'd talk to you in such a manner, that, when you parted, you would say, 'This is an extraordinary man.' "

In this chapter we emphasize one aspect of Burke: his role as advocate of political prudence and compromise, for which he was best known in the Thirteen Colonies. From the

American Revolution down to recent years, Burke's famous speech to the House of Commons on conciliation with the American colonies was studied in virtually every high school, as a model of political wisdom, logic, and rhetoric; editions of that address (1775) continue to appear. There was much more to Burke than his policy of conciliating the colonies, and political prudence was merely one among several teachings that have given Burke what he never expected, a high place in the history of political theory. Yet the long conciliation speech exerted more influence in America than did anything that Burke said or wrote later. Besides, an examination of Burke on conciliation leads us chronologically to the Declaration of Independence.

Burke, the son of a Dublin lawyer, meant to become a man of letters, and so settled in London. But in 1759 he was drawn into practical politics; soon he became the chief man of ideas among the Whigs. The Whig party, dominating England most of the time since the Glorious Revolution, had grown alarmed at the Tory opinions of King George III, who intended to rule as a "patriot king," whether the House of Commons should like it or not. But the Whigs were split into several factions. There came forward the Marquess of Rockingham, the head of one of the greatest Whig families, determined to reform his party and exert some check upon royal ambitions.

Rockingham saw in Burke a man who might help to heal the sickness of the Whigs. In 1765, when Lord Rockingham became prime minister because the king found it necessary to accept him, he appointed Burke to be his private secretary, and soon thereafter arranged that Burke should be elected to the House of Commons from the town of Wendover. At the age of thirty-five, Edmund Burke entered upon a parliamentary career that would endure for three decades. The first decade especially would be overshadowed by the political crisis in the American colonies.

Burke had some personal connection with America. In 1771, the General Assembly of the Province of New York appointed Burke as agent of that colony at London. (It then was common enough for members of Parliament to be engaged by the several colonies to represent their political interests in England, because such men understood the business of government; some agents, however, were sent out from America—Benjamin Franklin, for one.) Although he never visited America, Burke had been much interested in the colonies since his boyhood, had studied America closely in his capacity as editor of the *Annual Register,* and had written (in collaboration with a friend) *An Account of the European Settlements in America,* published in 1757. He would serve as New York's agent until 1775, when the moderate Whigs of New York who had chosen Burke would be swept out of power.

When the Rockingham ministry took office in 1765, the American colonists already were full of wrath at the Stamp Act passed by the Grenville ministry that had just left office. So the first enormous question that Burke confronted—indeed, on the very day, in 1766, when he took his seat in the House of Commons—was the political hurricane brewing in the American colonies. During the last third of the eighteenth century, Britain was losing an empire in North America and enlarging another empire in India. American affairs would involve Burke passionately until the end of the American Revolution.

There still lingers in the United States an erroneous impression that Burke was "in favor" of the American revolutionary cause. In truth, Burke never approved of any revolution, with the exception of the Glorious Revolution of 1688, which he called a revolution not made but prevented, and therefore no revolution at all. He did sympathize, true, with some of the complaints of the more moderate American opponents of George III's colonial policies. But revolution, and separation from the Empire, he believed to be evils. By timely concession and compromise, Burke and the Rockingham Whigs hoped in 1766, the loss of America might be averted.

Yet possibly America's secession from the British Empire could not have been prevented by any means. After the peace of 1763, ending the Seven Years' War, the American colonies no longer required British protection against the French.

Rapidly increasing in numbers and prosperity, and distant from Westminster and Windsor, two million Americans of European descent inclined toward self-government. Then, too, the old mercantilistic system of commerce, expressed in the Navigation Acts of Parliament, was giving at the seams. Soon its theoretical justification would be undermined by Adam Smith, and it could not coincide much longer with the economic interests of the Thirteen Colonies.

Still, the rupture between Britain and the colonies might have been postponed, or some loose connection with the British Empire retained almost indefinitely, had not George III and his ministers insisted upon asserting claims of absolute suzerainty over America that they could not enforce. The immediate dispute was as to whether, and how, the North American colonies should pay a share of the costs of defending the Empire. During the Seven Years' War, the several colonial assemblies had voted voluntary grants in aid of operations against the French; but sometimes these appropriations had been tardy, and sometimes niggardly. An attempt to raise revenue for this purpose on a regular basis, by either "external" or "internal" taxation of the colonies, was the fundamental error of King George III and most of his ministers.

Although this desire for revenue was not unreasonable, it was unseasonable, the French menace to the colonies being terminated already. (The Indians still menaced the frontiers, nevertheless.) And this demand affronted the pride of the colonists, who claimed all the "rights of Englishmen"—or, in fact, somewhat more than the rights possessed by subjects in Great Britain and Ireland.

George Grenville, prime minister from 1763 to 1765, had decided that the colonies should pay one-third of the cost of maintaining troops in America. Most of that sum he expected to raise by an "internal" tax on newspapers and official and legal documents, to which stamps must be affixed. So, early in 1765, Parliament passed the Stamp Act. For the first time, the British government was imposing internal taxes upon the colonists; and at once colonial opposition was clamorous.

Notwithstanding the assertions of many American

Patriots (and, on occasion, of Burke), George III was neither a tyrant nor a fool. He was a stubborn, well-intentioned ruler of limited talents. He meant to be a patriot, and looked upon himself as the champion of the common good against the Whig oligarchy which, he believed, had usurped powers properly reserved to the Crown. When George died, he was mourned loudly by the people of England—though he had been mad in his later years. He forfeited an empire by his imprudence, but George III was a king of good private character, the first real Englishman of the Hanoverian line. He contended inflexibly, sometimes not overscrupulous in his means, against the political drift of his age.

Burke would oppose the king and most of his ministers for three decades. He struggled with George with particular bitterness during the debate over American policy, believing that should the king succeed in diminishing American liberties, soon he might turn to English policies as arbitrary as those of James II.

But in 1765, when the Grenville cabinet that had invented the Stamp Act was dismissed by the king, George III found it unpleasantly necessary to accept Lord Rockingham's moderate Whig ministry, if the government were to be carried on at all. Burke was Rockingham's counsellor. The new prime minister and Burke knew that they must walk carefully: they were not beloved by the king, who sometimes acted as if Rockingham did not exist. They knew that the more irascible men among the colonists were at least as obdurate as the king. What compromise might be contrived, prudently reconciling freedom and order?

Already, from Boston to Savannah, the slogan "no taxation without representation" was being shouted. This meant, really, "no taxation by Parliament." The colonial leaders detested the Stamp Act, or any other from of internal taxation; if they might help it, they would not be taxed by Britain at all.

Nevertheless, the Patriots had no real expectation of parliamentary representation either. Some token colonial members in the House of Commons would not have given the Thirteen Colonies influence proportionate to their population or aspirations: not in the unreformed Parliament of the eighteenth century, for the House of Commons in those days admitted more members from the rotten and pocket boroughs of thinly-populated Cornwall than from the whole of Scotland. Even had the colonies been granted a number of seats proportionate to their population, still they would have been hopelessly outnumbered by the British members in any test of conflicting interest—as, not long later, the Irish members were outnumbered in the nineteenth-century House of Commons. Besides, Boston and New York and Philadelphia and Charleston were too distant from London for effective participation in the Mother of Parliaments, the slowness of eighteenth-century communication considered. Really, the colonial Patriot politicians desired neither taxation nor representation: they sought guarantees of political autonomy for every colony, the condition which had prevailed (with a few partial and brief exceptions) ever since North America had been settled.

Grenville's Stamp Act, desperately unpopular both as innovating internal taxation and as the intended means for supporting a permanent civil and military establishment of the Crown in North America (which, in effect, might have diminished the powers of the colonial assemblies), had provoked some colonists to think of insurrection. Thus the first necessity of the new Rockingham government was to remove the cause of discontent, while still asserting royal and parliamentary supremacy over North America, and satisfying George III that they were not yielding feebly to colonial insolence.

In their determination to repeal the Stamp Act, the Rockinghams had the powerful support of William Pitt and his faction of Whigs—who, going farther than Rockingham, Burke, and the cabinet, declared that any form of taxing the colonies would be unconstitutional. Promptly the speeches of Pitt and Burke prevailed: the House of Commons repealed the Stamp Act.

But Parliament and Privy Council, in part to placate the king, also passed the Declaratory Act, which asserted the right of the Crown in Parliament to legislate for the colonies—although this act omitted any direct reference to taxation. For different reasons, this satisfied fairly well both the king and Pitt; yet it was to remain a thorn in the flesh of the more radical colonial leaders, who maintained that though they owed allegiance to the Crown, they were not constitutionally subject to Parliament—both because their charters came from the king alone, and because the Americans went unrepresented at Westminster.

Burke did not desire that the Americans should obtain seats in the House of Commons; that project was impractical. Besides, as he had written in the *Annual Register* for 1765, to give parliamentary seats to colonies in which black slavery was supported by the colonial laws would be inconsonant with a free Parliament: ". . . common sense, nay self-preservation, seem to forbid, that those who allow themselves unlimited right over the liberties and lives of others, should have any share in making laws for those who have long renounced such unjust and cruel distinctions."

The repeal of the Stamp Act and the adoption of the Declaratory Act were almost the only important accomplishments of the first Rockingham ministry, which endured little more than a year. Pitt, with his popular appeal, seemed more useful to the king than did Rockingham. Also, despite his opinion that the constitution prohibited taxing the colonists, Pitt was more resolved than Rockingham that the colonial assemblies must acknowledge the British government's supremacy.

Before leaving office, Rockingham, Burke, and their colleagues did succeed in modifying Grenville's Revenue Act, to the considerable advantage of the colonies. Removal of the preferential duties on molasses imported into North America was especially applauded in New England. Together with the repeal of the Stamp Act, these reforming measures made Burke one of the English politicians most popular in North America.

But the Rockinghams had served the king's turn; now they were dismissed. In the following years, George III would run through a whole series of prime ministers, settling at last on Lord North and the "King's Friends." When the Mar-

quess of Rockingham departed from office, his whole reforming faction went into the political wilderness, to enjoy office again only for one brief interval, years later. Burke thus
became what he was to remain nearly all the time until the
end of his parliamentary years—a leader of the opposition.
He directed his talents toward saving America for the Empire.

The approach of the American Revolution is an unhappy
story. The king, the faction called the King's Friends, and the
Bedford Whigs must bear much of the blame; so must
demagogues and extremists in Boston, New York, and other
American towns. Townshend's Revenue Act, levying new
duties, enraged the colonists afresh. For nearly three years the
Rockinghams remained disheartened. But at the beginning of
1769, Burke spoke repeatedly against measures of increasing
severity and dubious legality on the part of the government—particularly against the Duke of Bedford's motion to
transport to England for trial all those Americans who were
accused of treasonable actions. His arguments against
Townshend's duties, though delivered somewhat tardily,
began to have weight.

Burke's American popularity soon stood at its height. A
friend of the colonists he was, but no friend of revolution.
Thus he said, in 1770, concerning parliamentary reform at
home, "Indeed, all that wise men ever aim at is to keep things
from coming to the worst. Those who expect perfect reformations, either deceive or are deceived miserably." In the
colonies, many people still subscribed to that prudent statement.

Early in 1770, there came to head the government Lord
North, wholly obedient to the king. The Rockinghams, joined
by Grenville and his followers, concentrated their opposition
upon the ruinous American policy of the King's Friends.
Burke's attacks upon Lord North, if sometimes intemperate,
confirmed the Americans in their high opinion of Burke; and
North has remained ever since something of a bogeyman to
popular American historians. Although North proposed to
repeal all the detested duties except the tax upon tea, it was
found necessary to station two British regiments in Boston to
restrain the Massachusetts radicals.

On March 5, 1770, occurred the Boston Massacre, in which five Americans were killed. Samuel Adams, who had encouraged the harassing of the British garrison in Boston, called it a "massacre." But his kinsman John Adams, then a rising lawyer, undertook the defense of the British officer commanding the detachment that had fired upon the mob—and a Massachusetts court acquitted that officer.*

Massachusetts could not be quieted. Shortly after taking office, Lord North had repealed most of the Townshend duties, but had retained the tax on tea. Men of the kidney of Samuel Adams would not pay it, or permit it to be paid. On December 16, 1773, pseudo-Indians tossed into Boston Harbor a whole shipload of tea.

North retaliated with the Boston Port Act, passed by a heavy majority in both houses of Parliament; Boston was to be strangled economically. Only Burke and William Dowdeswell protested vehemently. "One town in proscription, the rest in rebellion, can never be a remedial measure for general disturbances," Burke told the ministers. "Have you considered whether you have troops and ships sufficient to enforce an universal proscription to the trade of the whole continent of Europe? If you have not, the attempt is childish, and the operation fruitless."

On April 19, 1774, Burke delivered a general assault upon the North policy—his celebrated speech on American taxation. Some of his previous activity in American policy had been inconsistent, tempered to suit such occasional allies as Grenville, or partially unjust to the ministry. Now, however, he did become the philosopher in action, appealing for prudence, as opposed to abstract assertions of absolute right.

The duty on tea, said Burke, must be repealed for the sake of tolerable relations with America, for the sake of the East India Company (caught hopelessly between Scylla and Charybdis, in Boston Harbor), and, most of all, for the sake of the British imperial system, with all its benefits. America should

---

*"There is reason to suspect that Sam Adams provoked the entire incident—one of the victims made this accusation on his deathbed—to inflame the populace." (Mark M. Boatner, III, [ed.], *Encyclopedia of the American Revolution* [New York, 1966] p. 94.)

not be taxed to raise British revenue, for the Navigation Acts provided sufficient economic advantage to Britain, by promoting British trade. Taxation of the colonies should be undertaken only in some emergency, and then only if a colony had refused to contribute money toward the common defense. The "inferior legislatures" within the British Empire ordinarily should manage the concerns of the people whom they represented—even though by right, as expressed in the Declaratory Act, the King in Parliament possessed sovereign power to govern the whole Empire. The essence of Burke's position lies in these lines:

"Again, and again, revert to your old principles—seek peace and insure it—leave America, if she has taxable matter in her, to tax herself. I am not going here into the distinctions of rights, nor attempting to mark their boundaries; I hate the very sound of them." To haggle forever about abstract rights and powers, Burke would argue repeatedly, must result in injury to the real welfare of any nation; by compromise and conciliation, settle for the practicable.

"Leave the Americans as they anciently stood," he continued, "and these distinctions, born of our unhappy contest, will die along with it. They and we, and their and our ancestors, have been happy under that system. Let the memory of all actions in contradiction of that good old mode, on both sides, be extinguished forever . . . Do not burden them by taxes; you were not used to do so from the beginning. Let this be your reason for not taxing. These are the arguments of states and kingdoms. Leave the rest to the schools; for only there may they be discussed with safety. But if, intemperately, unwisely, fatally, you sophisticate and poison the very source of government, by urging subtle deductions, and consequences odious to those you govern, from the unlimited and illimitable nature of supreme sovereignty, you will teach them by these means to call that sovereignty itself in question. When you drive him hard, the boar will surely turn upon the hunters. If that sovereignty and their freedom cannot be reconciled, which will they take? They will cast your sovereignty in your face. Nobody will be argued into slavery."

Custom and usage, Burke is saying, provide firm ground

for justice and for voluntary acceptance of necessary authority. But pushing claims of abstract right upon metaphysical premises, and endeavoring to govern the commonwealth by notions of perfection, must end by setting great interest against opposing great interest. Accustomed to a high degree of liberty, the Americans must be indulged in their old ways; the whole Empire would prosper by a prudent shunning of extreme doctrines.

Yet Burke's wisdom and eloquence won few votes in the House of Commons. Early in May, Parliament approved two severe bills, making the Massachusetts constitution far more subject to royal authority, and altering that province's courts. The stern spirit of the Bay Colony would not submit to this. New York, too, at last was preparing to resist the duty on tea. Almost as Burke spoke on American taxation, action commenced. The acting governor of New York, a gentleman eighty-seven years old, was unable to resist the "Mohawks" who, going aboard the vessel "London", held New York's Tea Party. To prevent radicals from seizing control of the protest against the Boston Port Act, the conservative Whig proprietors and merchants who were Burke's New York principals and correspondents—the Delanceys, Crugers, and others—then joined a committee to defend the rights of all the colonies.

Yet the ministry would not return to the old policy of salutary neglect. On June 13, 1774, the House of Commons passed the Quebec Act, intended in part to make Canada a counterpoise against the English-speaking colonies. New York and Pennsylvania, previously less restive than New England and Virginia, now were thoroughly alarmed. The first Continental Congress was taking form: the Patriot delegates met at Philadelphia in September, to concert colonial resistance short of rebellion, if possible. It was the beginning of the end of British power in the Thirteen Colonies.

By early February, 1775, Lord North was pushing for a declaration that Massachusetts was in rebellion: Parliament so resolved. Later in the month, additional steps were authorized for subduing resistance in America. In March, North extended the restraints to four more colonies.

Late in February, Lord North had induced Parliament to offer certain conciliatory proposals to the Americans—chiefly a scheme to abandon taxation (though not the *right* to tax) if the colonial assemblies would promise to make grants at the Crown's request—the amount of every grant, and its use, to be determined by the English government. This plan was impractical, Burke thought, and the colonists would not put their trust in North's word. On March 22, therefore, Burke delivered his most famous speech, "On Moving Resolutions for Conciliation with America." This was the opposition's counter-proposal.

The grand plea was twice vain. There existed no possibility that Parliament would be won over by Burke and the Rockinghams, at this hour; and by April 19, Paul Revere had ridden, the shots heard round the world were fired at Lexington, and Bunker Hill was in prospect. The Revolution had commenced a month before "Conciliation" was published as a pamphlet, and well before word of Burke's speech had reached America.

Yet as a piece of political wisdom, the Speech on Conciliation has endured down to our time, and does not ring hollow today. Both Lord Chatham and Horace Walpole, no friends to Burke, praised this address heartily. The House of Commons voted down his first resolution by 270 to 78; but posterity voted with Burke.

"A great empire and little minds go ill together." Burke's six conciliatory resolutions amounted to a formal admission that the colonies lacked representation in Parliament; that taxation without representation had produced severe discontent; that the distance of the colonies from England, and other circumstances, had made representation in Parliament impractical; that colonial assemblies were competent to levy taxes; that the assemblies had made voluntary grants to the Crown for the common defense; that such voluntary grants from colonial assemblies were more agreeable to colonial subjects, and accorded better with the imperial interest, than taxation by parliament. His appeal was to English generosity and imperial prosperity. The speech added little to Burke's previous arguments on this subject, but so combined rational exposition, moral imagination, and passionate intensity that it has been ever since a principal school-model of English eloquence.

Perhaps Burke's proposals would not have satisfied the American Patriots, even had Parliament embraced them and even had there been opportunity for discussion in the colonies. They did not touch upon the Navigation Acts, which in general Burke had defended; and the mercantilism of that system for regulating commerce was bound up with American discontents, even though the colonial declarations of grievance did not emphasize this point. Still, had Burke and the Rockingham Whigs not gone out of office years before, possibly Burke's program might have been a basis for compromise and gradual accommodation and reform—if adopted earlier.

Burke declared that he did not know the method for drawing up an indictment against a whole people. The ministry's measures were directed not merely against the extreme Patriots, but were calculated to ruin all North Americans. "The mode of inquisition and dragooning is going out of fashion in the Old World, and I should not confide much to their efficacy in the New. The education of the Americans is also on the same unalterable bottom of their religion. You cannot persuade them to burn their books of curious science, to banish their lawyers from their courts of law, or to quench the lights of their assemblies by refusing to choose those persons who are best read in their privileges. It would be no less impracticable to think of wholly annihilating the popular assemblies in which these lawyers sit. The army, by which we must govern in their place, would be far more chargeable to us, not quite so effectual, and perhaps, in the end, full as difficult to be kept in obedience."

By denying the Americans their prescriptive liberties, Burke went on, the Crown must imperil the chartered rights of Englishmen. "As we must give away some natural liberties to enjoy civil liberties, so we must sacrifice some civil liberties for the advantages to be derived from the communion and fellowship of a great empire." In any political order, Burke is saying, obedience to laws is required. If those laws are reasonable, the benefit of security compensates for the diminishing of perfect freedom to do whatever one wishes. But any Englishman, and any American, would risk his life rather than submit to an *arbitrary* government on the model of Hobbes.

If the people are given adequate liberty, Burke reasoned, they will not risk their valuable existing rights merely for the sake of trying to obtain total freedom from all authority. Let the Americans, then, retain the liberties they always had enjoyed: to keep those old liberties, they will refrain from demanding perfect independence. The government of Britain should cease to insist on the full exercise of sovereignty, should settle for the possible: such was the gist of Burke's three hours of eloquence. The classical virtue of prudence —the art of calculating the eventual results of policies and actions, of avoiding extremes, of shunning haste—never was better described. But already the colonial militia were exchanging volleys with the British troops.

Though the war had commenced, might it not be arrested, even now? Burke still hoped that something might be accomplished by an energetic appeal to the British people, who could petition Parliament for peace; but he found Lord Rockingham and his following discouraged and faint-hearted. Desperate, he urged Rockingham to employ his powerful influence in Ireland to persuade the Irish Parliament to refuse to contribute troops and supplies to the American campaign; Ireland might mediate the quarrel. Of this, too, nothing came.

As the struggle in America ebbed and flowed, over the succeeding years, Burke contended against the king, the vast majority in Parliament, and predominant public opinion. After two years of fighting, he still demanded a negotiated peace. On April 3, 1777, there was published his *Letter to the Sheriffs of the City of Bristol,* denouncing the ministry's partial suspension of writs of *habeas corpus,* and lamenting a war undertaken and conducted without regard for prudence—which with a wise statesman takes precedence over right and power. He concluded with a passage on civil liberty, containing the kernel of his argument about the balance which ought to be maintained between freedom and power. This particular truth of Burke's, says Hans Barth, makes Burke the most important of modern political philosophers.[9]

Civil liberty is not an abstract speculation, Burke declared. How much freedom a people have, and how it is to be enjoyed, must depend upon "the temper and circumstances of every community." Those who demand total freedom may end under a perfect tyranny; those who demand total authority may be overthrown by popular resentment. "The *extreme* of liberty (which is its abstract perfection, but its real fault) obtains nowhere, nor ought to obtain anywhere; because extremes, as we all know, in every point which relates either to our duties or satisfactions in life, are destructive both to virtue and enjoyment. Liberty, too, must be limited to be possessed. The degree of restraint it is impossible in any case to settle precisely. But it ought to be the constant aim of every wise public counsel to find out by cautious experiments, and rational, cool endeavors, with how little, not how much, of this restraint the community can subsist; for liberty is a good to be improved, and not an evil to be lessened."

Ardent though Burke had been, all those years, in advocating conciliation and peace, still he had not much sympathized with the colonists' appeal to alleged natural rights, as embodied by 1776 in the Declaration of Independence. Civil liberty, as suggested in the preceding passage, is the product of social experience, convention, and compromise, not of an original and unalterable Nature. Americans were entitled to the "chartered rights of Englishmen"; but they possessed no "natural" right to defy constituted authority whenever it might suit their temporary purposes. The only liberty worth possessing is an ordered freedom.

As Burke had predicted, the stubborn American spirit was not to be crushed. The Rockingham Whigs had been denied opportunity to effect conciliation while compromise still had been possible; they had been ignored in their efforts to make peace while the Revolution raged. But in 1782, a few months after Cornwallis' troops laid down their arms at Yorktown, the North ministry fell at last. Much though the king disliked the Rockinghams, he was compelled to let the Marquess kiss hands and to permit the second Rockingham ministry to treat with the victorious Continental Congress. In a melancholy success, Rockingham, Burke, and their friends resumed the government they had relinquished sixteen years earlier. Meanwhile, an empire had collapsed and a new nation had emerged.

Seven years later, Burke would break with his party and many of his closest friends, to oppose the French Revolution with all his power. His *Reflections on the Revolution in France*, and his later writings on that struggle, would turn against him many leaders in America—until the fierce course of the French Revolution, and then the tyranny of Napoleon, justified Burke's prophecies.

In the long run, Burke's influence upon Americans was strong. Public men so various as Alexander Hamilton, John Randolph, Justice Story, and Chancellor Kent drew much from him; so, later, did John C. Calhoun in the South and James Russell Lowell in the North. Some well-known Americans paid him the highest form of flattery that can be offered to a man of letters: plagiarism. Burke's long articles on the course of the American Revolution, published in his influential *Annual Register* as the struggle progressed from year to year, later were raided by American historical writers of the early Republic. They boldly appropriated and published under their own names not only Burke's opinions but lengthy passages of his prose. Large reputations were built upon these thefts of literary property—and one of the plagiarists was John Marshall. Burke's view of the American Revolution was so widely disseminated by these borrowers that the conventional American interpretation of the Revolution and its causes is derived chiefly from Burke.[10]

"Burke was right, and was himself, when he wrought to keep the French infection out of England." So Woodrow Wilson would write, before he became President of the United States.[11] In America, Burke had seen hardheaded colonials asserting the old chartered rights of Englishmen—working no social revolution at all, really, but merely a political separation from Britain. In France, Burke saw a wholly different set of revolutionaries, destroying an order that might have been reformed peaceably: revolutionaries who, moved by the "idyllic imagination" of Jean Jacques Rousseau, tore a society apart. Unlike the Americans, the French innovators were pursuing the dream of an imaginary "social contract" that never had existed nor could come into being.

When only seventeen years old, Burke had written to a friend that the complacent society of the eighteenth century was not long for this world: the age, despite its deceptive flush, was decadent. "We are just on the verge of Darkness and one push drives us in—we shall all live, if we live long, to see the prophecy of the Dunciad fulfilled and the age of ignorance come round once more. . . .Is there no one to relieve the world from the curse of obscurity? No not one—I would therefore advise more to your reading the writings of those who have gone before us than our Contemporaries. . . ." And he quoted, in Latin, Virgil's Fourth Eclogue: "The Saturnian age returns, and the great order of the centuries is born anew."[12]

What with the American Revolution and the French Revolution, half a century later it seemed as if this undergraduate's prophecy had been fulfilled: the great order of the centuries was transformed by those events. But unlike the revolutionary French, the revolutionary Americans did not reject their patrimony of order. In refuting Rousseau's theory of the social contract, Burke described the *true* "contract of eternal society" out of which a high civil social order arises. "It is a partnership in all science," Burke wrote; "a partnership in all art; a partnership in every virtue, and in all perfection. As the ends of such a partnership cannot be obtained in many generations, it becomes a partnership not only between those who are living, but between those who are living, those who are dead, and those who are to be born."

Some of the men of the early American Republic would understand Burke in this, and would pray that their commonwealth might be such a moral and social partnership, joining generation with generation.

Notes

[1] Paul Hazard, *European Thought in the Eighteenth Century, from Montesquieu to Lessing* (translated by J. Lewis May; London: Hollis and Carter, 1954), p. 153.

[2] Basil Willey, *The Eighteenth Century Background* (London: Chatto and Windus, 1949), p. 135.

[3] C. E. Vaughan, *Studies in the History of Political Philosophy* (Manchester: University of Manchester Press, 1925), Vol. I, p. 331.

[4] Irving Brant, *James Madison* (Indianapolis: Bobbs Merrill, 1948), Vol. II, p. 415.

[5] Daniel Boorstin, *The Americans: the Colonial Experience* (New York: Random House, 1958), p. 203.

[6] Roscoe Pound, *The Formative Era of American Law* (Boston: Little, Brown, 1938), p. 153.

[7] Sir William Holdsworth, *A History of English Law* (London: Methuen, 1938), Vol. XII, p. 736.

[8] Alexis de Tocqueville, *Democracy in America* (edited by J. P. Mayer; Anchor Books edition, New York: Doubleday, 1969), pp. 268-69.

[9] See Hans Barth, *The Idea of Order: Contributions to a Philosophy of Politics* (Dordrecht: D. Reidel, 1960), Chapter II.

[10] See Harvey Wish, *The American Historian* (New York: Oxford University Press, 1960), p. 40; also *The Burke Newsletter,* Vol. IV, No. 2 (winter, 1962-3), pp. 179-81.

[11] Woodrow Wilson, "Edmund Burke and the French Revolution", *The Century Magazine,* Vol. LXII (N.S., XL), September, 1901, p. 784.

[12] See *The Correspondence of Edmund Burke* (edited by Thomas W. Copeland; Chicago: University of Chicago Press, 1958), Vol. I, p. 74.

CHAPTER XI

DECLARATION

AND CONSTITUTION

A Revolution Not Made, but Prevented?

Two centuries after the Americans vindicated the independence of their order, the American Republic still asserts the validity of its old moral principles and the practicality of its established institutions. Of other great states, Britain is almost alone in making a similar claim.

Into the writing of the Declaration of Independence and of the Constitution of the United States went much of the legacy of institutions and thought described in earlier chapters of this book. In different ways, those two documents express the American understanding of order. Once adopted, those documents themselves became part of the American order, being received as authoritative sources of public wisdom by which future generations of Americans should be guided.

To apprehend the meaning of Declaration and Constitution, we need to recall something of the causes of the War for Independence that began in 1775. Was that war fought merely to avoid payment of a threepenny duty on a pound canister of tea? If so, the Revolution would have been a bad miscalculation, economically: for material damage to Americans' property was tremendous during those years of violent conflict, and many of the men who led the resistance to Britain

393

(most especially the planters of the Chesapeake region) lost their fortunes by the war, when not their lives.

If one judges by modern rates of taxation in America, the economic grievance of the colonies was remarkably insignificant. Moreover, the British government repeatedly had yielded to colonial protests against taxation. The Stamp Act had been repealed; the Townshend duties on imported paper, glass, painters' colors, and lead had been abandoned; only the Tea Act of 1773 was still in force, when the first shots were fired at Lexington in 1775.

And actually that Tea Act had *reduced* the price of tea in the colonies. For although a tax of threepence per pound had been imposed on the importation of tea, at the same time the Act had abolished a previous duty of twelvepence a pound on all tea imported into England. Now tea might be re-exported to America, free of the twelvepenny duty: net gain to the colonial tea-drinkers, ninepence a pound in diminished taxation. The British government's only purpose in demanding a threepenny tax at American ports was to assert the right of the King in Parliament to levy such duties if he so chose.

For a peculiar reason, nevertheless, this actual reduction in the price of imported tea was unpopular with certain vigorous Americans, particularly in Boston. For merchants had grown rich by smuggling tea into the colonies, paying no duty at all. Now that the lawful price of tea had fallen, smuggling became unprofitable. In Boston, the well-born demagogue Samuel Adams was enabled to obtain backing against imperial policy by the respectable tea-smugglers—not because they objected to a high duty on tea, but because they suffered from lowering of the duty! The Boston Tea Party, then, was meant to increase the price of tea, not to diminish it. And so, in effect, were other successful acts of resistance against permitting the East India Company's duty-paid tea to be landed at New York, Philadelphia, Charleston, Annapolis, and other ports. A mad world, my masters: so thought many English friends of the American cause, and so thought Benjamin Franklin, Patriot though he was.

Certainly the motives of the men who made the Revolution were mixed. Yet the War of Independence really was not fought about cups of tea. The truly fundamental question was whether the Crown in Parliament might levy taxes upon the Americans without the consent of colonial assemblies.

If they should give way on the Tea Act, the Patriots believed, then before long they might be governed directly by Parliament, as they never had been governed before—or, in effect, governed by the King operating upon a Parliament which he could control, more or less, through the creation of new peers in the House of Lords and through using the Crown's patronage powers to influence elections to the House of Commons. What Whiggish America stood for was the long-established chartered right of the colonies to govern themselves. They looked upon George III as a monarch who intended to make a revolution, by subverting their old ways of self-government; they protested that they, in resisting Crown and Parliament, were preventing this royal revolution. Their argument, that is, closely resembled the argument of the English Whigs against the policies of James II—the protest that had triumphed in the Glorious Revolution of 1688.

The vast majority of the Patriots were well enough satisfied with the colonial society into which they had been born: it was a society of rising expectations, and of expectations that were being gratified. They sought to preserve that society from arbitrary political change for the worse. Their appeal was to established constitutional usage. Certainly almost none of the leading Patriots thought of himself as a social revolutionary. Below the surface of the Patriot movement, true, there seethed now and again the unrest of a more radical minority; occasionally such extremists alarmed the Continental Congress or the governors of the new states during the Revolution; but without much difficulty, the leaders in the War of Independence succeeded in controlling such dissidents. If the long-run consequences of the War of Independence would modify greatly the American social structure, still that was not the desire nor the expectation of the Patriots when the Revolution began.

In this, the American Revolution differed vastly from the French Revolution. The Americans, in essence, meant to keep their old order and defend it against external interference; but the French rising was what Edmund Burke called "a revolution of theoretic dogma," intended to bring down the Old Regime and substitute something quite new. (Just what that something new might be, the French revolutionary factions disputed violently among themselves.)

This point deserves a digression. The best brief early analysis of the distinction between these two revolutions was made by a writer who participated in neither: a young man of German culture, Friedrich Gentz. Often the perspective of a neutral observer is to be preferred to the conclusions of a man personally involved in a cause.

In the last year of the eighteenth century, John Quincy Adams, only thirty-three years old, was Minister Plenipotentiary of the United States to Prussia. Adams was educating himself the whole of his life; and, perfecting his German during his residence in Berlin, he translated from the Berlin *Historisches Journal* (April and May, 1800) a long essay on the American and French revolutions by Gentz, a rising Prussian man of letters, three years older than the precocious Adams.

Gentz was founder and editor of that journal of ideas, and sole contributor to it. These were men of mark: Adams would become the sixth President of the United States, and Gentz (as associate of Prince Metternich) a principal architect of the reconstruction of Europe after Napoleon's fall. "It cannot but afford a gratification to every American attached to his country," Adams wrote to Gentz in June, 1800, "to see its revolution so ably vindicated from the imputation of having originated, or having been conducted upon the same principle, as that of France."

Gentz had studied under the innovating philosopher Kant; but Burke's *Reflections* had converted the young Prussian to conservative principles. Abhorring the theories and consequences of the French Revolution, Gentz had translated the *Reflections* into German, so exerting his first influence upon European politics and making his reputation. Like Gentz, the younger Adams had been much struck by Burke; and though he tried to play arbiter between Edmund Burke and Thomas Paine, really Adams was persuaded by Burke's principal arguments. His *Letters of Publicola,* published in 1791, had demolished Paine's *Rights of Man* and had denounced the French revolutionaries, much to Thomas Jefferson's vexation. The Americans, young Adams had written, had not fallen into the pit of radical abstract doctrine:

"Happy, thrice happy the people of America! whose gentleness of manners and habits of virtue are still sufficient to reconcile the enjoyment of their natural rights, with the peace and tranquillity of their country; whose principles of religious liberty did not result from an indiscriminate contempt of all religion whatever, and whose equal representation in their legislative councils was founded upon an equality really existing among them, and not upon the metaphysical speculations of fanciful politicians, vainly contending against the unalterable course of events, and the established order of nature."[1]

So Adams was of one mind with Gentz, and saw in Gentz's essay the most succinct and forceful contrast between the moderate polity of the American colonies (founded upon a respect for prescriptive rights and customs), and the levelling theories of French radicalism. Only the word "Republic" was common to the two new dominations, Adams declared; and the French Republic already had ceased to contain any element of true representative government. Adams' translation of Gentz was published anonymously at Philadelphia in 1800.

The little book has Adams' style imprinted upon it in translation. But in thought and structure, Gentz's writing bears the mark of Burke's *Reflections* and Schiller's *Thirty Years' War*. The folly of true and thoroughgoing revolution was the theme of Gentz's thought and action from 1791 until the end of his life. By the power of his pen, the obscure Gentz (half Jewish by birth, as was a later Prussian, Karl Marx) rose to be the associate of kings and a designer of the concert of Europe.

With Burke, and with John and John Quincy Adams, Gentz perceived that disaster would come from the fallacies of Turgot and Condorcet and Rousseau and Paine and other movers of the French Revolution. His essay, *The American and French Revolutions Compared*, contrasts the theories and the course of the two movements. The American Revolution,

Gentz argues, was what Burke had called the Glorious Revolution: "a revolution not made, but prevented." The American Patriots had stood up for their inherited rights; their claims and expectations were moderate, and founded upon a sound apprehension of human nature and natural rights; their new written constitutions were conservative. But the French revolutionaries, hoping to transform utterly human society and even human nature, broke with the past, defied history, embraced theoretic dogmas, and so fell under the cruel domination of Giant Ideology.

Prudence and prescription guided the steps of the Americans, who simply preserved and continued the English institutions of representative government and private rights; fanaticism and vain expectations led the French to their own destruction. Burke, at the outbreak of the troubles in America, had maintained that the colonists were trying to conserve, not to destroy; they sought to keep liberties gained over the centuries, not to claim fanciful liberties conjured up by closet philosophers; they were "not only devoted to liberty, but to liberty according to English principles," in Burke's phrases. "Abstract liberty like other mere abstractions is not to be found. Liberty inheres in some sensible object."

Repeatedly, in his comparison, Gentz touches upon the broad differences between American and French principles that the course of history, since 1776, has made more clear. He compares, for instance, the Americans' sound understanding of natural rights with the French illusion of the abstract "Rights of Man"—"a sort of magic spell, with which all the ties of nations and of humanity were insensibly dissolved." The pretended right of an abstract "people" to do whatever they might like, Gentz insisted, would swallow up all the old hard-earned rights of groups and individuals. The Americans sought security; the French, through their armed doctrine, irresponsible power. "As the American revolution was a defensive revolution, it was of course finished, at the moment when it had overcome the attack, by which it had been occasioned. The French Revolution, true to the character of a most violent revolution, could not but proceed as long as there remained objects for it to attack, and it retained strength for the assault."

Later in the nineteenth century, the talented French writers Alexis de Tocqueville and Hippolyte Taine would judge the French Revolution similarly. In the twentieth century, American historians tend to confirm Gentz's verdict. "The Americans of 1776," Clinton Rossiter writes, "were among the first men in modern history to defend rather than to seek an open society and constitutional liberty; their political faith, like the appeal to arms it supported, was therefore surprisingly sober. . . .Perhaps the most remarkable characteristic of this political theory was its deep-seated conservatism. However radical the principles of the Revolution may have seemed to the rest of the world, in the minds of the colonists they were thoroughly preservative and respectful of the past. . . . The political theory of the American Revolution, in contrast to that of the French Revolution, was not a theory designed to make the world over."[2]

With the French revolutionaries, the whole attitude toward history, continuity, and the "contract of eternal society" was ruinously different. "So France, exhausted by fasting under the monarchy," Taine puts it, "made drunk by the bad drug of the *Social Contract*, and countless other adulterated or fiery beverages, is suddenly struck with paralysis of the brain; at once she is convulsed in every limb through the incoherent play and contradictory twitchings of her discordant organs. At this time she has traversed the period of joyous madness, and is about to enter upon the period of sombre delirium; behold her capable of daring, suffering, and doing all, capable of incredible exploits and abominable barbarities, the moment her guides, as erratic as herself, indicate an enemy or an obstacle to her fury."[3]

As Gentz points out, there occurred persecutions, cruelties, confiscations, and exiling of honest people in the course of the American Revolution also. "But what are all these single instances of injustice and oppression, compared with the universal flood of misery and ruin, which the French revolution let loose upon France, and all the neighbouring countries? If, even in America, private hatred, or local circumstances, threatened property or personal security; if here and there even the public authorities became the instruments of injustice, of revenge, and of a persecuting spirit, yet did the poison never flow into every vein of the social body; never, as in France, was the contempt of all rights, and of the very simplest precepts of humanity, made the general maxim of legislation, and the unqualified prescription of systematic tyranny."[4]

What made this enormous difference in the conduct of the two revolutions? Circumstances and theories. The Americans had nothing to overthrow within North America but a few English civil officers and an English army of occupation; while the French revolutionaries had a powerful and complex establishment, the Old Regime, to pull down. The Americans not only appealed to old "chartered rights," but firmly believed in those established rights and institutions; the French were enraptured by "theoretic dogma," which we now call ideology, and justified their fierceness by their visions of a future earthly paradise. As Tocqueville would write, halfway down the stairs the French revolutionaries threw themselves out of the window, in order to get to the ground more quickly.

A recent writer, Daniel Boorstin, comes to a conclusion identical with that of Gentz: "The American Revolution was in a very special way conceived as both a vindication of the British past and an affirmation of an American future. The British past was contained in ancient and living institutions rather than in doctrines; and the American future was never to be contained in a theory. The Revolution was thus a prudential decision taken by men of principle rather than the affirmation of a theory."[5]

Gentz drew a contrast between principle and ideology; between prudence and fanaticism; between prescriptive rights and extravagant ambitions; between historical experience and utopianism; between representative government and democratic despotism (or what J.L. Talmon calls "totalitarian democracy"). In examining the Declaration of Independence and the Constitution of the United States, those differences between the two Revolutions must be borne in mind. The Declaration was meant as a call for unity of purpose among the Patriots; as Franklin said, either they must all hang together, or else they would all hang separately. Also it was an apology to the world—France in particular—for the

Patriots' armed rising, in hope of assistance from abroad. Hastily drawn up by Jefferson and a committee of four others, the Declaration is not an original work of political theory: instead, it reflects theories that had been discussed in America for the preceding decade and longer. Nor is the Constitution—except for implications that may be drawn from it—a theoretical document at all.

"I have but one lamp by which my feet are guided," Patrick Henry told the Patriot planters of Virginia in 1775, "and that is the lamp of experience. I know of no way of judging the future but by the past." In the beginning, Henry was one of the more radical Patriots, but even he desired no revolution of theoretic dogma. The Americans looked for guidance to their own historical past in America, and to the past of the civilization, European and Christian, in which they shared. For novel abstract theories of human nature and society, most of the men who subscribed to the Declaration and the Constitution had no relish.

Justifying the Separation

More than any other people, Americans today look to certain basic documents for the written principles of their social order—to the Declaration of Independence, the Constitution, Washington's Farewell Address, and Lincoln's Gettysburg Address, most notably. The first of these, the Declaration, is of enduring importance chiefly for the six sentences with which it commences.

After those, the Declaration is a recounting of grievances against the King of England—some of them historically sustained, others calculated more to rouse sympathy abroad than strictly accurate in their expression. In this latter part of the Declaration there ring phrases from the English Petition of Right and the English Bill of Rights. Some of the charges—that against the quartering of troops, for one—directly echo the Bill of Rights that William and Mary had accepted. These charges do not constitute an explanation of the underlying causes of the Revolution, really: for the most part, they are stern complaints against the British government's actions since 1773, and some of them against British military measures since regiments had begun to march the previous year.

The fundamental political motive of the Patriots is mentioned only in a clause, "For imposing Taxes on us without our Consent . . ." Earlier, it is declared that "The history of the present King of Great Britain is a history of repeated injuries and usurpations, all having in direct object the establishment of an absolute Tyranny over these States." In reality, George III never intended to go so far, and many of the signers of the Declaration, in a less desperate hour, would not have charged him with precisely that. Nor had the King deliberately followed a systematic policy of usurpation: the measures of the North ministry were unimaginative and imprudent, rather than a scheme of contrived malice.

But such concerns are more matters of political history than they are questions of the American order. For our purpose, those beginning half-dozen sentences are what signify.

On what ground could separation from the British Empire be justified in theory? The Declaration recognizes the gravity of the decision: "Prudence, indeed, will dictate that Governments long established should not be changed for light and transient causes; and accordingly all experience hath shown, that mankind are more disposed to suffer, while evils are sufferable, than to right themselves by abolishing the forms to which they are accustomed." The tone of Hooker and Blackstone and Burke is in that sentence. Why is this separation not imprudent?

Why, because the Americans' petitions for redress of their unbearable grievances have gone unanswered, the Declaration asserts. What recourse remains? To whom or to what can a people appeal, if the king will not hear them?

The Continental Congress appeals to "the Laws of Nature and of Nature's God": that is, to natural law. They could have referred to the authority of the judicious Hooker; however, Thomas Jefferson, who wrote that phrase, knew his Locke and his Blackstone better than Hooker. Jefferson was influenced, too, by Algernon Sidney's compact-doctrine in

Sidney's *Discourses Concerning Government,* written at the beginning of England's Civil Wars. (Sidney, by the way, was no democrat, but the advocate of aristocratic ascendancy, as opposed to pure monarchy.) Whether the signers of the Declaration understood clearly what was meant by natural law, or could have agreed upon any clear definition of that term, has been inconclusively discussed. Yet their general appeal to natural law runs back to the principles of Cicero (sometimes mentioned by Jefferson) and of the medieval Schoolmen; it is connected, through another line of descent, with the claims of Parliament over several centuries, and especially with those of the Whig Parliaments of the seventeenth century.

In English constitutional assumptions, the king too is under the law. What if the king breaks the law? "The king can do no wrong" is an English legal aphorism of long standing, reaffirmed by Blackstone. It does not mean that the occupant of the throne is incapable of sinning: rather, it signifies that because the king is the indispensable axis upon which the whole realm revolves, he cannot be punished for the acts of his government—not if the bed of justice and the defense of the realm are to be maintained. It is the king's ministers who will be punished for encroachments upon liberty—if necessary, by impeachment and even execution; they *can* do wrong. So "the king can do no wrong" is a useful fiction—which does not mean that it is false. (*Pilgrim's Progress* also is a useful fiction.) The attempt to hold King Charles I personally responsible for the acts of his government, ending in his execution, had been disastrous for the English nation. (Few among the leaders of the American Revolution ever ventured to cite the actions and words of Cromwell, the Regicides, and the "Saints" of the Commonwealth as excuse for their own rising in arms: those would have been ill-omened precedents.)

The Americans, nevertheless, could not call to account the ministers of George III, because the colonies (or states, now) had no members in Parliament, and could not command the good will of a majority of the British people. There remained for the colonists only their appeal to natural law and the laws decreed by the Author of Nature. That is the extreme medicine of a people lacking any other means of redress.

Although the old doctrine of natural law had close connections with Christian teaching, Jefferson's phrase is Deistic, rather than strictly Christian. That phrase seems to have encountered no serious opposition from the members of the committee of the Congress for whom Jefferson drafted the Declaration. In 1776, Deistic sentiments still remained fairly common among certain Patriot leaders, though losing ground in public opinion at large. The "Nature's God" of Jefferson, in Jefferson's understanding and in that of several other eminent members of the Congress, was a deity who set the universe in motion and gave their "nature" to things, but who did not intervene in human lives directly—or work miracles. (In an early rough draft of the Declaration, submitted to Franklin by Jefferson, appears the phrase "We hold these truths to be sacred and undeniable": this may have been changed by Dr. Franklin, also a Deist, to its final wording of "self-evident.") Yet if the Declaration did not cry to the living God of Abraham, Isaac, and Jacob, still it looked to a deity who had ordained the laws of nature, and was himself bound by those laws—a placid constitutional monarch in the heavens, submissive to his own laws, never a tyrant.

Probably most delegates to the Continental Congress did not reflect overmuch on this choice of phrases; necessarily they acted with some haste, the situation of the Patriot forces being precarious. In the last sentence of the Declaration, nevertheless, the signers express reliance upon "the protection of Divine Providence"—a concept more orthodox Christian than Deistic. That affirming of trust in God's presence in the world does not appear in Jefferson's early drafts of the Declaration; it was added by the Congress, many of whose members were uneasy with Deism.

To what laws of nature, precisely, does the Declaration look? Why, "We hold these truths to be self-evident, that all men are created equal, that they are endowed by their Creator with certain unalienable Rights, that among these are Life, Liberty and the pursuit of Happiness." To secure those rights, government had been instituted among men.

Why "happiness" instead of Locke's and Blackstone's "property"? Presumably because it is possible to be happy without possessing property—and because the protection of property alone, tacitly excluding other benefits of a good civil social order beyond life and liberty, was not a notion especially attractive to those supporters of the Revolutionary cause who were poor in the world's goods. The employment of this word "happiness" has been ascribed by some writers to the writings of Burlamaqui, then widely circulated in the colonies; but it is unnecessary to look so far afield. James Wilson, for instance, one of the more intelligent and vigorous members of the Continental Congress, a principal signer of the Declaration, had written ten years earlier (though his pamphlet was not published until 1774) that "the happiness of the society is the first law of every government."

By "self-evident" (or, in the earlier draft, "sacred and undeniable"), it was meant that these truths flowed from the nature of things; that they were reasonable, in the sense of according with right reason; that they were bound up inseparably with the nature of man; that they came from the Creator. They are premises taken for granted, and every political order must be founded upon some such unquestioned premises. All men ardently desire life, liberty, and happiness: therefore those blessings are natural, and whoever deprives man of them acts in contempt of human nature. There is something Stoic in this conviction. These rights are "unalienable" because they are man's birthright: whoever violates them deprives man of his manhood, and with justice man may reclaim what has been snatched from him.

Presumably no member of the Continental Congress thought of these rights as quite unlimited. The right to life, after all, must be limited by the necessities of society: a man who tries to deprive others of life must not expect to be spared himself, and in 1776 no one proposed to abolish capital punishment. The right to liberty, too, must depend in some degree upon circumstances: no one stands at liberty to treat his neighbors and their property however he likes; "liberty under law" was the understanding of the American leaders. As for happiness, no government can guarantee the attainment of that: all government can do is to refrain from malign or bumbling interference, or to remove large general obstacles to the pursuit of happiness.

It has been remarked that this bold affirmation of the right to liberty ignored a considerable part of America's population, which had no voice in the Congress—the Negro slaves. Was it liberty simply for those already free? Jefferson, in his original draft, included a denunciation of slavery and the slave trade (though a considerable slaveholder himself); but this was deleted, out of deference to the sensibilities of delegates from South Carolina and Georgia, states in which slavery seemed essential to the economy, and where the slave trade still prospered. This glaring inconsistency would trouble the United States for nine decades longer—and in its consequences, for longer still. During the Revolution, the Tories of England would point out derisively the hypocrisy of such an affirmation.

This point returns us to the doctrine that "all men are created equal." What was meant by this? Jefferson, not unaware of his own remarkable talents, scarcely could have thought that every man (even if improved by the system of schooling Jefferson would outline for Virginians) could become the intellectual peer of Thomas Jefferson. As for equality in strength, swiftness, and beauty, those obviously are not articles in the Laws of Nature. John Adams, after Jefferson the committee-member with the largest hand in the Declaration, was given throughout his life to noting the inequality of human beings in many respects. If taken literally, the Declaration's equality clause would fly in the face of common sense.

Yet Jefferson did write "created equal," and the Congress did not strike out the phrase. Jefferson, though not necessarily most delegates to the Congress, may have been swayed here by John Locke's notion of the baby's blank tablet of the mind, the *tabula rasa*. Locke had known nothing of the modern science of genetics, nor did Jefferson. If indeed babies possess no innate ideas, does that general ignorance make them intellectually all equals? Half a century later, John Randolph of Roanoke would point out that whether or not babies are born with innate ideas, certainly they are born with differing capabilities: they are not equal in their genetic inheritance from their parents and their ancestors.

Randolph was an ardent breeder of horses and a considerable genealogist. Some members of the Continental Congress also bred horses, and were interested in family trees; they must have been aware, as was Randolph, that congenital inequalities exist between one individual of a species and other individuals. Yet "created equal" had a certain sweet ring to it; and it was not essential that other delegates should ascertain precisely what Jefferson had in mind; they might interpret this phrase, and other phrases of the Declaration, much as they liked. Such ambiguities in the Declaration have been debated among politicians and scholars ever since 1776.

The demagogue may find "created equal" a slogan useful to him; in Mark Twain's witticism, "One man is as good as another, or maybe a little better." There were some demagogues in the Continental Congress, but Jefferson was not of their number, and the large majority of the Declaration's signers were realists with broad experience of the world, not given to sentimental or false slogans. Later in American affairs, down to the present, a literal appeal to the doctrine of congenital equality would do mischief. Randolph of Roanoke—who early in his career was Jefferson's valuable ally, but later Jefferson's harshest enemy—had in mind that power for mischief when, in 1826, he would tell the Senate of the United States that "created free and equal" is a "pernicious falsehood."

"In regard to this principle, that all men are born free and equal," Randolph would cry, "if there is an animal on earth to which it does not apply—that is not born free, it is man—he is born in a state of the most abject want, and a state of perfect helplessness and ignorance, which is the foundation of the connubial tie. . . . Who should say that all the soil in the world is equally rich, the first rate land in Kentucky and the Highlands of Scotland, because the superficial content of the acre is the same, would be just as right, as he who should maintain the absolute equality of man in virtue of his birth. The ricketty and scrofulous little wretch who first sees the light in a work-house, or in a brothel, and feels the effects of alcohol before the effects of vital air, is not equal in any respect to the ruddy offspring of the honest yeoman; nay, I will go further, and say that a prince, provided that he is no better born than royal blood will make him, is not equal to the healthy son of a peasant."[6]

The men of the Continental Congress, however, did not take Jefferson's equality clause as an affirmation of literal equality in body and mind. (In one early draft of the Declaration, the phrase is "equal & independent"; in another rough draft, "& independent" is crossed out, presumably because Dr. Franklin or some other realist thought that assertion difficult to defend: a baby, as Senator Randolph suggested, is absolutely dependent.) Rightly, they did not look upon the average American, let alone the average man everywhere, as their literal equals. They did subscribe to two venerable concepts of human equality: equality before the law, and equality in the judgment of God.

In English law, no persons were privileged when brought before the bar of justice (though noblemen must be tried for serious crimes by the House of Lords, "a jury of their peers"): the law being no respecter of persons, justice must be administered regardless of the rank and wealth of a litigant. In that sense, all Americans, too, were born equal. It was not so in positive law then in all nations; but the Patriots believed that equality before the law was true according to the laws of nature.

In Christian teaching, as in Jewish, there exists moral equality among all men: that is, God judges men not according to their station in life, but according to their deserts as persons; Dives and Lazarus are punished or rewarded in the divine knowledge of how well or badly they have obeyed God's commandments, not with regard to their worldly success. Some are weighed in the balance, and found wanting, but not because of their rank here below. To this doctrine, too, the members of the Continental Congress assented: it was a pillar of the Laws of Nature's God.

Probably Jefferson's phrase implied to some Patriots the relative equality of condition in America, by contrast with the aristocratic society of England. Yet the delegates to the Continental Congress were not social and economic levellers on principle. Most of them had done well in the world by their own exertions; they might hope to open the way for others to do well also, but not by levelling downward. "Created equal," then, meant to the signers of the Declaration substantially the social arrangements into which they had been born in America: they found those relatively equal arrangements very natural indeed.

So the natural-right and natural-law beliefs of 1776 were a blending of Hebraic, Christian, classical, and seventeenth- and eighteenth-century theories. That life, liberty, and the pursuit of happiness were natural rights (or at least ordained through the laws of Nature's God) was a conviction as general in Britain, in that age, as in America; it would be carried to extravagant lengths, under a secularized version of natural-rights theory, in France within a few years. Few men of the time would have denied that governments are instituted to secure these rights.

But do governments derive "their just powers from the consent of the governed"? In that phrase, Jefferson and his colleagues were worked upon in varying degrees by certain social-compact theories, notably Locke's—though not by Rousseau's, for not even Jefferson had read Rousseau by 1776. Probably many members of the Continental Congress were aware of Montesquieu's and Hume's criticisms of the idea of the social compact. As Whigs, the Patriots respected Locke. His authority alone, nevertheless, might not have sufficed to bring "the consent of the governed" into the Declaration.

By "consent of the governed," the delegates to the Congress were affirming not so much a political philosopher's theory as an experienced institutional reality. That consent, after all, obtained in England, George III notwithstanding (the Patriots holding only that the King *intended* to make himself a tyrant, not that he was despotic already). Through Parliament, the consent of the governed was realized; divine-right theories of kingship virtually had been abandoned, even among the High Tories, by 1776. And as for America, from the first, in corporate colonies, proprietary colonies, and royal colonies alike, colonial assemblies had fulfilled the right of the governed to be represented in government. "Consent of the governed," therefore, did not necessarily imply firm belief in some primitive social compact, whether the type of Locke or the type of Hobbes. The image which that phrase summoned to most Americans' minds was representative government on existing British and American models.

With Montesquieu, the Americans thought of this form of "consent of the governed" as natural to the human condition. (For Montesquieu, either a monarchy or a republic might exist with the consent of the governed; it was a despotism that defied the principle.) Accordingly, "consent of the governed" was taken to be a part of the laws of nature, the many existing unnatural governments not withstanding.

It may have been as well that the Declaration did not probe more deeply into the precise character of "consent of the people." For just how many of the American "governed," in that year of 1776, willingly acknowledged the political authority of the Continental Congress? Candid John Adams, knowing much about such matters, later estimated that one third of the free inhabitants of the Thirteen Colonies favored the Patriot cause, another third adhered to the Crown, and the remainder were neutral or indifferent. After the victory at Yorktown, indeed, the Congress might claim to represent a majority of citizens—but only because many of the Loyalists who cast their lot with royal authority had fled over the mountains to Kentucky and Tennessee, to the Maritime Provinces of Canada, to Bermuda, to the West Indies, or to Britain; and those who remained were prudently silent. Definitions of "the governed" or "the people" vary often with the interest of the governors. How many of the slaves consciously and willingly assented to either Crown or Congress in power?

But let that pass. Suppose that a government "becomes destructive of these ends"—what shall be done? The Declaration asserts "the Right of the People to alter or abolish it, and to institute new Government, laying its foundations on such principles and organizing its powers in such form, as to them shall seem most likely to effect their Safety and Happiness." Just that was what the Continental Congress began to accomplish in 1776—or to accomplish the altering and abolishing, rather.

The Declaration did not precisely proclaim a right of revolution; yet soon, in Europe and Latin America, the Declaration would be regarded as justifying such a right. In London, a few years later, a radical Unitarian preacher, Dr. Richard Price, would talk of "cashiering kings." But the Patriots did not talk of cashiering George III, much though they detested him; and in England, it was Burke who would come to the defense of the King against Price. George's right to rule as King of England, Scotland, and Ireland was not their direct concern. (George III did have the consent of the governed there, after all, being popular with his subjects usually.) The question for the Patriots was whether George III had any right to govern *them,* beyond the rather vague sovereignty that English kings had asserted over the colonies from the beginning—whether he had the right to terminate the policy of salutary neglect and commence a policy of unhealthy meddling. It was George III and his ministers, the Patriots contended, who were trying to work a revolution.

One needs to note, moreover, that the Declaration's word is "government"—not "state." Eighteenth-century writers made a clear distinction between the two. "Government" implied the temporary possessors of power and their current political policies: whenever the king dismissed his ministers and chose new ones, a new "government" was formed. "State," on the other hand, meant what today we tend to call "society"—the established civil social order, permanent in character, with some sort of enduring constitution. The Declaration spoke of instituting "new Government," not of overthrowing the state itself, or the social order. That is another aspect of the moderation of the American "revolutionaries": they argued that *governments* might be altered or abolished, but contemplated no pulling down of fundamental institutions and ways of life. If in effect they declared a right of revolution, it was a right only to change a people's government for the better, and not a right to hack through the roots of the permanent things in a nation.

For justifying a thorough change in government, the

Patriots did not have to turn to radical theorists. They could cite the father of the common law, Henry Bracton, in the middle of the thirteenth century: "Let the king render back to the Law what the Law gives to him, namely, dominion and power; for there is no king where will, and not Law, wields dominion." They could turn to Richard Hooker, in the sixteenth century, on how an unjust king should be resisted. They looked, most of all, to the precedent of 1688, in which a government had been unseated and even a king dethroned—but the fabric of society had been uninjured.

So it was that even the overthrowing of a form of government "destructive of these ends" seemed natural to the men of 1776. By nature, the civil social order was intended to promote safety of life, enlarged liberty, and the pursuit of happiness: a government that acted otherwise was unnatural. Even such a government, they believed, should not be overthrown imprudently, for they had learned from old Aesop that King Stork may be more voracious than King Log. Only when evils are insufferable must nature assert itself again, in the perilous task of bringing down an unredeemably oppressive government, so that a tolerable government (with the help of Divine Providence) may be set up.

All in all, the Declaration's understanding of "natural law" is consonant with old "right reason," and is not an infatuation with the Goddess Reason whom the French revolutionaries would enthrone. "Whenever men become sufficiently dissatisfied with what is, with the existing regime of positive law and custom, they will be found reaching out beyond it for the rational basis of what they conceive ought to be," Carl Becker writes. "This is what the Americans did in their controversy with Great Britain; and this rational basis they found in that underlying preconception which shaped the thought of their age—the idea of natural law and natural rights."[7]

Although the Declaration describes the colonial past only in general terms, it was not by natural-law arguments alone that the Patriots could justify their separation from the Empire. For the preceding decade, their orators and pamphleteers had been defending the Americans' cause by

412

citing precedents of colonial history; so had Burke and others in England. One reason why such accounts of colonial history do not appear in the Declaration is that the Declaration was meant, in large part, as a plea to France and other conceivable allies against the British government; and while a claim of natural rights might wake the sympathies of such potential enlightened friends, a claim upon the "chartered rights of Englishmen" would have little meaning for Europeans. After all, it was against Englishmen that the French must fight, once they should ally themselves with the Americans. Therefore the Declaration goes so far in circumspection as to avoid mentioning even Parliament, calling that body merely "the Legislature."

The Patriots' historical and constitutional argument did not conflict with their natural-law principles; even so, it was a separate argument, and one more readily apprehended today. In essence, it is this: why should America be subject to Parliament, and why should the King assert powers rarely or never employed in America before, when the greatest benefit conferred upon the colonies by Crown and Parliament had been salutary neglect? Only in Georgia had the king's government assisted with funds the settling of the colony: all the other colonies had been built up by private proprietors or corporate bodies, or by the exertions of individual colonists—the Crown doing nothing more than to make grants of lands over which Britain then possessed no effectual control.

True, British armies and fleets had helped to defend the colonies against external enemies. But much of the cost of military operations had been borne by the colonial people themselves, and most of the brunt of French and Indian attacks. Had British governments defended the colonies out of pure charity? Not at all: Britain had gained mightily from commerce with the colonies, under the Navigation Acts, and with the help of colonial forces had succeeded in defeating Britain's most formidable rival in the world, the French imperial system. If one must talk of obligation, the larger debt was that of Britain to the North American colonies.

Self-governing from the first, the colonists asked only that they continue to possess the rights of all Englishmen, secured in Britain by the constitution. To be taxed only with the consent of their parliamentary representatives was the key to all other English political rights. The colonies having no members in Parliament, was it not reasonable that they should be taxed only by their own colonial representative assemblies?

In short, from the earliest times in America the colonial people had been a people separate from the British people, though linked to the British by willing ties of culture and friendship, and by common allegiance to a king. Rather than pulling down a government, the Patriots were defending their own prescriptive governments against what had become an alien government. In their act of separating from Britain, Americans did no more than reassert a political autonomy, or independence, rooted in the North American continent ever since the landings at Jamestown and Plymouth.

Such were some of the historical and constitutional points which might have been included in the Declaration. They were not so included because they would not have stirred Frenchmen gravely; because to detail them would have made that document far too long for its exhortatory and apologetic purpose; because they already were familiar to the mass of Americans. So if the first part of the Declaration seems somewhat abstract to twentieth-century readers, that is not because the members of the committee which drew it up, nor the delegates to the Continental Congress, were abstracted *philosophes*. Far from being closet philosophers, those men of 1776 were intensely practical lawyers and planters and merchants, none of them sheltered from the rough reality of colonial America. Republican virtue they possessed, but not cloistered virtue. They were men, most of them, who had held public offices or at least had directed and led many of their fellow-citizens. In essence, the Declaration of Independence was a world apart from the later French Declaration of the Rights of Man and Citizen (1789)—quite as the members of the Continental Congress were a different breed from the members of revolutionary France's National Assembly, or from the members of France's National Convention that supplanted the National Assembly.

By force of arms and power of belief, the men of the Declaration expelled British government from the Thirteen States, once colonies. Now could the Americans "institute new Government . . . likely to effect their Safety and Happiness"? Could they restore and improve an order, moral and social, which the War of Independence had weakened perilously? Eleven years later, the Americans would meet that challenge in the Constitutional Convention.

The Spirit of Laws Realized: the New Constitution

In 1787, at Philadelphia, there was drawn up the Constitution of the United States; no other written constitution of modern times has endured so long. The eighteenth century had been an age of absolutism in great states, Britain excepted. Now there emerged a strong republic of vast extent, whose constitution would be emulated, with varying degrees of success, in other continents.

The word "republic" means public concerns—the general welfare as expressed in political forms. Although a republic may choose a powerful executive head, it has no hereditary monarch. A republic may be either aristocratic or democratic. What took form in America was a democratic republic, but not a "totalitarian democracy," or government directly and absolutely controlled by the masses.

The American Republic was a government on a national scale, but with the powers of the general government limited; also the powers of that Republic's component states were restricted. The most remarkable features of this Republic would be its independent national judiciary, endowed with power to rule upon the constitutionality of the acts of national and state legislatures; and its successful "federal" character, "out of many, one," reconciling national needs and self-government in its member states. It would be a democracy of elevation, not of mediocrity, with strong guarantees for the security of life, liberty, property, and other private rights. The United States, John C. Calhoun would write in a later era of

415

American politics, "is, of course, a Republic, a constitutional democracy, in contradistinction to an absolute democracy; and . . . the theory which regards it as a government of the mere numerical majority rests on a gross and groundless misconception."[8]

The true constitution of any political state is not merely a piece of parchment, but rather a body of fundamental laws and customs that join together the various regions and classes and interests of a country, in a political pattern that is just. The English constitution is said to be "unwritten": that is, there exists no single formal document which can be called the Constitution of the United Kingdom. Certain great permanent charters, statutes, usages, and long-accepted political conventions make up that system of practices and principles, vaguely delimited but strongly entrenched, which is British constitutional government.

Similarly, even the American Republic possesses an underlying unwritten constitution—of which the written Constitution of the United States is an expression. The written Constitution has survived and has retained authority because it is in harmony with laws, customs, habits, and popular beliefs that existed before the Constitutional Convention met at Philadelphia—and which still work among Americans today. The written Constitution produced by the delegates from the several states drew upon the political experience of the colonies, upon their legacy of English law and institutions, upon the lessons of America under the Articles of Confederation, upon popular consensus about certain moral and social questions. Thus the Constitution was no abstract or utopian document, but a reflection and embodiment of political reality in America. Once ratified, the Constitution could obtain the willing compliance of most Americans because it set down formally and in practical fashion much of the "unwritten" constitution of American society.

Nor were the delegates who assembled at Philadelphia without recent precedents and experience in the framing of formal constitutions: for they profited from the several state constitutions that had been drawn up between 1776 and 1783, most notably the constitution of Virginia (1776) and that of

Massachusetts (not ratified until 1780.) Some of these constitutions were adopted by the Revolutionary assemblies, others by state constitutional conventions.

All these state constitutions were discussed at some length, and none was a radical departure from the colonial experience of politics—though a good deal of reference to eighteenth-century political theories took place during debate, particularly in the patiently-conceived Massachusetts constitution. Connecticut and Rhode Island found it possible simply to retain their colonial charters, with a few improvements. In his massive *Defense of the Constitutions of Government of the United States,* John Adams (a principal framer of the Massachusetts constitution) would point out that the United States Constitution was developed from these several state constitutions.

So the Federal Constitution, profiting from a decade's experience of constitution-drawing among the states, was realistic and closely related to the colonial and Revolutionary background of politics. Effective functioning was the primary concern of its framers.

It would go otherwise, during the nineteenth and twentieth centuries, with the formal written constitutions produced in other countries. France, Germany, Italy, the Latin-American republics, and nearly all other modern nation-states repeatedly have abrogated one formal constitution, adopted another, dropped that in favor of a third—and so on, without prospect of constitutional stability and permanence. (The constitutions of the several states within the American Republic, too, never have lasted long.) These other constitutions failed to endure for a number of reasons. Sometimes they did not genuinely reflect the underlying "unwritten constitution" of a people; sometimes they were too rigid and too detailed to survive when circumstances altered; sometimes they did not succeed in attracting the support and trust of the people whose fundamental instruments of government they were supposed to be.

The Constitution of the United States, on the contrary, steadily grew in authority, acquiring a symbolic value as well as a practical efficacy. For many Americans, with the passing of the years, their Constitution almost would acquire the divinity that "doth hedge a king": the Constitution became the monarch.

The new American nation's first attempt at a general government, the Articles of Confederation (drafted by Congress in 1777), had failed by 1787. This loose league of the new states could not have offered much defense against foreign enemies; did not satisfactorily settle disputes among the states; was unable to establish a sound currency; and had no means for protecting property, or other private rights, within states that might fall under the influence of demagogues and radical factions.

To improve the Articles of Confederation, the several states sent to Philadelphia a remarkably able body of delegates. Many of them were surprisingly young; and of the delegates who actually attended the Constitutional Convention, only eight had been signers of the Declaration of Independence. The trials of the Revolution and of the confused years that had followed, though they had injured the prosperity and sometimes the morals of Americans, had brought forth a courageous and intelligent generation of young leaders, some of them men of genius. If another constitutional convention had been held at any later period in American history, it may be doubted whether such a talented group of delegates could have been assembled. George Washington, strong, calm, and incorruptible, presided over the Convention.

What this Convention produced was not a revised version of the Articles of Confederation, but a new Constitution, in part on different principles. It was an impressive accomplishment; yet sometimes the Constitution is praised indiscriminately. Actually, the Constitution was not recorded by angels or prophets, but was put together by highly reasonable and prudent men who were willing to compromise with one another on many points, that they might agree on some strong instrument of government.

No matter how well conceived, the Constitution could not have functioned, once ratified, had not the statesmen of the early Republic been unusually able and vigorous. If someone less upright than George Washington had been the first President; if the Congresses of the Republic's first decade had been composed mostly of mediocrities; if, later, John Marshall had not dominated the Supreme Court—why, the Constitution might have fallen apart like that "rope of sand," the Articles, sharing the fate of other formal constitutions which have been badly implemented.

And if the Constitution, however ingenious in the abstract, had not been supported willingly in its early years by a majority of the citizens, then it would have gone the way of the several impractical republican constitutions of France. The American Constitution functioned not because it was a consistent, far-sighted contrivance (though it was that), but because, more important still, the Constitution accorded with social realities and necessities in the new Republic.

How might the infant American nation maintain a strong order, and yet guarantee personal liberties and a measure of democracy? The delegates found it necessary to deliberate on the most persistent and perplexing of all political problems: on the tension between the claims of order and the claims of freedom. National freedom they had obtained through the War of Independence; but private freedom still was insecure within the country, and even national independence was menaced by the great powers of Europe. Rash popular impulses, injudicious state legislatures, and the feebleness of the government of the Articles could not be endured. The men of the Convention were men both of freedom and of order; they found it well, at that moment in American affairs, to redress the American balance in favor of order.

As a sample of their concern for a more secure order, take the remarks of Elbridge Gerry, a delegate from Massachusetts, on May 31, 1787: "The evils we experience flow from the excess of democracy. The people do not want virtue, but are the dupes of pretended patriots. In Massachusetts it had been fully confirmed by experience that they are daily misled into the most baneful measures and opinions by the false reports circulated by designing men, and which no one on the spot can refute. . . . He had, he said, been too republican heretofore: he was still however republican, but had been taught by experience the danger of the levelling spirit."⁹

Among the delegates were men able to apprehend that healthful tension between order and freedom, so well as it ever has been obtained through a formal constitutional instrument. James Madison of Virginia did most of all, but there were others whose abilities ranked with his: Rufus King of Massachusetts, Alexander Hamilton of New York, James Wilson and Gouverneur Morris of Pennsylvania, John Dickinson of Delaware, Luther Martin of Maryland, George Mason and George Wythe of Virginia, John Rutledge and Charles Pinckney of South Carolina. (Thomas Jefferson and John Adams were not delegates; both were abroad as ministers, respectively, to Paris and London.)

The new general government which this Convention was to institute must possess adequate power; but it must not be so overwhelmingly powerful as to reduce the several states to mere provinces. (Most of the delegates did not desire such total eclipse of the states; even if they had, no such constitutional proposal would have obtained ratification by the states.) It must uphold order; but it must not reduce true liberty. It must work out some sound separation of powers, and provide checks upon power and balances in power, after the fashion commended by Montesquieu and suggested by the English constitution and certain other historical examples. It must arrange for an executive stronger than a mere presiding officer of Congress, but not so all-powerful as to become a king or a dictator. It must provide for a national legislature in which both the several states and the American people at large would obtain representation; and that legislature, like Parliament, should consist of two houses, chosen on different principles and balancing one the other. It must establish an independent national judiciary. It must be a government able to pursue sound fiscal policies and to promote the growth of commerce and industry. And it must be a government which foreign powers would respect, able to wage war and make peace.

All this the Constitutional Convention achieved. Some provisions of the Constitution never would function as they were meant to work—the Electoral College to choose

Presidents, for one—but in general the document was admirably practicable, and within a few years the functioning Constitution would command such respect that it would not be seriously challenged until the Civil War. Here we must concentrate upon two especially important aspects of the new Constitution: first, the "federal" concept and reality; second, the separation of powers within the general government.

The new political pattern of the United States must reconcile the claims of authority and the claims of freedom. In structure, it must provide a general government with sufficient power to ensure the common defense, conduct successful diplomacy, prevent struggles among the states or insurrection within the states, maintain a sound national currency and fiscal policy, and promote the general welfare. But also, in structure, it must provide for the survival and vigor of the several state governments, including the free and relatively democratic forms of local government which had developed first in the colonies and then in the states. In short, the national Constitution must so allocate powers that both national strength and state self-government in many matters would be maintained.

This dividing of powers between a general government (soon situated in the District of Columbia) and the governments of the several states (with their subordinate local governments) we now call the American federal system. Yet "federalism" is not altogether a satisfactory term for what was contrived by the Constitution of the United States.

In earlier times, the terms "federalism" and "federal government" implied "league," rather than union. Probably the majority of Americans who voted to ratify the Constitution thought that they were approving merely a more efficient form of the Articles of Confederation. It was sufficiently difficult, indeed, to persuade them to accept the new Constitution even upon such an understanding. Yet the structure created at Philadelphia amounted to a new pattern of government, not truly "federal" in the old sense. As Adams put it, in the concluding observations of his *Defence:*

"The former confederation of the United States was formed upon the model and example of all the confederacies, ancient and modern, in which the federal council was only a diplomatic body. . . . The magnitude of territory, the population, the wealth and commerce, and especially the rapid growth of the United States, have shown such a government to be inadequate to their wants; and the new system, which seems admirably calculated to unite their interests and affections, and bring them to an uniformity of principles and sentiments, is equally well combined to unite their wills and forces as a single nation.''[10]

The Constitution, then, abandoned the plan of a confederacy, and substituted that of a single nation. Thus the success of the American Republic has altered the very usage of the word "federalism," which no longer is generally taken to mean a simple league of sovereign states. Nowadays the meaning of this term is adequately expressed by the third definition in the most ample of American dictionaries, *The Century Dictionary* (edition of 1904): "Pertaining to a union of states in some essential degree constituted by and deriving its power from the people of all, considered as an entirety, and not solely by and from each of the states separately; as, a *federal* government, such as the governments of the United States, Switzerland, and some of the Spanish-American republics. A *federal* government is properly one in which the federal authority is independent of any of its component parts within the sphere of the federal action: distinguished from a *confederate* government, in which the states alone are sovereign, and which possesses no inherent power."

Many Americans during the last decade of the eighteenth century and the early decades of the nineteenth century would try to maintain that the Constitution had divided sovereignty, giving some sovereignty to the Washington government and the rest to the state governments. This interpretation would be opposed by the Federalists (most of the time) and later by the Whigs and the anti-slavery Republicans; also it would be opposed, for different reasons, by the more forceful advocates of "states' rights" (better called states' powers). This constitutional dispute would nearly provoke a call to arms during the Nullification controversy, in 1832; it would be a major cause of the Civil War. But actually, whether or not the people of America so intended it, sovereignty passed to the general government of the United States, not long after the Constitution was ratified. John Randolph, a mordant champion of state sovereignty, observed that a state can no more surrender *part* of its sovereignty than a woman can surrender *part* of her chastity. The "federal" system created by the Constitution established a true general government—which, nevertheless, was not a centralized, unitary, absolute government.

The word "federalism" today implies a voluntary and limited union for certain defined purposes, rather than a concentrated central system. A Zurich scholar of the twentieth century, Werner Kägi, makes this clear, distinguishing five characteristics of federalism: (1) federalism is an order of "multiplicity in unity"; (2) federalism is an order based upon the autonomy of the narrower communities; (3) federalism is an order in which the smaller circles and communities are granted the maximum possible power to direct their own affairs; (4) federalism is an order which makes it possible for minorities to live together in freedom; (5) federalism is an order built upwards from the smaller communities, in which the conditions can be seen at a glance, and in which relationships have remained, in some degree, on a personal footing.[11]

Also the spirit of federalism sometimes subsists in political systems that do not bear the formal label "federal"—as in Britain, even today as in the eighteenth century, where in practice county and town authorities retain large permanent powers, though in theory Parliament is supreme. And some orders that still are called "federal" have ceased, for the most part, to operate that way. In general, one may say that a modern federal order (on the model of the American Constitution) divides practical power between a general government and territorial governments, with the aim of safeguarding local liberties and choices while securing national interests.

The general government of the United States, established under the Constitution, was not democratic, but representative and republican. In James Madison's phrases, "A democracy . . . will be confined to a small spot. A republic may be extended over a large region." Jean Jacques Rousseau, the most enthusiastic of democrats, did not expect true democracy to be realized in a national government: "God alone can rule the *world*," he wrote, "and to govern great nations requires superhuman qualities." The American leaders of the Convention years knew perfectly well that a centralized "democracy" would be no better than a play upon words. The French reformer Turgot, who had been a high official in the Old Regime, was disappointed that the Americans had not established a centralized and unitary form of democratic government; he wrote to Dr. Richard Price, the London democrat, that in America the people should collect "all authority into one centre, the nation." To this, John Adams replied tartly:

"It is easily understood how all authority may be collected into 'one centre' in a despot or a monarch; but how it can be done when the centre is to be the nation, is much more difficult to comprehend. . . . If, after the pains of 'collecting all authority into one centre,' that centre is to be the nation, we shall remain exactly where we began, and no collection of authority at all will be made. The nation will be the authority, and the authority the nation. The centre will be the circle and the circle the centre. When a number of men, women, and children, are simply congregated together, there is no political authority among them; nor any natural authority but that of parents over their children."[12]

Centralization on Turgot's plan would have required worship of an abstract People—for whom some fallible human oracle must speak. Even though Alexander Hamilton would have liked a national government with greater powers than those the ratified Constitution would confer, nobody among the delegates at the Constitutional Convention desired such democratic centralization as Turgot advocated; indeed, such centralization would have been impossible to attain in America, even by force of arms. The "federalism" developed by the Convention of 1787 was a device to reconcile state governments with the exigencies of the American nation-state. Half a century later, Tocqueville would point out the ingenuity and real benefits of the American "federal" contrivance:

"The human understanding more easily invents new things than new words, and we are hence constrained to employ many improper and inadequate expressions. When several nations form a permanent league and establish a supreme authority, which, although it cannot act upon private individuals like a national government, still acts upon each of the confederate states in a body, this government, which is so essentially different from all others, is called Federal. Another form of society is afterwards discovered in which several states are fused into one with regard to certain common interests, although they remain distinct, or only confederate, with regard to all other concerns. In this case the central power acts directly upon the governed, whom it rules and judges in the same manner as a national government, but in a more limited circle. Evidently this is no longer a federal government, but an incomplete national government, which is neither exactly national nor exactly federal; but the new word which ought to express this novel idea does not yet exist.

"Ignorance of this new species of confederation has been the cause that has brought all unions to civil war, to servitude, or to inertness; and the states which formed these leagues have been either too dull to discern, or too pusillanimous to apply, this great remedy. The first American Confederation perished by the same defects."[13]

What Tocqueville described as an "incomplete national government," created by the Constitution of 1787, now is called the federal system of the United States. The Articles of Confederation had fallen because those who drew up the ephemeral Articles had not foreseen how feeble and incompetent that government would be. The general government made by the Constitutional Convention of 1787 was misunderstood by many, and so there came about the American Civil War. Aside from that prolonged struggle, the American federal system has worked well enough, from 1789 to the present, fulfilling the five characteristics of real federalism that Kägi distinguishes. It has worked better and endured longer, at any rate, than any other modern governmental pattern with the possible exception of Britain's. It would function adequately under a variety of presidents and parties. And although in the twentieth century the general government's powers have increased steadily at the expense of states' powers, and though there are Americans today who would like a still higher degree of political centralization, nevertheless the formal framework of 1787's "federalism" still stands. Tocqueville suggests that in modern times, centralization is the strong tendency everywhere, and local freedom is a garden plant, requiring much watering. Whether the "incomplete national government" called the American federal system indeed will be completed as a centralized and unitary structure remains to be seen; that question may be decided by developments in the closing quarter of the twentieth century.

Doubtless Montesquieu would have been delighted with America's federalism. (Centralization, which he detested, plagues France to this day.) Power to resist external enemies, to put down any serious domestic disorders, and to secure freedom of commerce within the Union, was conferred upon the general government; but control over the bulk of internal affairs was guaranteed to state governments and their subordinate units.

Montesquieu's chapters on centralization and political freedom were quoted at the Constitutional Convention, and his ideas reinforced Madison and other architects of the new federal structure; Montesquieu's sentences would dot the pages of *The Federalist,* those essays written by James Madison and Alexander Hamilton and John Jay to explain the proposed new Constitution to those who must ratify it. It would be putting the cart before the horse, for all that, to say that America's federal government was fathered by Montesquieu; for circumstances, not books, led to the federal plan for the new Republic. The several states, already existing, were jealous of their powers. How might those states be reconciled to the erection of a general government greater than any state government? Why, by conferring indispensable powers upon the general or national government, but reserving all other powers to the state governments, or to the people; and by the representation of all states, large or small, as peers in one house of the Congress. Federalism, then, was a happy practical compromise: Montesquieu's lucid arguments against centralization merely sanctioned that necessary reconciling of national security with the states' autonomy.

The other feature of America's Constitution which would have gratified Montesquieu is the careful separation of powers within the general government. A century later, Sir Henry Maine would write of the American Constitution, "It would seem that, by a wise Constitution, Democracy may be made nearly as calm as water in a great artificial reservoir; but if there is a weak point anywhere in the structure, the mighty force which it controls will burst through it and spread destruction far and near."[14] (Because the framers of the Constitution equivocated about slavery, Maine pointed out, the Civil War erupted seventy-four years after the Convention.) In the separation of powers made by the Constitution, there were virtually no weak points: that system continues to function today.

The executive branch of America's general government consists of the President, surrounded by his cabinet and an inner circle of White House advisors and assistants; and, of course, the mass of civil and military employees of the national government scattered throughout the country and abroad. (Nowadays the inner circle of the President's staff often is referred to as the Executive Force—a body of several hundred people today, but smaller than the comparable body of courtiers and functionaries who used to surround a king at the larger European courts of the eighteenth century.)

As Henry Maine notes, the office of the President really is the office of a king—the chief difference being that the American President is subject to election, at fixed terms, and that the office is not hereditary. Maine even suggests that the framers of the Constitution may have had in mind the powers of George III, when they established the powers of the

American presidency. In one way, the President today is more powerful than was that King: his cabinet is not responsible to any parliamentary body, but only to himself. (In 1787, England's present system of "cabinet" government had not developed fully.) The lack of a strong executive had been one of the conspicuous defects of the Articles of Confederation, and the framers of the Constitution deliberately gave the President greater authority than any mere prime minister could have possessed. Besides, without a titular king, whose minister could such a prime minister have been? Commander-in-chief of the armed forces and director of the national civil administration, the President would be comparable to the Roman emperor—except that he is given no judicial powers by the Constitution. The first six presidents, from Washington to John Quincy Adams, were men of good education and a high sense of duty who deliberately restrained themselves in the use of their powers; had they been autocrats or demagogues, the executive branch of the American government might have reduced the legislative and judicial branches to insignificance.

The Congress of the United States, the legislative branch, took Parliament for its model in most respects. Like Parliament, it consists of two houses; of those, the one more directly connected with popular opinion, the House of Representatives, is given the more direct control over taxation and appropriations, while the Senate is given primacy in foreign affairs and in the confirming of the President's major appointments to office.

Until passage of the Seventeenth Amendment to the Constitution, in 1913, United States senators were chosen by the legislatures of the several states; and those legislatures tended to select distinguished men. That, and the six-year senatorial term (by contrast with the two-year term of the House of Representatives) gave to the Senate more continuity and independence within its membership—which is just what the framers of the Constitution intended. To some degree, Senate and House would check and balance each other; it would be difficult to legislate rashly. Although less aristocratic than the English House of Lords (where every peer, in theory, represents no one but himself), the Senate was intended to curb democratic impulses of the hour. Also the allotment of two senatorial seats to every state, regardless of population or area, satisfied the smaller states' demand for equality of treatment.

Unlike the executive and legislative branches, the judicial branch under the new Constitution of the United States was virtually unprecedented. England, France, and some other states had made their judges more or less independent, with life tenure of office; but never before had an independent judiciary been permitted to decide fundamental constitutional questions for the whole country. "There is no liberty, if the Judicial power be not separated from the Legislative and the Executive," Montesquieu had written. The framers of the Constitution, clearly influenced by Montesquieu, made the Supreme Court a "depository of laws," removing questions of constitutional interpretation from the national and state legislative bodies—or, rather, much diminishing debate on such questions among legislators; also the powers of the new American national judiciary reduced the danger that disagreement over constitutional questions might lead to armed conflict, as had occurred often in history, especially in classical times.

Upon the Supreme Court of the United States, the Constitution conferred original jurisdiction over cases affecting ambassadors and other representatives of foreign powers, and cases to which a state might be a party. That Court was given appellate jurisdiction over a considerable range of other cases, in effect those cases involving international disputes, litigation between states, controversies to which the general government might be a party, interpretation of the Constitution and of the laws of the United States, and other cases for which the jurisdiction of state courts seemed insufficient; this appellate jurisdiction was narrowed somewhat by the Eleventh Amendment, ratified in 1798. The great bulk of jurisdiction in civil and criminal cases was left to the state courts, or was dealt with by the inferior federal courts. Some check was retained upon the federal judiciary's power by the constitutional provision that Congress might regulate the appellate jurisdiction; this restraint has been applied several times in the history of the federal courts.

Also it was left possible for Congress to authorize, and the President to appoint, additional justices to the Supreme Court; and impeachment of federal judges was authorized by the Constitution—although this latter action never has been employed successfully for partisan motives. Despite these checks upon possible encroachment of the judicial branch on the executive and legislative powers, the federal courts were given by the Constitution a degree of autonomy previously unknown. Federal judges were guaranteed office "during good Behaviour," and that their salaries should not be diminished while in office.

The federal courts would come to exercise the real power to declare unconstitutional acts of Congress, acts of state legislatures, and executive measures: something no judiciary in any realm ever had possessed before. This power, though latent in the Constitution, might not have been employed to its full extent, had not the strong-willed Chief Justice John Marshall exercised it repeatedly—sometimes to the wrath of President and Congress—during his thirty-four years in office.

It was not merely by the system of formal separation of powers that Montesquieu's ideas of ordered liberty were given reality: a variety of checks and balances entered into the Constitution. Some were checks upon the legislative branch—notably the President's veto-power and the Supreme Court's power to declare legislation unconstitutional. The executive branch, too, was checked potentially in a number of ways, among them the power of Congress to override a veto, the reserving to Congress of the power to declare war, and the Senate's power of accepting or rejecting treaties and major appointments. In addition to checks upon the judicial branch suggested above, Congress or the several states could introduce constitutional amendments.

The men who drew up this Constitution declared that

they had framed a government of laws, not of men; and of laws which must be applied by a regular and impartial process. Stability and security in the Republic, and protection of the citizens against arbitrary power, received equal attention in the Constitution.

In a few respects, the Constitution does not function today as its authors had expected it to. The Electoral College failed to operate successfully, because the framers had not anticipated the rise of strong political parties to whose choice of presidential candidates, in effect, prospective Electors would bind themselves. (In 1787, coherent political parties with recognizable principles were only beginning to arise in England; President Washington vainly hoped that "faction," or party, would not appear in America.) In the long run, because of the Seventeenth Amendment, the United States Senate became a more directly popular body than had been intended. The President's effective powers have been enlarged gradually—especially in the twentieth century—by the necessities of a great nation, especially in time of war or economic crisis. The Supreme Court has become more active than most Americans (especially the Jeffersonians) of 1787 intended it to be. The powers of state governments have diminished somewhat before the advance of the government in Washington.

And yet the main features of the original Constitution have endured, despite the adoption of more than a score of amendments from that time to this. The federal design, the separation of powers, the reign of law, and the requirement of "due process" still function vigorously enough. Only once, with the coming of the Civil War, has the Constitution's supremacy been seriously challenged by an appeal to arms.

As an instrument of order, the Constitution of the United States would be more successful than any other formal written device in the history of mankind; in the nineteenth and twentieth centuries, some British juridical writers would perceive virtues in the American Constitution which the British Constitution does not possess—most notably, restraints upon the power of a temporary majority in the legislative branch. Strong in its general principles, yet adaptable to changed circumstances through judicial interpretation and subject to formal amendments, the Constitution has preserved continuity of political order through nearly two centuries of tremendous social and economic change. The Constitution arose out of America's experience of order, and out of Americans' knowledge of earlier principles of order; the Constitution would become itself a living source of order, as the successful instrument of liberty under law.

The Federal Constitution and Religious Belief

In 1791, ten amendments to the Constitution, the American "Bill of Rights," were ratified. In several particulars, these resembled the English Bill of Rights, and were adopted to afford specific protections under the Constitution, or prohibitions against invasions of private rights by government. At first, the Bill of Rights operated only upon Congress; in the twentieth century, its effect would be extended to state legislatures and state courts. Most of these rights were familiar liberties to anyone acquainted with the English constitution: freedom of religion, speech, the press, and assembly; the right to bear arms; a prohibition against quartering troops; security against search and seizure; due process of law in a variety of circumstances; trial by jury; a forbidding of excessive bail, excessive fines, and cruel or unusual punishments. It is unnecessary to examine in detail here liberties that are part of America's inheritance from English law.

The first clause of the first of these amendments, however, deserves some close attention. It is concerned with freedom of religion, and an examination of that clause will suggest the relationships between church and state—between the moral order and the political order—in America's society of "religious pluralism." Also such an examination will illustrate how a constitutional provision may be variously interpreted as the years pass.

The first clause of the First Amendment is brief and

432

simple: "Congress shall make no law respecting an establish-ment of religion, or prohibiting the free exercise thereof." Nothing, at first glance, could seem more lucid. Yet the significance of this provision is still being debated today.

That the founders of the American Republic believed in a religious basis for society can be illustrated abundantly from their speeches and writings. The wise politician, according to Alexander Hamilton, "knows that morality overthrown (and morality *must* fall with religion), the terrors of despotism can alone curb the impetuous passions of man, and confine him within the bounds of social duty."[15] It would be better far to turn back to the gods of the Greeks, said John Adams, than to endure a government of atheists.

What the statesmen of the young Republic professed, the American people at large professed quite as earnestly. James Madison feared that the zeal of the people for Christianity might lead to intolerance. Tocqueville, writing in the 1830's, recognized the primacy of religious principles in American politics: "I do not know whether all Americans have a sincere faith in their religion—for who can search the human heart?—but I am certain that they hold it to be indispensable to the maintenance of republican institutions. This opinion is not peculiar to a class of citizens or to a party, but it belongs to the whole nation and to every rank of society."[16]

That had been as true when the First Amendment had been ratified, four decades earlier. Not only was there no pop-ular hostility toward Christianity in late colonial times and in the early Republic, but there was little opposition to church establishments. In nine of the Thirteen Colonies, on the eve of the Revolution, some church was established by law: the Anglican in Virginia, Maryland, the Carolinas, Georgia, and the southern counties of New York; the Congregational in Massachusetts and its dependencies, Connecticut, and New Hampshire.

Because of the links between the Church of England and the British Crown, the Anglican Church was disestablished in all colonies by the end of the Revolution—although the Revolutionary leaders acted so only with reluctance. (At the Virginia Convention of 1776, James Madison had been unable to obtain any support for his proposal to disestablish the Church of England in Virginia.) John Randolph of Roanoke, that passionate Old Republican, could say as late as the 1830's, "I am not a member of your American Episcopal Church, sir. I am a member of the Church of England, sir—the good old Church of England."

Congregationalism, however, remained established in Massachusetts, Connecticut, and New Hampshire, for more than half a century after the Revolution—although this was a tolerant establishment in its later days, allowing Episcopalians to pay their rates to their own church, and exempting from church-rates altogether the Quakers and the Baptists. These established churches were hard upon only one minority: the Catholics. Colonial governors had been instructed to indulge liberty of conscience "to all persons except Papists"; and at the time the Revolution commenced, only in Pennsylvania could Catholic masses be celebrated publicly.

Such was the climate of religious opinion in America when the Jeffersonian faction, in 1788 and 1789, demanded a Bill of Rights to supplement the Constitution that the Convention delegates had signed on September 17, 1787. To insure the states' ratification of this Constitution, James Madison and other moderate Federalists found it expedient to give way to this demand, and so to prepare a series of constitutional amendments, incorporating the principal rights listed by Jefferson's supporters (soon to take the name of Republicans). Several states drew up declarations of rights to be attached to the Constitution; and the declarations of Virginia, North Carolina, and Rhode Island contained identical passages which are the sources of the first clause of the First Amendment. They ran thus:

"That religion or the duty which we owe to our Creator, and the manner of discharging it, can be directed only by reason and conviction, not by force or violence, and therefore all men have an equal, natural and unalienable right to the free exercise of religion according to the dictates of conscience, and that no particular religious sect or society ought to be favored or established by Law in preference to others."

For the most part, these resolutions were copies of the article on religion (written by James Madison) in the Virginia

Declaration of Rights (1776). Madison, indeed, was both indirectly and directly the principal author of the first clause of the First Amendment. He was second only to Jefferson in opposition to established churches—that is, to special recognition of one particular church by the state, with state enforcement of that church's claim to the right of collecting tithes or rates from the citizens. Baptized in the Church of England, Madison had been educated in the Presbyterian college of Princeton; he was much read in theology, but gradually drifted in the direction of Deism, though never going so far that way as did Jefferson and Franklin. Religious toleration was among his principal interests, and he was opposed not merely to any national establishment of religion, but to the separate state establishments.

Although the established churches of the states had many adherents, particularly in New England, no one of importance in America desired to establish a *national* church. Thus Madison was able to incorporate into the First Amendment the general principles of toleration and impartiality that he had advocated for fifteen years previously.

At first, Madison proposed to Congress this draft of a religious-freedom amendment: "The civil rights of none shall be abridged on account of religious belief or worship, nor shall any national religion be established, nor shall the full and equal rights of conscience be in any manner, or on any pretext, abridged." It was feared by some that this clause might provide an excuse for national interference with the separate established churches of the states; and so, at length, the House adopted a substitute proposed by Fisher Ames, of Massachusetts. The Ames draft more nearly resembled the present first clause of the First Amendment, running thus: "Congress shall make no law establishing religion, or to prevent the free exercise thereof, or to infringe the rights of conscience." The Senate adopted a version more friendly toward church establishments. From the conference committee of Senate and House there emerged, finally, the present first clause of the First Amendment: "Congress shall make no law respecting an establishment of religion or prohibiting the free exercise thereof." Again, Madison appears to have been the author of this accepted version.

And so this clause became part of the Constitution, and was ratified by the states with no serious difficulty. It satisfied two bodies of opinion: first, the defenders of the established state churches in New England, and the friends of establishment elsewhere, because it prohibited Congress from disestablishing or otherwise interfering with these state establishments; second, the friends of complete toleration and the foes of any national religious establishment, because it prohibited Congress from entering upon this field at all. By both factions, this clause of the First Amendment was looked upon as a safeguard of religious convictions, not as an act of disavowing religious principles.

Madison had long maintained that the union of State and Church could only harm the Church. This was no new doctrine: the separation of Church and State was an ancient Christian teaching, enunciated by Pope Gelasius at the end of the fifth century, in his exposition of the "two swords": "Two there are by whom this world is ruled." The insertion of this clause in the First Amendment was particularly satisfying to the forlorn minority of American Catholics, for it insured that never would they suffer under a national Protestant establishment.

Here in the religious-freedom clause of the First Amendment, then, was no philosophe's Deistical declaration, and no Encyclopedist's rationalistic denunciation of Christianity. What the few words of the clause intended to convey was the essence of the article on religion drafted by George Mason for the Virginia Declaration of Rights in 1776, as modified then by Madison: "That Religion or the duty we owe to our Creator, and the manner of discharging it, being under the direction of reason and conviction only, not of violence or compulsion, all men are equally entitled to the free exercise of religion, according to the dictates of conscience, unpunished, and unrestrained by the magistrate, unless the preservation of equal liberty and the existence of the State are manifestly endangered. And that it is the mutual duty of all, to practice Christian forbearance, love and charity toward each other."

Such, indeed, had been the attitude of the tolerant Anglican establishment in Virginia before the Revolution. In 1789, incidentally, it still seemed possible that some of the southern states might re-establish the Episcopal church; this was seriously considered by the legislature of Virginia. There was no necessary opposition between established churches in the several states and the kind of religious freedom protected by the English Toleration Act of 1689.

This American doctrine of toleration had the sanction of experience in the New World; it embodied what already, with a few exceptions, had become practice in the several states of the new Republic. This principle owed almost nothing to the theories of the Enlightenment, then popular in France. So far as this doctrine was derived from any modern philosopher, it came from Locke—not from Voltaire or Diderot.

Now the First Amendment, and the other nine amendments ratified in 1791, were binding only upon the national government, not upon the states—until 1925, when, in the case of Gitlow v. New York, the United States Supreme Court ruled that the Fourteenth Amendment had made the free-speech and free-press guarantees of the First Amendment operative within the several states. In 1940, in the case of Cantwell v. Connecticut, this doctrine was specifically extended to the religious-freedom clause of the First Amendment. Until a few decades ago, then, the several states could have established state churches and in other ways have regulated religious observance, had they desired to do so.

The First Amendment established no "wall of separation" between State and Church; that phrase and that concept appear nowhere in the Constitution, or in any other official national document. Thomas Jefferson, in 1802, wrote a letter to an assembly of Baptists in which he argued that the First Amendment was intended to construct "a wall of separation between Church and State." But though doubtless that is what Jefferson desired from the First Amendment, it is by no means what Congress—and particularly the Senate—had in mind when it passed the Amendment in 1789; nor was the phrase "wall of separation" employed by Madison or any other notable advocate of the Amendment.

Justice Joseph Story, in his *Commentaries on the Constitution* (1833), offered a fuller and more adequate explanation of the purpose of this religious-freedom clause. It was adopted, Story wrote, because different sects predominated in different states; and "it was impossible that there should not arise perpetual strife and perpetual jealousy on the subject of ecclesiastical ascendency, if the national government were left free to create a religious establishment. The only security was in extirpating the power. . . . Probably at the time of the adoption of the Constitution, and of the amendment to it now under consideration, the general if not the universal sentiment in America was, that Christianity ought to receive encouragement from the state so far as was not incompatible with the private rights of conscience and the freedom of religious worship. An attempt to level all religions, and to make it a matter of state policy to hold all in utter indifference, would have created universal disapprobation, if not universal indignation."[17]

Careful examination of the opinions of members of the Congress in 1789, and of the public press of that time, confirms Story's opinion: the Americans approved religious toleration, and left the field of religious establishments solely to the separate states; but Americans generally endorsed the idea of a religious foundation for their political order. This stand was reaffirmed by Justice William O Douglas, distinctly liberal in his principles, in the Zorach case (1952), when he wrote the Supreme Court's majority opinion:

"We are a religious people whose institutions presuppose a Supreme Being. We guarantee the freedom to worship as one chooses. We make room for as wide a variety of beliefs and creeds as the spiritual needs of man deem necessary. We sponsor an attitude on the part of government that shows no partiality to any one group and that lets each flourish according to the zeal of its adherents and the appeal of its dogma. . . . To hold that government may not encourage religious instruction would be to find in the Constitution a requirement that the government show a callous indifference to religious groups. That would be preferring those who believe in no religion over those who do believe. . . . We find no constitutional requirement which makes it necessary for government to be hostile to religion and to throw its weight against efforts to widen the effective scope of religious influence."[18]

So the first clause of the First Amendment, like much of

the Constitution, may have been a bundle of compromises; but it did succeed in expressing the general sense of the American people on the relationship between State and Church. And that sense was not an arid secularism, hostile toward the religious consecration of the civil social order. "While the law permits the Americans to do what they please," Tocqueville would write, "religion prevents them from conceiving, and forbids them to commit, what is rash or unjust." The religious freedom of the First Amendment reaffirms Gelasius' principle that "two there are." But it does not set up those two, State and Church, in fortified camps, at feud.

Unlike the Declaration of Independence, the Constitution contains no reference whatever to the Creator, or even to "Nature's God." Indeed, except for the First Amendment, the Constitution's only mention of religion occurs in Article VI, where it is declared that "no religious Test shall ever be required as a Qualification to any Office or public Trust under the United States." This neutrality notwithstanding, the framers of the Constitution took it for granted that a moral order, founded upon religious beliefs, supports and parallels the political order. The Constitution was and is purely an instrument for practical government—not a philosophical disquisition. Yet practical government in the United States, and in every other nation, is possible only because most people in that nation accept the existence of some moral order, by which they govern their conduct—the order of the soul.

Notes

[1] John Quincy Adams to Friedrich Gentz, June 16, 1800, and his "Letters of Publicola", June-July, 1791, in *Writings of John Quincy Adams* (edited by Worthington Chauncy Ford; New York: Macmillan, 1913), Vol. II, p. 463, and Vol. I, p. 98.

[2] Clinton Rossiter, *Seedtime of the Republic: the Origin of the American Tradition of Political Liberty* (New York: Harcourt, Brace 1953), p. 448.

[3] Hippolyte Taine, *The French Revolution* (translated by John Durand; New York: Henry Holt, 1897), Vol. I, pp. 355-56.

[4] Friedrich Gentz, *The French and American Revolutions Compared* (edited by Russell Kirk; Chicago: Henry Regnery, 1955), pp. 44, 60, 81.

[5] Daniel Boorstin, *The Genius of American Politics* (Chicago: University of Chicago Press, 1953), pp. 94-5.

[6] John Randolph, speech on Negro slavery in South America, *Register of Debates* (Nineteenth Congress, second session), II, 125-26.

[7] Carl L. Becker, *The Declaration of Independence: a Study in the History of Ideas* (revised edition, New York: Peter Smith, 1942), p. 135.

[8] John C. Calhoun, *A Discourse on the Constitution and Government of the United States*, in Richard K. Crallé (ed.), *The Works of John C. Calhoun* (Columbia: A. S. Johnston, 1851), Vol. I, p. 185.

[9] Elbridge Gerry, recorded in "Debates in the Federal Convention of 1787 as Reported by James Madison", in *Documents Illustrative of the Formation of the Union of the American States*, selected by Charles C. Tansill (Washington: Government Printing Office, 1927), p. 125.

[10] John Adams, *A Defence of the Constitutions of Government of the United States of America*, in Charles Francis Adams (ed.), *The Life and Works of John Adams* (Boston: Little, Brown, 1851), Vol. VI, p. 219.

[11] Werner Kägi, "Federalism and Freedom", in Albert Hunold (ed.), *Freedom and Serfdom, an Anthology of Western Thought* (Dordrecht: D. Reidel, 1961), pp. 220-25.

[12] John Adams, *Defence of the Constitutions, op. cit.*, Vol. VI, p. 301.

[13] Alexis de Tocqueville, *Democracy in America* (edited by Phillips Bradley; New York: Knopf, 1945), Vol. I, pp. 158-59.

[14] Sir Henry Maine, *Popular Government* (London: John Murray, 1886), p. 111.

[15] Alexander Hamilton, "The Stand", in Henry Cabot Lodge (ed.), *The Works of Alexander Hamilton* (New York: Macmillan, 1904), Vol. V, p. 410.

[16] Alexis de Tocqueville, *Democracy in America*, Bradley edition, *op. cit.*, Vol. I, pp. 305-6.

[17] Joseph Story, *Commentaries on the Constitution*, as quoted in *The Constitution of the United States of America: Analysis and Interpretation* (edited by Edward S. Corwin; Washington: Government Printing Office, 1952), pp. 758-59.

[18] *Zorach v. Clauson*, 343 U. S. 313-314 (1952), as quoted in Corwin (ed.), *The Constitution of the United States, op. cit.*, pp. 762-63.

CHAPTER XII
CONTENDING AGAINST
AMERICAN DISORDER

The Power of Laws and Mores

This being a book about the *roots* of American order, we had best not slide into a survey of the struggle between order and disorder in the history of the United States. Yet it is necessary in this chapter to say something about the troubled reality of order, and the idea of order, in nineteenth-century America. In every age, among every people, disorder rises up in one shape or another; and so it happened in swelling democratic America after the generation of men who made the Constitution passed away. Jefferson said that liberty can be maintained only by ceaseless vigilance; it is as true that order can be sustained only by endless patience.

At the beginning of the nineteenth century, there were well rooted in the United States the institutions and the beliefs which still underlie this country's order today. During the first century and a half of civilization along North America's Atlantic seaboard, a moral order was introduced from the Old World that took root in the New World. During that century and a half, a European social order, expressed in class, family, church, and community, underwent in America something of a sea-change—and yet did not lose continuity with three thousand years of social experience in Europe and Asia. Both moral and social order would encounter rough challenges, once the American people had separated themselves politically from the Old World. It is no wonder that much disorder occurred in American life after 1800 (the year of the "Jeffersonian revolution," bringing to power the more democratic leaders); it is no wonder that disorder grew more ominous after 1825 (the year when the "Jacksonian revolution" commenced, though Jackson did not enter the White House until four years later). It is more remarkable that despite stern trials, the moral order and the social order described in earlier chapters of this book have endured in considerable part down to our day.

"The history of American society strongly suggests that if men subvert or abandon the values embodied in a well-ordained institutional structure, and so dismantle the social foundations for cultural achievement and spiritual serenity, they proceed at their own grave peril," writes Rowland Berthoff, in his recent ground-breaking study of order and disorder in American social history. Just such subverting or abandoning occurred in nineteenth-century America, Berthoff continues. One may add that nevertheless the essence of America's early order survived through the most materialistic and violent times of that century; and (as Berthoff suggests) a renewed strength of the basic American moral and social order may be discerned in the closing decades of the twentieth century. Although Berthoff is concerned immediately with the American social framework, he points out that social stability is far from being the whole of order:

"At the base of the hierarchy lie the economic values, necessary but subservient, of adequate production and equitable distribution of material goods. Upon that system rest the specifically social values of satisfactory relationships among men in a reasonably stable, secure institutional structure, the system with which social history is primarily concerned. But a stable social structure is less important in itself than as the foundation, in turn, for other, loftier values of mind and spirit—esthetic and intellectual achievement of some excellence and perhaps even what is variously called self-fulfillment, redemption from sin, and salvation of the soul."[1]

Nineteenth-century America, eager for material gain, often neglected the roots of order in class, family, church, and community; and despite the zeal of evangelical preachers, the common man of nineteenth-century America sought less earnestly after salvation of his soul than had Bunyan's Christian. Here we can merely suggest the difficulties which the "permanent things," the ideas and institutions of an abiding order, encountered in the United States during the era when the American people swept on to the Pacific, and grew more prosperous and powerful than any other great people ever had been.

The growing danger to American order during that era was not political, primarily: rather, practical political measures were the mirror of an increasing confusion in the moral and the social order. Beginning about 1800, America entered upon that progressive triumph of democratic impulses in which the Jeffersonian and Jacksonian campaigns were stages. Nationally, power escaped from the hands of the Federalists who had brought into being the Constitution; in every state, the "gentlemen freeholders" were compelled to admit to the franchise all free white males, property qualifications for voting going by the board. This political struggle—between East and West in every state, between the propertied and the unpropertied, often between the older generation and the younger—ended with the total triumph of the democrats.

When Jefferson defeated John Adams in their contest for the presidency of the country, and when Jackson defeated John Quincy Adams twenty-eight years later, there occurred a partial collapse of the leadership of the "American gentleman" who had guided America for more than a century and a half. (Both Henry Adams and T.S. Eliot, in the twentieth century, would write that the America which their families had represented had ended with the election of Andrew Jackson.) Until the Civil War loomed, less able men would be elected to the presidency; public policies would be less enlightened; sectionalism would divide the nation, self-interest would swell; it would seem as if, in Emerson's later line, "Things are in the saddle, and ride mankind."

Yet probably some historians have exaggerated the effect of the democratic triumph upon America's moral and social order. American politics would survive the "spoils system" of the Jackson administration, and even the fierce animosities of the controversy over slavery. Democratic elections would not result in economic levelling—quite the contrary. American literary culture, far from being undone by these political changes, would burst into vigor shortly after this alleged "social revolution." And the American gentleman would not be extirpated, even if less conspicuous in public office. In Europe and Britain, the aspirations of democratic forces during these same years resulted in more marked changes.

So it was not America's outward political order, really, that sustained serious damage during the nineteenth century. The true social revolution of that time resulted from America's swift enormous increase in wealth and territory. Industrial production, stimulated initially by America's isolation during the Napoleonic wars and by the War of 1812, rapidly came to dwarf the old agricultural and commercial economy of the Atlantic seaboard; cities (so dreaded by Jefferson) grew in formless fashion, and Irish immigrants rushed into them. First over the Alleghenies, then across the Mississippi, poured the frontiersmen, sweeping the Indian tribes and all other opposition before them; by 1846, they would reach the Pacific, accomplishing what a New York editor called America's "Manifest Destiny." In the raw new states and territories, class, family, church, and community seemed to count for little; even the authority of the general government was difficult enough to maintain. Could much order prevail there but the principle "That they shall take who have the power, and they shall keep who can"?

Material success often seemed directly proportionate to lack of moral worth. "Put money in thy purse, and yet again, put money in thy purse": no social and moral order can preserve harmony if dominated by that maxim. An individualism ruthless as that of Hobbes asserted itself on the frontier and sometimes in the new industry, with no restraining Leviathan. "A people who made economic progress their pre-eminent value," as Berthoff puts it, "could discern only dimly the fundamental but far less salutary upheaval that was undermining the primary institutions of their social order. . . . It was one thing . . . to free the individual enterpriser for the material development of the country. It proved quite another for the individual to get along without the non-economic values of life that had been embedded in the old social order."[2]

From about 1825 onward, Berthoff argues, American society fell into disorder, with the decay of moral imagination and the neglect of true community. Commercial acuteness often was confounded with wisdom and integrity; community became "real estate," for sale at a profit; the jerry-built new cities and towns commonly were dismal enough; even the sacrament of marriage was corrupted into "copartnership." As climax of a half-century of confusion, there would come the grand disaster of the Civil War, brought on by the inflexible dogmas of Abolitionist and Fire-eater. What remained of the old order?

In the early years of this era of appetite and passion, there travelled in America Alexis de Tocqueville, who would become for the United States such a commentator upon order as Montesquieu had been for England—who, indeed, would surpass Montesquieu's insights. To understand the threats to genuine order in nineteenth-century America, and the means by which the "permanent things" survived nevertheless, one turns to Tocqueville's *Democracy in America*.

In 1831 and 1832, two young French men of law, Tocqueville and Charles de Beaumont, saw a great deal of America and the Americans while studying penal systems. From a single year's tour, the genius of Tocqueville obtained the materials for his penetrating book. After the publication of *Democracy in America,* Tocqueville rose to some eminence in French politics. It was his hope that democracy, the wave of the future, might follow in Europe the course of American democracy, despite the failings he found in the United States; for whatever American democratic society might lack, it had not lost an understanding of order; and in that society was high promise, as well as present difficulty.

Tocqueville describes candidly the Americans' indiffer-

445

ence to polite learning and pure science, their avarice and materialism, the rawness and isolation· of backwoods life, their suspicion of unusual talents and their tendency toward mediocrity. He touches upon the decay of class, of family, of religious imagination, of community. He finds modern democracies, even the American, in danger of succumbing to a new servitude: their materialism and their desire for equality may entice them into a "democratic despotism," a boring society under an omnicompetent state:

"Equality has prepared men for all this, predisposing them to endure it and often regard it as beneficial.

"Having thus taken each citizen in turn in its powerful grasp and shaped him to its will, government then extends its embrace to include the whole of society. It covers the whole of social life with a network of petty, complicated rules that are both minute and uniform, through which even men of the greatest originality and the most vigorous temperament cannot force their heads above the crowd. It does not break men's will, but softens, bends, and guides it; it seldom enjoins, but often inhibits, action; it does not destroy anything, but prevents much being born; it is not at all tyrannical, but it hinders, restrains, enervates, stifles, and stultifies so much that in the end each nation is no more than a flock of timid and hardworking animals with the government as its shepherd."[3]

That was not the condition of America when Tocqueville made his way through New York to the Great Lakes, explored New England, visited Philadelphia and Baltimore, made his way down the Ohio and the Mississippi to New Orleans, and then voyaged from Mobile to Washington. What he and Beaumont encountered then, often, was an extreme individualism and isolation, sufficiently typified on the frontier by the Michigan wilderness homestead where a bear was chained in the yard to keep watch. But it was to the possible future order that Tocqueville had an eye: an order, all too conceivable, of the dull mass-man.

Yet the common man of America whom Tocqueville encountered—eagerly acquisitive, emancipated from many of the old bonds of community, apparently free to act as his appetities and impulses might suggest—nevertheless had not fallen into personal and public anarchy. America was reasonably orderly and prosperous. Though there were few soldiers and police, in strong contrast with Europe, life and property were safe enough: more secure, indeed, than in many lands long civilized. How might one explain this relative orderliness of democratic America? "The American has always seen order and public prosperity linked together and marching in step; it never strikes him that they could be separate; consequently he has nothing to forget and has no need to unlearn, as Europeans must, the lessons of his early education." Could it be the circumstances (as Montesquieu had described national "circumstances") of the Americans that maintained their order? Could it be America's laws? Or could it be their mores—that is, their customs and deep-rooted ways of conduct, their moral habits of thought and action?

This American order did not arise out of favorable circumstances to any marked extent, Tocqueville reflected. As for Americans' laws, indeed those were of assistance. The federal form of government gave America "the power of a great republic and the security of a small one"; the communal or local institutions (what Brownson would call "territorial democracy") operated to "moderate the despotism of the majority and give the people both a taste for freedom and the skill to be free"; the judicial power, checking and directing the movements of the majority, helped to correct "the aberrations of democracy."

But the strongest prop of American order, Tocqueville found, was their body of moral habits. "I here mean the term 'mores' (*moeurs*) to have its original Latin meaning; I mean it to apply not only to '*moeurs*' in the strict sense, which might be called the habits of the heart, but also to the different notions possessed by men, the various opinions current among them, and the sum of ideas that shape mental habits."[4] Their religious beliefs in particular, and also their general literacy and their education through practical experience, gave to the Americans a set of moral convictions—one almost might say moral prejudices, as Edmund Burke would have put it—that compensated for the lack of imaginative leadership and institutional controls.

"It is their mores, then, that make the Americans of the United States, alone among Americans, capable of maintaining the rule of democracy; and it is mores again that make the various Anglo-American democracies more or less orderly and prosperous," Tocqueville concluded.

"Europeans exaggerate the influence of geography on the lasting powers of democratic institutions. Too much importance is attached to laws and too little to mores. Unquestionably those are the three great influences which regulate and direct American democracy, but if they are to be classed in order, I should say that the contribution of physical causes is less than that of the laws, and that of laws less than mores. . . . The importance of mores is a universal truth to which study and experience continually bring us back. I find it occupies the central position in my thoughts; all my ideas come back to it in the end."[5]

It was America's moral order, then, that sustained America's social order. Even though class, family, and community were enfeebled west of the Alleghenies; even though the institutional Church might be reduced to circuit-riding preachers there; even though the common man of the West seemed interested chiefly in his own material aggrandizement—still he read his Bible, accepted as good the political framework which he inherited from the Atlantic seaboard and from Britain, and took for granted a moral order that was his custom and his habit. That is why the American frontiersmen and backwoodsmen and entrepreneurs of the vast newly-opened country were not men "in a state of nature." And that is why the American democracy was not a democracy of degradation. "For the Americans," Tocqueville found, "the ideas of Christianity and liberty are so completely mingled that it is almost impossible to get them to conceive of one without the other; it is not a question with them of sterile beliefs bequeathed by the past and vegetating rather than living in the depths of the soul." In the middle of the nineteenth century, American society might have sunk into an irresponsible disintegrating individualism, had it not still been held together by the cement of Christian teaching.

Resting upon its laws and its mores, American society was sound enough, Tocqueville found. But where might this society find leaders qualified to uphold the mores and the laws? No great man would risk his life and his honor to become President, Tocqueville said: the rewards of that chief magistracy were not enticing enough. The invisible power of public opinion, enforcing conformity to the convictions or interests of the common man, deterred politicans from taking strong stands. There were many ambitions in America, but few of those ambitions were lofty.

In the American Republic, nevertheless, there would occur times when hard irrevocable decisions must be made upon grand questions. One of these questions—the most pressing of them, Tocqueville perceived—was the problem of Negro slavery. "Whatever efforts the Americans of the South make to maintain slavery," he foresaw, "they will not forever succeed. Slavery is limited to one point on the globe and attacked by Christianity as unjust and by political economy as fatal: slavery, amid the democratic liberty and enlightenment of our age, is not an institution that can last. Either the slave or the master will put an end to it. In either case great misfortunes are to be anticipated."[6]

Thirty years after Tocqueville landed in America, that dilemma would have to be confronted. And in that hour, a man of the old mores would be brought forward to maintain the laws. He would be a man of modest ambition, slowly risen from the humblest origins. In Abraham Lincoln, the American democracy would find, at its sternest crisis of disorder, its most capable and self-sacrificing man of order.

Lincoln and the Defense of the American Order

The Roman Republic had been at the back of the minds of the men who made the Constitution: they had hoped that the President of the United States would be like the model of a

Roman consul, governed by the high old Roman virtue. George Washington, endowed with what Burke had called "the unbought grace of life," set the presidential standard high. Some seventy years later there was elected a President of very different origins, who nevertheless has come to stand as Washington's equal in republican virtue.

Abraham Lincoln had only one thing in common with a Roman barracks-emperor: that he had risen, as did Diocletian and others, from a poverty-stricken rural background. As he said, quoting Thomas Gray's "Elegy in a Country Churchyard," his family's story was only "the short and simple annals of the poor." He was born in a primitive log cabin in Kentucky; when he was seven years old, and the family had shifted to Indiana, their shelter was a "half-faced camp," open on one side to the winter wind. The boy knew nothing of the unbought grace of life. Only toward the end of his life would he attain a certain sombre dignity, after greatness had been thrust upon him.

One of the saddest aspects of the War Between the States was that it pitted against each other those men who best understood both the claims of order and the claims of freedom. Were there space here, a section could be included about General Robert E. Lee as representing the best in the order of the South: the opponent of slavery, disliking secession, who found that his loyalty lay with the commonwealth of Virginia, and not with the government in Washington that he had served so well. But planter-gentlemen of Lee's background have been discussed earlier. With Lincoln, for the first time we see a man from the common clay as defender of order.

James Russell Lowell, from the Brahmin urbanity of Tory Row, in Cambridge, would write the most moving tribute to the rough-hewn politician who was President when the questions of slavery and sectionalism burst into flame. In truth, as Lowell says, Abraham Lincoln's election to the presidency is the great line of demarcation in the history of America: "We should be irrevocably cut off from our past, and be forced to splice the ragged ends of our lives upon whatever new conditions chance might leave dangling for us." And yet Lincoln prevented the victory of disorder.

From youth, Lincoln was a man of few books. But he did read those books which imparted the mores that Tocqueville had described: the Bible, *The Pilgrim's Progress*, Aesop's *Fables, Robinson Crusoe*, Weems' *Life of Washington*, a popular history of the United States. Most of what he learned beyond those, Lincoln learned from hard experience in the disorderly America of his time.

From a poor-white background there emerged a man who, until quite late in life, seemed thoroughly unlikely ever to become a molder of opinion or a leader of a party, let alone a statesman. He was a man who entered politics merely with the humble hope of making a tolerable living from public office—the American "desire for place" that Tocqueville had mentioned. He was clumsy always, often feckless. In his debates with Stephen Douglas, he declared that it is "better to be a live dog than a dead lion." For years he was defeated in every endeavor to influence national politics. He was a self-taught country lawyer (his preparation having begun with a copy of Blackstone's *Commentaries* he picked up at an auction), sunk in melancholy, married to a neurotic woman, eclipsed in his own party by men whose talents seemed to outshine his immeasurably.

Through the eyes of his partner, William Herndon, we see Lincoln enduring the excesses of his disorderly children, who "would tear up the office, scatter the books, smash up pens, spill the ink," and urinate on the floor.[7] We see him apparently unfit for regular business of any description, his office all higgledy-piggledy; amid its confusion an envelope marked, in Lincoln's hand, "When you can't find *it* anywhere else, look into this." We see him, only three years before he won the presidential election of 1860, still an obscure and gawky backlands attorney, attending court in Cincinnati in his rumpled clothes, a blue cotton umbrella in his hands, snubbed by Edwin Stanton (later Secretary of War in Lincoln's cabinet) and other distinguished lawyers. The man seemed pathetic at best, if not downright ludicrous: all the majesty and all the loneliness of his tragic triumph were yet to come.

So Lincoln seemed to the casual observer. For all that, ever since his boyhood some friends had perceived in this curious being a dim touch of greatness. Lincoln possessed the incongruous dignity of those who have stood up under hard knocks. It always has been true that melancholy men are the wittiest; and Lincoln's off-color yarns, told behind a log barn or in some dingy Springfield office, were part and parcel of his consciousness that this is a world of vanities. When Lincoln gave orders from the White House, this wry humor of his would become an element of the high old Roman virtue; it was *comitas,* or the relief that seasons *gravitas*—that is, the sense of heavy responsibility.

The attempts of Herndon and other biographers to find the source of this brooding sorrowfulness in some early blighted love are puerile. "What? Would you cry for a little girl?" Epictetus asks. So it was with Lincoln. He was no woman's man, and his marriage was made tolerable only by his own boundless charity and tenderness; but he never was one to weep over his own blemishes or blunders. "In my poor, lean, lank face," he said, "nobody has ever seen any cabbages sprouting out."

Strong in his sadness, the man found the power to endure with humility and generosity the burden of his presidential office. When Chief Justice Taney, "old, shrunken, and shrivelled like 'a galvanized corpse,'" administered the inaugural oath to the first President elected by the Republican Party, the vanity of human wishes was stamped across the face of the strange giant in the new black suit, whose lacklustre eyes stared down upon the crowd, the soldiers, and the cannon. *Gravitas* had been conferred upon him.

Not until Lincoln's course was almost run did even his more intelligent supporters come to apprehend the real character of their President: their initial impressions had been different indeed. When, at the commencement of his administration, Lincoln called Charles Francis Adams to Washington to appoint him Minister to England, the formal and nearly humorless son of John Quincy Adams was confounded by the boorish and almost inane manner of the chief magistrate of the Republic. The President, lounging slipper-shod in his office, addressed a few brusque and inconsequential remarks to the representative of the most distinguished family in America, about to assume the most important diplomatic post in the world; then, as if forgetting Adams' existence, he turned aside to discuss a postmastership with a member of his cabinet.

Lincoln was a puzzle. Most of the leaders of his own party detested him, or despised him, or thought he would be the ruin of the Republicans. "We asked for a rail-splitter, and we have got one." It was a surprise to nearly everyone that he was nominated for the presidency, and a bigger surprise that he was elected by a plurality. It was the war which made Lincoln great: the war brought out from within him fortitude and dignity.

"As for dignity," the younger Charles Francis Adams wrote to his father as late as February 7, 1865, "I do not look to President Lincoln for that. I do look to him for honesty and shrewdness and I see no evidence that in this matter [the episode of the Peace Commissioners] he has been wanting in these respects." But Lincoln's essential dignity soon would be manifest even to the Adams family.

Precisely one month later, indeed, Charles Francis Adams, Jr., came to acknowledge the stature of the President, by that date inaugurated for the second time. "What do you think of the inaugural?" the young Colonel Adams wrote then to his father, the American Minister to the Court of St. James's. "That rail-splitting lawyer is one of the wonders of the day. Once at Gettysburg and now on a greater occasion he has shown a capacity for rising to the demands of the hour which we should not expect from orators or men of the schools. This inaugural strikes me in its grand simplicity and directness as being for all time the historical keynote of this war; in it a people seemed to speak in the sublimely simple utterance of ruder times. What will Europe think of this utterance of the rude ruler, of whom they have nourished so lofty a contempt? Not a prince or minister in all Europe could have risen to such an equality with the occasion."[8]

So President Lincoln acquired in office the old Roman *gravitas.* And the virtue of *pietas,* too, became his, in the old Roman sense: willing subordination to the claims of the divine, of neighbors, of country. Lincoln had begun as a naïve skeptic, receiving next to no religious instruction of any sort. Solitary reading of the Bible gave majesty to his style, but never brought to him any faith less cloudy and austere than a solemn theism. Yet the New Testament shone out from his acts of mercy; and the Old Testament from his direction of the war. A deep piety suffuses his Gettysburg Address, and occurs in some of his letters—for instance, in his letter to General Hooker upon appointing that ambitious soldier to the command of the Army of the Potomac: "And now, beware of rashness. Beware of rashness, but with energy, and sleepless vigilance, go forward, and give us victories."

This prophetic majesty was not often Lincoln's mood, nor was it discernible in him until the War. Once evoked, however, the Roman qualities of *pietas* and *officium*—duty and service—endured until his end. Here was a man; and as the best of life is tragic, and as the highest reward of virtuous life is a good end, so this man was fortunate in the hour of his death.

Lincoln was struck down at the height of his powers, having confronted the agony of the Civil War with firmness of purpose—which the Romans had called *constantia*. He fulfilled his office with *disciplina*, or steadiness of character; with *industria*, or hard labor; with *clementia*, or forgoing his own rights; with *frugalitas*, or austere abstinence; with *virtus*, or energetic manliness. He died at the moment when his hopes were rewarded and his acts justified. He passed from life unaffected by the rancor and corruption of the Reconstruction era, so that the intended evil of Booth's bullet was in reality, for Lincoln, relief and blessing. He left to the Republic somthing better than military or political victory: the example of strong probity.

Prudent amidst passion, Lincoln never had been a doctrinaire. In sentences about Lincoln that have lost nothing of their meaning, Lowell wrote of this: "Among the lessons taught by the French Revolution there is none sadder or more striking than this, that you may make everything else out of the passions of men except a political system that will work, and that there is nothing so pitilessly and unconsciously cruel as sincerity formulated into dogma."[9] Lincoln was a man of order, not a man of theoretic dogmas in politics. Having risen from very low estate, he knew the savagery that lies close beneath the skin of man, and he saw that most men are law-abiding only out of obedience to routine and custom and convention. The self-righteous Abolitionist and the reckless Fire-eater were abhorrent to him; yet he took the middle path between them not out of any misapplication of Aristotle's doctrine of the golden mean, but because he held that the unity and security of the United States transcended any fanatic scheme of perfectibility. In his immediate object, the preserving of the Union, he succeeded through the ancient virtue of *prudentia*.

Misunderstood in life, Lincoln the statesman often has been misinterpreted since his death. The Radical Republicans detested him as cordially as did the Southern zealots. He never was an Abolitionist, and the act for which he is most celebrated, the Emancipation Proclamation, he undertook as a measure of military expediency, not as a moral judgment. If he could have preserved the Union, short of war, by tolerating slavery, he would have done so, he said: he was no rash transformer of society overnight. The maintaining of order, as expressed in Declaration and Constitution, was his steady aim.

As a statesman, Lincoln upheld the nation-state against the passions of the American democracy, northern and southern. This made him popular with no violent faction. For a long while, Lincoln resisted the importunities of the Radicals who were eager for immediate Negro emancipation; he yielded, at length, out of the hard necessities of the Union cause; and once the thing was done, he engaged in unsuccessful endeavors to settle the freed blacks in the West Indies or in Latin America. Lincoln tried to persuade the members of his cabinet to agree to a monetary compensation to former slaveholders in the loyal states, at least—and was saddened by their unanimous refusal to support him in this. His proposals for Reconstruction in the South might have saved the southern states from much of the ignominy, and some of the material damage, that the Radicals meant to inflict upon them: had his moderate proposals for the gradual improvement of the freedmen been made effectual, the whole problem of later racial antagonism in America might have been diminished.

In Lincoln there was no presumption; much, he knew, must be left to Providence. To an enthusiastic clergyman who assured him that God was on "our side," Lincoln replied with a stern dignity that he knew nothing of the sort; he only hoped that we might be on His. "In the present civil war," Lincoln wrote in 1862, "it is quite possible that God's purpose is something different from the purpose of either party. . . . The will of God prevails. In great contests each party claims to act in accordance with the will of God. Both may be, and one must be, wrong. God cannot be for and against the same thing at the same time."

Man's order, Lincoln was saying, is subordinate to a providential order. That conviction—though few other Americans have been able to express it so powerfully as Lincoln did—has helped to keep the American democracy from a variety of foolish undertakings. Tocqueville would have subscribed wholly to those words of Lincoln.

In the era after Lincoln, James Bryce suggested that no longer were great men chosen for the American presidency. "The ordinary American voter," Bryce wrote, "does not object to mediocrity. He has a lower conception of the qualities requisite to make a stateman than those who direct public opinion in Europe have. He likes his candidate to be sensible, vigorous, and, above all, what he calls 'magnetic', and does not value, because he sees no need for originality or profundity, a fine culture or a wide range of knowledge."[10]

Lincoln had seemed mediocre enough, in 1860; certainly he had no magnetism, until his last months. Virtue, however, he did possess; and from that soil of virtue there sprang up dignity, the soil being sprinkled with blood. The model of that virtue and that final dignity still is respected by the American democracy. In a democratic society, as in every society, order must have primacy: that was the meaning of Lincoln's successful struggle to maintain the Union. To that cause he rendered up the last full measure of devotion. Probably he read no political thinker except Sir William Blackstone, aside from the speeches and public papers of earlier American statesmen. Out of the American democratic experience he came; and his life proved that a democracy of elevation can uphold resolutely the public order and the moral order.

Brownson and the Just Society

A few months after the murder of Lincoln, Orestes Brownson published a systematic treatise on American order, *The American Republic*. Brownson (who disliked Lincoln, but disliked the Secessionists even more) is intellectually one of the most interesting of all Americans, and his examination of order in the United States is an original work—though it is a kind of summary of what he had been writing in periodicals for the preceding quarter of a century. Although long neglected by most historians of American politics and thought, in recent years Brownson and his writings have received considerable attention, and *The American Republic* has been reprinted. There is good reason for this: late in the twentieth century, Americans confront the fundamental problems of personal and social order in which Brownson was passionately interested.

Lord Acton, who possessed one of the best intellects of nineteenth-century England, thought that Orestes Brownson was the most penetrating American thinker of his day; and that is a high compliment, for it was the day of Hawthorne, Melville, Emerson, and a half-dozen other men of the first rank in the works of the mind. The versatility of the man has made it difficult to fit him into any convenient category. He was a considerable political philosopher, a seminal essayist on religion, a literary critic of discernment, a serious journalist of fighting vigor, and one of the shrewder observers of American character and institutions. The long span of Brownson's career, too—for, born in 1803, he was engaged in controversy all the while from 1827 to his death in 1876—prevents his being classified within any conventional literary era. Nor was he a regional writer: a New Englander by birth, he spent much of his life in New York and Detroit, and died in Michigan; he is buried in the chapel of the University of Notre Dame, in Indiana. Midway in his life, Brownson became a Catholic, so departing from what the typical historian of culture likes to call the "mainstream" of American intellectual development; this deviation accounts in part for the neglect of Orestes Brownson in most books about American intellectual history. Yet he called himself "a true-born Yankee," and so he was —with the forthrightness, energy, and intellectual belligerence of his kind.

Brownson's course in partisan politics was intricate, from the time of Jackson to the time of Hayes; the course of his political and religious thought was equally perplexed, until 1844. Born into poverty, and chiefly self-educated, Brownson had to grope his way through the sects and factions of New England until he reached that understanding of things sacred and secular for which he had been seeking. He was a Bible-reader from early childhood; his quest for religious certitude led him from the Congregationalism of his boyhood successively to Presbyterianism, Universalism, humanitarianism, Unitarianism, and Transcendentalism. He was a Universalist minister at one time, and a Unitarian minister later; he was active in the socialistic undertakings of Robert Owen and Fanny Wright; for a year he was a militant atheist and revolutionary conspirator. But in none of these movements did he find intellectual or emotional satisfaction. Somewhere, Brownson believed, there must exist a source of religious authority, without which men are at sea; he found that in the Catholic faith, being baptized and confirmed in 1844.

His social ideas went through a succession of changes closely parallel to those in his religious convictions. Brownson was a socialist long before the name of Marx was known, and in several respects anticipated Marx's thought—which made him the more formidable as an opponent of socialism in his maturity. He was besides, in his early years, a complete democrat, taking equality of condition for a natural right—the principle upon which the civil social existence ought to be ordered.

Brownson always believed that if a principle were sound, there could be no danger in pushing it to its logical consequences. This he did with the principle of democratic equality, in his "Essay on the Laboring Classes," published in 1840. Equality of civil rights, he argued, must lead to equality of condition—to economic equality. The inheritance of private property, the system of bank credit, and all other principal features of what Marx would call "capitalism" must be abolished, then, so that equality of condition might triumph. Brownson defended this thesis stoutly; it did much mischief to the cause of the Democratic party, which he then supported. Ironically enough, the election of 1840 disillusioned this unequivocal egalitarian. The "Tippecanoe and Tyler Too" campaign, with its gross demagoguery, compelled Brownson to ask himself whether a republic could endure without recognizing clear principles of moral authority. When the American people elected a President on the strength of the assertions that General William Henry Harrison had been born in a log cabin (which was not strictly accurate) and drank hard cider, something was lacking in the social order. "We for one confess," Brownson wrote later, "that what we saw during the presidential election of 1840 shook, nay, gave to the winds all our remaining confidence in the popular democratic doctrines."

So after 1840 Brownson defended the permanent things. He had concluded from close observation of the American people that pure democracy and economic equality were miserable shams, which could lead only to the destruction of liberty and justice in any country. But if the idea of equality of condition was false, upon what principle ought an intelligent man to found his politics? Brownson came to perceive that somewhere there must reside an authority, in the original Latin meaning of that word—a source of moral knowledge, a sanction for justice and order.

Brownson did not become the defender of everything that existed in American society about the middle of the nineteenth century: he remained a mordant critic of many aspects of that society, but stood up for the principles of order which (however much obscured) made possible the American

Republic. His politics were the politics of a religious man, not of a Benthamite who looks upon the Church as a moral police-force. Brownson understood that we cannot separate the world of spirit and the world of society into distinct entities; but he had no intention of using the Church to advance his political beliefs, or of using his political convictions to advance the interests of the Church. Religion and politics are forever joined in this: mundane justice and order require a moral sanction; and that sanction cannot be found outside religious principle. He courted no man's favor, and was as fierce against the Utilitarian intellectual and the money-obsessed entrepreneur as against the Marxist fanatic and the doctrinaire social revolutionary.

Brownson was more than a vigorous controversalist: he was a political philosopher, something rare in the United States. Before Brownson wrote, only two important American books could be considered treatises on political philosophy —Adams' *Defense of the Constitutions* and *The Federalist*—and even those were apologies for a political situation and a particular set of circumstances, rather than analyses of the essence of political order. In Brownson's own time, his friend John C. Calhoun would write two logical political dissertations of a philosophical character, in defense of the South's stand. Yet in general Brownson's essays and his *American Republic* retain more meaning for our time than do Calhoun's works.

Brownson told Americans how even they, in their seemingly triumphant materialism and swaggering individualism, could not long endure without knowing the meaning of Justice. In reminding Americans of this, Brownson did not make himself popular. Ordinarily he was on the losing side at national elections. He had a following, but he strove against the current in his day. Yet the subtle influence of Brownson's writings, though it may be difficult to trace down to our time, has done something to chasten American impulsiveness and materialism. Today he can be read with interest and sympathy, which is more than can be said for most polemicists of yesteryear, popular though they may have been at the height of reputation.

Brownson waged intellectual battle upon several fronts. First, he had to contend against the radical doctrine of the Rights of Man—not those natural rights of which the Church long had spoken, but instead the arrogant abstract rights of Paine and Priestley and the French revolutionaries, divorced from duties and shorn of religious sanctions. Second, he had to deal with the delusion that "the voice of the people is the voice of God," which in America was put forward as an excuse for majorities to alter all law as they might choose, regardless of justice toward minorities and individuals. Third, he was confronted by an aggressive individualism—in part an American growth, in part the spirit of the age—which often sacrificed the common good in public affairs to immediate money-getting and private advantage. Fourth, he struggled against a sentimentality like that of Jean Jacques Rousseau, which mistook a misty-eyed compassion for Justice. Fifth, he defended Justice against a smug secularism, which looked upon Sin as merely a vestigial survival from barbarous times, sure to disappear with the march of progress. Sixth, he had to stand fast against the disintegrating competition of sectarianism, a chaos of cults which diminished the teaching authority of the Christian Church.

Brownson's was a lonely labor. For generations, the New England conscience had been some support for a just social order; but in Brownson's day, the old puritanical uprightness of New England was awash in a sea of innovating doctrines—later-day Congregationalism, Unitarianism, Universalism, Transcendentalism, and the rest. Brownson knew all these well, and found them unable to bear the weight of Justice. At the same time, the old planter-society of the South, resentful and fearful, was struggling against the North's new industrialism; saddled with its Peculiar Institution, slavery, the South moved toward violence. In the North, the zealots for Abolition, bent upon the destruction of one evil at the risk of aggravating other social afflictions, mistook social surgery for Justice. And beyond these American difficulties, Brownson discerned the rise of the "labor question" and the approach of socialism—an ideology that confounded Justice with absolute equality of condition.

Yet Brownson did not lose heart. Tireless, he labored to persuade his fellow-Americans of their common need for a principle of authority. Justice, he said, requires Authority —not the authority of soldier or policeman, but the authority of religious truth. No people can enjoy a just society without some standard of judgment superior to the mood of the moment; and this is especially true in democratic states, which have no hereditary class of magistrates to sustain the laws. Now this abiding standard of righteousness, or principle of authority, must be ethical in its nature; and to receive habitual assent from the people, that ethical system must refer to religious sanctions. This standard must be interpreted authoritatively by some body fitted for that function: the Church is required. Simple popular opinion never can maintain Justice:

"But we are told, once more, that practically it can make no difference whether we say the will of God is sovereign, or the will of the people; for the will of the people is the will of God. . . . We deny it. The will of God is eternal and immutable justice, which the will of the people is not. The people may do and often actually do wrong. We have no more confidence in the assertion, 'The people can do no wrong,' than we have in its brother fiction, 'The king can do no wrong'. . . . For very shame's sake, after denying, as most of you do, the possibility of an infallible church immediately constituted and assisted by infinite wisdom, do not stultify yourselves by coming forward now to assert the infallibility of the people." So Brownson wrote in his essay on "Legitimism and Revolution" in 1848, the year of the *Communist Manifesto*.

"In most cases," Brownson continued, "the sufferings of a people spring from moral causes beyond the reach of civil government, and they are rarely the best patriots who paint them in the most vivid colors, and rouse up popular indignation against the civil authorities. Much more effectual service could be rendered in a more quiet and peaceful way, by each one seeking, in his own immediate sphere, to remove the moral causes of the evils endured."[11]

Without Authority vested somewhere, without regular moral principles that may be consulted confidently, Justice cannot long endure anywhere. Yet modern liberalism and democracy are contemptuous of the whole concept of moral authority; if not checked in their assaults upon habitual reverence and prescriptive morality, the liberals and democrats will destroy Justice not only for their enemies, but for themselves. *Under God,* the will of the people ought to prevail; but many liberals and democrats ignore that prefatory clause. In America, particularly since 1825, there had been distressingly obvious a tendency to make over the government into a pure and simple democracy, centralized and intolerant of local rights and powers, upon the model of Rousseau. That "pure" democracy, if triumphant, would destroy the beneficent "territorial democracy" (a phrase Brownson borrowed from Disraeli) of the United States, with its roots in place. This would be a change from a civilized constitution to a barbaric one. The Civil War, said Brownson, had accelerated the process.

"But the humanitarian democracy, which scorns all geographical lines, effaces all individualities, and professes to plant itself on humanity alone, has acquired by the war new strength, and is not without menace to your future. . . ." The humanitarian presently will attack distinctions between the sexes; he will assail private property, as unequally distributed. "Nor can our humanitarian stop there. Individuals are, and as long as there are individuals will be, unequal: some are handsomer and some are uglier, some wiser or sillier, more or less gifted, stronger or weaker, taller and shorter, stouter or thinner than others, and therefore some have natural advantages which others have not. There is inequality, therefore injustice, which can be remedied only by the abolition of all individualities, and the reduction of all individuals to the race, or humanity, man in general. He can find no limit to his agitation this side of vague generality, which is no reality, but a pure nullity, for he respects no territorial or individual circumscriptions, and must regard creation itself as a blunder."[12]

The humanitarian, or social democrat (here Brownson uses those terms almost interchangeably), is by definition a person who denies that any divine order exists. Having rejected the supernatural order and the possibility of a Justice more than human, the humanitarian tends to erect Envy into a pseudo-moral principle. It leads him, this principle of Envy, straight toward a dreary tableland of featureless social equality—toward Tocqueville's democratic despotism, from which not only God seems to have disappeared, but even old-fangled individual man is lacking.

Yet the social democrat is not the only enemy of Justice and Authority in our time. The disciples of Bentham, with their moral calculus, their exalting of self-interest, and their social atomism, are the other side of the coin. Their principle of universal competition, and their fallacy that political constitutions can be created overnight, damage Justice in society as much as do the illusions of the socialistic leveller: because some men are more able and energetic than others, we cannot leave Justice to pure competition in society. For then "they in whom selfishness is the strongest will gain the preponderance, and, having the power, must, being governed only by selfishness, wield the government for their own private ends. And this is precisely what has happened, and which a little reflection might have enabled anyone to have foretold. The attempt to obtain wise and equitable government by means of universal competition, then, must always fail. But this is not the worst. It, being a direct appeal to selfishness, promotes the growth of selfishness, and therefore increases the very evil from which government is primarily needed to protect us."[13]

Both the socialist and the enthusiast for perfect competition, then, would undo Justice. But this descent of modern society into injustice may be arrested, Brownson argues: roused to their peril, men may renew true Justice. Suppose that modern men return to their belief in a Justice divinely ordained: what will be the shape of a just society, when the character of true human wants is better understood?

The just society will seek to give unto each man his due: not through the release of selfish impulse, not through a sentimental and enervating socialism, but by recognizing both the Christian virtue of charity and the profound natural differences that distinguish one human being from another. The just society will not repudiate democracy, properly understood, though it will turn away from both the atomistic "Jacksonian" democracy and the oppressive humanitarian democracy:

"Democracy, understood not as a form of government, but as the end government is to seek, to wit, the common good, the advance in civilization of the people, the poorer and more numerous, as well as the richer and less numerous, classes, not of a privileged caste or class, is a good thing, and a tendency toward it is really an evidence of social progress."[14] Such a democracy, if it is to remain just, must be restrained by solemn and prudent constitutions and by an enlightened faith. Nevertheless, its government will not hesitate to conduct itself with courage, or to undertake large projects. It is shallow sophistry to say that government is a necessary evil: government is no evil, but a device of divine wisdom to supply human wants. The function of government is not repressive merely:

"Its office is positive as well as negative. It is needed to render effective the solidarity of the individuals of a nation, and to render the nation an organism, not a mere organization—to combine men in one living body, and to strengthen all with the strength of each, and each with the strength of all—to develop, strengthen, and sustain individual liberty, and to utilize and direct it to the promotion of the common weal—to be a social providence, imitating in its order and degree the action of divine providence itself, and, while it provides for the common good of all, to protect each, the lowest and meanest, with the whole force and majesty of society. . . . Next after religion, it is man's greatest good; and even religion without it can do only a small portion of her work. They wrong it who call it a necessary evil; it is a great good, and instead of being distrusted, hated, or resisted, except in its abuses, it should be loved, respected, obeyed, and, if need be, defended at the cost of all earthly goods, and even of life itself."[15]

The government justly may perform all those labors which surpass the reach of individual abilities; and justly may do all that can be done to secure every man in his natural liberty, and to advance the culture of society. But the success of this

465

just government will be dependent upon those men of superior abilities who alone can provide for the progress of humanity and the preservation of the wisdom of our ancestors. Out of a solemn concern for the operation of Justice, Brownson argues, society ought to take every care that superior abilities should not be disparaged or positively repressed, that superior energies be not denied their reward, that learning be not trodden down by men without imagination. To each his own: to the natural entrepreneur, the fruits of industry; to the natural scholar, the contemplative leisure which is his need and his reward.

In any particular country, Brownson maintains, the form of government must be suited to the traditions and the organic experience of the people: in some lands that will be monarchy, in others aristocracy, in America republicanism, or democracy *under God*. It will not stoop to the degradation of the democratic dogma; it will not contest the sovereignty of God, which is absolute over all of us. It will secure to every man his freedom. And that freedom obtains the justice of which Plato wrote in his *Republic*, and Cicero in his *On Duty:* the right of every man to do his work, free of the meddling of others; the right of every man to what is his due.

Such is the nature of true social justice, Brownson declares: not the selfish loneliness of the Benthamite philosophy, nor the mean equality of the Socialists, but a liberation of every man, under God, to do the best that is in him. Poverty is no evil, in itself; obscurity is no evil; labor is no evil; even physical pain may be no evil, as it was no evil to the martyrs. This world is a place of trial and struggle, so that we may find our higher nature in right response to challenge.

To the Socialist, says Brownson, poverty, obscurity, and physical suffering are positive evils, because the Socialist does not perceive that these challenges are put into the world to save us from apathy and sloth and indifference. The Socialist would condemn humanity to a condition of permanent injustice, in which no man could hope for what is his due, the right to exercise his talents given him by God; the Socialist would keep us all in perpetual childhood:

"Veiling itself under Christian forms, attempting to distinguish between Christianity and the Church, claiming for itself the authority and immense popularity of the Gospel, denouncing Christianity in the name of Christianity, discarding the Bible in the name of the Bible, and defying God in the name of God, Socialism conceals from the undiscriminating multitude its true character, and, appealing to the dominant sentiment of the age and to some of our strongest natural inclinations and passions, it asserts itself with terrific power, and rolls on its career of devastation and death with a force that human beings, in themselves, are impotent to resist. Men are assimilated to it by all the power of their own nature, and by all their reverence for religion. Their very faith and charity are perverted, and their noblest sympathies and their sublimest hopes are made subservient to their basest passions and their most grovelling propensities. Here is the secret of the strength of Socialism, and here is the principal source of its danger."[16]

Those lines were written only a few months after the proclaiming of the Communist Manifesto. At that early date, Orestes Brownson had seen the dread strength of the Marxist heresy, an attempt at total destruction of the old order of human existence.

The United States was not brought into being to accomplish the work of Socialism. For every living nation, Brownson wrote in *The American Republic*, "has an idea given it by Providence to realize, and whose realization is its special work, mission, or destiny." The Jews were chosen to preserve traditions, and so that the Messiah might arise; the Greeks were chosen for the realizing of art, science, and philosophy; the Romans were chosen for the developing of the state, law, and jurisprudence. And the Americans, too, have been appointed to a providential mission, continuing the work of Greece and Rome, but accomplishing yet more. The American Republic is to reconcile liberty with law:

"Yet its mission is not so much the realization of liberty as the realization of the true idea of the state, which secures at once the authority of the public and the freedom of the individual—the sovereignty of the people without social despotism, and individual freedom without anarchy. In other words, its mission is to bring out in its life the dialectic union of authority and liberty, of the natural rights of man and those of society. The Greek and Roman republics asserted the state to the detriment of individual freedom; modern republics either do the same, or assert individual freedom to the detriment of the state. The American republic has been instituted by Providence to realize the freedom of each with advantage to the other."[17]

The reconciling of authority and liberty, so that justice might be realized in the good state: that mission for America is not accomplished, a century later, but is not forgotten. During the blighted years of "Reconstruction" in the South (a failure anticipated by Brownson, who despised the Radical Republicans), that mission of ordered freedom would seem infinitely remote from fulfillment.

Yet Brownson labored on, an old man in Detroit, exhorting Americans to vigor. *Under God*, said Brownson in his emphatic way, the American Republic may grow in virtue and justice. A century later, the words "under God" would be added to the American pledge of allegiance. Brownson's principles of justice, after all, expressed those American moral habits of thought and action that Tocqueville had found strong. The violence and confusion of Brownson's time would diminish somewhat; Marxism would make little headway in the United States. So thoroughly American himself, Orestes Brownson knew that there was more to America's great expectations than the almighty dollar.

In God's Own Good Time

"The United States is one of the great creations of history, like Rome or the Spanish Empire, realities which we enthusiastically study and understand today." So writes a Spanish scholar, Julián Marías, who knows intimately the America of our own day. "And the United States is being created before our very eyes, at an accelerated rate that allows us to observe it within our lifetime, or even in less than a lifetime. . . . Is this not an intellectually exciting spectacle? Has there been a greater social and historical experiment available for man's contemplation in many centuries?"[18]

The American order, far from being stagnant, still is developing. This word "order" implies membership: an order is something that one belongs to. All American citizens are born into this American order, or else formally naturalized into it. Active participation in this order is both a right and an obligation, and whether this order improves or decays must depend upon the quality of that participation.

From the Declaration and the Constitution onward, the American order stood open to newcomers from Europe. The Irish laborers who crowded into New York and Boston and many other cities during Brownson's lifetime were only the first great wave of post-Revolutionary immigration. In their hundreds of thousands the Irish and the Germans came, and presently millions of immigrants from southern and central Europe, and farther afield. Except for the Irish, English, Scottish, and Welsh newcomers, few of these spoke English on arrival, or knew much of Anglo-American civilization; most were Catholics, many were Jews.

Yet with surprising speed these masses of immigrants made themselves members of the American moral and social order. Only here and there, in city or countryside, did little islands of dissent resist the attraction of the predominant American order. The new citizens accepted Declaration and Constitution, and the whole complex of social and political institutions, with readiness; sometimes they surpassed the native Americans in their knowledge of the fundamental documents of American order, and even in their new-found attachment to American principles. The Negroes, emancipated during the Civil War, labored under greater social and economic handicaps than did the immigrants, but not until the 1950's would there arise among America's black citizens any nation-wide strong protest against their condition. America's society was pluralistic and tolerant enough, generally, cemented by willing allegiance to the written and unwritten constitutions.

Lest this book become an intellectual and institutional

history of the United States, we do not carry the close examination of American order beyond Orestes Brownson and his times, a century past. The roots have been described; the living tree of order is the society in which we find ourselves today.

Although the tree of American order has grown in height and breadth during the past hundred years, it could not have flourished so if those roots had been unhealthy. Those roots go deep, but they require watering from time to time. Whatever the failings of America in the eighth decade of the twentieth century, the American order has been a conspicuous success in the perspective of human history. Under God, a large measure of justice has been achieved; the state is strong and energetic; personal freedom is protected by laws and customs; and a sense of community endures. As the chapters of this book have suggested, the history of most societies is a record of painful striving, brief success (if success at all), and then decay and ruin. No man can know the future, but most Americans believe that their order will continue to "bring out in its life the dialectic union of authority and liberty." That will be true so long as the roots of order have proliferating life in them.

By the shock of the Civil War, Brownson wrote in 1865, "The nation has been suddenly compelled to study itself, and henceforth must act from reflection, understanding, science, statesmanship, not from instinct, impulse, passion, or caprice, knowing well what it does, and wherefore it does it." That sentence applies equally well to the circumstances of the United States in our present decade, when domestic and foreign troubles have induced many Americans to inquire into the character of the order to which they belong. That awakening, Brownson continued, "is sure to give it the seriousness, the gravity, the manliness it has heretofore lacked."[19] If Brownson's expectation was not altogether fulfilled during the last quarter of the nineteenth century, still it may come to pass during the last quarter of the twentieth.

By comparison with any other major nation of modern times, the United States has preserved and nurtured its essential order ever since Brownson wrote. Most of the world, during the past century, has experienced revolution after revolution, almost effacing the past and bringing forth hard new orders—often orders directed by squalid oligarchs. Even Britain has broken more clearly with its prescriptive pattern of politics and social institutions and general beliefs than has America. This is the only powerful nation-state, during the past century, that has not been ridden over by the Four Horsemen of the Apocalypse: America's wars have been fought thousands of miles distant from the American coasts, and not even one serious attempt at armed revolution has occurred.

The American order has been shaken from time to time, true: by enormous technological innovations; by massive shifts of population from one region to another, and from countryside to city; by economic dislocations; by partisan quarrels; by the coming of new mass media and a "mass culture" that those media feed; by hot disputes between management and labor; by challenges to moral assumptions and habits; in very recent years, by protest and rioting over questions of color and questions of war. And yet the general character of that American order remains little altered. The circumstances have changed markedly, from time to time, but the laws and the mores have endured; and as Tocqueville knew, the American democracy is the creation of its laws and (in still larger degree) of its moral habits. From time to time, small circles of dissenters have advocated radical alteration of the American order, but they have been rebuffed by public opinion; substantial reforms, however, have been accepted, and have not yet operated to impair the order itself. And whatever America's incertitudes today, it is difficult to find American citizens who can sketch any convincing ideal new order as an alternative to the one long rooted here.

In more ways than one, the American order has improved since Brownson's day. If class, family, church, and community have suffered during the past century, nevertheless many Americans have become aware of the need for reinvigorating those chief indispensable features of their order. Rowland Berthoff concludes his historical examination of America's order and disorder on a sanguine note:

"Fortunately the curious cycle through which American society had passed in its first 360 years left a growing sense that the good society could not be built merely by cutting the individual adrift from all institutions and structures. For a higher freedom—liberation of his energy and talents for cultural and spiritual self-fulfillment—evidently the support of a stable, well-founded social structure was as necessary as the checks and balances of the new economic system," Berthoff writes.* He ventures to hope for a "positive and many-sided liberty," rooted in the American inheritance of laws and mores.[20]

That patrimony, as traced in this book, is not a dead thing. The roots of order twist back to the Hebrew perceptions of a purposeful moral existence under God. They extend to the philosophical and political self-awareness of the old Greeks. They are nurtured by the Roman experience of law and social organization. They are entwined with the Christian understanding of human duties and human hopes, of man redeemed. They are quickened by medieval custom, learning, and valor. They grip the religious ferment of the sixteenth century. They come from the ground of English liberty under law, so painfully achieved. They are secured by a century and a half of community in colonial America. They benefit from the debates of the eighteenth century. They approach the surface through Declaration and Constitution. They emerge full of life from the ordeal of the Civil War. "A reformer hewing so near to the tree's root never knows how much he may be felling," George Santayana remarked, by way of caution, in 1915. Those who would assist in America's providential mission, as Brownson saw it, need to understand where these thick roots of moral and social order may be found.

One of the more pressing perils of our time is that people may be cut off from their roots in culture and community. "The rootless are always violent," Hannah Arendt says. In the 1960's, hostility toward the American order was con-

---

* By "new economic system," Rowland Berthoff means the reconciliation of free enterprise with a number of public controls on the economy.

spicuous among two very different groups of people: the impoverished and "culturally deprived" inhabitants, black and white, of the cities' decayed cores; and a restless element among college and university students, often bored, the children of American affluence. The first group had lost their roots in place and community, most of them being rural people (or the children of rural people) abruptly and bewilderingly shifted to urban existence; the second group had lost their roots in culture and moral habits, in paradoxical consequence of the material success of their parents, with a resulting disappearance of responsibilities and incentives. Whenever people cease to be aware of membership in an order—an order that joins the dead, the living, and the unborn, as well as an order that connects individual to family, family to community, community to nation—those people will form a "lonely crowd," alienated from the world in which they wander. And to the person and the republic, the consequences of such alienation will be baneful.

"The first of the soul's needs, the one which touches most nearly its eternal destiny, is order," Simone Weil writes in her moving little book *The Need for Roots*: "that is to say, a texture of social relationships such that no one is compelled to violate imperative obligations in order to carry out other ones. . . . The great instigators of violence have encouraged themselves with the thought of how blind, mechanical force is sovereign throughout the whole universe.

"By looking at the world with keener senses than theirs, we shall find a more powerful encouragement in the thought of how these innumerable blind forces are limited, made to balance one against the other, brought to form a united whole by something which we do not understand, but which we call beauty. . . ." Indeed, human order is "something to which a total sacrifice is due should the need arise. . . ."[21]

Sometimes that total sacrifice for the sake of order is required. Moral and social order, or a vast part of it, may be destroyed by a few years of violence or a few decades of contemptuous neglect. Then hope is lost, for many generations: for order is a kind of organic growth, developing slowly over many centuries; it cannot be created by public proclamation.

The caricature of order established by "men on horseback" like Cromwell or Napoleon—or, worse, like Hitler or Stalin—is a harsh pseudo-order, and it does not endure: in the phrase of Talleyrand, "You can do everything with bayonets—except sit upon them." The rootless are empty of hope, because disordered, and therefore they grow angry and destructive.

To live within a just order is to live within a pattern that has beauty. The individual finds purpose within an order, and security—whether it is the order of the soul or the order of the community. Without order, indeed the life of man is poor, nasty, brutish, and short. No order is perfect, but any tolerable order may be improved. Although in recent years the American order may have been deficient in imagination—in dealing with its problems of urban life, technology, shifts of population, and education, for instances—nevertheless this American order has maintained a high degree of freedom, opportunity, and prosperity. The conscientious citizen works to improve that order: for the alternative to a tolerable order is not Utopia, but an intolerable disorder.

It is quite possible, as Julián Marías suggests, to support an order stupidly and ineffectually; he writes of those "who immoderately espouse the cause of 'Law and Order.'" Failing to understand that order is subtle and complex, "They are the people who believe that problems can be solved with more and sterner police. If there is juvenile delinquency, they would not seek its causes and try to eventually modify the social conditions of wayward youth. They think it must be stopped 'right now'. . . . If some unwanted tendency appears within the country, no time should be lost in persuading others that it is bad; it must be immediately and inexorably cut out at the root."

But the man who truly understands order does not hack rashly through roots; he does not imitate extremists. The real accomplishments, Marías tells us, "belong to those who have known how to wait, those who know how long it takes for a tree to grow, those who, instead of shouting 'Right now!', have worked for the day when certain things would be possible. They know that things come about, as men used to say in earlier times, 'in God's own good time.' "

The intemperate zealot for instant "law and order," and the ingenuous radical who demands perfection right now, are especially misguided in America, Marías concludes in a Tocqueville-like passage. For happiness, recognized in the Declaration of Independence, "always has been probable and frequent in the United States, perhaps more so than in most other countries." The present problems of American order are far less dismaying than were those of the past or are those of other countries today; and Americans make headway against their present discontents. "Today's youth have not learned 'to see humor in misfortune', because they have hardly known what misfortune is. They are being urged to do the opposite: they are being asked to declare a state of mourning and to make sadness and protest the rule in the midst of what must be considered—in view of the true state of the world—an incomparable example of well-being, justice, freedom, and prosperity." And Marías quotes Miguel Unamuno, a philosopher of dignity and freedom: "Let us not protest, for protest kills happiness."[22]

To protest against the existence of order is to protest against well-being, justice, freedom, and prosperity. Happiness is found in imaginative affirmation, not in sullen negation. Gratitude is one form of happiness; and anyone who appreciates the legacy of moral and social order which he has inherited in America will feel gratitude. The pursuit of happiness is not altogether vain. One finds happiness in restoring and improving the order of the soul and the order of the republic—not in acts of devastation that make a desert of spirit and of society.

America's order rose out of acts of affirmation, from what Thomas Carlyle called "the Everlasting Yea." Upon the classical and the theological virtues, upon the social experience of the Old World and the New, there was built by self-sacrifice and high imagination the intricate structure of personal and public order. Although no single human mind planned this order of ours, the wisdom and the toil of countless men and women have gone into its making.

Two hundred years after the ferment which produced Declaration and Constitution, America's order is in ferment still—but in a ferment of renewal, for change is the means of our preservation. This book has sketched the principal features of the order that the United States inherited and developed. Other hands may renew that order's structure and improve it with prudence and love, in God's own good time.

Notes

[1] Rowland Berthoff, *An Unsettled People: Social Order and Disorder in American History* (New York: Harper and Row, 1971), p. xiii.

[2] *Ibid.*, p. 174.

[3] Alexis de Tocqueville, *Democracy in America* (edited by J. P. Mayer and translated by George Lawrence; Anchor Books edition, New York: Doubleday, 1969), p. 692.

[4] *Ibid.*, p. 287.

[5] *Ibid.*, p. 308.

[6] *Ibid.*, p. 363.

[7] Emanuel Hertz (ed.), *The Hidden Lincoln, from the Letters and Papers of William H. Herndon* (New York: Viking Press, 1938), p. 105.

[8] Charles Francis Adams, Jr. to Charles Francis Adams, February 7, 1865, and March 7, 1865, in Worthington C. Ford (ed.), *A Cycle of Adams Letters, 1861-1865* (Cambridge, Mass.: Houghton, Mifflin, 1920), Vol. II, pp. 253, 257-58.

[9] James Russell Lowell, "Abraham Lincoln", *Political Essays* (Boston: Houghton, Mifflin, 1888), p. 186.

[10] James Bryce, *The American Commonwealth* (New York: Macmillan, 1919), Vol. I, p. 79.

[11] Orestes A. Brownson, "Legitimacy and Revolutionism" (1848), in Henry F. Brownson (ed.), *The Works of Orestes A. Brownson* (Detroit: Brownson, 1882-87), Vol. XVI, pp. 68, 81.

[12] Brownson, *The American Republic* (facsimile edition, Clifton, N. J.: A. M. Kelley, 1972), pp. 363-64.

[13] Brownson, "Demagoguism", *Works*, XV, p. 438.

¹⁴ Brownson, "Liberalism and Progress" (1864), *Works*, XX, p. 354.

¹⁵ Brownson, *The American Republic, op. cit.*, pp. 18-19.

¹⁶ Brownson, "Socialism and the Church", *Essays and Reviews, chiefly on Theology, Politics, and Socialism* (New York: Smith, 1852), p. 499.

¹⁷ Brownson, *The American Republic, op. cit.*, pp. 4-5.

¹⁸ Julián Marías, *America in the Fifties and Sixties* (edited by Aaron Rockland; University Park, Penna.: Pennsylvania State University Press, 1972), p. 412.

¹⁹ Brownson, *The American Republic, op. cit.*, pp. 2-3.

²⁰ Berthoff, *An Unsettled Society, op. cit.*, pp. 478-79.

²¹ Simone Weil, *The Need for Roots: Prelude to a Declaration of Duties toward Mankind* (translated by Arthur Wills; Boston: Beacon Press, 1952), pp. 10-11.

²² Julián Marías, *America in the Fifties and Sixties, op. cit.*, pp. 420-21, 442, 444.

EPILOGUE

by Frank Shakespeare

The *Roots of American Order*, one of Russell Kirk's many wonderful scholarly achievements, first appeared in 1974. At that time our country was preparing to celebrate the bicentennial of the Declaration of Independence, a magnificent statement of core principles that continues to inspire people struggling for freedom all over the world. In those years the country was also emerging from a tumultuous period during which its institutions—the family, religious tradition, private property, social authority, and government—had suffered serious assaults. Radicals, bent on challenging and even destroying the foundations of Western culture, had sought to repudiate our shared history and national character. Young leftists were using Watergate to foment skepticism. Our nation's religious denominations were losing confidence in their ability to promote permanent values. The country as a whole seemed to have lost its direction.

Dr. Kirk's book was an antidote to all such confusion of the era. He lucidly argued that our nation, if it is to remain great, must remember and understand the roots from which it grew. As Dr. Kirk put it, "these roots go deep, but they require watering from time to time." Dr. Kirk saw that the then-fashionable attempt to pull up these roots and to reconstruct our country from scratch would in fact kill it. To prevent such destruction, he guided his reader on a sweeping tour of some thirty-two centuries of intellectual history. It was an exhilarating tour, one that gave anyone who read it a new appreciation of our heritage and our country. He made it clear that those who want to remake the nation and reinvent its moral codes had better understand the nature and magnitude of their mission, because they war against the greatest accumulation of wisdom in the history of man.

Today's America is a more peaceful place. The voices of revolution have quieted, especially in the wake of the disintegration of communism and third-world liberationist ideology. The threats to American social order today are less obvious. But we have not entirely overcome many of the problems that plagued our nation when Dr. Kirk's book first appeared. The revolutionaries are still among us, although they have become more subtle in their strategies.

Despite the extraordinary carnage caused by Marxist-Leninist ideology and the unchecked state power it unleashed, leftist intellectuals in American universities have continued their Gramscian march through our cultural institutions. The most recent ideological threat is "multiculturalism," a thinly-disguised assault on Western thought and ideas. This new ideology, one completely foreign to our shared history, has become deeply entrenched, not only in academia, but in the media and popular culture as well.

We should not underestimate the threat posed by this so-called multiculturalism. Multiculturalism posits that the values undergirding Western civilization were destined only for certain groups, usually labeled "oppressor classes," and that other groups, usually racial and ethnic groups, require special treatment, separate curricular, and independent political organizations. What the advocates of multiculturalism have failed to realize is that the cornerstones of Western civilization— the dignity of the individual, the integrity of private property, the bedrock importance of religious faith,—and the necessity for constitutional checks on government power—have universal applicability. These institutions were not designed to give this or that group certain privileges at others' expense, but to protect the rights of *all* individuals and groups. Earlier in this century Marxists and secularists did much to undermine religious faith; now multiculturalism is in the process of repudiating even the value of logic and reason. These ideologues fail to realize that, without faith and without reason, all that remains is an existence much like the Hobbesian state of nature.

There are other threats as well, ranging from radical environmentalism, which seeks to exchange our prosperity for a nature-adoring poverty rooted in paganism, to the new racism, which uses rigid racial quotas to war on the voluntary wage contract and the autonomy of our educational institutions.

As the struggle builds between those who embrace our heritage and those who reject it, it is a blessing to have Dr. Kirk's book back in print. His entire intellectual life has been devoted to one end—helping our modern age regain a lost sense of perspective. This book accomplishes this task as well as any ever written. More than most studies produced during this era, *The Roots of American Order* asks us to consider the sweep of history, philosophy, and even theology in order to understand what constitutes the Western social order. Dr. Kirk demands that we slow down, leave the op-eds and the microscholarship behind, and *think*—think about what defines us as individuals, as a community, and as a nation.

The Roots of American Order begins by tracing our intellectual roots to the Hebraic understanding of a purposeful universe under God's dominion. The Jewish people understood their God to be omniscient and omnipotent, the author of both the moral law and the terms of justice. They understood that He watched over them and gave them a moral nature. In turn, they were obliged to keep the moral law and to suffer the consequences if they failed to do so. This moral law was not intended to be adapted to every new political trend. Moral law is, by definition, not infinitely malleable. Instead, the moral law stands implacably against arrogant ideological claims.

The American order was further strengthened by the philosophical reflections of the Greeks, with their high regard for the uses of reason, and by the stern virtues of such exemplary Romans as Cicero. When the Word became Flesh, our ancestors learned to better understand the duties and limitations of Man, as well as the importance of the Transcendent in our lives. The roots of our order also include the magnificent traditions and universities of the medieval world, the religious zeal of the Reformation and the response to it, the development of British common law, the debates and discord of the eighteenth century, and the written words of our Declaration and Constitution.

We must always remember that those who originally advanced the ideas which today undergird our institutions were actual and potential martyrs. They believed that more was at stake than their own material betterment; they were subject to a higher law that imposed a duty to construct a better future for generations to come. Their strivings—so brilliantly and engagingly described in Kirk's pages—resulted in the ordered liberty of our predecessors, and, we can hope, that of our children as well.

Dr. Kirk's historical survey ends a century before our own. This is significant since most modern historians treat American history as if it began only with the expansion of the franchise and the rise of the ever-expanding panoply of special interest protests which now define our political life. By contrast, Dr. Kirk undoubtedly regards our own century as one in which the traditional order began to erode, endangering both our present and our future.

It should be clear that by "order" Dr. Kirk means more than positive law, those general rules that "make possible the tolerable functioning of an order," or even the written words of our founding documents. We also have what he calls our unwritten constitution, and it constitutes the strongest thread of our social fabric. Our unwritten constitution includes elements always beyond ourselves: our ingrained habits and customs, our implied rights and obligations, our unstated doctrines and beliefs, the things we take for granted, the things we would notice only if we were deprived of them. This unwritten constitution is enforced by informal but powerful courts of social sanction. It is a crucial element of our order. Yet it is characteristic of our age that positive law has become the sum total of our nation's purpose. We legislate for or against anything and everything, and this is somehow supposed to change our nature. But a comprehensive order is more organic, less concrete; it is integral to our national character, albeit in ways which we may not fully understand. An order is a tradition which we must respect. "No single human mind planned this order of ours," Kirk writes, "The wisdom and the toil of countless men and women have gone into its making."

To be sure, Dr. Kirk dissents from the conventional understanding of American intellectual history on several points. He is less willing than most, for example, to credit Locke and Hobbes with constructing our essential intellectual edifice, and he is more appreciative of the Jewish and Christian contributions. He views America's War of Independence as the affirmation of an order already existing, rather than a revolutionary overthrow of an established order. And, unlike many intellectuals, his sympathies lie not with egalitarianism and majoritarian democracy but with restrained democracy; he shows how the slow cultivation of an American gentleman led to an insistence on placing *limits* on democratic rule in order to keep it from becoming mob rule.

What of our present age? Is our order, so ancient in its origins, in danger of cracking? Dr. Kirk reminds us that "the history of most societies is a record of painful striving, brief success (if success at all), and then decay and ruin." We have no guarantee that America has been providentially appointed to carry the tradition through future ages. To preserve our position we need not another revolution, but a renewal of tradition. We must avoid frantic rushes into new intellectual and political fads. We must eschew ideology, which he defines as "servitude to political dogmas and abstract ideas not founded upon historical experience," and embrace philosophy and intellectual history. We must reject utopian millenarianism, that insidious force that, from time immemorial, has tempted man to exchange what is right and good for a rootless and radically uncertain future. In short, we had better take the time, if we can find it between elections and media feeding frenzies, to be tutored by the wisdom of the ages.

In spite of everything, Dr. Kirk remains hopeful for America's future, for "the general character of American order remains little altered." Our prayer should be that it will always be so, and that the long-lived ordered liberty of America will continue to be a blessing to its own citizens and a beacon to other peoples.

SUGGESTED READINGS

This list of books, arranged to parallel the several chapters, is not a bibliography: rather, it is meant merely to introduce readers to some important and readable studies related to American order, most of them recent and readily available. A number of other books are cited in the chapter-notes.

Chapter I

For theoretical and historical examinations of social order and its links with personal order, the following general studies are recommended; many others might be listed.

Barth, Hans. *The Idea of Order: Contributions to a Philosophy of Politics.* Dordrecht, Holland: D. Reidel, 1960.
Burckhardt, Jacob. *Force and Freedom: Reflections on History.* Edited by James Hastings Nichols. New York: Pantheon Books, 1943.
Curtis, Lionel. *Civitas Dei.* London: Allen and Unwin, 1950.
D'Arcy, M.C. *The Sense of History, Secular and Sacred.* London: Faber and Faber, 1959.
Dawson, Christopher. *The Dynamics of World History.* Edited by John J. Mulloy. New York: Sheed and Ward, 1956.
Heer, Friedrich. *The Intellectual History of Europe.* Translated by Jonathan Steinberg. 2 vols. New York: Anchor Books edition, Doubleday, 1968.

Löwith, Karl. *Meaning in History: the Theological Implications of the Philosophy of History.* Chicago: University of Chicago Press, 1949.

Lukacs, John. *Historical Consciousness, or the Remembered Past.* New York: Harper and Row, 1968.

McNeill, William H. *The Rise of the West: a History of Human Community.* Chicago: University of Chicago Press, 1963.

Nisbet, Robert A. *Social Change and History: Aspects of the Western Theory of Development.* New York: Oxford University Press, 1969.

Voegelin, Eric. *Order and History.* 3 vols. Baton Rouge: Louisiana State University Press, 1956-1957.

Chapter II

For this chapter and for Chapter V, it may be well to consult a good dictionary of the Bible. Two recent ones are *The Interpreter's Dictionary of the Bible,* edited by George Arthur Buttrick (New York: Abingdon Press, 1962) in four volumes; and *Dictionary of the Bible,* edited by John L. McKenzie (Milwaukee: Bruce, 1965). From the vast scholarship about the Hebrews and the Jews, the Bible, and Judaism, the following books are selected.

Brandon, S.G.F. *The Judgment of the Dead: the Idea of Life after Death in the Major Religions.* New York: Scribners, 1967.

Cheyne, T.K. *Traditions and Beliefs of Ancient Israel.* London: Black, 1907.

Dawson, Christopher. *The Age of the Gods.* London: Sheed and Ward, 1934.

Glover, T.R. *Progress and Religion.* London: Student Christian Movements, 1922.

Heaton, E.W. *The Old Testament Prophets.* London: Penguin Books, 1958.

Heschel, Abraham J. *The Prophets.* 2 vols. Harper Torchbooks edition, Harper and Row, 1971.

Meilsheim, David. *The World of Ancient Israel.* Translated by Grace Jackman. New York: Tudor, 1973.

Roth, Cecil. *A Short History of the Jewish People.* New York: revised edition, Hartmore, 1968.

Scott, R.B.Y. *The Relevance of the Prophets.* New York: revised edition, Macmillan, 1968.

Smith, W. Robertson. *The Religion of the Semites: the Fundamental Institutions.* New York: Meridian Library edition, Meridian, 1957.

Thomas, D. Winton (ed.). *Documents from Old Testament Times.* New York: Torchbooks edition, Harper and Row, 1961.

Toynbee, Arnold. *An Historian's Approach to Religion.* New York: Oxford University Press, 1956.

Vaux, Roland de. *Ancient Israel.* 2 vols. New York: paperback edition, McGraw-Hill, 1961.

Ward, James M. *Amos and Isaiah: Prophets of the Word of God.* Nashville: Abingdon Press, 1969.

Chapter III

Because of the great variety of translations and editions of Greek philosophers, poets, and historians, no regular attempt is made here to list the original sources—although occasionally in this chapter, as in later ones, a particular edition or translation is commended. The following works of interpretation and commentary are representative of a broad field.

Adams, Charles D. *Demosthenes and his Influence.* New York: Longmans, Green, 1927.

Barker, Ernest. *The Political Thought of Plato and Aristotle.* New York: Dover, 1959.

Bevan, Edwyn R. (ed.). *Later Greek Religion.* Boston: Beacon Press, 1950.

Bowra, C.M. *The Greek Experience.* Cleveland: World, 1957.

Burnet, John. *Early Greek Philosophy.* New York: Meridian Library edition, Meridian, 1957.

Cairns, Huntington. *Legal Philosophy from Plato to Hegel.* Baltimore: Johns Hopkins University Press, 1949.

Cornford, F.M. (ed.). *Greek Religious Thought.* Boston: Beacon Press, 1950.

Dodds, E.R. *The Greeks and the Irrational.* Boston: Beacon Press, 1957.

Dudley, Donald R. *A History of Cynicism, from Diogenes to the Sixth Century, A.D.* London: Methuen, 1937.

Field, G.C. *The Philosophy of Plato.* London: Cumberledge, 1949.

Freeman, Edward H. *The Story of Sicily: Phoenician, Greek, and Roman.* New York: Putnam, 1892.

Glover, T.R. *Springs of Hellas, and other Essays*. Cambridge: Cambridge University Press, 1945.

Greene, William Chase. *The Achievement of Greece: a Chapter in Human Experience*. New York: Barnes and Noble, 1966.

Grene, David. *Man in his Pride: a Study in the Political Philosophy of Thucydides and Plato*. Chicago: University of Chicago Press, 1950.

Griffo, Pietro. *Gela: the Ancient Greeks in Sicily*. Greenwich, Conn.: New York Graphic Society, 1968.

Gutherie, W.K.C. *The Greeks and their Gods*. Boston: Beacon Press, 1955.

Hamilton, Edith. *The Greek Way to Western Civilization*. New York: Norton, 1942.

Hamilton, Edith, and Cairns, Huntington (eds.). *The Collected Dialogues of Plato*. New York: Pantheon, 1961.

Hammond, N.G.L. *A History of Greece to 332 B.C.* Oxford: Clarendon Press, 1959.

Harrison, Jane. *Prolegomena to the Study of Greek Religion*. New York: Meridian edition, Meridian, 1955.

Harrison, Jane. *Themis: a Study of the Social Origins of Greek Religion*. Cleveland: revised edition, World, 1969.

Kerényi, C. *The Gods of the Greeks*. London: Thames and Hudson, 1951.

Kitto, H.D.F. *Greek Tragedy: a Literary Study*. Garden City, N.Y.: Anchor edition, Doubleday, 1954.

Livingstone, R.W. *The Greek Genius and its Meaning to Us*. Oxford: Clarendon Press, 1952.

Livingstone, R.W. (ed.). *The Legacy of Greece*. Oxford: Clarendon Press, 1921.

Mahaffy, J.P. *Social Life in Greece, from Homer to Menander*. London: Macmillan, 1883.

Miller, Helen H. *Sicily and the Western Colonies of Greece*. New York: Scribners, 1965.

More, Paul Elmer. *Platonism*. Princeton: Princeton University Press, 1931.

Murray, Gilbert. *Hellenism and the Modern World*. London: Allen and Unwin, 1953.

Murray, Gilbert. *The Literature of Ancient Greece*. Chicago: Phoenix edition, University of Chicago Press, 1956.

Otto, Walter F. *The Homeric Gods: the Spiritual Significance of Greek Religion*. Translated by Moses Hadas. New York: Pantheon, 1954.

Robinson, C.E. *Hellas: a Shory History of Ancient Greece.* Boston: Beacon paperback edition, Beacon Press, 1955.

Rose, H.J. *Ancient Greek Religion.* London: Hutchinson's University Library, 1946.

Rose, H.J. *A Handbook of Greek Mythology, including its Extension to Rome.* London: fifth edition, Methuen, 1953.

Sinclair, T.S. *A History of Greek Thought.* New York: Meridian edition, Meridian, 1967.

Snell, Bruno. *The Discovery of the Mind: the Greek Origins of European Thought.* Translated by T.G. Rosenmeyer. New York: Harper Torchbooks edition, Harper, 1960.

Tarn, W.W. *Alexander the Great.* Boston: Beacon paperback, Beacon Press, 1956.

Taylor, A.E. *The Mind of Plato.* Ann Arbor: University of Michigan Press, 1960.

Thucydides. *The Peloponnesian War.* Thomas Hobbes' translation, edited by David Grene. 2 vols. Ann Arbor: University of Michigan Press, 1959.

Walsh, James J. *Aristotle's Concept of Moral Weakness.* New York: Columbia University Press, 1963.

Zeller, Eduard. *Outlines of the History of Greek Philosophy.* Translated by L.R. Palmer. New York: Meridian edition, Meridian, 1955.

Zimmern, Alfred E. *The Greek Commonwealth: Politics and Economics in Fifth-Century Athens.* Oxford: Clarendon Press, 1911.

Chapter IV

Several translations exist of all the Latin writers discussed in this chapter. The books mentioned below include both general studies and some more specialized examinations of Roman mores and culture.

Barrow, R.H. *The Romans.* London: Penguin Books, 1951.

Berenson, Bernard. *The Arch of Constantine, or the Decline of Form.* London: Chapman and Hall, 1954.

Bloch, Raymond. *The Origins of Rome.* London: Thames and Hudson, 1960.

Burckhardt, Jacob. *The Age of Constantine the Great.* Translated by Moses Hadas. New York: Pantheon, 1949.

Cairns, Huntington. *Theory of Legal Science.* New York: reprint, Kelley, 1941.

Carcopino, Jerôme. *Daily Life in Ancient Rome: the People and the City at the Height of the Empire.* Edited by Henry T. Rowell. London: Penguin Books, 1956.

De Burgh, William George. *The Legacy of the Ancient World.* 2 vols. London: Pelican Books edition, Penguin Books, 1953.

D'Entrèves, A.P. *Natural Law: an Introduction to Legal Philosophy.* London: Hutchinson's University Library, 1951.

Duruy, Victor. *The World of the Romans.* Translated by Gwenn Lansdell. Geneva: Minerva, 1972.

Dill, Samuel. *Roman Society from Nero to Marcus Aurelius.* New York: Meridian edition, Meridian, 1956.

Dill, Samuel. *Roman Society in the Last Century of the Western Empire.* Meridian edition, Meridian, 1958.

Frothingham, A.L. *Roman Cities in Italy and Dalmatia.* New York: Sturgis and Walton, 1919.

Glover, T.R. *The Conflict of Religions in the Early Roman Empire.* London: Methuen, 1909.

Gummere, Richard M. *Seneca the Philosopher, and his Modern Message.* New York: Cooper Square Publishers, 1963.

Howe, Laurence Lee. *The Pretorian Prefect from Commodus to Diocletian.* Chicago: University of Chicago Press, 1942.

Maine, Henry. *Ancient Law: its Connection with the Early History of Society and its Relation to Modern Ideas.* London: John Murray, 1897.

Meigs, Russell. *Roman Ostia.* Oxford: Clarendon Press, 1960.

Renan, Ernest. *Marcus Aurelius.* Translated by William G. Hutchinson. London: Walter Scott, 1903.

Rose, H.J. *A Handbook of Latin Literature.* London: Methuen, 1947.

Rostovtzeff, M. *Rome.* New York: Galaxy edition, Oxford University Press, 1960.

Rostovtzeff, M. *Social and Economic History of the Roman Empire.* Oxford: Clarendon Press, 1926.

Smith, R.E. *Cicero the Statesman.* Cambridge: Cambridge University Press, 1966.

Stark, Freya. *Rome on the Euphrates: the Story of a Frontier.* London: John Murray, 1966.

Trollope, Anthony. *The Life of Cicero.* 2 vols. New York: Harper, 1881.

Wilkes, J.J. *Dalmatia.* Cambridge, Mass.: Harvard University Press, 1969.

Zane, John M. *The Story of Law*. Garden City, N.Y.: Garden City Publishing Company, 1927.

Chapter V

The New Testament, Josephus' *History of the Jews*, the later Roman historians, and the Fathers of the Church are our chief original sources for this period. Some twentieth-century studies are listed below.

Buck, Charles, and Taylor, Greer. *Saint Paul*. New York: Scribners, 1969.

Butterfield, Herbert. *Christianity and History*. London: Bell, 1950.

Clark, Mary T. *Augustine, Philosopher of Freedom*. New York: Desclee, 1958.

Cochrane, Charles N. *Christianity and Classical Culture*. New York: Galaxy edition, Oxford University Press, 1957.

Daniel-Rops, Henri. *The Church in the Dark Ages*. Translated by Audrey Butler. New York: Dutton, 1950.

D'Arcy, M.C. *The Meaning and Matter of History: a Christian View*. New York: Noonday, 1967.

Dawson, Christopher. *The Formation of Christendom*. New York: Sheed and Ward, 1967.

Dawson, Christopher. *The Making of Europe*. London: Sheed and Ward, 1948.

Dawson, Christopher. *Religion and the Rise of Western Culture*. London: Sheed and Ward, 1950.

Deane, Herbert A. *The Political and Social Ideas of St. Augustine*. New York: Columbia University Press, 1963.

Enslin, Morton Scott. *Christian Beginnings*. 2 vols. New York: Torchbooks edition, Harper, 1956.

Glover, T.R. *The Christian Tradition and its Verification*. London: Methuen, 1913.

Guardini, Romano. *The Lord*. Translated by Elinor Castendyk Briefs. Chicago: Regnery, 1954.

Harnack, Adolf. *Outlines of the History of Dogma*. Translated by Edwin Knox Mitchell. Boston: Beacon paperback edition, Beacon, 1959.

Hoare, F.R. (ed.). *The Western Fathers, being the Lives of SS. Martin of Tours, Ambrose, Augustine of Hippo, Honoratus of Arles, and Germanus of Auxerre*. New York: Sheed and Ward, 1954.

Howe, Quincy, Jr. (ed.). *Selected Sermons of St. Augustine*. New York: Holt, 1966.

Krook, Dorothea. *Three Traditions of Moral Thought*. Cambridge: Cambridge University Press, 1959.

Ladner, Gerhart B. *The Idea of Reform: its Impact on Christian Thought and Action in the Age of the Fathers*. Cambridge, Mass.: Harvard University Press, 1959.

Lecky, W.E.H. *History of European Morals, from Augustus to Charlemagne*. 2 vols. New York: third edition, Appleton, 1906.

McGiffert, Arthur C. *A History of Christian Thought*. 2 vols. New York: Scribners, 1953.

More, Paul Elmer. *The Catholic Faith*. Princeton: Princeton University Press, 1931.

More, Paul Elmer. *The Christ of the New Testament*. Princeton: Princeton University Press, 1924.

Palanque, J.R.; Bardy, G.; and de Labriolle, P. *The Church in the Christian Roman Empire*. Vol. I, *The Church and the Arian Crisis*. Translated by Ernest C. Messenger. New York: Macmillan, 1953.

Paolucci, Henry (ed.). *The Political Writings of St. Augustine*. Chicago: Gateway edition, Regnery, 1965.

Pelikan, Jaroslav. *The Emergence of the Catholic Tradition (100-600)*. Chicago: University of Chicago Press, 1974.

Pelikan, Jaroslav. *The Shape of Death: Life, Death, and Immortality in the Early Fathers*. Nashville: Abingdon Press, 1961.

Pope, Hugh. *St. Augustine of Hippo*. Garden City, N.Y.: Image Books edition, Doubleday, 1961.

Prat, Ferdinand. *Jesus Christ: His Life, His Teaching, and His Work*. Translated by John J. Heenan. 2 vols. Milwaukee: Bruce, 1950.

Przywara, Erich (ed.). *An Augustine Synthesis*. New York: Torchbooks edition, Harper, 1958.

Ricciotti, Giuseppe. *Paul the Apostle*. Translated by Alba I. Zizzamia. Milwaukee: Bruce, 1953.

Richardson, Alan. *An Introduction to the Theology of the Testament*. London: SCM Press, 1961.

Santayana, George. *The Idea of Christ in the Gospels, or God in Man*. New York: Scribners, 1946.

Sittler, Joseph. *The Structure of Christian Ethics*. Baton Rouge: Louisiana State University Press, 1958.

Toal, M.F. (ed.). *The Sunday Sermons of the Great Fathers*. 4 vols. Chicago: Regnery, 1963.

Van der Meer, F. *Augustine the Bishop: Religion and Society at the Dawn of the Middle Ages.* Translated by Brian Battershaw and C.R. Lamb. New York: Torchbooks edition, Harper, 1965.

Chapter VI

The books listed below have to do chiefly with the development of law and political institutions in medieval times, with medieval thought and universities, and with the character of feudal life.

Adams, George Burton. *Civilization during the Middle Ages.* New York: revised edition, Barnes and Noble, 1966.

Adams, George Burton. *Constitutional History of England.* New York: Henry Holt, 1936.

Adams, Henry. *Mont-Saint-Michel and Chartres.* Boston: Houghton Mifflin, 1913.

Anselm, Saint. *Basic Writings.* Translated by S.N. Deane, with an introduction by Charles Hartshorne. La Salle, Ill.: Open Court, 1966.

Aquinas, Thomas, Saint. *Basic Writings.* Edited by Anton C. Pegis. 2 vols. New York: Random House, 1945.

Butterfield, Herbert. *Christianity in European History.* London: Collins, 1952.

Cairns, Huntington. *Legal Philosophy from Plato to Hegel.* Baltimore: Johns Hopkins Press, 1949.

Cairns, Huntington. *Theory of Legal Science.* New York: reprint, Kelley, 1941.

Cant, Ronald G. *The College of St. Salvator.* Edinburgh: Oliver and Boyd, 1950.

Cant, Ronald G. *The University of St. Andrews: a Short History.* Edinburgh: Oliver and Boyd, 1946.

Church, R.W. *Dante and Other Essays.* London: Macmillan, 1888.

Church, R.W. *Saint Anselm.* London: Macmillan, 1899.

Claggett, Marshall; Post, Gaines; and Reynolds, Robert (eds.). *Twelfth-Century Europe and the Foundations of Modern Society.* Madison: University of Wisconsin Press, 1966.

Copleston, Frederick G. *Medieval Philosophy.* London: Methuen, 1952.

Coulton, G.G. *Studies in Medieval Thought.* London: Nelson, 1940.

Daniel-Rops, Henri. *Cathedral and Crusade: Studies of the Medieval Church.* New York: Dutton, 1957.

D'Arcy, M.C. *St. Thomas Aquinas*. Westminster, Maryland: Newman, 1953.

Dawson, Christopher. *Medieval Essays*. London: Sheed and Ward, 1953.

Dawson, Christopher. *Religion and the Rise of Western Culture*. London: Sheed and Ward, 1950.

DeWulf, Maurice. *Philosophy and Civilization in the Middle Ages*. New York: Dover, 1953.

Dicey, A.V. *Introduction to the Study of the Law of the Constitution*. London: Macmillan, 1889.

Duckett, Eleanor S. *The Gateway to the Middle Ages*. 3 vols. Ann Arbor: University of Michigan Press, 1961.

Dunlop, Annie I. *The Life and Times of James Kennedy, Bishop of St. Andrews*. Edinburgh: Oliver and Boyd, 1950.

Every, George. *Christian Mythology*. London: Hamlyn, 1970.

Froissart, John. *Chronicles*. Translated by Geoffrey Brereton. Baltimore: Penguin Books, 1968.

Gabriel, A.L. *Skara House at the Medieval University of Paris*. Notre Dame, Ind.: University of Notre Dame Press, 1960.

Gabriel, A.L. *Student Life in Ave Maria College, Medieval Paris*. Notre Dame, Ind.: University of Notre Dame Press, 1955.

Gilson, Etienne. *Reason and Revelation in the Middle Ages*. New York: Scribners, 1938.

Gilson, Etienne. *The Spirit of Medieval Philosophy*. New York: Scribners, 1940.

Giraldus Cambrensis. *Autobiography*. Edited and translated by H.E. Butler. London: Cape, 1937.

Harrison, Frederick. *Life in a Medieval College*. London: John Murray, 1952.

Holdsworth, William. *A History of English Law*. Vols. II and III. London: Methuen, 1966 and 1942.

Jacobus de Voragine. *The Golden Legend*. Translated by Granger Ryan and Helmut Ripperger. New York: Longmans, Green, 1948.

Jerrold, Douglas. *England: Past, Present, and Future*. London: Dent, 1950.

Joinville, Jean de, and Villehardouin, Geoffrey de. *Chronicles of the Crusades*. Translated by Margaret M. Shaw. Baltimore: Penguin Books, 1963.

Kirk, Russell. *St. Andrews*. London: Batsford, 1954.

Maine, Henry. *The Early History of Institutions*. London: John Murray, 1890.

Pirenne, Henry. *Economic and Social History of Medieval Europe*. New York: Harcourt, Brace, 1937.

Pirenne, Henri. *Mohammed and Charlemagne*. London: Allen and Unwin, 1954.

Power, Eileen. *Medieval People*. London: Penguin Books, 1939.

Previté-Orton, C.W. *The Shorter Cambridge Medieval History*. 2 vols. Cambridge: Cambridge University Press, 1952.

Rashdall, Hastings. *The Universities of Europe in the Middle Ages*. Edited by F.M. Powicke and A.B. Emden. 3 vols. New York: Oxford University Press, 1936.

Runciman, Steven. *A History of the Crusades*. 3 vols. Cambridge: Cambridge University Press, 1954.

Salusbury, G.T. *Street Life in Medieval England*. Oxford: Pen-in-Hand, 1948.

Stenton, Frank Merry. *William the Conqueror and the Rule of the Normans*. New York: revised edition, Barnes and Noble, 1966.

Stephenson, Carl, and Marcham, F.G. (eds.). *Sources of English Constitutional Law*. New York: Harper, 1937.

Talbot, C.H. (translator and editor). *The Anglo-Saxon Missionaries in Germany*. New York: Sheed and Ward, 1954.

Taylor, Henry Osborn. *The Medieval Mind*. 2 vols. Cambridge, Mass.: fourth edition, Harvard University Press, 1951.

Thomas, Charles. *Britain and Ireland in Early Christian Times, A.D. 400-800*. New York: McGraw-Hill, 1971.

Thorndike, Lynn. *University Records and Life in the Middle Ages*. New York: Octagon Press, 1944.

Trevelyan, George Macaulay. *England in the Age of Wycliffe*. London: Longmans, Green, 1946.

Wallace-Hadrill, J.M. *The Barbarian West, 400-1000*. London: Hutchinson's University Library, 1952.

Chapter VII

For this period and most of the succeeding chapters, a sound general work of reference is *The New Cambridge Modern History*, edited by G.R. Potter (14 vols., Cambridge University Press, 1957-70). Two other useful historical works are Oscar Halecki's *The Millenium of Europe* (University of Notre Dame Press, 1963) and the latter two volumes of H.A.L. Fisher's *History of Europe* (3 vols., Eyre and Spottiswoode, London, 1935). For a survey of moral ideas, see the latter half of Crane Brinton's *A History of Western Morals* (New York: Harcourt, Brace, 1959).

Bainton, Roland H. *The Reformation of the Sixteenth Century*. Boston: Beacon Press, 1952.

(Burnet, Gilbert). *Bishop Burnet's History of the Reformation of the Church of England*. 6 vols. London: Priestley, 1820.

Calvin, John. *On God and Political Duty*. Edited by John T. McNeill. New York: Liberal Arts Press, 1956.

Cassirer, Ernst; Kristeller, Paul O.; Randall, J.H. (eds.). *The Renaissance Philosophy of Man*. Chicago: Phoenix edition, University of Chicago Press, 1956.

Chambers, R.W. *Thomas More*. Ann Arbor: University of Michigan Press, 1958.

Dante Aligheri. *Monarchy, and Three Political Letters*. Translated by Donald Nicholl and Colin Hardie. New York: Noonday, 1954.

Dante Aligheri. *The Portable Dante*. Edited by Paolo Milano. New York: Viking, 1957.

Dawson, Christopher. *The Dividing of Christendom*. New York: Sheed and Ward, 1954.

Dillenberger, John, and Welch, Claude. *Protestant Christianity, Interpreted through its Development*. New York: Scribners, 1954.

Eliot, T.S. *Dante*. London: Faber and Faber, 1965.

Friedell, Egon. *A Cultural History of the Modern Age*. Vol. I. New York: Knopf, 1953.

Gilson, Etienne. *Dante the Philosopher*. New York: Sheed and Ward, 1949.

Habsburg, Otto von. *Charles V*. New York: Prager, 1970.

Hearnshaw, F.J.C. (ed.). *Social and Political Ideas of the Renaissance and Reformation*. New York: Barnes and Noble. 1949.

Hooker, Richard. *Works*. 2 vols. Oxford: Clarendon Press, 1890.

Knox, John. *The History of the Reformation of Religion within the Realm of Scotland*. Glasgow: Galbraith, 1761.

Lang, Andrew. *John Knox and the Reformation*. London: Longmans, Green, 1905.

More, Paul Elmer; and Cross, Frank L. (eds.). *Anglicanism*. London: SPCK Press, 1951.

Munz, Peter. *The Place of Hooker in the History of Thought*. London: Routledge and Kegan Paul, 1952.

Olin, John C. *The Catholic Reformation: Savonarola to Ignatius Loyola*. New York: Harper and Row, 1969.

Pelikan, Jaroslav. *Spirit versus Structure: Luther and the Institutions of the Church.* New York: Random House, 1968.

Pica della Mirandola, Giovanni. *Oration on the Dignity of Man.* Translated by A. Robert Caponigri. Chicago: Gateway edition, Regnery, 1956.

Reid, J.M. *Kirk and Nation: the Story of the Reformed Church of Scotland.* London: Skeffington, 1960.

Sayers, Dorothy L. *Introductory Papers on Dante.* London: Methuen, 1954.

Schwarzenfeld, Gertrude von. *Charles V, Father of Europe.* Chicago: Regnery, 1957.

Scott-Moncrieff, George. *The Mirror and the Cross.* London: Burns and Oates, 1960.

Shirley, F.J. *Richard Hooker and Contemporary Political Ideas.* London: SPCK Press, 1949.

Symonds, John Addington. *Renaissance in Italy.* 6 vols. London: Smith, Elder, 1882-1907.

Weber, Max. *The Protestant Ethic and the Spirit of Capitalism.* New York: Scribners, 1958.

Whale, J.S. *The Protestant Tradition: an Essay in Interpretation.* Cambridge: Cambridge University Press, 1955.

Willey, Basil. *The English Moralists.* London: Chatto and Windus, 1964.

Chapter VIII

The complex events in this chapter will be made clearer if one consults a standard history of England—for instance, Keith Feiling's *A History of England, from the Coming of the English to 1918* (London: Macmillan, 1950). For intellectual movements of the seventeenth century, see particularly Friedrich Heer's *Intellectual History of Europe* (2 vols., Anchor edition, New York, 1968).

Acton, John Emerich Edward Dalberg (first Baron Acton). *Lectures on Modern History.* Edited by Figgis and Lawrence. London: Macmillan, 1950.

Ashley, Maurice. *Cromwell's Generals.* London: Cape, 1954.

Ashley, Maurice. *England in the Seventeenth Century.* London: Penguin Books, 1952.

Ashley, Maurice. *The Glorious Revolution of 1688.* New York: Scribners, 1966.

Bosher, Robert S. *The Making of the Restoration Settlement: the Influence of the Laudians.* London: Dacre Press, 1951.

Browne, Sir Thomas. *Works.* Edited by Charles Sayle. 3 vols. Edinburgh: John Grant, 1912.

Bunyan, John. *The Pilgrim's Progress.* Edited by Louis Martz. New York: Rinehart, 1949.

Butterfield, Herbert. *The Englishman and his History.* Cambridge: Cambridge University Press, 1945.

Butterfield, Herbert. *The Whig Interpretation of History.* London: G. Bell, 1950.

Carswell, John. *The Descent on England: a Study of the English Revolution of 1688 and its European Background.* New York: John Day, 1969.

Clark, George. *War and Society in the Seventheenth Century.* Cambridge: Cambridge University Press, 1958.

Daniel-Rops, Henri. *The Church in the Seventeenth Century.* New York: Dutton, 1963.

Dicey, A.V. *Lectures on the Relation between Law and Opinion in England.* London: Macmillan, 1905.

Filmer, Robert. *Patriarcha, and other Political Works.* Edited by Peter Laslett. Oxford: Alden Press, 1949.

Finch, Jeremish S. *Sir Thomas Browne: a Doctor's Life of Science and Faith.* New York: Collier Books, 1961.

Fuller, Thomas. *The Holy State and the Profane State.* Cambridge: Williams, 1648.

Harrington, James. *Oceana, and his Other Works.* London: the booksellers of London and Westminster, 1700.

Hazard, Paul. *The European Mind (1680-1715).* London: Hollis and Carter, 1953.

Hearnshaw, J.F.C. (ed.). *Social and Political Ideas of the Sixteenth and Seventeenth Centuries.* New York: Barnes and Noble, 1949.

Hobbes, Thomas. *Leviathan: or Matter, Form and Power of a Commonwealth.* Edited by Michael Oakeshott. New York: Collier Books, 1966.

Keir, David Lindsay. *The Constitutional History of Modern Britain, 1485-1937.* London: A. and C. Black, 1950.

Krook, Dorothea. *Three Traditions of Moral Thought.* Cambridge: Cambridge University Press, 1959.

Linklater, Eric. *The Royal House.* Garden City, N.Y.: Doubleday, 1970.

Locke, John. *Two Treatises of Government.* Edited by Peter Laslett. Cambridge: Cambridge University Press, 1960.

Mackenzie, Agnes Mure. *The Passing of the Stuarts*. Edinburgh: Oliver and Boyd, 1958.

Mathew, David. *The Age of Charles I*. London: Eyre and Spottiswoode, 1951.

Nef, John U. *War and Human Progress: an Essay on the Rise of Industrial Civilization*. London: Routledge and Kegan Paul, 1950.

O'Connor, D.J. *John Locke*. London: Penguin Books, 1952.

Roots, Ivan. *Commonwealth and Protectorate: the English Civil War and its Aftermath*. New York: Schocken, 1966.

Spragens, Thomas, A., Jr. *The Politics of Motion: the World of Thomas Hobbes*. Lexington: University Press of Kentucky, 1973.

Strauss, Leo. *Hobbes' Political Philosophy: its Basis and its Genesis*. Oxford: Clarendon Press, 1936.

Strauss, Leo. *Natural Right and History*. Chicago: University of Chicago Press, 1953.

Vaughan, C.E. *Studies in the History of Political Philosophy before and after Rousseau*. 2 vols. Manchester: University of Manchester Press, 1925.

Venables, Edmund. *Life of John Bunyan*. London: Scott, 1888.

Wedgwood, C.V. *Thomas Wentworth, First Earl of Strafford, 1593-1641*. New York: Macmillan, 1962.

Willey, Basil. *The Seventeenth Century Background*. London: Chatto and Windus, 1962.

Williams, Basil. *The Whig Supremacy, 1714-1760*. Oxford: Clarendon Press, 1949.

Williams, Charles. *James I*. London: Arthur Barker, 1951.

Wingfield-Stratford, Esmé. *Charles King of England, 1600-1637*.

Wingfield-Stratford, Esmé. *King Charles and King Pym, 1643-1649*.

Wingfield-Stratford, Esmé. *King Charles the Martyr, 1649-1660*. (A three-volume biography; London: Hollis and Carter, 1949.)

Wormald, B.H.G. *Clarendon: Politics, History and Religion, 1640-1660*. Cambridge: Cambridge University Press, 1951.

Chapter IX

As with other chapters, we list here some books of a popular character, some more specialized studies, and a number of narratives or treatises by men who wrote during the age under discussion.

Adams, Brooks. *The Emancipation of Massachusetts: the Dream and the Reality*. Introduction by Perry Miller. Boston: Sentry edition, Houghton Mifflin, 1962.

Andrews, Charles McLean. *The Colonial Period*. New York: Holt, 1912.

Andrews, Charles McLean. *The Fathers of New England: a Chronicle of the Puritan Commonwealth*. New Haven: Yale University Press, 1920.

Berthoff, Rowland. *An Unsettled People: Social Order and Disorder in American History*. New York: Harper and Row, 1971.

Black, Robert C. *The Younger John Winthrop*. New York: Columbia University Press, 1966.

Boorstin, Daniel J. *The Americans: the Colonial Experience*. New York: Random House, 1958.

Boorstin, Daniel J. *The Genius of American Politics*. Chicago: University of Chicago Press, 1953.

Bradford, William. *Of Plymouth Plantation, 1620-1647*. Edited by Samuel Eliot Morrison. New York: Knopf, 1952.

Carse, James. *Jonathan Edwards and the Visibility of God*. New York: Scribners, 1967.

(Cresswell, Nicholas). *The Journal of Nicholas Cresswell, 1774-1777*. Edited by Lincoln McVeagh. New York: Dial, 1924.

Dodd, William E. *The Old South: Struggles for Democracy*. New York: Macmillan, 1937.

(Fithian, Philip Vickers). *Journal and Letters of Philip Vickers Fithian, 1773-1774: a Plantation Tutor of the Old Dominion*. Williamsburg: Colonial Williamsburg, Inc., 1943.

Gummere, Richard M. *The American Colonial Mind and the Classical Tradition*. Cambridge, Mass.: Harvard University Press, 1963.

Gummere, Richard M. *Seven Wise Men of Colonial America*. Cambridge, Mass.: Harvard University Press, 1967.

Jefferson, Thomas. *Notes on the State of Virginia*. New York: Torchbooks edition, Harper and Row, 1964.

Labaree, Leonard Woods. *Conservatism in Early American History*. New York: New York University Press, 1948.

Leach, Douglas Edward. *The Northern Colonial Frontier, 1607-1763*. New York: Holt, Rinehart and Winston, 1966.

Miller, Perry. *The New England Mind*. 2 vols. Boston: Beacon Press, 1961.

Miller, Perry. *Orthodoxy in Massachusetts, 1630-1650*. Boston: Beacon Press, 1959.

Miller, Perry. *Roger Williams: his Contribution to the American Tradition.* New York: Atheneum, 1962.

Parkes, Henry Bamford. *Jonathan Edwards: the Fiery Puritan.* New York: Milton, Balch, 1930.

Rossiter, Clinton. *Seedtime of the Republic: the Origin of the American Tradition of Political Liberty.* New York: Harcourt, Brace, 1953.

Rowse, A.L. *The Elizabethans and America.* New York: Harper Colophon edition, Harper, 1965.

Sydnor, Charles S. *Gentlemen Freeholders: Political Practices in Washington's Virginia.* Chapel Hill: University of North Carolina Press, 1952.

Wertenbaker, Thomas Jefferson. *The Founding of American Civilization.* 3 vols. New York: Cooper Square Publishers, 1938-1947.

Wertenbaker, Thomas Jefferson. *The Government of Virginia in the Seventeenth Century.* Charlottesville: University of Virginia Press, 1957.

(Winthrop, John). *Winthrop's Journal: "History of New England", 1630-1649.* Edited by James Kendall Hosmer. 2 vols. New York: reprint, Barnes and Noble, 1966.

Wright, Louis B. *The Atlantic Frontier: Colonial American Civilization, 1607-1763.* New York: Knopf, 1947.

Wright, Louis B. *Culture on the Moving Frontier.* Bloomington: Indiana University Press, 1955.

Wright, Louis B. *The First Gentlemen of Virginia: Intellectual Qualities of the Early Colonial Ruling Class.* Charlottesville: Dominion Books, 1964.

Chapter X

The writings of Montesquieu, Hume, Blackstone, and Burke are readily available; some scholarly editions are included in the list below, together with commentaries on the thought of the eighteenth century.

Basson, A.H. *David Hume.* London: Penguin Books, 1958.

Becker, Carl L. *The Heavenly City of the Eighteenth-Century Philosophers.* New Haven: Yale University Press, 1946.

Beloff, Max (ed.) *The Debate on the American Revolution, 1761-1783.* London: Kaye, 1949.

(Blackstone, William). *Blackstone's Commentaries, with Notes of Reference to the Constitution and Laws of the Federal Government of the United States and of the Commonwealth of Virginia.* Edited by St. George Tucker. 5 vols. South Hackensack, N.J.: reprint, Rothman, 1969.

Boorstin, Daniel J. *The Lost World of Thomas Jefferson.* Boston: Beacon edition, Beacon Press, 1960.

Boulton, James T. *The Language of Politics in the Age of Wilkes and Burke.* Toronto: University of Toronto Press, 1963.

Bredvold, Louis I. *The Brave New World of the Enlightenment.* Ann Arbor: University of Michigan Press, 1961.

Brinton, Crane. *The Anatomy of Revolution.* New York: Vintage Books, 1957.

Burke, Edmund. *Correspondence.* Edited by Thomas Copeland and others. 9 vols. Chicago: University of Chicago Press, 1958-1970.

Burke, Edmund. *Reflections on the Revolution in France.* Introduction by Russell Kirk. New Rochelle, N.Y.: Arlington House, 1966.

Burke, Edmund. *Speech on Conciliation with the Colonies.* Introduction by Jeffrey Hart. Chicago: Gateway edition, Regnery, 1964.

Butterfield, Herbert. *George III and the Historians.* London: Collins, 1957.

Butterfield, Herbert. *George III, Lord North, and the People, 1779-1780.* London: G. Bell, 1949.

Canavan, Francis. *The Political Reason of Edmund Burke.* Durham, N.C.: Duke University Press, 1960.

Carswell, John. *The Old Cause: Three Biographical Studies in Whiggism.* London: Cresset, 1954.

Cassirer, Ernst. *The Philosophy of the Enlightenment.* Translated by Fritz C.A. Koelln and James Pettegrove. Princeton: Princeton University Press, 1951.

Chapman, Gerald W. *Edmund Burke: the Practical Imagination.* Cambridge, Mass.: Harvard University Press, 1967.

Colbourn, H. Trevor. *The Lamp of Experience: Whig History and the Intellectual Origins of the American Revolution.* Chapel Hill: University of North Carolina Press, 1965.

Cone, Carl B. *Burke and the Nature of Politics.* 2 vols. Lexington: University of Kentucky Press, 1957 and 1964.

Cone, Carl B. *The English Jacobins: Reformers in the Late Eighteenth Century.* New York: Scribners, 1968.

Haraszti, Zoltán. *John Adams and the Prophets of Progress.* Cambridge, Mass.: Harvard University Press, 1952.

Hazard, Paul. *European Thought in the Eighteenth Century, from Montesquieu to Lessing.* London: Hollis and Carter, 1954.

Hearnshaw, F.J.C. (ed.). *The Social and Political Ideas of Some Great French Thinkers of the Age of Reason.* New York: Barnes and Noble, 1931.

Hoffman, Ross J.S. *Edmund Burke, New York Agent.* Philadelphia: American Philosophical Society, 1956.

Hume, David. *Enquiries concerning the Human Understanding and concerning the Principles of Morals.* Edited by L.A. Selby-Bigge. Oxford: second edition, Clarendon Press, 1902.

Hume, David. *A Treatise of Human Nature.* Edited by L.A. Selby-Bigge. Oxford: Clarendon Press, 1949.

Kirk, Russell. *Edmund Burke: a Genius Reconsidered.* New Rochelle, N.Y.: Arlington House, 1967.

Lecky, William Edward Hartpole. *A History of England in the Eighteenth Century.* 7 vols. London: Longmans, Green, 1911.

Letwin, Shirley R. *The Pursuit of Certainty.* Cambridge: Cambridge University Press, 1965.

MacNabb, D.G.C. *David Hume: His Theory of Knowledge and Morality.* London: Hutchinson's University Library, 1951.

Montesquieu, Charles de Secondat, Baron de. *The Spirit of Laws.* 2 vols. London: Nourse and Vaillant, 1750.

Mossner, Ernest Campbell. *The Life of David Hume.* London: Nelson, 1954.

Pound, Roscoe. *The Formative Era of American Law.* Boston: Little, Brown, 1938.

Stanlis, Peter. *Edmund Burke and the Natural Law.* Preface by Russell Kirk. Ann Arbor: University of Michigan Press, 1958.

Stephen, Leslie. *History of English Thought in the Eighteenth Century.* 2 vols. New York: reprint, Peter Smith, 1949.

Taine, Hippolyte Adolphe. *The Ancient Regime.* Translated by John Durand. New York: Holt, 1881.

Talmon, J.L. *The Origins of Totalitarian Democracy.* London: Secker and Warburg, 1952.

Tocqueville, Alexis de. *The Old Regime and the French Revolution.* Translated by Stuart Gilbert. Garden City, N.Y.: Anchor Books, 1955.

Willey, Basil. *The Eighteenth Century Background.* London: Chatto and Windus, 1949.

Wu, John C.H. *Fountain of Justice: a Study in the Natural Law.* New York: Sheed and Ward, 1955.

Chapter XI

To understand the political principles and experience that entered into the Constitution of the United States, everyone should read closely the *Federalist Papers,* of which several editions are in print. There exist hundreds of books about this period; a few of them, especially useful or readable, are listed below, together with some of the writings of the men who made Declaration and Constitution.

Adams, John. *Works.* Edited by Charles Francis Adams. 10 vols. Boston: Little, Brown, 1851-1856.

(Adams, John). *Diary and Autobiography of John Adams.* Edited by L.H. Butterfield. 4 vols. Cambridge, Mass.: Belknap Press, 1961.

(Adams, John). *Familiar Letters of John Adams and His Wife.* Edited by Charles Francis Adams. New York: Hurd and Houghton, 1876.

Becker, Carl. *The Declaration of Independence.* New York: Vintage Books edition, Random House, c. 1960.

Becker, Carl. *The Eve of the Revolution.* New Haven: Yale University Press, 1921.

Beloff, Max. *Thomas Jefferson and American Democracy.* London: English Universities Press, 1965.

Bemis, Samuel Flagg. *The Diplomacy of the American Revolution.* Bloomington: Indiana University Press, 1957.

Bernard, E.A. *Fisher Ames, Federalist and Statesman, 1758-1808.* Chapel Hill: University of North Carolina Press, 1965.

Boorstin, Daniel. *The Americans: the National Experience.* New York: Random House, 1966.

Bowers, Claude G. *The Young Jefferson.* Boston: Sentry edition, Houghton, Mifflin, 1969.

Brant, Irving, *James Madison.* 4 vols. Indianapolis: Bobbs-Merrill, 1941-1953.

Burleigh, Ann Husted. *John Adams.* New Rochelle, N.Y.: Arlington House, 1964.

Chinard, Gilbert. *Honest John Adams.* Boston: Little, Brown, 1964.

Chinard, Gilbert. *Thomas Jefferson, the Apostle of Americanism.* Ann Arbor: second edition, revised, University of Michigan Press, 1966.

Cobbett, William. *A Year's Residence in America.* London: Chapman and Dodd, c. 1920.

Corwin, Edward S. *The "Higher Law" Background of American Constitutional Law*. Ithaca: Cornell University Press, 1955.

Corwin, Edward S. *John Marshall and the Constitution: a Chronicle of the Supreme Court*. New Haven: Yale University Press, 1920.

Dauer, Manning J. *The Adams Federalists*. Baltimore: John Hopkins Press, 1953.

Dawson, Christopher. *The Gods of Revolution*. Introduction by Arnold Toynbee. New York: New York University Press, 1972.

Dietze, Gottfried. *The Federalist*. Baltimore: Johns Hopkins Press, 1962.

Dos Passos, John. *The Head and Heart of Thomas Jefferson*. Garden City, N.Y.: Doubleday, 1954.

Dos Passos, John. *The Shackles of Power: Three Jeffersonian Decades*. Garden City, N.Y.: Doubleday, 1966.

Dunne, Gerald T. *Justice Joseph Story and the Rise of the Supreme Court*. New York: Simon and Shuster, 1970.

Farrand, Max. *The Fathers of the Constitution: a Chronicle of the Establishment of the Union*. New Haven: Yale University Press, 1921.

Farrand, Max. *The Framing of the Constitution of the United States*. New Haven: Yale University Press, 1968.

Hacker, Louis M. *Alexander Hamilton in the American Tradition*. New York: McGraw-Hill, 1957.

Hacker, Louis M. (ed.). *The Shaping of the American Tradition*. 2 vols. New York: Columbia University Press, 1947.

(Hamilton, Alexander). *The Papers of Alexander Hamilton*. 10 vols. New York: Columbia University Press, 1961-1966.

Horton, Theodore. *James Kent: a Study in Conservatism*. New York: Da Capo Press, 1969.

(Jefferson, Thomas). *Correspondence between Thomas Jefferson and Samuel du Pont de Nemours*. Edited by Dumas Malone. Boston: Houghton Mifflin, 1930.

(Jefferson, Thomas). *The Jefferson Bible: the Life and Morals of Jesus of Nazareth*. Edited by Douglas E. Lurton. Cleveland: World, 1942.

Kurtz, Stephen G. *The Presidency of John Adams*. Philadelphia: University of Pennsylvania Press, 1957.

Lipsky, George A. *John Quincy Adams: his Theory and Ideas*. New York: Crowell, 1950.

(Madison, James). *The Complete Madison: His Basic Writings*. Edited by Saul K. Padover. New York: Harper, 1953.

Madison, James. *Notes of Debates in the Federal Convention of 1787.* Edited by Adrienne Koch. New York: Norton, 1966.

McClellan, James. *Joseph Story and the American Constitution.* Norman: University of Oklahoma Press, 1971.

Miller, John C. *Alexander Hamilton: Portrait in Paradox.* New York: Harper and Row, 1959.

Miller, John C. *Crisis in Freedom: the Alien and Sedition Acts.* Boston: Little, Brown, 1951.

Miller, John C. *The Federalist Era.* New York: Harper, 1960.

Miller, John C. *Origins of the American Revolution.* Boston: Little, Brown, 1943.

Morgan, Edmund S. *The Birth of the Republic, 1763-1789.* Chicago: University of Chicago Press, 1956.

Morris, Richard B. (ed.). *The Basic Ideas of Alexander Hamilton.* New York: Pocket Library edition, Pocket Books. 1957.

McMaster, John Bach. *The Political Depravity of the Founding Fathers.* Introduction by Louis Filler. New York: Noonday, 1964.

Murray, John Courtney. *We Hold These Truths.* New York: Sheed and Ward, 1961.

Nock, Albert Jay. *Jefferson.* New York: Hill and Wang, 1960.

Peterson, Merrill D. *Jefferson Image in the American Mind.* New York: Galaxy edition, Oxford University Press, 1960.

Read, Conyers (ed.). *The Constitution Reconsidered.* Preface by Richard B. Morris. New York: Harper Torchbooks edition, Harper and Row, 1968.

Riemer, Neal. *The Democratic Experiment: American Political Theory.* Princeton, N.J.: Van Nostrand, 1967.

Rogers, George C., Jr. *Charleston in the Age of the Pinckneys.* Norman: University of Oklahoma Press, 1969.

Rossiter, Clinton. *Alexander Hamilton and the Constitution.* New York: Harcourt, Brace, and World, 1964.

Rossiter, Clinton. *1787: the Grand Convention.* New York: Mentor edition, Mentor Books, 1966.

Rutland, Robert A. *George Mason, Reluctant Statesman.* Williamsburg: Colonial Williamsburg, Inc., 1961.

Smith, David G. *The Convention and the Constitution: the Political Ideas of the Founding Fathers.* New York: St. Martin's Press, 1965.

Smith, Page, *John Adams.* 2 vols. New York: Doubleday, 1963.

White, Leonard D. *The Federalists: a Study in Administrative History.* New York: Macmillan, 1948.

Williamson, Chilton. *American Suffrage from Property to Democracy, 1760-1860.* Princeton: Princeton University Press, 1960.

Williamson, René de Visme. *Independence and Involvement: a Christian Reorientation in Political Science.* Baton Rouge: Louisiana State University Press, 1964.

Chapter XII

For additional study of subjects discussed in this and the preceding chapter, a useful work of reference is *The Literature of American History: a Bibliographical Guide,* edited by J.N. Larned (New York: Ungar, 1966). The following list of books about nineteenth-century America and Americans does no more than to suggest a few of the aspects of the problems of order since 1800.

Adams, Henry. *History of the United States during the Administrations of Jefferson and Madison.* 9 vols. New York: Scribners, 1885-1891.

Bemis, Samuel Flagg. *John Quincy Adams and the Foundations of American Foreign Policy.*

Bemis, Samuel Flagg. *John Quincy Adams and the Union* (a two-volume biography.) New York: Knopf, 1950 and 1956.

Boorstin, Daniel. *The Americans: the Democratic Experience.* New York: Random House, 1973.

Bowers, Claude G. *Jefferson in Power.* Boston: Sentry edition, Houghton Mifflin, 1967.

Brownson, Orestes. *The American Republic: its Constitution, Tendencies, and Destiny.* New York: reprint, A.M. Kelley, 1972.

Bryce, James. *The American Commonwealth.* 2 vols. New York: Macmillan, 1919-21.

(Calhoun, John C.). *Calhoun: Basic Documents.* Edited by John M. Anderson. State College, Pa.: Bald Eagle Press, 1952.

(Calhoun, John C.). *The Papers of John C. Calhoun.* Edited by Robert L. Meriwether and W. Edwin Hemphill. 7 vols. Columbia: University of South Carolina Press, 1959-1973.

Coit, Margaret L. *John C. Calhoun, American Portrait.* Boston: Houghton Mifflin, 1950.

Cooper, James Fenimore. *The American Democrat.* Edited by H.L. Mencken. New York: Knopf, 1931.

Costanzo, Joseph F. *The Nation under God.* New York: Herder and Herder, 1964.

Current, Richard N. *Daniel Webster and the Rise of National Conservatism.* Boston: Little, Brown, 1950.

Ellis, John Tracy. *American Catholicism.* Chicago: University of Chicago Press, 1957.

Filler, Louis. *Slavery in the United States of America.* New York: Van Nostrand, 1972.

Fox, Dixon Ryan. *The Decline of Aristocracy in the Politics of New York.* New York: Longmans, Green, 1919.

Gilhooley, Leonard. *Contradition and Dilemma: Orestes Brownson and the American Idea.* New York: Fordham University Press, 1973.

Green, Fletcher. *Constitutional Development in the South Atlantic States, 1776-1860.* Chapel Hill: University of North Carolina Press, 1930.

Grigsby, Hugh Blair. *The Virginia Convention of 1829-30.* New York: reprint, Da Capo Press, 1969.

(Herndon, William H.) *The Hidden Lincoln, from the Letters and Papers of William H. Herndon.* Edited by Emanuel Hertz. New York: Viking Press, 1938.

Kirk, Russell. *The Conservative Mind, from Burke to Eliot.* Chicago: fifth revised edition, Regnery, 1973.

Kirk, Russell. *John Randolph of Roanoke: a Study in American Politics.* Chicago: Regnery, 1964.

Lively, Jack. *The Social and Political Thought of Alexis de Tocqueville.* Oxford: Clarendon Press, 1965.

Livermore, Shaw. *The Twilight of Federalism: the Disintegration of the Federalist Party, 1815-1830.* Princeton: Princeton University Press, 1962.

Marshall, Hugh. *Orestes Brownson and the American Republic.* Washington: Catholic University of America Press, 1971.

(Marshall, John). *The Marshall Reader: the Life and Contributions of Chief Justice John Marshall.* Edited by Edwin C. Surrency. New York: Oceana, 1955.

Mayer, J.P. *Alexis de Tocqueville: a Biographical Study in Political Science.* New York: Harper, 1960.

McMaster, John Bach. *History of the People of the United States from the Revolution to the Civil War.* Selected and edited by Louis Filler. New York: Noonday, 1964.

Morley, Felix. *Freedom and Federalism.* Chicago: Regnery, 1959.

Niebuhr, Reinhold. *The Irony of American History.* New York: Scribners, 1952.

Nisbet, Robert A. *The Quest for Community.* New York: Oxford University Press, 1972.

Peterson, Merrill D. (ed.). *Democracy, Liberty, and Property: the State Constitutional Conventions of the 1820's.* New York: Bobbs-Merrill, 1966.

Pierson, George W. *Tocqueville and Beaumont in America.* New York: Oxford University Press, 1938.

Risjord, Norman K. *The Old Republicans: Southern Conservatism in the Age of Jackson.* New York: Columbia University Press, 1965.

Ryan, Thomas R. *The Sailor's Snug Harbor: Studies in Brownson's Thought.* Westminster, Md.: Newman, 1952.

Santayana, George. *Character and Opinion in the United States.* New York: Scribners, 1924.

Spain, August O. *The Political Theory of John C. Calhoun.* New York: Bookman Associates, 1951.

Taylor, John, of Carolina. *An Inquiry into the Principles and Policy of the Government of the United States.* London: reprint, Routledge and Kegan Paul, 1950.

Thomas, Benjamin P. *Abraham Lincoln.* New York: Knopf, 1953.

Tocqueville, Alexis de. *Democracy in America.* Edited by J.P. Mayer. Garden City, N.Y.: Anchor edition, Doubleday, 1969.

Weaver, Richard M. *The Southern Tradition at Bay: a History of Postbellum Thought.* Edited by George Core and M.E. Bradford. New Rochelle, N.Y.: Arlington House, 1968.

Wilson, Francis Graham. *The American Political Mind.* New York: McGraw-Hill, 1949.

CHRONOLOGY

This list of dates includes the chief events mentioned in this book, with the addition of certain other dates of major historical significance. It may serve to relate, in point of "linear" time, events occurring during the same centuries in the Levant, Greece, and Rome, for instance.

B.C.	
2850-2190	The Old Kingdom of Egypt
2190-2052	First Intermediate Period in Egypt
2052	Beginning of Middle Kingdom in Egypt
1800?-1600?	Patriarchal period of the Israelites (Abraham, Isaac, Jacob)
1778	End of the Middle Kingdom in Egypt
1778-1610	Second Intermediate Period in Egypt
1600?	Israelites in Egypt
1670-1570 ,	Hyksos Period in Egypt
1610	The New Kingdom in Egypt begins
1280?	Exodus of the Israelites, led by Moses and Aaron, from Egypt
1260?	Entrance of the Israelites into Caanan; beginning of rule by the Judges
1200?	Troy falls to the Greeks
1030?	Saul chosen first king of Israel
1000?	David becomes king of Israel
970-931	Solomon, king of Israel
926	The tribes of Israel divide into two kingdoms, Israel (Samaria) and Judah

900?-800?	Homer composes the *Iliad* and the *Odyssey*
800	Carthage founded
766	Traditional date of First Olympiad in Greece
765?	The prophet Amos in Samaria
753	Traditional date of the founding of Rome
750?	Hesiod composes his *Theogony* and *Works and Days*
740?	The prophets Isaiah I and Micah in Judah
734	Founding of Syracuse, in Sicily
734-732	The prophet Hosea in Samaria
721	Samaria conquered by the Assyrians
715	End of the New Kingdom in Egypt
700	Aristocracies dominate Greek city-states
672	Assyrians conquer Egypt
627	Jeremiah begins to prophesy in Judah
621	The laws of Draco in Athens
600?	The prophet Habakkuk in Judah; the prophet Ezekiel
587	Jerusalem destroyed by the Babylonians, and its inhabitants carried off to Babylon
594	Solon begins to reform the laws of Athens
561	Peisistratus first seizes power in Athens
550?	Prophecies of Isaiah II (Deutero-Isaiah)
546	Cyrus, king of Persia, conquers Croesus, king of Lydia
539	Cyrus and the Persians and Medes Conquer Babylon
538	Cyrus permits the Jews to return to Jerusalem
520	The Second Temple founded at Jerusalem
521	Darius becomes king of Persia
510	Athenians overthrow the sons of Peisistratus
490	The Greeks defeat the Persians at Marathon
480	The Greeks defeat the Persians at Salamis and the Carthaginians at Himera
461	Ephialtes establishes a democratic Constitution in Athens
443-429	Pericles leads Athens
431	Peloponnesian War in Greece begins
427	Plato born
413	Athenians suffer disaster at Syracuse
406	Akragas falls to the Carthaginians
404	Athens surrenders to the Spartans
399	Socrates condemned by an Athenian jury
390	Rome sacked by the Gauls
384	Aristotle born; goes to Athens in 362
347	Plato dies
343	Aristotle appointed tutor to Alexander

340	Alexander becomes regent of Macedonia
323	Alexander dies in Asia
322	Aristotle dies in exile
298-290	Romans defeat Samnites, Etruscans, and Gauls
286	Plebians admitted to full Roman citizenship
264-241	First Punic War between Rome and Carthage
218-201	Second Punic War
215	The Romans invade Macedonia
212	The Romans conquer Syracuse
200-196	Second Macedonian War
169-151	Polybius a Roman hostage
149-146	Third Punic War
146	The Romans destroy Carthage and Corinth
133-121	The Gracchi attempt radical reform of the Roman Republic
90-88	The Social War in Italy
86-78	Constitution of Sulla
73-71	The Servile War in Italy
70	Cicero prosecutes Verres
64	Cicero, as consul, crushes Catiline's conspiracy
60-54	First Triumvirate
58-51	Conquest of Gaul by Julius Caesar
49-46	War between Caesar and the Senate
43	Second Triumvirate; murder of Cicero
31	Octavian wins the battle of Actium
27	Octavian (Augustus) made Princeps
19	Virgil dies
3?	Seneca born

Beginning of the Christian era (actually, it is now held that Jesus of Nazareth may have been born in the year which we call 4 A. D.)

A.D.

14	Augustus dies; Tiberius made emperor
30	Jesus of Nazareth crucified
35?	Paul of Tarsus beholds Christ on the road to Damascus
43?	London resettled by the Romans
46	Plutarch born
55	Tacitus born
60?	Epictetus born

570	Mohammed born
590	Gregory made pope
597	St. Augustine of Canterbury begins to convert England to Christianity
614	Avars and Slavs overrun Dalmatia
632	Mohammed dies
638	The Moslems take Jerusalem
663	Synod of Whitby, by which Roman Christianity triumphs in Britain
688	The Mosque of Omar, or Dome of the Rock, built in Jerusalem
731	Bede's *Ecclesiastical History*
732	Charles Martel defeats the Moslems at Tours
787	First landing of the Vikings in England
800	Coronation of Charlemagne as emperor, in Rome
843	Division of the Frankish Empire
871	Alfred the Great becomes king of Wessex
880?	Death of Duns Scotus Erigena, philosopher
911	Dukedom of Normandy established
962	Otto the Great crowned emperor of the West
987	Hugh Capet crowned king of France
1016	Cnut of Denmark crowned king of England
1042	Edward the Confessor crowned king of England
1054	The Great Schism of the Eastern and Western Churches
1066	William of Normandy conquers England
1093	St. Anselm consecrated archbishop of Canterbury
1095	Pope Urban II proclaims the First Crusade
1099	The Latin Crusaders establish the kingdom of Jerusalem
1100	Henry I crowned king of England
1121	Condemnation of the philosopher Abelard at Soissons
1139	Civil war in England between Stephen and Matilda commences
1141	Death of Hugh of St. Victor, schoolman
1147	Beginning of Second Crusade
1164	Constitutions of Clarendon
1164?	Death of Peter Lombard, author of the *Sentences*
1170	Archbishop Thomas Becket murdered
1180	Death of the philosopher John of Salisbury
1187	Saladin captures Jerusalem
1189	Beginning of Third Crusade
1200	King Philip Augustus grants a charter to the University of Paris
1201	Beginning of the Fourth Crusade
1204	Latin Crusaders capture Constantinople
1208	Francis of Assissi embraces a religious vocation

	John of Brienne made king of Jerusalem
1215	King of John of England seals Magna Carta
1219	John of Brienne leads the Fifth Crusade into Egypt
1225	The Emperor Frederick II marries Yolande, daughter of John of Brienne
1226	St. Francis of Assisi dies
1231	John of Brienne becomes Latin emperor of Constantinople
	Robert Grosseteste begins lecturing at Oxford
1245	Death of Alexander of Hales, schoolman
1249	University College, Oxford, founded
1254	Knights of the shire summoned to the English parliament
1260	Publication of Bracton's *De Legibus et Consuetudinibus Angliae*
1265	Representatives of the towns summoned to the English parliament
1274	Death of St. Thomas Aquinas
1280	Death of Albertus Magnus, schoolman
1284	Peterhouse College, Cambridge, founded
1294	Death of Roger Bacon
1295	"Model Parliament" summoned by Edward I of England
1297	Confirmation of the Charters by Edward I
	William Wallace leads Scots against Edward's rule
1308	Death of Duns Scotus, schoolman
1313	Death of the Emperor Henry VIII, at Siena
1314	The English defeated by the Scots at Bannockburn
1321	Death of Dante
1322	By the Statute of York, the Commons are recognized as an essential part of the English parliament
1324	Marsilius of Padua publishes his *Defensor Pacis*
1337	The Hundred Years' War begins
1340	By statute, taxation without consent of the English parliament is forbidden
1348	University of Prague founded
1348?	William of Ockham, the Nominalist, dies
1374	Death of Petrarch
1377	John Wycliffe's teaching is condemned by Pope Gregory XI
1378	Beginning of the Great Schism in the Western Church
1381	Peasants' Revolt in England
1399	Coronation of Henry of Bolingbroke in England, with assertion of parliamentary authority over succession to the throne
1407	John Resby, Lollard preacher, burnt in Scotland
1408	France forsakes Benedict XII, the Avignon pope
1413	Papal bulls issued to confirm the charter of the University of St. Andrews

1415	John Huss burnt as a heretic at Constance
1420	The Hussite wars commence
1424	John Zizka's skin made into a Hussite drum
1430	The English parliament establishes permanent qualifications for county electors
1433	Paul Craw, Hussite, burnt at St. Andrews
1450	St. Salvator's College founded at St. Andrews
1453	Constantinople falls to the Turks
1454	Beginning of the Wars of the Roses in England
1485	Henry Tudor wins the English throne
1486	Pico della Mirandola arrives at Rome
1492	Columbus discovers the West Indies
1493	Pico purged of heresy by Alexander VI
1503	Death of Pope Alexander VI
1512	St. Leonard's College founded at St. Andrews
	Ponce de Leon discovers Florida
1513	Balboa discovers the Pacific Ocean
1517	Martin Luther nails his Ninety-five Theses to a church door
1519	Cortez lands in Mexico
1520	Magellan discovers the straits which bear his name
	Luther is excommunicated
1521	The Emperor Charles V summons the Diet of Worms to deal with the Reformers
1522	Luther publishes his translation of the New Testament
1524	Luther debates with Erasmus on freedom of the will
1526	Pizarro discovers Peru
1527	Patrick Hamilton preaches Lutheran doctrines in Scotland, and is executed
1529	Bezerro and Grijalva discover California
1531	Death of Ulrich Zwingli at Kappel
1532	Machiavelli's *Il Principe* is published
1533	Cartier lands on the coast of Canada
1534	Anabaptists seize Munster, in Germany
	The Act of Supremacy overthrows the Catholic establishment in England
1535	John Calvin publishes his *Institutes of the Christian Religion*
	Sir Thomas More executed by Henry VIII
	First French Protestant Bible published
1537	St. Mary's College founded at St. Andrews
1538	Henry VIII excommunicated
1539	Cranmer's Bible published in England

1540	De Soto discovers the Mississippi
	Ignatius Loyola's Company of Jesus confirmed
1542	English forces defeat the Scots at Solway Moss
1543	The infant Mary Stuart is crowned queen of Scotland
1545	The Council of Trent convenes, commencing the Counter-Reformation
1546	Luther dies
	George Wishart is burnt at St. Andrews for heresy
	Cardinal Beaton is murdered in St. Andrews castle
1547	King Henry VIII dies, and is succeeded by his young son Edward VI, backed by the Protestant interest
1549	The English Book of Common Prayer is published
1553	The University of Lima, in Peru, is founded
	Edward VI dies, and is succeeded by Mary Tudor, a Catholic
1558	Elizabeth I crowned queen of England
1559	John Knox leads a violent reformation in Scotland, resisted by the regent, Mary of Guise, mother of Mary Queen of Scots
1560	Catholicism is suppressed in Scotland, and the Reformed Kirk of Scotland is established
1563	The Anglican Convocation ratifies the Thirty-Nine Articles, fixing the doctrines of the Church of England
1577	Sir Francis Drake sails round the world
1578	The Scottish Kirk's *Second Book of Discipline* is published
1582	The University of Edinburgh is founded
1583	Sir Walter Raleigh lands in Virginia
1587	Queen Mary Stuart is beheaded in England
1588	The Spanish Armada is defeated
1591	Trinity College, Dublin, is founded
1593-1594	Part I of Richard Hooker's *Laws of Ecclesiastical Polity* is published
1595	Raleigh makes his first expedition to the Orinoco
1600	The East India Company is founded
1603	James VI of Scotland, Mary Stuart's son, is crowned James I of England
1607	Jamestown, in Virginia, is founded by the Virginia Company
1608	Champlain founds Quebec
1609	Hudson discovers the Hudson and Delaware rivers
1611	Publication of the Authorized Version of the Bible (King James's Bible)
1618	Thirty Years' War commences
1619	The first black slaves are sold in Virginia
	The first House of Burgesses convenes in Virginia

CHRONOLOGY

1620	The Pilgrim Fathers land in Massachusetts
1625	Charles I is crowned king of England
1626	The Dutch found New Amsterdam (now New York)
1628	King Charles reluctantly accepts the Petition of Right
1630	The Puritans found Boston, Massachusetts
1632	Lord Baltimore founds Maryland
1635	Maryland's assembly asserts the right to make its own statutes
1636	Puritans settle Connecticut
	Roger Williams founds Rhode Island
1637	Pequot War in Massachusetts
1639	Charles I marches on Scotland
1640	Thomas Hobbes flees to France
1643	The English Civil War begins
	Sir Thomas Browne's *Religio Medici* is published
1644	The Royalists are beaten in the first stage of the Civil War
	John Milton's *Areopagitica* is published
1646	The Levellers make their appearance
1648	Thomas Fuller's book *The Holy State and the Profane State* is published
1649	Charles I is beheaded
	The Diggers are dispersed by Cromwell's troops
	Cromwell crushes the Irish
1650	Harvard College founded in Massachusetts
1651	Hobbes' *Leviathan* is published
1653	Cromwell dissolves the Rump Parliament
	Settlement of North Carolina begins
1660	The Protectorate is overthrown; Charles II assumes the English throne
1664	The English take New Amsterdam
	Settlement of New Jersey begins
1669	La Salle discovers Niagara Falls and the Ohio river
1670	Charleston founded in South Carolina
1676	Bacon's Rebellion in Virginia
1677	Maine is added to Massachusetts
1678	John Bunyan's *Pilgrim's Progress* is published
1679	New Hampshire becomes a royal province
1681	Pennsylvania and Delaware are granted to William Penn
1682	Penn founds Philadelphia
1685	James II, a Catholic, succeeds to the throne
1687	James II publishes the Declaration of Indulgence
1688	The "Glorious Revolution": William and Mary thrust James from the throne

1689	The Bill of Rights is accepted by King William and Queen Mary
	John Locke's two *Treatises of Civil Government* are published
	In North America, King William's War against the French and Indians begins—lasting until 1697
1690	Locke publishes his *Human Understanding*
1692	Witchcraft trials are held at Salem, Massachusetts
1693	The College of William and Mary is chartered in Virginia
1696	The Board of Trade and Plantations is established
1701	Cadillac founds Detroit
1702	Anne, daughter of William and Mary, is crowned queen
	In North America, Queen Anne's War begins, lasting until 1713
1714	George, elector of Hanover, is crowned as George I of the United Kingdom of England and Scotland
1718	Yale College is founded at New Haven, Connecticut
1719	The proprietary administration is overthrown in South Carolina, which becomes a royal province
1727	George II succeeds to the throne
1733	General Oglethorpe founds Savannah, in Georgia
1735	John Wesley goes out to Georgia, where he preaches until 1738.
1737	George Whitefield goes out to Georgia for a year; he preaches in Massachusetts in 1740
1740	David Hume publishes *A Treatise of Human Nature*
1744	King George's War begins, lasting until 1748
1748	College of New Jersey (later Princeton) is chartered
	Montesquieu publishes *De l'Esprit des Lois*
1749	Bolingbroke publishes his *Idea of a Patriot King*
1750	English translation of *The Spirit of Laws* appears
1751-1752	The French *Encyclopedia* is published
1753	Colonel George Washington resists the French at Fort Necessity
1754	Benjamin Franklin, at the Albany Congress, proposes a plan of union for the colonies
	Jonathan Edwards publishes *The Freedom of the Will*
	King's College (later Columbia) is founded in New York
	David Hume begins to publish his *History of England*
1755	The French and Indian War begins, lasting until 1763; Braddock's expedition is defeated
1759	The British, under Wolfe, capture Quebec from the French
1760	George III is crowned king
	Capture of Montreal by the British
1763	By the Treaty of Paris, France surrenders most of its North American possessions to Britain

1764	Grenville's Sugar Act vexes the colonies
1765	The Stamp Act meets with strong opposition in America
	Lord Rockingham, with Edmund Burke as his private secretary, is reluctantly accepted as prime minister by George III
	Sir William Blackstone begins to publish his *Commentaries on the Laws of England*
1766	The Rockingham ministry succeeds in repealing the Stamp Act, but passes the Declaratory Act
	Lord Rockingham's government gives way to a ministry dominated by the elder Pitt
1766-1770	The Townshend Acts rouse furious opposition in America
1770	Lord North's government repeals most of the Townshend duties, but retains a tax upon tea—and stations regiments in Boston
	The Boston "Massacre" (March 5)
1771	Burke appointed London agent for the province of New York
	The Regulators' War in North Carolina
1773	The Tea Act (May)
	The Boston Tea Party (December 16)
1774	The "Intolerable Acts", including the Boston Port Act, passed by parliament; the Quebec Act also passed
	Lord Dunmore's War in Virginia
	The First Continental Congress assembles in Philadelphia
1775	Burke's speech on conciliation (March 22)
	The fights at Lexington and Concord (April 19)
	The battle of Bunker Hill (June 17)
1776	Thomas Paine publishes *Common Sense*
	Adam Smith's *The Wealth of Nations* is published
	The Declaration of Independence (July 4)
	Americans defeated in the battle of Brooklyn Heights (August 27)
	Edward Gibbon publishes his *Decline and Fall of the Roman Empire*
	David Hume dies
1777	Burke publishes his *Letter to the Sheriffs of Bristol* (April 30), denouncing the British conduct of the war
	General Burgoyne surrenders to the Americans at Saratoga (October 17)
	The Continental Congress draws up the Articles of Confederation
1778	The United States obtains the alliance of France
1779	George Rogers Clark gains American victories in the West
1780	The war is fought chiefly in the South

1781	The Articles of Confederation are ratified
	Lord Cornwallis surrenders the British forces at Yorktown
1782	George III finds it necessary to return the Rockingham Whigs to office, to treat for peace
	The Treaty of Paris is concluded
1787	John Adams publishes his *Defence of the Constitutions*
	The Constitutional Convention draws up the Constitution of the United States
1788	Hamilton, Madison, and Jay publish *The Federalist*
	The Constitution is ratified
1789	George Washington takes office as the first president
	The French Estates-General assemble; the Bastille is stormed
	French Declaration of the Rights of Man and Citizen
1791	John Quincy Adams publishes his *Letters of Publicola*
	The first ten amendments to the Constitution, the "Bill of Rights", are ratified
1796	John Adams is elected president
1800	Friedrich Gentz publishes his *American and French Revolutions Compared;* it is translated into English by J. Q. Adams
	Thomas Jefferson defeats John Adams in the presidential election; beginnings of the "Jeffersonian revolution"
1801-1824	The "Virginia Dynasty" in national executive power
1825	John Quincy Adams inaugurated as president
	Beginnings of the "Jacksonian revolution"
1826	James Kent begins to publish his *Commentaries on American Law*
1828	Andrew Jackson wins the presidential election
1829-1830	The Virginia Constitutional Convention, most interesting of the several state conventions which enlarged the franchise during the 1820's and 1830's
1831-1832	Tocqueville and Beaumont travel in America
1840	"Tippecanoe and Tyler too" presidential election
1846	The United States expands to the Pacific
1848	Orestes Brownson publishes his essay "Legitimism and Revolution"
1851	John C. Calhoun's *Discourse on the Constitution and Government of the United States* is published
1860	Abraham Lincoln is elected president
1861-1865	The American Civil War
1865	Lincoln is assassinated
1866	Orestes Brownson publishes his *American Republic*

A Note of Acknowledgement

In the preparation of this third edition of *The Roots of American Order*, the author has had the advantage of the advice of Professor Forrest McDonald, today's principal authority on the economic and intellectual origins of the Constitution of the United States.

In the labor of revising the text, I was much helped at my library in the backwoods of Michigan by Mr. Charles Brown and Mr. Christopher Briggs.

I remain most grateful to the late Romuald Gantkowski, of Pepperdine University, who two decades ago prevailed upon me to write this fat book; and to Pepperdine University for its making possible the book's earlier editions.

—RUSSELL KIRK

About the Author

R ussell Kirk, the author of thirty books, has been in the thick of many of the literary and political struggles of our time. He is the president of two educational foundations and the editor of the quarterly *University Bookman*. He was first published nationally in 1936; he has contributed to more than a hundred serious periodicals on either side of the Atlantic.

He is the editor of The Library of Conservative Thought, published by Transaction Books; editor of, or contributor to, nearly fifty other volumes, aside from his own books. He has been a Senior Fellow of the American Council of Learned Societies, a Guggenheim Fellow, a Constitutional Fellow of the National Endowment for the Humanities, a Fulbright Lecturer in Scotland. He is the only American to hold the highest earned degree of the senior Scottish university—doctor of letters of St. Andrews University.

He has been distinguished visiting professor at a dozen universities and colleges and has spoken on hundreds of campuses. In 1989 he was awarded the Presidential Citizens' Medal.

Among his better-known books are *The Conservative Mind, Eliot and His Age, Enemies of the Permanent Things, Randolph of Roanoke*, and *Beyond the Dreams of Avarice*. Also he is the author of several volumes of fiction.

INDEX

influence upon, 368–374; Browne's influence upon, 278; Bunyan's influence upon, 278–279, 281–282; Burke's connection with, 375–376, 389–390; colleges in, 212–213; and England's Civil Wars, 267–268; governmental development in, 301–312, 323–332; Hobbes' influence upon, 274; individualism in, 270; philosophy in, 291–293, 348–368; political factions in, 294–295; Reformation in, 208; religion in, 25, 28–30, 45–49, 230, 236–238, 257, 332–344

Comitas, Roman virtue, 452

Comitia, Roman political term, 100, 114

Commentaries on American Law, Kent's, 369

Commentaries on the Constitution, Story's, 437

Commentaries on the Laws of England, Blackstone's, 191–192, 350, 368–370, 373

Commodus, Lucius Aelius Aurelius, Roman emperor, 125

Common law, 184–192, 194, 218, 370–373

Common Pleas, court of, 183–184

Communism, 7, 9, 264–266, 271, 460–463

Community, social, 12–15, 21, 26, 36, 218, 444–445

Conciliation with American colonies, Burke on, 384–387

Confessions, St. Augustine's, 158–160

Confirmation of the Charters, English, 197–198

Confucius, Chinese sage, 13–14, 144

Congregationalism, 261, 263, 307, 333, 340, 433, 461

Congress of the United States, 428–429

Consent of the governed, doctrines of, 90–92, 196–197, 243–245, 254–256, 263–266, 270–272, 285–288, 324–325, 353–354, 362–364, 409–413

Considerations on the Revolution of Empires, Volney's, 134n.

Constantia, Roman virtue, 454

Constantine the Great, Roman emperor, 120, 127, 130, 132, 155–158, 224

Constantinople (Byzantium), 133, 135, 156, 157, 169, 200, 202, 204, 205, 222, 223

Constitution, British, 194–200, 241–247, 259–268, 282–283, 284–289, 293–299, 379–380, 386–388, 415–416

Constitutions, Greek, 61–70, 90–93; Aristotle on, 90–93; of Cleisthenes, 68; of Draco, 62; of Ephialtes, 69–70; of Solon, 63–65

Constitution, Roman, 100–105, 114, 126–128

Constitution of the United States, 415–439; Bill of Rights added, 432; Electoral College in, 430–431; executive branch in, 427–428; federal concept of, 422–427; judicial branch in, 429–430; legislative branch in, 428–429; necessities of, 419–420; separation of powers in, 426–427; as a source of order, 431–432; and religious belief, 432–439; not utopian, 416–418

Constitutional Convention of the United States, 134, 415–421

Continental Congress, 405, 407, 407–411, 414

Continuity, Richard Hooker on, 244–247

Contra Faustum, St. Augustine's, quoted, 164

Convention Parliament (1688), 293, 296–299

Cooper, Anthony Ashley (Earl of Shaftesbury), 314–317

Cooper, James Fenimore, American novelist, quoted, 322

Convocation of the Clergy, 196–197

Corinth, Greek city, 62

Corpus juris civilis, 135

Council of the Areopagus, Athenian, 64, 69

Council of Four Hundred, Athenian, 64

Council of Nicaea, 155–158

County government in America, 327–328

Covenant, concept of, in American government, 29–30; of the Hebrews, 24–29, 31–32, 40, 42; New Covenant of the Hebrews, 34–35; Scottish National Covenant, 255–257

Crassus, Marcus Licinius, Roman general, 105

Craw, Paul, Hussite reformer, 217, 252

Creon, in *Antigone*, 58n.

Croesus, king of Lydia, 64

Cromwell, Oliver, Lord Protector, 156, 262–270, 279, 309, 403

Crusades, 200–206

Culdees, Christian sect, 213

Custom, 276, 352–354, 361, 383–384; Burke on, 383–384; Hume on, 360–362; Montesquieu on, 352–354

Damietta, Egyptian city, 201

Danakils, African people, 45